The Lord Is the Spirit

The Evangelical Theological Society Monograph Series

Volume 4
Did Jesus Teach Salvation By Works?
The Role of Works in Salvation in the Synoptic Gospels
—Alan P. Stanley

Volume 5
Has God Said?
Scripture, the Word of God, and the Crisis of Theological Authority
—John Douglas Morrison

Volume 6
The Light of Discovery:
Studies in Honor of Edwin M. Yamauchi
—John D. Wineland, editor

Volume 7
The Lord Is the Spirit:
The Authority of the Holy Spirit in Contemporary Theology
—John A. Studebaker Jr.

Volume 8
The Sinner in Luke
—Dwayne Adams

The Lord Is the Spirit

The Authority of the Holy Spirit in Contemporary Theology and Church Practice

JOHN A. STUDEBAKER JR.

◅PICKWICK *Publications* • Eugene, Oregon

THE LORD IS THE SPIRIT
The Authority of the Holy Spirit in Contemporary Theology and Church Practice

Evangelical Theological Society Monograph Series

Copyright © 2008 John A. Studebaker Jr. All rights reserved. Except for brief quotations in critical publications or reviews, no part of this book may be reproduced in any manner without prior written permission from the publisher. Write: Permissions, Wipf & Stock, 199 W. 8th Ave., Suite 3, Eugene, OR 97401.

ISBN 13: 978-1-55635-436-6

Cataloging-in-Publication data:

Studebaker, John A., Jr.
  The Lord is the Spirit : the authority of the Holy Spirit in contemporary theology and church practice / by John A. Studebaker Jr.

  Eugene, Ore.: Pickwick Publications, 2008
  The Evangelical Theological Society Monograph Series 7

  xiv + 392 p. ; 23 cm.

  ISBN 13: 978-1-55635-436-6

  1. Holy Spirit. 2. Holy Spirit—Biblical teaching. 3. Holy Spirit—History of Doctrine—20th century. I. Title. II. Series.

BT121.2 S75 2008

Manufactured in the U.S.A.

*To my parents, John and Joanne Studebaker,
who have always loved me
and have walked this journey with me
over the past ten years*

Contents

List of Figures / viii
Preface / ix
Acknowledgements / xi
Abbreviations / xii

1 Introduction / 1
2 The Authority of the Holy Spirit and Historical Theology: Assessing Historical Debates / 17
3 The Authority of the Holy Spirit and Systematic Theology: Part 1 / 91
4 The Authority of the Holy Spirit and Systematic Theology: Part 2 / 155
5 The Authority of The Holy Spirit and Practical Theology: Hermeneutics / 235
6 The Authority of the Holy Spirit and Practical Theology: The Structure and Guidance of the Church / 277
7 The Authority of the Holy Spirit and Practical Theology: Christian Spirituality / 315
8 Conclusions and Implications of the Doctrine of the Authority of the Holy Spirit / 361

Bibliography / 375

List of Figures

1. A Summary of Biblical and Postmodern Perspectives with Respect to the Authority of the Holy Spirit / 222

Preface

❧ THE EVIDENCE for "the authority of the Holy Spirit" within the Church is certainly more abundant than the books written on the subject! This critical yet undefined doctrine, however, can no longer be ignored. Contemporary theology is often challenging the Church's understanding of the person and work of the Holy Spirit with "non-authoritative" (i.e., panentheistic, universalistic, experiential, and domesticating) approaches.

The Spirit's authority with respect to the Church, however, can be demonstrated through a proper understanding of the Spirit's place within the "pattern of divine authority" derived from Scripture. Chapter one shall define this pattern as the revelation of God's authority with respect to Christ, the Scriptures, and the Holy Spirit. The principle of authority introduced here holds that divine authority is located in the Triune God (Father, Son, and Spirit) and is revealed through an execution of this pattern.

Chapter two delves into the several debates in Church history concerning the doctrine of the Holy Spirit ("pneumatology"). These debates will allow us to discern provisional "definitions" of the Spirit's authority in relation to the pattern of divine authority.

Chapters three and four probe the most critical passages of Scripture for developing a biblical and systematic understanding of the Spirit's authority. These passages are exegeted and utilized according to a specified methodology. Then they are used to respond to postmodern and contemporary "pneumatologists" and to develop formal descriptions of the Spirit's authority for Systematic Theology.

Chapters five, six, and seven present three specific areas of local church life and practice—Hermeneutics, Church structure and guidance, and Christian spirituality—where our model of the Holy Spirit's authority (developed in chapters three and four) may be applied. This application will

Preface

also allow a biblical response to be made to contemporary theologians who are attempting to associate the Spirit with such practices.

Chapter eight offers specific conclusions and further implications of this "new" doctrine—with respect to evangelical theology, contemporary theology, and other practical fields not yet studied.

Acknowledgments

❦ SPECIAL THANKS to Kevin Vanhoozer, Bruce Fields, James Borchert, Joanne Studebaker, Susan Vrobel, Ken Walbridge, Nancy Smith, and Don Sosnowski for their assistance on this project.

Abbreviations

AB	Anchor Bible
BAGD	*A Greek-English Lexicon of the New Testament*
BDB	*The New Brown-Driver-Briggs-Gesenius Hebrew and English Lexicon*
BibSac	*Bibliotheca Sacra*
CBQ	*Catholic Biblical Quarterly*
CH	*Church History*
CurTM	*Currents in Theology and Mission*
EDOT	*Evangelical Dictionary of Theology*
EphTL	*Ephemerides Théologiques et Lovanienses*
EvQ	*Evangelical Quarterly*
EvT	*Evangelische Theologie*
ExpT	*Expository Times*
IBMR	*International Bulletin of Missionary Research*
JAAR	*Journal of the American Academy of Religion*
JETS	*The Journal of the Evangelical Theological Society*
JPT	*Journal of Pentecostal Theology*
JTS	*Journal of Theological Studies*
LQ	*Lutheran Quarterly*
NAC	*The New American Commentary*
NICNT	*New International Commentary on the New Testament*
NICOT	*New International Commentary on the Old Testament*
NIDNTT	*New International Dictionary of New Testament Theology*
NIDOTTE	*New International Dictionary to Old Testament Theology and Exegesis*
NIGTC	*The New International Greek Testament Commentary*
PRS	*Perspectives in Religious Studies*
RR	*Reformed Review*
RTR	*Reformed Theological Review*
SBET	*Scottish Bulletin of Evangelical Theology*

Abbreviations

ScEs	*Science et Esprit*
SJT	*Scottish Journal of Theology*
SNTU	Studien zum Neuen Testament und seiner Umwelt
ST	*Studia Theologica*
TJ	*Trinity Journal*
TNTC	Tyndale New Testament Commentaries
TS	*Theological Studies*
TTo	*Theology Today*
VC	*Vigiliae christianae*
WBC	Word Biblical Commentary
WTJ	*Westminster Theological Journal*

1

Introduction

> How much do we hear about the Holy Spirit and His authority? If I were to hazard an opinion I would say that no aspect of the Christian faith has been so totally neglected and perhaps misunderstood. . . . Here, I truly believe, we are dealing with the main source of weakness in modern Evangelicalism.[1]

❈ THE VERY IDEA of "the authority of the Holy Spirit" probably sounds new to many Christians. Some may be skeptical that this relatively unknown concept could be our "main source of weakness." Others may wonder why such a crucial topic has been so neglected.

Many Christians feel that a general disrespect for authority marked the twentieth century, and that this disrespect is now blooming into a full crisis in our century. Hall points out that today's postmodern culture tends to ignore the existential element of authority, particularly regarding one's standing before God.[2] In addition, our culture no longer regards any one version of "truth" as having priority over another. As a result, the Church seems to have become just one more voice among many.

Several contemporary theologians have responded to this crisis of authority by re-asserting the doctrine of Christian pneumatology ("the doctrine of the Holy Spirit"). Postmodern theologians claim that traditional models of pneumatology were constructed on "modernist" approaches to systematic theology and, in doing so, placed undue reliance on metaphysics or on the "authority" of theological methodology itself. Such models, they hold, are now inadequate for providing a new sense of authority. "The house

---

1. Lloyd-Jones, *Authority*, 65.
2. Hall, *Word and Spirit*, 187–89.

of [theological] authority has collapsed," proclaims Ed Farley, because it was "propped up with mythical, historical and doctrinal rationalization" that can no longer stand on their own.[3] Postmodern theologians claim that, while the God of modernism was abstract and transcendent, in the Holy Spirit we rediscover God's concreteness and immanence, as well as God's power to liberate people from bondage. Michael Welker, for example, holds that,

> authoritarian theologies of one-upmanship have sought to grasp and expound God and God's revelation in numerous abstract formulas: God comes "from above," God always "precedes," God is the "all-determining" reality. The theology of the Holy Spirit will challenge us to replace these formulas or render them superfluous.[4]

Another postmodern theologian, Peter Hodgson, presents an even more radical assessment of the Western marginalization of the Holy Spirit.

> In Western theology and philosophy the very concept of "spirit" has for the most part been fraught with difficulties, conveying something vapid and dualistic, implying a separation of and a hierarchy between the mental and the physical, the soul and the body, the human and the natural, the male and the female, the holy and the profane. The hierarchy reflects a suspicion and fear of the suppressed poles: nature, the body, the feminine.[5]

Such theologians usually want to promote a re-emphasis of the Spirit with respect to several doctrines of systematic theology, particularly the Trinity and ecclesiology. Such a re-emphasis sounds very appealing to the Church today, as witnessed by the many churches that are promoting an experience of the Spirit as well as the many evangelical theologians who are sympathetic with postmodern cries of marginalization and are writing on pneumatology as well. In that more theologians are taking up biblical pneumatology as a way of revitalizing the Church, the postmodern project is to be commended.

Many of these contemporary theologians, however, seem to have granted the Spirit an "authority" unchecked by biblical boundaries. Some have divorced the Spirit's authority from the authority of Christ or the

---

3. Farley, *Ecclesial Reflection*, 157, 165.
4. Welker, *God the Spirit*, xi.
5. Hodgson, *Winds of the Spirit*, 276.

Introduction

authority of Scripture. Others have adopted "panentheistic"[6] portrayals of "Spirit" that often reduce the Holy Spirit's status as divine Person to that of a divine "force," "world spirit," or "function" within communities. Welker, for example, borrows from the field of magnetism in referring to the Holy Spirit as a "force field" in the world.[7] Hodgson refers to "Spirit" as a "primal energy" that "takes on the shape of many created spirits, not just of living persons but of ancestors and animals as well as plants, trees, rivers."[8]

Evangelicals hold that Scripture lays out specific identifying characteristics regarding the Spirit's nature and work. Since the Spirit is clearly referred to in Scripture as "God" (i.e., Acts 5:3–5), he must possess "divine authority" in some sense. Indeed a "divine authority" proper to the Spirit seems to have explicit backing in Scripture (i.e., John 3:3–8; 14–16; 1 Cor 2:10–14; 2 Pet 1:20–21). "Authority" is certainly implied when the Spirit is referred to as "Lord" in Scripture (i.e., 2 Cor 3:17–18) and in the Nicene Creed. Because of this abundant evidence, evangelicals proclaim that theologians are not to define the Spirit, nor his "authority," in any way they desire.

At the same time, evangelicals must also admit that a general confusion reigns today regarding the precise nature of "the authority of the Holy Spirit." It seems there are several nagging yet critical theological questions that have never been adequately answered, such as: (1) What is the biblical data regarding the Spirit's authority? (2) How is the Spirit's authority related to the authority of Jesus Christ and to the authority of Scripture? (3) How might a biblical understanding of the Spirit's authority expose and correct deficiencies in postmodern pneumatology?

Such a study also intersects the sort of practical issues and questions local churches continually wrestle with—questions regarding hermeneutics (i.e., how do we interpret Scripture "through" the Spirit?), church govern-

---

6. "Panentheism" is defined in *The Evangelical Dictionary of Theology* as "a doctrine of God that attempts to combine the strengths of classical theism with those of classical pantheism" (Franklin, "Panentheism," 819–20). God is the "supreme effect"—everything that happens affects and changes God. To be the supreme effect, "God must not only be affected by each event in the world, he must also retain his own integrity and wholeness during this process" (ibid., 819–20).

7. Welker, *God the Spirit*, 21–22.

8. Hodgson, *Winds of the Spirit*, 284.

ment (i.e., how does the Spirit structure and guide a church?), and Christian spirituality (i.e., what does it mean to "respond" to the Spirit?)

Lloyd-Jones asserts that the Spirit's authority is indeed *practical* in nature. After investigating the authority of Christ and the authority of Scripture, he exhorts:

> I would remind you first of all that, from a practical standpoint, this third division of our study is the most important of all . . . Only when the authority of the Holy Spirit comes to bear upon us do these things [i.e., the authority of Christ and the authority of the Scriptures] become real and living and powerful to us. More than that, all that we believe about the Scriptures and about the Lord Himself can only be applied in our ministry and so become relevant to the world and its situation, as we are under the authority and power of the Spirit.[9]

A theological understanding of the Holy Spirit's authority must therefore be reconstructed for today's Church as it wrestles with postmodern and contemporary theology on both a theoretical and a practical level. This reconstruction certainly does not require a reversion to modern "authoritarianism," but a fresh, biblical examination and articulation of the authoritative character and work of God the Holy Spirit in the Church today. With the doctrine of the Holy Spirit receiving such attention today, is it not time in the historical development of Church doctrine to develop biblical and yet practical clarity regarding "the authority of the Holy Spirit?"

Purpose

My Thesis Question is, "How might evangelicals recover a biblical conception of the Holy Spirit's authority in and over the Church, one that could serve to provide a response to contemporary misconceptions of 'Spirit?'"[10] My Thesis Statement is, "In order to meet the challenge posed by contemporary misconceptions of 'Spirit,' a biblical conception of the Holy Spirit's authority to establish and govern the Church must be recovered in systematic theology." I will demonstrate this recovery both theoretically (by

---

9. Lloyd-Jones, *Authority*, 62.

10. In speaking of the "Church," I am referring broadly to Christ's universal Church, unless referring to the local "church" (as I shall frequently in chapter six).

Introduction

discerning the nature of the Spirit's authority within the overall pattern of divine authority), and "practically" (by showing how the Spirit's authority is brought to bear with respect to hermeneutics, the structure and guidance of the church, and Christian spirituality).[11]

A Framework for Understanding and Defining "The Authority of the Holy Spirit"

In order to introduce the notion of "the authority of the Holy Spirit" we need to (1) define the general concept of authority and the specific "principle" of authority to be used throughout this work, (2) understand the basic "pattern of authority" exhibited within biblical Christianity, and (3) provide an initial determination of the Holy Spirit's place within this pattern.[12] Then, in the remainder of this thesis, we will have clear starting points for discussing the theological nature of the Spirit's authority in a biblical/systematic way and for discerning the "practical" nature of this authority with respect to the Church.

Defining the General Concept of Authority and the Christian Principle of Authority

A good secular definition of "authority," according to Ramm, is as follows:

> Authority itself means that right or power to command action or compliance, or to determine belief or custom, expecting obedience from those under authority, and in turn giving responsible account for the claim to right or power.[13]

Webster's dictionary defines authority as "the power or a right to command, act, enforce obedience, or make final decisions."[14] As a result,

---

11. I am defining "practical theology" as the application of the results of systematic theology to the development of the church's overall "ministry," both theoretically and practically (i.e. "practical theology" would thereby include the theory and practice of hermeneutics, church government, and spirituality).

12. One of the best discussions of the "principle" and "pattern" of authority in Christianity is found in Bernard Ramm's *The Pattern of Authority*. This book will serve as a basis for understanding many of the essential concepts used herein.

13. Ramm, *The Pattern of Authority*, 10.

14. Webster and McKechnie, "Authority," 126.

"authority" might be thought of according to two interrelated categories: (1) an authority *over* particular domains and people, and (2) an authority to act *in* a given situation. These two "perspectives" on authority might be referred to as *imperial authority* and *executive authority*, respectively.[15]

"Authority" appears in many areas of investigation (i.e., law, politics, education, etc), each developing their own "principle" of authority that specifies the general definition within a particular field or context. We can thereby expect a specific principle of authority to emerge with respect to religion as well. Ramm demonstrates that the common problem faced by all religions is the need for an understanding of authority that goes beyond a "bare monistic principle."[16]

> Most treatises on religious authority assert that God is the final authority in religion, but this bare assertion does not make its way. Unless the assertion is expressed in a more concrete fashion it becomes mere platitude. A *principle* of religious authority, along with its *pattern* designed for its practical and concrete expression and execution, should incorporate all the necessary elements associated with such a complex notion as religious authority.[17]

Only in Christianity do we encounter a divine *principle* of authority (one that incorporates the notion of a "final" imperial authority) along with an extensive *pattern* of authority through which the principle is graciously expressed and executed in practical ways. According to Ramm,

> God's imperial authority is graciously expressed. When God binds His authority upon man, it is an act of grace. In God's supreme revelation, Jesus Christ, exists the epitome of God's authority—grace and truth (John 1:17). There is no impersonal force in grace, and God's authority is sealed by grace, not by impersonal force. Bound to God by love and grace, the believer's mind is free from all traces of imposed authoritarianism or forced obedience.[18]

---

15. Imperial authority is that which is "possessed by persons or ruling bodies by reason of superior position such as that of a king" (Ramm, *The Pattern of Authority*, 10); DeGeorge defines executive authority as "the right or the power to act in certain ways" (DeGeorge, *The Nature and Limits of Authority*, 62).

16. Such a principle only leads to "authoritarianism," which is "the sheer appeal to authority, or the excessive claims of an authority" (Ramm, *The Pattern of Authority*, 19).

17. Ibid., 18 (emphasis mine).

18. Ibid., 21.

Introduction

As a result, the Triune God should be thought of as the One who demonstrates "imperial authority" *over* the world, but this authority includes a divine "executive authority" to act *in* the world. "Imperial authority" is portrayed in Scripture in terms of God's position as the one sovereign, holy, eternal, omniscient, and omnipotent Lord who reigns over all. Scripture tells us that "The Lord reigns, let the nations tremble . . . . He is exalted over all the nations . . . . He is Holy" (Ps 99:1–2). According to Ramm, "God as God occupies the highest conceivable personal station, and possesses all the authority which derives from that station."[19] For sake of discussion, however, when speaking of imperial authority in relation to God, I will from this point on refer to it as simply "divine authority." Divine authority will thus refer to God's imperial authority *over* the world, one that incorporates an authority to act *in* and *toward* the world. It will thus serve as our general definition for the sort of authority located in God the Father, God the Son, and God the Holy Spirit.

"Divine authority" is distinguished from other authorities by its intimate association with several of God's "absolute" or "supreme" characteristics. Most significant characteristics would include God's absolute metaphysical *primacy, eternality,* and *necessity* (see Exod 3:14; Deut 33:27). Such characteristics in themselves do not constitute divine authority, but instead substantiate God's *transcendence*, which is a relational term identifying God as uniquely *other* than creation and *above* all creation.

Our study of "divine authority" in Christianity (and with respect to the Holy Spirit) will therefore proceed along two lines: the Christian *principle* of authority (defining the *nature* of divine authority) and the associated *pattern* of authority (the execution of the principle). First, what is this *principle* of authority in Christianity? Ramm states,

> *In Christianity the authority-principle is the Triune God in self-revelation.* This is the central piece of the mosaic of authority, and the first and most impressive link in the chain of authority. This is the Object of religion declaring Himself to men, and in this declaration there is not only the imperial authority of God ("hallowed be thy name") but the truth from God about God.[20]

---

19. Ibid., 26.
20. Ibid., 21 (emphasis his).

This "authority-principle" tells us that "divine authority" not only possesses a quality of supremacy *over* the world but also that it must be revealed *in* the world. The principle thus alludes to a triune God whose authority is both transcendent (it "comes to the fore when God is presented to us as exalted above creation") and immanent (God's authority is "as far removed as possible from any notion of God as 'wholly other' or as 'infinitely distant'").[21] Divine transcendence can be witnessed in God's intellectual attributes (omniscience, faithfulness, wisdom), ethical attributes (holiness, righteousness), and existential attributes (freedom, authenticity).[22] Divine transcendence, however, translates into *divine authority* when such divine attributes are *immanently brought to bear* on the world and revealed to the world in all components of human existence.[23] As a result, *God is the highest authority in the world*; he above all is to be honored and obeyed. Frame points out the "absoluteness" of God's authority:

> Authority is God's right to be obeyed . . . To say that God's authority is absolute means that His commands many not be questioned (Job 40:11ff.; Rom 4:18–20, 9:30; Heb. 11:4, 7, 8, 17, passim), that divine authority transcends all other loyalties (Exod 20:3; Deut 6:4f; Matt 8:19–22, 10:34–38; Phil 3:8), and that this authority extends to all areas of human life (Exodus; Leviticus; Numbers; Deuteronomy; Rom 14:23; 1 Cor 10:31; 2 Cor 10:5; Col 3:17, 23).[24]

---

21. Frame, *The Doctrine of the Knowledge of God*, 16.

22. See Lewis, "Attributes of God," 453–58. Divine transcendence has traditionally been a watershed attribute for "theism." "The incomparable divine transcendence involves a radical dualism between God and the world. . . . A biblical theist not only believes that the one, living God is separate from the world, as against pantheism and panentheism, but also that God is continually active throughout the world providentially, in contrast to deism" (Lewis, "Attributes of God," 458).

23. While Frame holds that both divine *authority* and divine *control* demonstrate transcendence ("divine transcendence in Scripture seems to center on the concepts of control and authority"), he also seems to distinguish the way they do so. Divine authority demonstrates transcendence in that "divine authority transcends all other loyalties (Exod 20:3; Deut 6:4f; Matt 8:19–22, 10:34–38; Phil 3:8)" (Frame, *The Doctrine of the Knowledge of God*, 15–16). Divine control, however, is made evident "by God's sovereign power" (p. 15).

24. Frame, *The Doctrine of the Knowledge of God*, 16.

Introduction

Nevertheless, while God's authority is "absolute," it also remains "personal." Frame continues:

> But this metaphysical absoluteness does not (as in non-Christian thought) force God into the role of an abstract principle. The non-Christian, of course, can accept an absolute only if that absolute is impersonal and therefore makes no demands and has no power to bless or curse. There are personal gods in paganism, but none of them is absolute; there are absolutes in paganism, but none is personal. Only in Christianity (and in other religions influences by the Bible) is there such a concept as a "personal absolute."[25]

The Christian principle of authority ("the triune God in self-revelation") thus identifies both the "who" and the "how" of divine authority. Regarding the "who," this principle has a specific locus in *Divine Persons*. Ramm states that "in a very real sense all authority is at root *personal*. . . . Authority is the right and power of a person or persons to compel action, thought, or custom."[26] He is "God in three *Persons*"—Father, Son, and Holy Spirit.[27] As a result, any discussion of the Spirit's "authority" must be built upon this notion of his *divine Personhood*. This implies that the Spirit has authority because (1) he is a *Person* (rather than a "force field" or "primal energy"; see Mark 3:29; Acts 5:3; Eph 4:30), and (2) he has a special kind of authority—namely, *divine* (see Acts 5:3–5; 1 Cor 2:10–12).

This principle also identifies "how" divine authority is expressed (but without explaining it). Ramm parts with many other theologians on this very point: "Most books on religious authority state that God is the final authority in religion. Here is where the discussion begins, and it begins with this question: *How does God express His authority?*"[28] The obvious an-

---

25. Ibid., 16.
26. Ramm, *The Pattern of Authority*, 14. This is confirmed by the Latin word for authority, *auctoritas,* which refers to "personal influence" and is derived from the *auctor,* a person who "brings about the existence of any object" (Watt, *Authority*, 11).
27. This also implies that our principle of authority is free from *subjectivism*—it finds its locus not in the individual "under" authority but in the Father, Son, and Spirit who "possess" divine authority (see Ramm, *The Pattern of Authority*, 21).
28. Ramm, *The Pattern of Authority*, 19.

swer is "by divine self-revelation."[29] The idea is that God does not need an intermediary to communicate his divine authority to others. Instead, it is revealed through the interrelated contributions of the Father, Son, and Holy Spirit. In general, the Father is the *author* of divine revelation (establishing its final authority), the Son is the *focus* of divine revelation (establishing its content), and the Spirit is the *revealer* and *executor* of divine revelation (revealing God's authority in the world).[30]

The Pattern of Authority

As mentioned earlier, the *principle* of authority in Christianity is associated with a *pattern* of authority, which is "designed for its practical and concrete expression and execution." In other words, while "divine authority" is located in divine Persons and is revealed by God himself, the Christian "pattern of authority" expands this self-revelation into a full description of the means by which divine authority is revealed and executed. Ramm contends that divine revelation requires a specific pattern of delegation through which such execution occurs.[31] We might say that divine authority is revealed through a specific pattern involving a delegated *executive authority*. In the Old Testament this pattern first includes the Holy Spirit and the prophets. The Spirit spoke the revealed word through the prophets to a particular generation of people. This was "the actual authority for the Old Testament believer."[32] This pattern later came to include a written word of revelation available for subsequent generations. As a result, divine author-

---

29. Ramm explains, "All authority must be *personally recognized*. This is not, to be very sure, the grounds of authority. An authority becomes authoritative to a person only as that person accepts the authority through personal decision. This would appear to taint all authority with the leaven of subjectivism, but this is so only if the grounds of authority are confused with the personal acceptance of authority" (Ramm, *The Pattern of Authority*, 14).

30. Ramm defines divine revelation as "the religious object determining the character and truth of religion to the subjects of religion" (ibid., 20). See also Oden, *Life in the Spirit*, 23.

31. Ramm adds, "It must be understood that there is not dilution of authority in its delegation" (Ramm, *The Pattern of Authority*, 27).

32. Ibid., 27.

Introduction

ity is delegated through a basic pattern involving *Word* and *Spirit*.³³ This basic pattern tells us that what gets communicated is not just the *content* of authority through the Word of God but also, in a very real sense, the actual *saying* of authority *through the Spirit of God*. Divine authority, in other words, consists of the intimate association of *content* (from the mind of God) and *rightful force* (of a divine Person).

The NT, however, presents a radical *focusing* of this essential pattern. The center of divine revelation becomes the person and work of Jesus Christ. "Christ is the supreme object of the witness of the Spirit, and Christ is the supreme content of the Scriptures."³⁴ Ramm thus presents God's indivisible "pattern" of authority in terms of these three interrelated elements of God's self-revelation:

(1) *Christ*, who is the personal Word of God, the living, supreme revelation of God, and supreme depository of the knowledge of God (Col 2:3)

(2) *The Holy Spirit*, who conveys revelation, who delegates its authority, and who witnesses to its divinity

(3) *The Sacred Scriptures*, which are inspired by the Holy Spirit and therefore the document of revelation, which witness to Jesus Christ, and which are the Spirit's instrument in effecting illumination.³⁵

---

33. Ramm proclaims, "The duality of the Word and the Spirit must always be maintained, for it is in this duality that the Protestant and Christian principle of authority exists" (ibid., 30). Ramm also provides helpful documentation of this thesis in Protestant theology. This includes: Calvin, who entitles one chapter in his Institutes, "The Testimony of the Spirit Necessary to Confirm the Scripture, in Order to the Complete Establishment of Its Authority" (Calvin, *Institutes of the Christian Religion*, chap. VII); Luther, who states, "I believe that I can not by my own reason or strength believe in Jesus Christ my Lord, or come to him; but the Holy Ghost has called me through the Gospel . . ." (Luther, *Small Catechism*); and Arminius, who asserts, "the Holy Spirit, by whose inspiration holy men of God have spoken this word . . . is the author of that light by the aid of which we obtain a perception and an understanding of the divine meanings of the word, and is the Effector of that Certainty by which we believed those meanings to be truly divine" (Arminius, *The Writings of Arminius*, 1:140).

34. Ramm, *The Pattern of Authority*, 37.

35. Ibid., 36.

The Spirit's Place within the Pattern of Divine Authority

This pattern of authority involves both objective and subjective factors. God's *objective* revelation results in the written and authoritative Scriptures. Scripture possesses "delegated imperial authority and veracious authority in all matters in which it intends to teach."[36] The objective truth of the Word of God moves first from the utterance of the Father to Christ as his Supreme Revelation. Then,

> [Christ] delegates His word to His chosen apostles, who complete their oral witness to the supreme Person of divine revelation with a written document, the New Testament. There is no decay of authority nor lessening of authority from the utterance of the Father to the written word of the Scripture.[37]

This pattern of authority also involves the *subjective* operation of the Spirit of God that parallels the objective revelation. The Spirit inspires the Scriptures and then illuminates this written revelation in the mind and heart of the believer. "Thus the objective Word of the Father, and the subjective ministry of the Spirit intersect in the heart of the believer to create a true knowledge of God and to call into being the Christian principle of authority."[38] The Westminster Confession proclaims the crucial importance of this intersection for the authoritative determination and discernment of truth in all things.

> The Supreme Judge, by which all controversies of religion are to be determined, and all decrees of councils, opinions of ancient writers, doctrines of men, and private spirits, are to be examined, are in whose sentences we are to rest, can be no other but the Holy Spirit speaking in the Scriptures.[39]

In this work, the doctrine of the Spirit's authority will be developed as an outworking of our "pattern of divine authority. The Spirit is involved in this pattern as an *executor* of Christ's will in the world (John 15:26; 16:14–15). The Spirit's involvement in the world has been described in the

---

36. Ibid., 38.
37. Ibid., 62.
38. Ibid., 62.
39. *The Westminster Confession of Faith*, ch. 1, no. 10.

Introduction

historic notion of the "economic Trinity." Whereas the "immanent Trinity" is the perspective on God that explains who he is "antecedently and eternally in his own divine life,"[40] the economic Trinity is the perspective that demonstrates the priority and distinctive role of each of the three Persons as they act *in relation to us*. In the economic Trinity we witness a subordination of authority—the Son to the Father, and the Spirit to the Son. This subordination certainly does not imply inferiority. Forsyth states,

> Subordination is *not* inferiority, and it *is* Godlike. The principle is imbedded in the very cohesion of the eternal Trinity. . . . It is not a mark of inferiority to be subordinate, to have an authority, to obey. It is divine.[41]

Within the pattern of divine authority, the Son and the Spirit may be thought of as authoritative "agents" of the Father, each being equal with the Father and having the Father's full authority with respect to their nature (as God) and their right to execute the Father's will. Such "agency," therefore, retains divine authority. The Spirit is also given the specific assignment of executing Christ's will, an authority I will define in chapters two and three as "executorial authority." Such an authority shall be examined in two specific ways in chapter four: (1) the authority to act as *Spirit of Truth*, bringing the truth that is in Christ to the believer (through his "veracious authority"[42]) and (2) the authority to act as *Governor* of the Church, bringing the Church *under* the authority of Christ the King and delegating to her

---

40. Thompson, *Modern Trinitarian Perspectives*, 25.
41. Forsyth, "The Divine Self-Emptying," 42.
42. Veracious authority is defined by Ramm as "that authority possessed by men, books, or principles which either posses truth or aid in the determination of truth" (Ramm, *The Pattern of Authority*, 12).

a limited "functional"[43] or "ministerial" authority[44] in the world (through his "governing authority"[45]).

A Limitation of This Study

This study will wrestle primarily with the Spirit's inherent *authority* rather than with the display of his *power*. The Spirit's authority can be seen as that which provides appropriate parameters for understanding and experiencing the Spirit's power. The Greek words ἐξουσία and δύναμις illustrate the general distinction between "authority" and "power." Ἐξουσία is used in the New Testament 105 times and is closely related to, though distinguishable from, divine δύναμις. Barrett catches the crucial distinctions:

> Ἐξουσία corresponds to potential energy; it is the divine authority which may at any moment become manifest as power, δύναμις, through the impulse of God's will . . . ἐξουσία could be used for an office, or magistracy, which afforded authority, the capacity for wielding δύναμις. Thus ἐξουσία belongs to a state of effectiveness which lies behind δύναμις, which δύναμις reveals and on which δύναμις depends.[46]

These comments indicate that, while there is a close relationship in the New Testament between authority and power, these two concepts should not be confused.

43. Ramm thinks of "functional authority" as a "substitutional authority" (ibid., 12). For further explanations see chapters four and six in this work.

44. As we shall see, the emphasis of Scripture regarding the Spirit's authority *in* the Church is that of a "ministerial authority" rather than a "magisterial authority." A general parallel can be drawn between present debates regarding the Spirit's authority and Reformation debates regarding Church authority. "Catholic" authority "understands the *magisterium* to be the living authority of the Church"; the Church "specifies the rules for interpreting the Bible, and even (at times) restricts the use of the Bible" (Shelley, *By What Authority?*, 140). Whereas Catholicism replaced the authority of the believer to interpret Scripture with the authority of the Church, postmodernists often replace the authority of the Bible as truth with the power of the Spirit, and the absolute authority of Christ with a "pluralistic" authority of the Spirit.

45. Governing authority might be seen as a fully delegated right to govern within a particular structure.

46 Barrett, *The Holy Spirit and the Gospel Tradition*, 78. Henry points out that in the NT, "*exousia* appears as a dual-sense word meaning both authority and power. These two ideas are closely related" (Henry, *God, Revelation, and Authority*, VI:24). Ἐξουσία, however, is almost always translated "authority" or "right" (NASB).

Introduction

Methodology

Each chapter will build upon the previous chapters. In this chapter, I show the need for this study, define its purpose, develop a basic framework for understanding and discussing "The Authority of the Holy Spirit," mention an important limitation, and present an overview of the chapters.

Chapter two will be entitled "The Authority of the Holy Spirit and Historical Theology: Assessing Historical Debates." Here I shall examine the critical debates regarding the doctrine of the Holy Spirit found in five periods of historical theology: Patristic, Medieval, Protestant, Modern, and Postmodern. I shall discern four provisional definitions of the Spirit's authority that emerge from these debates (divine, executorial, veracious, and governing authority) that display his authority in various "realms."

Chapters three and four will be entitled "The Authority of the Holy Spirit and Systematic Theology" (Parts 1 and 2). In chapter three, I shall develop a systematic understanding of the Spirit's divine and executorial authority, two critical perspectives on his authority that are foundational for any further understanding (in that they establish the essential "nature" of his authority as well as his "authority to act"). In chapter four, I shall develop a systematic understanding of two critical "domains" of the Spirit's executorial authority: veracious authority and governing authority. I will develop these two chapters by exegeting key passages of Scripture, by attempting to find specific evidence of the Spirit's authority therein for systematic theology, and by developing "dialogue" with contemporary pneumatologists.

In chapters five, six, and seven, I will attempt to demonstrate the way my systematic model (developed in chapters three and four) comes to bear upon three "practical" applications with respect to the Church. These three chapters will be entitled "The Authority of the Holy Spirit and Practical Theology" and subtitled "Hermeneutics," "The Structure and Guidance of the Church," and "Christian Spirituality," respectively. Within these chapters I will also provide an evangelical response to contemporary versions of "practical theology" that attempt to incorporate the work of the Holy Spirit in various ways.

2

The Authority of the Holy Spirit and Historical Theology: Assessing Historical Debates

❧ IN THIS CHAPTER I will examine and compare various perspectives on "the authority of the Holy Spirit" that emerge from critical debates in theological history. Then I will propose provisional definitions of the Spirit's authority that emerge from the debates. These debated center around five periods of historical theology: (1) Patristic theology: First through Fourth Centuries (including both "early" and "late" Patristics), (2) Medieval theology: Fifth Century to the Reformation (including Eastern Orthodox and Roman Catholic theology), (3) Protestant theology: Reformation to Twentieth Century, (4) Modern theology, and (5) Postmodern and Contemporary theology.[1] In each period I will consider the arguments and contributions of those theologians who (1) sought to

---

1. Griffith Thomas divides pneumatological Church history into two main epochs. The first, extending from the Sub-Apostolic age to the Reformation, "was concerned with the Personality and Deity of the Holy Spirit and His relation to the Father and the Son. . . . The second took rise at the Reformation, and has been connected almost wholly with the Work of the Spirit" (Thomas, *The Holy Spirit of God*, 114). Morris Inch makes a tripartite division: "Early Church," (first through fourth centuries), "Establishment of Christendom as State Religion" (fifth century through the Reformation), and the Post-establishment era or "The Modern Era" (from the Reformation to today) (Inch, *Saga of the Spirit*, 199). Inch's scheme closely aligns with mine, except that I have divided his third period into "Reformation" and "Modern" periods, and have added the postmodern period.

provide significant clarification of the doctrine of pneumatology, and (2) did so within the context of the discussion of divine authority.

Assumptions

In the last chapter, we defined the "principle of authority" in Christianity along with its corresponding "pattern of authority." Our principle of authority revealed the possibility of the Spirit's "divine authority" as a *divine Person* within the Triune God. The pattern of authority (incorporating Christ, the Scriptures, and the Holy Spirit) revealed the possibility of the Spirit's "executive authority." So, we can assume that since the Spirit is an essential partner in both our principle of authority and our pattern of authority, *the authority of the Holy Spirit should be evaluated in relation to the authority of the Triune God (who possesses divine authority over the world) as well as in relation to the authority of Christ and the authority of Scripture.* In addition, *since this work is concerned with the implications of the Spirit's authority in the Church, such a relation should be evaluated as well.*

The Progressive Development of the Doctrine of the Holy Spirit in Theological History

As we can evaluate these critical debates in Church history, we will begin to observe a progressive development of the doctrine of the Holy Spirit. In fact, each major period of theological history contained a critical debate that focused on one of the "relations" mentioned above. Thus, each debate seemed to result in further clarification of the doctrine of the Holy Spirit. Since each debate revolved around a very significant ecclesiastical problem of the time (i.e., a heresy or conflicting views of sanctification) each served to shape and define that theological period in a significant way. As a result, the "storyline" development of the doctrine of the Spirit's authority, though often unnoticed, emerges as a hidden theme in the storyline of the Church itself. The doctrine progressively unfolds—unwittingly and covertly—on the pages of theological history.

According to Oden, the history of the doctrine of the Spirit can be traced in parallel to the earthly history of Christ. Whereas the story of Christ in the New Testament is available for historical inquiry, the earthly "story" of the Spirit is open to investigation in the form of Church history.[2] The Spirit has "a history that can be narrated by remembered events."[3] In the Church age, these events include the substantive debates that arise between orthodoxy and "heterodoxy."

> The councils thought that the Spirit was providentially allowing heterodoxy to challenge the truth of Scripture in order that the Spirit would lead the Church to search Scripture more deliberately to consider a more cohesive reflection upon the triunity of God.[4]

Therefore, we must not only acknowledge the Spirit's role in the authorship of Scripture, but also in the historical development of orthodox theology. Ramm notes that the interpreter of revelation must pay due regard to the Spirit in the history of theology. "The Holy Spirit is the Teacher of the Church, and surely in some manner the history of theology reflects this teaching ministry."[5] Ramm warns that "every generation of Christian theologians must be prepared to take seriously the history of theology (broadly interpreted to include symbols, councils, theologians, treatises) as possessing manifestations of the teaching ministry of the Holy Spirit."[6] This teaching ministry of the Spirit, of course, manifests the progressive "story" of the doctrine of the Holy Spirit as well!

The Discernment of "The Authority of the Holy Spirit" in Theological History

We must admit that most theologians in Church history do not specifically refer to "the authority of the Holy Spirit" in their writings (though there are exceptions[7]). Rather than attempting to "force" such language into the writings of these theologians, I will examine their writings within the context of the particular theological debates, looking to discern notions of the Spirit's authority in relation to the triune God, to Christ, to Scripture (both its inspiration and illumination), and to the Church. In other words, though

2. Oden, *Life in the Spirit*, 50.
3. Ibid., 25–26.
4. Ibid., 27.
5 Ramm, *The Pattern of Authority*, 59.
6. Ibid., 57.
7. Such as Tertullian, Calvin (*Institutes*), and Carl Henry (*God, Revelation, and Authority*).

most theologians do not use the word "authority" in discussing or debating the Holy Spirit, we can analyze these debates in an attempt to gather information for discerning provisional definitions of the Spirit's authority. Of course, any information gathered or conclusions drawn will need to be confirmed (or disaffirmed) by an exegetical study of the Scriptures (which will be the task of chapters three and four).

Historical Methodology

An overview of the five debates is as follows:

1. Patristic theology. In the period marked by the development of Patristic theology we find a critical debate over the *divinity* of the Spirit. The question here is essentially, "Is the Spirit a divine Being or merely a creature?" Two significant figures in this debate are Arius and Athanasius. While Arius argues for a "creature" view of the Spirit, Athanasius argues for the Spirit's divinity based on an analysis of the Spirit's relationship with the world.

2. Medieval theology. In this period a debate ensues regarding the relationship between the Spirit and *the authority of Christ*. The crucial question in this debate is: "Does the Spirit have an authority 'independent' of the authority of Christ (i.e., a purely 'executive authority' of his own), or does the Spirit always act 'under' the authority of Christ (i.e., an 'executorial authority')?" This debate begins with Augustine and the Cappadocians, continues through medieval and orthodox theology and persists to this very day.

3. Reformation theology. In the period a debate concerning the relationship between the Spirit and *the Scriptures* ensues. The question here is: "Does the Spirit authorize the Church to serve as authoritative interpreter of Scripture, or does this 'interpretive authority' ultimately lie with the Spirit alone, speaking through Scripture?" This debate begins with Martin Luther and the Roman Catholic Church and continues its development through John Calvin and subsequent theological movements.

4. Modern Theology. In this period, which arguably begins with nineteenth-century liberal theology (i.e., Friedrich Schleiermacher) and continues through twentieth century Protestant Evangelicalism (i.e., Carl Henry), we find a continuous debate brewing with regard to the Spirit's relationship to *the individual believer interpreting the Word of God*. "How does the Holy Spirit execute his authority in the life—and particularly the mind—of the believer attempting to interpret Scripture?" The "debate" in this period might indeed be drafted between Schleiermacher, who took an experiential tack to the question of the Spirit's authority with respect to the believer, versus Henry, who opted for a rationalistic approach.

5. Postmodern theology. Finally, in postmodern theology we discover yet another critical debate—this time concerning the relationship between the Spirit and *the Church community*. The question here is: "What is the nature of the Spirit's authority *within* the Church?" This question has to do with the way we should understand the Spirit's authority to govern the Church. Here we discover that "evangelical" theologians generally want to retain an understanding of the Spirit's authority within the Church that corresponds with our principle and pattern of divine authority (i.e., his authority *over* the world, *under* the authority of Christ, and *speaking through* the Word of God), while postmodern or contemporary theologians, in general, seem to be more concerned with the Spirit's *power* and *function* within the Church. Since the discernment of postmodern theology is such a critical part of this entire study, I will survey several theologians (whom we might more or less consider "postmodern") in order to investigate the general "landscape" of this debate in contemporary theology. This will allow me to develop an initial understanding of some critical "dialogue partners" that will need to be addressed in the remainder of this study.

In evaluating these debates I will follow a specific pattern of investigation. At the beginning of each section I will briefly investigate the various conceptions of "authority" that predominate within that particular historical period (including political, philosophical, and/or theological conceptions). Then I will identify two or more prominent theologians within that period who emerged as primary contributors to the specific debate. I will examine their arguments, paying particular attention to any discussion regarding the Spirit's place in relation to the Triune God (and to the world), to Christ, to the Scriptures and to the Church. After this I will briefly examine other theologians within that period that provided significant contribution to the debate. Finally, I will attempt to answer the question, "What provisional definition of the Holy Spirit's authority might evangelicals infer from this specific defense?"[8] I will conclude by attempting to account for the impact of that particular debate upon the developing "storyline" of the Spirit's authority in historical theology.

The goal of this chapter, therefore, is to attempt to find within historical theology initial confirmation that the Holy Spirit does indeed have an important place in our Christian "principle of authority" and our "pattern of authority" and to make initial discernment regarding the nature of the Spirit's authority within this principle and pattern. Such discernment will provide parameters for our exegetical analysis in chapters three and four. These insights will also allow us to grasp the significant contributions made by previous theologians, to avoid some of their exegetical mistakes, and to know what sort of questions to address in subsequent chapters.

Significant Resources

Three kinds of works are of crucial importance for this chapter. The first are those that discuss historical approaches to the "problem" of authority in the Church throughout her history. One of the most helpful works in this category is Harold J. Berman's *Law and Revolution: The Formation of the Western Legal Tradition* (which examines the interaction between political authority, Church authority, and theology through the patristic and medieval ages). Other important works include Gregory Bolich's *Authority and the Church* (which defines the witness of the Spirit to the Word of God in terms of a functional authority), Hans von Campenhausen's *Ecclesiastical Authority and Spiritual Power* (which investigates the Spirit's authority in the first three centuries), Rupert Davies' *Religious Authority in an Age of*

---

8. "Evangelical" will be defined as theology that attempts to honor the notion of the historic Trinity, the "inerrancy of Scripture" (properly understood according to its literary "genres"), and the authority of Scripture above the authority of "tradition."

Doubt (which examines issues of authority from Schleiermacher to today), P.T. Forsyth's *The Principle of Authority* (which views all authority in terms of the soul's relation to God), John Frame's *The Doctrine of the Knowledge of God* (with an excellent model of divine Lordship), Francis Hall's *Authority: Ecclesiastical and Biblical* (apologetics for a "modern" evangelical authority), Robert Johnson's *Authority in Protestant Theology* (especially helpful for understanding Luther, Calvin, and Schleiermacher), Karl Morrison's *Tradition and Authority in the Western Church: 300–1140*, and Bruce Shelley's *By What Authority* (which examines standards of truth in the early Church).

The second kind of works includes those that provide a "storyline" analysis of the historic doctrine of pneumatology and that occasionally relate this discussion to issues of divine authority. These include Gary Badcock's *Light of Truth and Fire of Love* (which attempts a "storyline" of pneumatology through the analysis of crucial episodes and debates; especially helpful on Moltmann), Yves Congar's *I Believe in the Holy Spirit*, volumes 1 and 3 (which provides technical analysis of pneumatological debates in the context of pneumatological history; especially helpful on Augustine), Alasdair Heron's *The Holy Spirit* (which presents the "story" in terms of key pneumatologists in Church history), Brian Gaybba's *The Spirit of Love* (a general history of pneumatology from a Catholic perspective), Thomas Oden's *Life in the Spirit* (which systematically analyses pneumatology in the Patristic period), Griffith Thomas' *The Holy Spirit of God* (which contains a very helpful section on "Historical Interpretation" that attempts to isolate the "essence" of pneumatology into specific Church "epochs"), and Morris Inch's *Saga of the Spirit* (which attempts to provides an "update of Griffith Thomas' volume").

The third kind of helpful works are those that examine the pneumatology of specific theologians. These include Regin Prenter's *Spiritus Creator* (on Martin Luther), Philip Rosato's *The Spirit as Lord* (on Karl Barth), Lycurgus Starkey's *The Work of the Holy Spirit* (on John Wesley), and John Thompson's *The Holy Spirit in the Theology of Karl Barth*. Articles include Eugene Osterhaven's "John Calvin: Order and the Holy Spirit" and Emilio Brito's "Hermeneutique et Pneumatologie Selon Schleiermacher."

The Development of the Doctrine of the Holy Spirit's Authority in Historical Theology

Now we shall examine the five periods of historical theology from the perspective of the development of the doctrine of the Holy Spirit's authority.

Patristic Theology

In the Patristic period (ca. 100–450), divine authority was understood in terms of Hebrew (i.e., Old Testament) understandings. The word ἐξουσία occurs fifty times in the LXX, with the book of Daniel providing important background material for understanding the New Testament use of the word. Daniel's usages imply dominion or power, and often refer to the whole world. The authority of the human world-rulers always originates from the supernatural realm; it is delegated by God, the Lord of history, whose rule is eternal (4:31), who installs and removes kings (2:21), and who can remove their dominion at any time (7:12). The "Son of Man" is invested with sovereign authority to rule all nations, and his dominion will never pass away (7:14). Old Testament authority was often conceived of in terms of Word and Spirit, two closely related "authorities" (i.e., Isa 59:21). Clement of Rome refers to the role of the Spirit in the inspiration of the Old Testament, saying "Look closely into the Scriptures, which are the true utterances of the Holy Ghost."[9] Clement also reported that the Apostles appointed bishops and deacons by the leading of the Spirit to govern the Church and that the gift of apostleship was given to continue the apostolic tradition into the patristic period (i.e., through inspired writings). According to Nielsen, Clement viewed the Spirit as "a reality connected with the . . . governmental structure of the Church."[10] Nielsen adds,

> It is significant, is it not, that the Holy Spirit is interested enough in the tradition of ecclesiastical succession to help guarantee it. According to Clement, one must keep contact with apostolic tradition simply because the Apostles had unique authority.[11]

---

9. Clement, *First Epistle to the Corinthians*, 1:17.
10. Nielsen, "Clement of Rome and Moralism," 142.
11. Ibid., 142.

The institutional Church eventually tried to gain political authority through symbiotic union with the Empire. Athanasius said that Constantius had attempted to make the Church a "civil senate" by "mingling Roman sovereignty with the constitution of the Church" and had led the Arians to consider "the Holy Place a house of merchandise and a house of juridical business for themselves."[12] Constantine's Rome not only began to guard against persecution but against the Empire's intrusion into the Church. The Church was given free reign to develop its tradition for preserving its own integrity. After Constantine, however, a "hostile separateness" between Empire and Church emerged and eventually grew so strong that the question of the day became, "What has the Emperor to do with the Church?" It was the Church's opportunity to search the Scripture and to draft a series of doctrinal precedents, developed only through a long series of controversies, upon which she could assert her own "authority." Imperial authority, whether paraded by Church or State, found its flourishing soil upon these semi-alienated grounds.

It is within this context that the debate over the Holy Spirit's divinity began to erupt—the Arian perspective often collaborating with the Empire and the orthodox "Fathers" at times finding themselves on the defensive, trying to protect the early Church from heresy.

Arius

Arius was a priest over the Church of Bacucalis in Alexandria (318) who systematically taught a subordinationism that thought of the Father alone as "God" and the Son and Spirit as "creatures."[13] The Arians held that the Spirit is really an angel, created by the Son, and one of the spirits ministering to God in heaven. Arianism is well known for denying the deity of the Son and particularly the idea of the Son being *homoousious* ("of one essence") with the Father. According to Arius,

> The essences [*ousia*] of the Father and the Son and the Holy Spirit are separate in nature. They are estranged, unconnected, alien . . .

---

12. Athanasius, *Historia Arianorum*, cc. 33–34.

13. According to Arius, there was no distinction drawn between the Son being begotten and being created; though the Son was the "first" created being, he also had a beginning and there was a time when the Son did not exist.

> and without participation in each other. . . . They are utterly dissimilar from each other with respect to both essences and glories to infinity.[14]

The "Arians" increased along with the Church's imperial authority, replacing the Scriptures with numerous creeds of their own. Athanasius referred to them as "modern Jews and disciples of Caiaphas."[15] As legalists, the Arians sought to justify their doctrines with an appeal to the authority of synods. Morrison claims that, for the Arians,

> Exegesis was therefore more important than the actual text. Theology and concepts of Church cohesion had shifted from repetition of scriptural passages to the right interpretation, from the text to the gloss. True believers were no longer simply those who upheld the Scriptures as true, but those who shared a particular understanding of the Scriptures' inner meaning or implications.[16]

The various "Arian Councils" were actually the first ones to attempt to draft a formal theology of the Holy Spirit for the Church at large. Before that time extensive writings on the Spirit were made by Clement of Rome and Ignatius, but their teaching "seems to be solely personal and experimental, and only indirectly doctrinal,"[17] serving only to confirm the presence of the Spirit in the Body of Christ. The Arian Councils (up until 360), however, expressed their theology of the work of the Spirit "in terms which were in thorough accord with the spiritual simplicity of the Holy Scripture."[18] Lest we discount the contribution of the Arians entirely, Swete acknowledges:

> The Church owes a debt, it may be freely admitted, to the Arian leaders who thus persistently called attention to the teaching and sanctifying influences of the Holy Spirit, at a time when there was grave risk of Christian thought being turned too entirely to theological controversy.[19]

---

14. Arius, as quoted by Athanasius, *Orations against the Arians*, 1.6.
15. Athanasius, *De decretis Nicaenae synodi*, c. 27.
16. Morrison, *Tradition and Authority*, 63.
17. Thomas, *The Holy Spirit of God*, 78.
18. Ibid., 85.
19. Swete, *The Holy Spirit in the Ancient Church*, 169.

Nevertheless, Arian and semi-Arian teaching on the mission and work of the Spirit made the doctrine of the Spirit's *nature* conspicuous by its absence. It was "unsatisfactory and even misleading; professing to be scriptural, it represents only one side of the teaching of Scripture."[20] As a result, new controversy regarding the deity of the Spirit arose throughout Christendom. While the "trinitarian" orthodoxy of the third century was both modalist and subordinationist—shaped largely by Origen, who saw the distinctions of the three Persons mainly in terms of three levels of divine outreach to the world—Arius drafted a radical metaphysical discontinuity amongst the Persons. Arius' denial of the Spirit's divinity emerged from his reaction to this third-century modalism.[21]

The council of Nicea sought to correct such heresy through an articulation of *homoousios*, which was employed to define the nature of the triune God. The Council constitutes a decisive step in a general movement in the fourth-century from economic to immanent trinitarianism. Many Christians, however, were horrified at the conclusions of Nicea (conclusions which were essentially unclear regarding the specific nature of *homoousios*), and thought that the idea of the Father and Son as one identical *ousia* implied modalism. Arianism took advantage of such fears, leading many believers to the conclusion that the Holy Spirit is less than divine. In reaction, the Church Fathers gave considerable attention to the *nature* of the Spirit (particularly in relation to the Son and to the Father) in their writings (up to and even after the Council of Constantinople in 381).[22]

Athanasius

Athanasius' *Letters Concerning the Holy Spirit* and *Letters to Serapion* present perhaps the best defense of the Spirit's divinity in the first millennium of the Church. As the chief elaborator and defender of the Nicene Creed after 325, Athanasius suffered considerable persecution from Arian politi-

---

20. Ibid., 169.

21. See Gregg and Groh, *Early Arianism*; also Badcock, *Light of Truth and Fire of Love*, 47–48.

22. Badcock, *Light of Truth and Fire of Love*, 50. This shift in thinking is illustrated by the emergence of the word *theologia*, which refers to the doctrine of the "immanent Trinity," as opposed to *oikonomia*, or economy, referring to everything else that the Trinity does in relation to creation (see LaCugna, *God with Us*, 37ff.).

cians. When Athanasius turned his attention to the doctrine of the Spirit he gained many converts from Arianism, such as the followers of Serapion, who had accepted the *homoousios* of the Son with the Father but continued to view the Spirit as a creature. In his *Letters to Serapion*, Athanasius uses divine attributes such as immutability and supremacy to convincingly demonstrate the Spirit's divinity. First, the Spirit's divinity is witnessed in His *immutability*.

> That the Spirit is above the creation, distinct in nature from things originated, and proper to the Godhead, can be seen from the following considerations also. The Holy Spirit is incapable of change and alteration. For it says, "The Holy Spirit of discipline will flee deceit and will start away from thoughts that are without understanding." (Wis. 1:5). And Peter said, "In the incorruptibility of the meek and quiet Spirit" (1 Pet 3:4). . . . The Holy Spirit, being in God, must be incapable of change, variation, and corruption.[23]

Second, the Spirit's divinity emerges from His supremacy over all things.

> Again, the Spirit of the Lord fills the universe. Thus David sings, "Whither shall I go from your Spirit?" (Psalm 139:7) Again, in Wisdom it is written, "Your incorruptible Spirit is in all things." (Wis. 12:1) . . . But if the Spirit fills all things, and if the angels, being his inferiors, are circumscribed, and where they are sent forth, there are they present; it is not to be doubted that the Spirit does not belong to things originated, nor is he an angel at all, as you say, but by nature is above the angels.[24]

While Origen took a "spiritualizing" approach to the exegesis of Scriptures, Athanasius emphasized the use of a "grammatical-historical" interpretive scheme.[25] Well known for his knowledge of Scripture, Athanasius actually moved beyond the letter of Scripture and theological tradition in

---

23. Athanasius, "First Letter to Serapion," 129–30.

24. Ibid., 129–30.

25. Hanson points out that "Athanasius unmistakably believed in the sufficiency and primacy of Scripture for doctrinal purposes . . . showing that he desired to prove tradition from Scripture" (Hanson, "Basil's Doctrine of Tradition in Relation to the Holy Spirit," 243). Athanasius says, "It is our task now to search the Bible and to examine and judge when it is speaking about the divinity of the Word, and when about his humanity" (Athanasius, "Third Letter to Serapion," 2.8).

order to confront sects that denied the deity of the Spirit. Perhaps his most famous argument lies in the contrast he drew between the nature of creatures and the nature of the Spirit. He employed Gen 1:1–23 to demonstrate that creatures are created from nothing and come into being at a particular time, and 1 Cor 2:11–12 to show that the Spirit is not created but emerges directly from God.[26] Athanasius backed this contrast with persuasive logic:

> They say also in their hearts "there is no God" (Ps. 14:1). For if, as no one knows the thoughts of a man save the spirit who is in him (εν αυτω): would it not be evil speech to call the Spirit who is in God (εν τω Θεω) a creature, him who searches even the depths of God? For from this the speaker will learn to say that the spirit of man is outside himself, and that the Word of God, who is in the Father (εν τω πατρι) is a creature.[27]

Athanasius also applies the logic of Nicean Christology and the concept of *homoousios* to the doctrine of the Holy Spirit, demonstrating that the Spirit bears the same rank and relative function to the Son as the Son does to the Father.

> And if the Son, because he is of the Father, is proper to his essence, it must be that the Spirit, who is said to be from God, is in essence proper to the Son. And so, as the Lord is Son, the Spirit is called Spirit of sonship. Again, as the Son is Wisdom and Truth, the Spirit is described as the Spirit of Wisdom and Truth. Again, the Son is the Power of God and Lord of Glory, and the Spirit is called Spirit of Power and of Glory. So Scripture refers to each of them. Paul wrote to the Corinthians, "Had they known, they would not have crucified the Lord of glory" (1 Cor 2:8). . . . Peter wrote, "If you are reproached for the name of Christ, blessed are you; because the Spirit of glory and of power rests upon you" (1 Pet. 4:14). The Lord is called the Spirit, "Spirit of truth" and "Paraclete;" whence he shows that the Triad is in him complete.[28]

Thus, for Athanasius, the Spirit's attributes of divine power and divine glory seem to be "lordship" attributes. Athanasius cites the baptismal formula, "in the name of the Father, and of the Son, and of the Holy

---

26. Athanasius, "Third Letter to Serapion," 2.28.
27. Athanasius, "First Letter to Serapion," 22.121.
28. Gregory of Nazianzus, "On the Holy Spirit," 325–26.

Spirit," maintaining that since we now know that the Son is God along with the Father, it makes no sense to introduce a creature (i.e., the Arian Holy Spirit) into the Trinity.[29] The Spirit must therefore be a *procession* of the Father and not a mere creation of the Father (Athanasius cites John 15:26, "the Spirit of truth who proceeds from the Father").

Even more central to Athanasius' argument, however, is his association of the Spirit with our sanctification (which is indeed a vital part of our salvation), concluding that the Spirit must therefore be our savior, together with the Father and the Son. The argument is inductive, beginning with the work of the Spirit and moving to the person of the Spirit. Since sanctification is a divine activity, the Spirit must be divine. Athanasius provided this argument at a synod in Alexandria in 362, at which the full divinity of the Spirit was clearly acknowledged.

OTHER CONTRIBUTORS

Eunomius (ca. 335–393), a relatively late Arian, regarded the Son as a creature of the Father and the Spirit as a creature of the Son (as the first and greatest work of the Son). Since "the Son is inferior to the Father, but superior to the Spirit,"[30] the Spirit is third not only in rank and dignity but also in *nature*. Such *pneumatomachi* (those who "fight against the Spirit") based their teaching on the notion that the Spirit is not specifically referred to as "God" in Scripture, but rather as a power that seems subordinate to God or placed between God and the creatures.[31]

The Cappadocian Fathers (Basil of Caesarea, Gregory of Nyssa, Gregory of Nazianzus) developed some of the most penetrating rebukes to such Arian theology. Their strategy, essentially, was to distinguish between *ousia* and *hypostases* (i.e., between divine oneness and the distinctiveness of the three Persons). Writing around the time of the Iconium Council (375), Basil continued in the logic of Athanasius (in his *On the Holy Spirit*), countering Arian assertions that the Spirit is a creature by insisting that the Spirit's equality and dignity qualifies the Spirit as a member of the Trinity. Basil's most penetrating questions to Eunomius are: "Why should 'third in

---

29. Badcock, *Light of Truth and Fire of Love*, 54.
30. Eunomius, quoted by Augustine, *de Haeresae*, LIV.
31. Congar, *I Believe in the Holy Spirit*, vol. 3, 29.

order' necessarily mean 'third in nature'?" and "How could the name of a created being have found place in the baptismal formula together with the Father and the Son?"[32] Arguing from the Spirit's work to his divinity, Basil essentially asked: "If the Spirit is the breath of God and has the power to sanctify, how can he be a mere creature? If the Spirit is an intelligent substance (*ousia*) of infinite power, unlimited by time, and naturally sought by all those seeking holiness and virtue, does this not establish his divinity?"

> [Basil] is describing the Spirit as the divine goodness that permeates the world and that the world somehow shares in; the Platonic philosophical basis of his thought, together with his Christian faith, certainly makes him inclined to see goodness in such metaphysical and indeed specifically theological terms.[33]

Gregory of Nyssa also used the baptismal formula in his defense of the Spirit's divinity. He went further than Athanasius, however, by developing this classical argument into a theological anthropology, which is witnessed in the Spirit's formation (*morphosis*) and perfection of the Christian. Gregory argued at Constantinople (ca. 381) that this action requires the Spirit to be God and to receive the same honor as the Father and the Son. The sanctifying Spirit is to be considered *consubstantial* (possessing the same nature or substance) with the Father and Son without losing his distinction in *hypostasis*. Gregory of Nyssa held to the conviction of the monarchy of the Father, which is illustrated by several metaphors—a lamp, for example, which communicates its light to another lamp and through that lamp to a third lamp. The Spirit alone shone in this way, he taught, eternally through the Son.[34] The result of this argument was a "new" view of the Spirit as deifier or sanctifier, the one who transforms various common or material elements through his sanctifying power. In turn, humans are transformed by partaking in the sacramental provision of the Spirit. It is "the visitation of the Spirit that comes sacramentally to set us free."[35]

Gregory of Nazianzus (ca. 330—ca. 385) is often called "the theologian" by the Eastern Church, and was the first of the Cappadocian Fathers

---

32. Swete, *On the Early History of the Doctrine of the Holy Spirit*, 63.
33. Badcock, *Light of Truth and Fire of Love*, 55.
34. Congar, *I Believe in the Holy Spirit*, 31.
35. Gregory of Nyssa, *On the Baptism of Christ*, 5:519.

The Lord Is the Spirit

to declare that the Spirit is "God." He proclaimed, "Each [of the three persons] is God by reason of 'consubstantiality,' the three are God by reason of monarchy."[36] He was called in 380 by the emperor to clarify the doctrine of the deity of the Spirit (which was considered the key debate of the day). Gregory's *Fifth Theological Oration* was as much of an attack upon the Orthodox Church (which seemed ambivalent on this issue) as it was upon the Arians. He argued, somewhat like Gregory of Nyssa, that there is one light that comes to us from the Father, through the Son, in the Spirit:

> Light, and light, and light, but one light, and one God. David anticipated this when he said, "In your light shall we see light." But now we have seen and we preach, receiving the light of the Son from the light of the Father, in the light of the Holy Spirit.[37]

For Gregory of Nazianzus, this divine outreach cannot be divided up between creature and Creator. The light that is received by the creature must be true God in itself—for if the Spirit in whom the light comes to us is not God, how can we be saved? "If he is ranked with me, how can he divinise me?"[38] he asks. Then he poses the rhetorical question, "Is the Spirit God?" to which Gregory answers, "Most certainly," and adds, "Is he *homoousios*? Yes, if he is God!"[39] Whereas the Arians objected that the plurality of the Father, Son, and Spirit is on the same level as the plurality of "three crabs," Gregory rebuts that consubstantiality makes such a ridiculous comparison impossible because "the fact that the three are consubstantial is affirmation enough of the divine unity, while also making simply numeration along creaturely lines logically and metaphysically inappropriate."[40]

One would think that the council of Constantinople (ca. 381) would recognize the impenetrable logic of Gregory's argument. However, because of the fear of a tumultuous reaction from the newly excommunicated Arians, their expansion of the Nicean creed settled on a *via media* position: "[We believe] in the Holy Spirit, the Lord and the Life-giver, who proceeds

---

36. Gregory of Nazianzus, *Select Orations*, XL:41.
37. Ibid., V:3.
38. Ibid., V:4.
39. Ibid., V:10.
40. Badcock, *Light of Truth and Fire of Love*, 57.

from the Father, who is worshipped and glorified together with the Father and Son, who spoke by the prophets."[41]

The "Divine Authority" of the Spirit—Definition and Storyline

Is there a provisional definition of the Holy Spirit's authority that we are able to infer from these defenses of the Spirit's divinity? If so, how might this definition: (1) correlate with our principle and pattern of divine authority? (2) provide a beginning or basis for the "storyline" of the Spirit's authority in theological history?

In order to assess these questions, we will need to borrow a bit of logic regarding authority from some contemporary theologians. Frame, for example, defines divine Lordship as "covenant headship."[42]

> [All created things] are appointed to be covenant servants, to obey God's law, and to be instruments of His gracious purpose. If God is covenant *head*, then He is exalted above His people; He is transcendent. If He is *covenant* head, then He is deeply involved with them; He is immanent. Note how beautifully these two concepts fit together when understood biblically.[43]

Divine *Lordship* thereby provides a key window into our understanding of divine authority and Personhood. According to Frame, Lordship involves control, authority, and presence.[44]

---

41. Kelly, *Early Christian Creeds*, 97–98.

42. Frame states that "Lord is the name God gives to himself as head of the Mosaic Covenant and the name given to Jesus Christ as head of the New Covenant" and cites the following Scriptures as examples: Exod 3:13–15; 6:1–8; 20:1–2; John 8:58; Acts 2:36; Rom 14:9 (Frame, *The Doctrine of the Knowledge of God*, 11–12). Lord" (*Yahweh* in Hebrew, *kyrios* in Greek) is also the name given in the New Testament to the exalted Christ (Acts 2:36; Rom 14:9) and to the Spirit (2 Cor 3:17–18).

43. Frame, *The Doctrine of the Knowledge of God*, 13 (emphasis his).

44. Frame adds, "It is important to see the three lordship attributes as forming a unit, not as separate from one another. God is 'simple' in the theological sense (not compounded of parts), so there is a sense in which if you have one attribute you have them all" (Frame, *The Doctrine of the Knowledge of God*, 17). Frame does interrelate these attributes further: "God's control, according to Scripture, involves authority, for God controls even the structure of truth and rightness. . . . Authority involves control, for God's commands presuppose His full ability to enforce them. Authority involves presence, for God's commands are clearly

> Control is evident in that the covenant is brought about by God's sovereign power. . . Authority is God's right to be obeyed, and since God has both control and authority, He embodies both might and right. To say that God's authority is absolute means that His commands may not be questioned (Job 40:11ff.; Rom 4:18–20; 9:20; Heb. 11:4, 7, 8, 17, passim), that divine authority transcends all other loyalties (Exod 20:3; Deut. 6:4f.; Matt. 8:19–22; 10:34–38; Phil. 3:8), and that this authority extends to all areas of human life (Exod.; Lev.; Num.; Deut.; Rom 14:32; 1 Cor 10:31; 2 Cor 10:5; Col. 3:17–23). Control and authority—these are the concepts that come to the fore when the Lord is present to us as exalted above creation and they are as far removed as possible from any notion of God as "wholly other" or as "infinitely distant."[45]

Several arguments in patristic pneumatology clearly allow us to infer the Spirit's "divine authority" as a *Divine Person*. Each looks to the Spirit as one whose supreme right with respect to the world can be described in both transcendent and immanent terms. Athanasius' argument from Gen 1:1–23 and 1 Cor 2:11–12 allows us to infer his belief in the Spirit as a *first cause*. Classical theology recognizes God to be the *principium essendi* ("first cause"), the foundation that underlies all activity. This attribute displays divine transcendence and yet is centered in immanence (as the divine causation of all creation). God is the beginning and the end, the "author" of all things and all authority. However, "this metaphysical absoluteness does not (as in non-Christian thought) force God in to the role of an abstract principle."[46] Athanasius' "absolute" language regarding the Spirit's divine immutability and divine supremacy over all things provides valuable contributions as well to our understanding of the Spirit's divine Personhood.

Basil's inductive reasoning (from the Spirit's activity as the breath of God and sanctifier to the Spirit's infinite power, eternality, and moral su-

---

revealed and are the means by which God acts in our midst to bless and curse. . . . Presence involves authority, for God is never present apart form His Word" (17–18). Nevertheless, these three critical attributes can and should be discerned when God's "Lordship" is revealed in Scripture, so that divine authority might not be confused with divine power or presence, particularly when discerning divine "authority" within the world or church community (15–18).

45. Frame, *The Doctrine of the Knowledge of God*, 15–16.
46. Ibid., 17.

premacy) employs similar logic. Basil's insistence on the Spirit's equality (with the Father and the Son), dignity, and demonstration of divine goodness also confirms the Spirit's authority as a divine Person. Here Basil does expose his platonic leanings, pointing to his preference for *transcendence* in theology. Nevertheless, Basil's thought did serve to pave the way for the popular notion of divine *ousia* and accounted for the "oneness" of the three "hypostases." The implication of a shared divinity is the sharing of divine authority amongst the three hypostases.

Gregory of Nyssa's theological anthropology demonstrates the Spirit's divine Personhood as well. Gregory's understanding of the Spirit's *sanctification* is described as an internal process *within us* arising from an external source that descends *upon us*. Forsythe clarifies this key distinction:

> An authority must be external, in some real sense, or it is none. It must be external to us. It must be something not ourselves, descending on us in a grand paradox. . . . [It] must reveal itself in a way of miracle. It does not arise out of human nature by any development, but descends upon it with an intervention, a revelation, a redemption.[47]

Such an authority, according to Forsythe, is not foreign or alien—it is "other." It represents a kind of pressure upon our souls. Gregory's *transcendent* understanding of the Spirit certainly drives a premeditated stake through the heart of the "modern soul"—that "transcendent ego" or individuality that refuses the sanctifying wisdom which comes "from above" (James 3:15, 17). According to Forsythe, such wisdom is dispensed by the "Grand State Secretary of heaven on earth, the Holy Spirit."[48]

In speaking of the Father and Son as being "consubstantial," Gregory of Nazianzen recognizes that the light of the Spirit must also be "true God in itself" in order to save us. While Athanasius argues for the Spirit's divinity from the Spirit's participation in the divine act of creation, Gregory argues from soteriology. Forsythe tightens this crucial link between divine authority and soteriology:

> If there is any authority over the natural man, it must be that of its Creator; and, if the New Humanity has any authority above it, that

---

47. Forsyth, *The Principle of Authority*, 271, 299.
48. Ibid., 190.

authority must be found in the act of *its* creation, which act is the Cross of Christ.[49]

This is where our "story" begins—the story of the progressive unveiling the Spirit's authority in theological Church history. This first substantial "unveiling" emerges through a heated debate regarding the Spirit's essential nature—the idea that the Spirit, as a divine Person, possesses divine authority. The Spirit retains authority *over* the world while revealing God's authority *to us*. The Patristic arguments for the Spirit's equality and shared divinity with the other Trinitarian Persons point toward his authority as a *divine Person*. Their arguments for the Spirit's divine transcendence, divine "absoluteness," and involvement in certain activities (i.e., creation, salvation, and sanctification) confirm this authority.[50]

As seen in the previous chapter, the "principle of authority" in Christianity grants the Spirit "divine authority" as a divine Person. This lies at the foundation of pattern of divine authority. The Church Fathers seem to claim that the Spirit, as a member of the Trinity, reveals himself *to* all humanity by demonstrating his authority *over* all humanity. This seems to become the first parameter within which a case for the Spirit's authority can be developed.[51] Any attempt to portray the Spirit's *nature* as subordinate, "creaturely," or in purely "anthropomorphic" terms will only run against these theological conclusions in that they only serve to reduce the Spirit to something less than a fully divine Person (and thus not able to possess divine authority at all).

Historians will rightly point out that the Nicene and Constantinople Creeds are ambiguous regarding the divinity of the Spirit. The reason for

49. Ibid., 58.

50. I would argue that Arian pneumatology not only sought to strip the Spirit of divinity, but, perhaps even more so, of divine authority. This intention seems apparent in various metaphors and conciliation: the Arian analogy of the Father, Son, and Spirit to gold, silver, and brass makes the Spirit seem inferior. According to Swete, Eunomius' reference to the Spirit as a created Person implies that "Spirit" remains "destitute indeed of Deity and of creative power" (Swete, *On the Early History of the Doctrine of the Holy Spirit*, 62).

51. As we shall see in the subsequent theological periods, such a parameter seems to provide a very specific limitation upon further discussion. The Medieval Church, for example, will require that subsequent investigations into the nature and work of the Spirit in relation to Christ conform to this foundational doctrine. Postmodern theology, on the other hand, will often violate this fundamental limitation.

this, however, is well-known—namely, the Church rightly saw the need for clarification of Christology before pneumatology.[52] Yet, interestingly, the word choice given in the Constantinople Creed in describing the Spirit as "the Lord, the Life-giver" represents the Spirit's *authority* more so than his divinity.[53] Yet this is only where the story begins.

Medieval Theology

In this section, I will evaluate the medieval debate over the *Filioque*[54] clause in an attempt to discern implications for the relationship between the Spirit's authority and Christ's authority. To begin this discernment it will be very helpful to trace the impact of political/theological history upon the development of Eastern and Western pneumatologies. In doing so we discover the true nature, potency, and impact of this debate.

Alexander the Great (356–323 BC) brought the center of civilization westward to Europe, and after Roman occupation the *pax Romana* eventually extended there as well. Though this might give the impression of a unified confederation, Ramm points out that this is a "mirage" because "the map fails to convey the enormous diversity that persisted in the Roman Empire. Underneath the apparent unity was a great cultural division of the East and West."[55] After the birth of Christianity, this division was only exacerbated by the rise of Byzantine (Eastern) Christianity (which eventually proved to be a serious threat to the primacy of Rome), the rapid rise of Islam (which created internal pressure within Christendom) and the even-

---

52. Badcock concedes, "Although one had to admit . . . the fact that any creed must be economical in order to be functional, a great deal about the work of the Spirit—about the relation between Spirit and Church, for example—has been left unsaid. Perhaps this is wise, as doctrinal definition is intended to point the way rather than to exhaust all possibilities, but perhaps it also reflects a general uncertainty concerning the Spirit's role in human salvation and in the spiritual life" (Badcock, *Light of Truth and Fire of Love*, 61).

53. Could it be that the Spirit's Lordship—his control and authority—are more recognizable in Scripture that his divinity? A brief perusal of pertinent Old Testament and New Testament passages seems to demonstrate this to be the case, but it also seems that, in Scripture, the Spirit's divinity is extrapolated, in part, from his divine authority.

54. *Filioque* is Latin for "and the Son," and was inserted into the Nicene Creed after the statement, "I believe . . . in the Holy Spirit, the Lord, the Giver of Life, who proceeds from the Father."

55. Ramm, *The Evangelical Heritage*, 17.

tual missionary movements of both Eastern and Western Churches (which further underscored the polarity).[56] This division found theological support as well, with the Eastern Church tending toward "mystical" theology and the Western Church toward a more "rational" one. The great modern pneumatologist Ives Congar cites T. de Regnon's studies of the Eastern and Western conceptions of the Trinity. According to de Regnon, "The Latins regarded the personality as the way in which nature was expressed, while the Greeks thought of nature as the content of the person. These are contrary ways of viewing things, throwing two concepts of the same reality on to different grounds."[57] The Latin theologian therefore says, "three persons in one God"; whereas the Greek says, "one God in three persons." The faith and the dogma are approximately the same in each model, but the mystery is presented in two different forms.

The impact of medieval history upon pneumatology becomes most apparent when one explores the tense cohabitation that developed between Church and State. This relationship stems back to the late patristic era, and particularly to Constantine, who attempted to "christianize" the Roman Empire in AD 312. Though Constantine was converted in 313, we learn from Berman's excellent analysis that Constantine's project may have actually stunted the early Church's growth.

> [It] raised in stark terms the question whether Christianity had anything positive to contribute to the ruler's role as supreme judge and supreme legislature in his domain. The question was reduced especially acute by the belief that the emperor was the head of the Church and represented Christ on earth.... The Christian emperors of Byzantium considered it their Christian responsibility to revise the laws, as they put it, "in the direction of greater humanity."[58]

Berman cites many positive changes that took place under Constantine—changes regarding women's rights in marriage and society, slave rights, judicial reform, and the systematization of law as a step toward a "humanized" Christianity.[59] Still, the elimination of anti-Christian laws

---

56. Inch, *Saga of the Spirit*, 221.
57. Congar, *I Believe in the Holy Spirit*, 3:xvi.
58. Berman, *Law and Revolution*, 167–68.
59. Ibid., 168.

was very difficult, and the Roman legal system was in decay throughout most of Byzantium history.

> Despite its generally humanizing influence on the law, Eastern Christianity may indeed have ultimately exerted, on the whole, a negative effect upon Byzantine legal science, since it robbed Roman law of its ultimate significance while offering no alternative system of justice in the world.[60]

This occurred, seemingly, because of a lack of significant "grounding" with respect to the Eastern Church's understanding of legal authority; in other words, there was a lack of true connection made between divine authority and such practical issues as law. Nevertheless, while this "authority vacuum" was developing in the East, an even greater one appeared in the West, but for a different reason. From 476 on, and particularly after 495 when Clovis was converted, the West began the process of independence from imperial rule. Clovis, who was called *Christus Pantocrator* ("Christ as ruler" over the world and especially over the emperor), began the process of setting the Church free from the secular empire, which resulted in the rise of a desacrilized secular state as well. The Popes attempted to fill this authority vacuum by vehemently asserting that their authority was derived from Peter and not from their political setting. It was Gelasius (Pope from 492 to 496) who, over against the emperors, began to intervene at will in ecclesiastical affairs, asserting an independent and higher political authority in religious matters. So, while the doctrine of the Spirit seemed to diminish considerably during this time (mostly because Church leaders were fearful of "enthusiasm") the authority of the Church itself was on the rise. Between Constantine and Clovis there was certain "deadness" in both Eastern and Western Churches. Though papal claims remained lofty throughout the Middle Ages, the actual ecclesial power of the Popes diminished considerably between 600 and 1050. Councils of Bishops often ruled in various Western territorial Churches with kings presiding over them. With the "prophets" of the early Church no longer exhibiting Church authority, with no official emperor, and with the diminishing influence of the papacy, Western Churches (those previously controlled by the emperor) were able to develop a greater degree of local ecclesial control.

60. Ibid., 169.

Within this context we can examine the importance of the *Filioque* debate. The clause was first inserted into the Nicene Creed at the third council of Toledo (ca. 589) under King Reccared (ca. 586–601). Though the Eastern Church objected to this emendation, they were more offended at not having been consulted about the change. The struggle reached its climax in 1054 with the "official" addition of the *Filioque clause* into the Nicene Creed. This amendment, performed by Pope Benedict VIII at the Council of Florence,[61] stated that, by begetting the Son, the Father also bestowed upon the Son that the Spirit should proceed from the Son as well as from Himself. This action factored heavily into the intense political upheaval that soon followed. Pope Hildebrand (1070s) proclaimed the legal supremacy of the Pope over all Christians and of the clergy over all secular authorities, and Pope Urban II launched the First Crusade in 1095. Berman demonstrates that *Filioque* gave the papacy theological grounds to capitalize on the schism. In attempting to use the crusades to export the Papal Revolution to Eastern Christendom, the schism eventually took the form of violence and conquest. *Filioque* was thereby a major contributor to the conception of the popular slogan, "the freedom of the Church."[62]

The Papal Revolution is described as *rapid* (with sweeping changes often occurring overnight) and *total* (including political, socioeconomic, cultural, and intellectual changes). Technological developments and new methods of cultivation contributed to the rapid increase in agricultural productivity, surplus, and trade. European population increased by more than half between 1050 and 1150, and thousands of new cities and towns emerged. Cultural changes include the creation of the first universities, the first use of scholastic methods of learning, and the rigorous systematization of theology, jurisprudence, philosophy, and science.[63] Behind these improvements stood a critical change in the conception of the Church itself and its responsibility to reform the world. This Papal Revolution resulted in

---

61. Charlemagne tried to have it formally confirmed at Frankfurt (794). He was attempting to correct the Second Council of Nicaea (787), which had received the profession of Tarasius, who stated that the Spirit proceeds "from the Father *per* ('through') the Son." The two Churches remained in communion through these challenges. It wasn't until Florence, when the East felt it views were unrepresented, that the departure become official.

62. Berman, *Law and Revolution*, 105.

63. See Berman, *Law and Revolution*, 99–106.

a political disengagement (but not separation) of the sacred from the secular, as well as the "desacrilization" of the state, granting various political and religious groups a relative freedom of religion (though the Popes attempted to rule in matters of faith and morals) along with freedom from state rule and oppression. "The freedom of the Church" became an apocalyptic struggle for a new order of things. As a result, the concept of the Church became one of dynamic involvement in the world and in its practical affairs (i.e., ethics, law, government, etc.).[64]

Is there any connection between the *Filioque* emendation and the change that occurred regarding the Church's understanding of its role in the world? This question is one to ponder as we examine two major contributors to the *Filioque* debate: Augustine and John of Damascus.

Augustine

Augustine (354–430) was intensely interested in the doctrine of the Holy Spirit. Though the *Filioque* doctrine had already been taught in one form or another by other Church Fathers (i.e., Tertullian, Hilary, Ambrose), Augustine's understanding of the Holy Spirit as the Spirit of love and the Spirit of unity between the first two Persons of the Trinity was considered novel for his time. Beginning with the idea of the Trinity as pure relation, Augustine calls the Spirit the *vinculum caritas* ("bond of love") between the Father and the Son,[65] and a *caritas* ("mutual gift") primarily from the Father to the Son, but also from the Son to the Father.[66] As the Spirit of the Father and of the Son, he "proceeds"[67] simultaneously from both the Father and the Son (and thus from only one source). Holding that the Spirit receives His

---

64. Berman points out that many historians mark this as the beginning of the modern era. See Berman, *Law and Revolution*, 87–88.

65. Augustine's approach, according to Badcock, "suggests a certain priority of the Father-Son relation over everything else; indeed, strictly speaking, the Spirit *is* this Father-Son relation" (Badcock, *Light of Truth and Fire of Love*, 77–78).

66. Augustine, "De Trinitate," VI:7–9.

67. Gregory of Nazianzus developed the concept of "divine procession." Referring to such Scriptures as John 15:26, Gregory says that the Spirit is neither Father nor Son; he is neither *unbegotten* (as is the Father), nor *begotten* (as is the Son), but *proceeds*—and none of these three concepts can be understood rationally. Thus, the Spirit is not a "second son" or a "grandson." See Gregory, *Select Oracles*, 31:8.

divinity from the Son (just as the Son receives His divinity from the Father), Augustine rules out the idea that the Son is only a *medium* through which the Spirit proceeds (as proposed in the Eastern view). Instead, the Spirit acts as the principle agent in the economy of Christ's salvation by bringing the sinner into the life of the Trinity, into the relationship of love provided therein. Augustine gives the following summary of the Spirit's work:

> According to Holy Scripture, this Holy Spirit is neither only the Spirit of the Father nor only the Spirit of the Son, but is the Spirit of both. Because of this, he is able to teach us that charity which is common both to the Father and to the Son and through which they love each other.[68]

Latin tradition regarding the trinitarian Persons exposes this understanding of the Spirit. In the unity of the godhead (which is defined in the word *homoousios*), the Persons are distinguished by the way they are relationally opposed to each other. Since the Spirit and Son proceed equally from the Father, there must be a processional relationship between Son and Spirit as well (proceeding from Son to Spirit) in order for them to be distinguished.[69] In *De Trinitate* Augustine confirms this Latin conception of procession by referring to the terms "Father," "Son," and "Holy Spirit" as "relative" terms—that is, expressions of relationship. Since such relational diversity exists within the same substance or "essence,"[70] absolute terms such as "good," "all-powerful," and "Creator" apply to each of the Persons without diversifying or multiplying the substance. Though all three Persons may rightly be called "Creator," this does not amount to three creators.[71]

---

68. Augustine, *De Trinitate*, XV:17, 27.

69. See Congar, *The Word and the Spirit*, 1:107–8. See Anselm for further detail.

70. Congar, *I Believe in the Holy Spirit*, 3:81.

71. Therefore, an Augustinian conception of the Trinity contains both relational and absolute aspects, and each Person exists by a relationship of "eternal source" or "eternal procession." Defining "Person" in terms of relationship actually coincides closely with the theology of the Cappadocian Fathers, on whom Augustine was possibly dependent. There are, however, important differences. Basil, for example, deduces from the divine relationships the unity of the divine essence, while Augustine begins with the divine identity and then deduces from this the divine relationships (See Congar, *I Believe in the Holy Spirit*, 3:82–83).

Augustine deals with the question of *Filioque* in *De Trinitate* as well, and his conclusions accord with the above thinking. In his writing he seems to make a deliberate effort to oppose the Eastern conception of the Spirit by associating divine *auctoritas* (i.e., authority or source or authorship) with the Father alone (rather than to all three Persons). Augustine states,

> Scripture enables us to know in the Father the principle, *auctoritas*, in the Son being begotten and born, *nativitas*, and in the Spirit the union of the Father and the Son, *Patris Filioque communitas*. . . . The society of the unity of the Church of God, outside of which there is no remission of sins, is in a sense the work of the Holy Spirit, with, or course, the co-operation of the Father and the Son, because the Holy Spirit himself is in a sense the society of the Father and Son.[72]

How does Augustine deal with John 15:26, which tells us that the Spirit "proceeds from the Father"? He replies that the Father communicated to the Son all that he is, apart from his being Father. Thus, all that the Son has comes from the Father.[73]

John of Damascus

John of Damascus (ca. 675—ca. 749) has been described as "the last great theologian of the Eastern Church." John's pneumatology is essentially a synthesis of the basic concepts provided by Athanasius and the Cappadocians. His *De Fide Orthodoxa* came to serve as a primary textbook for Eastern theology that provided Greek theologians with many theological standard concepts, including the monarchy of the Father, the distinction between the Son's begetting and the Spirit's ἐκπόρευσις ("procession"), and clarifications regarding the Son/Spirit relationship (i.e., the Spirit comes "through" the Son, "rests in" the Son, expresses the Son, and is communicated by the Son). He also provides one of the few early documents that literally grant "authority" to the Spirit:

> Likewise we become also in one Holy Spirit, the Lord and Giver of Life, which proceeds from the Father and rests in the Son, the object

---

72. Augustine, *Sermo* 71:18.
73. Augustine, *Commentary on John the Evangelist*, XCIX:8–9.

of equal adoration and glorification with the Father and the Son, since it is con-substantial and co-eternal, the Spirit of God, direct, *authoritative*, the foundation of wisdom and life and holiness; God existing and addressed along with the Father and the Son; uncreated, full, creative, all-ruling, all-effecting, all-powerful, of infinite power; Lord above all creation, and not under any Lord.[74]

Such an authority is associated with the *energies* of God, which Eastern theology distinguished from God's *essence*.[75] The divine energies function to make the incomprehensible and inaccessible essence of God comprehensible and accessible, thus providing a theoretical foundation for communion with God and for the Eastern understanding of the Trinity. John also popularized the use of the term *perichoresis* in the theology of the Trinity.[76] It was first used by Maximus the Confessor to express the oneness of action and effect resulting from the union of the two natures in Christ.

Perichoresis in the theology of the Trinity points to the in-existence of the Persons within each other, the fact that they are present to each other, that they contain one another and that they manifest each other. This in-existence is based on the unity and identity of

---

74. John of Damascus, *De fide orthod*. I:8 (emphasis mine).

75. "In his essence, God remains the unattainable, incomprehensible mystery; and at the heart of that mystery lies the generation of the Son and the sending forth of the Sprit, both issuing in their different modes from the Father. But God also reaches out by activity of his uncreated energies to create and to involve the creation in participation in the movement of his triune being. At the level of the energies . . . the Spirit shines out in the Son, reflects the Son, and manifests the glory incarnate in him. And what enables and underlies this activity of imaging and displaying the Son is the primal springing of the Spirit *from the same One who is Father of the Son*, not a procession of the Spirit *from both*. The abyss of the divine nature overflows doubly in the begetting of the Son and the sending forth of the Spirit, the Lord, the Life-giver, who proceeds from the Father" (Heron, *The Holy Spirit*, 85, emphasis his).

76. This term provides balance to the Eastern conception of the Trinity. Eastern theology argues that the Nicene Creed speaks of the Spirit as a distinct Person within the trinitarian Godhead, rather than as a subordinate agent of the Son. Eastern Churches have particularly emphasized the uniqueness of function of the three divine hypostases. The Trinity is not to be viewed, however, as a sort of tritheism, because of the balance provided by the concept of *perichoresis*, which implies that each member of the Trinity functions in vital correspondence and involvement with the other two.

substance between the three, even in the teaching of the Greek Fathers.[77]

The Greek ἐν was used to indicate the way that the Persons that exist within God "hypostatize" the same substance. They are "in" or "within" each other. Each one is also εἰς, turned "toward" the other and given "to" the other. John begins by speaking of the one God as the absolute being, rather than of the three hypostases. This one God, however, is also the Father, who by means of monarchy is Father by nature of the Son and the "Producer" of the Holy Spirit. The Spirit is not another Son—he does not proceed by begetting but by ἐκπορευτός.[78] In contrast to Augustine, John draws a parallel between the Son who is "begotten" and the Spirit who "proceeds": "We have learned through faith that there is a difference between begetting and proceeding, but faith tells us nothing about the nature of that difference."[79] The Spirit, therefore, proceeds from the Father alone. The crucial distinction between John's theology and Western theology thereby arises when we consider the relationship between the Spirit and the Son. John says, "We do not say that the Son is the cause, nor do we say that he is Father . . . We do not say that the Spirit comes from the Son (ἐκ τοῦ Υἱοῦ), but we do say that the Spirit is of the Son."[80] The idea here is that the Spirit's property—procession—is only accessible and intelligible to us in reference to the Son, and that the Spirit "penetrates" the Son until the Spirit remains and dwells in the Son while still dwelling in the Father.

OTHER CONTRIBUTORS

John of Damascus' conception of the procession of the Spirit from the Father and through the Son did not stand in direct opposition to *Filioque*. It was only with Photius that the issue became one of serious controversy, so much so that the *Filioque* addition became grounds for official separation. For Photius, "the distinction between the divine persons was adequately

---

77. Congar, *I Believe in the Holy Spirit*, 3:37.
78. John of Damascus, *De fide orthod*, I:8.
79. Ibid.
80. Ibid.

explained by the personal properties of each."[81] In 867, while Patriarch of Constantinople, Photius attacked *Filioque* on several fronts, arguing that: (1) it was a Western innovation, (2) it was unbiblical (nowhere in Scripture, he proclaimed, is the Son mentioned as the *source* of the Spirit within the divinity), (3) the Western position splits the divinity (because the Spirit appears to proceed from two principles), and (4) Augustinian thought (that the Father and Son form a single source) cancels the distinction between the Father and Son. Photius' most persuasive argument, however, is that the Augustinian view distorts the idea of personal source (the Father being that source), by replacing it with an essentially impersonal one—the *relationship* between the Father and the Son.

Anselm (1033–1109) begins with the common ground between the Latin and the Greek conceptions of the Trinity in order to attempt a reconciliation regarding *Filioque* (at the Council of Bari). He examines the identity of the Person (which is found in either origin or procession), and the Father and Son as source, and concludes that there is no inequality between the Father as principle source and the Son as a derived source. The Spirit's procession is from "God," who is the divine essence. This essence includes Father, Son, and Spirit—each possessing equality of divinity.[82] Anselm, however, broke from the previous tradition regarding procession. Augustine had regarded the Father as the sole origin (with the Holy Spirit proceeding originally [*principaliter*] from the Father but also from the Son), and Aquinas has affirmed the Father is the source and that the Son's procession is thereby derivative from the Father. Nevertheless, Anselm did not recognize the Father's originality, and has perhaps influenced Western theology more than any of his predecessors.

The "Executorial Authority" of the Spirit—Definition and Storyline

Medieval theology challenges the universal Church to consider whether or not the Holy Spirit's authority to execute God's will in the world is in any way related to the authority of Jesus Christ, the one who proclaims, "All authority in heaven and on earth has been given to me" (Matt 28:18). Is the

---

81. Gaybba, *The Spirit of Love*, 74.
82. See Congar, *I Believe in the Holy Spirit*, 3:98–110; Gaybba, *The Spirit of Love*, 74–75.

Spirit's authority executed *under* the authority of Christ or, as the Eastern tradition implies, is the Spirit somewhat "independent" of Christ's authority in his execution of God's will?

Whereas Patristic theology helps us discern a provisional definition of a generic "divine authority" with respect to the Spirit of God (the "who" of the Spirit's authority), in this section we begin to discern the nature of the Spirit's "executive authority" (the "how" of the Spirit's authority with respect to the pattern of divine authority). In other words, while both Eastern and Western theologies grant the Spirit some measure of divine authority *by nature*,[83] the difference between the two lies in the nature of the execution of this authority in the world. The two views are implied by their conceptions of the Spirit's procession:

1. The Eastern formulation (as expressed by John of Damascus as the procession of the Spirit from the Father *through* the Son) implies that the Spirit has an "authority" derived from or delegated by the Father alone. Photius, in particular, emphasizes the parallel between the Spirit's procession and the Son's generation, thus giving them distinct origins in and from the Father. The Spirit has his own complementary role alongside the Son, cooperating with the Son. Rather than the unity of the Trinity residing in the Spirit, as we have seen in Augustine, unity in the Orthodox tradition lies in the Father. A supreme "executive authority" of the Spirit (one that parallels the "executive authority" of Christ) is thereby implied by Eastern Orthodox theology.[84] The Spirit simply possesses an authority to execute the Father's will. This authority is not subject to Christological limitations, and there is no directly implied subordination of authority by the Spirit to the Son.[85]

---

83. As we shall see, some Western theologies—such as Augustine's—do bring the Spirit's divine authority with respect to the immanent Trinity into question. However, there is no prominent Western theologian who is both orthodox and has actually *denied* the fact that the Spirit possesses divine authority of some sort.

84. In the previous chapter we identified "executive authority" as simply "the right or the power to act in certain ways" (DeGeorge, *The Nature and Limits of Authority*, 62). This definition contains no specific limitations regarding the right or power to act.

85. Eastern Orthodoxy's mindset is grounded in the ideas that there exists a substantial continuation of the Spirit's authority from the days of the early Church until now. This

THE LORD IS THE SPIRIT

2. The Western view implies that the Spirit has an authority derived from and delegated by both the Father and the Son for the *primary* purpose of glorifying the Son (John 16:13–14). The Spirit does this by carrying out the Son's will *after* his departure. Therefore, we may infer that an analogy to an *executor of a will* may best describe the Western understanding of the Spirit, as one who has been given the authority to carry out Jesus' will on earth after Jesus has departed. It would then seem to be more accurate to speak of the Western understanding of the Spirit's authority as that of an "executorial authority" rather than as an "executive authority."

Is the *Filioque* debate solvable? Two ecumenical councils (Lyons in 1274, and Florence in 1438) both attempted and yet failed to resolve the struggle. Florence concluded that "from the Son" and "through the Son" means essentially the same thing, but this was later dismissed by the East. These councils probably failed because they only sought to persuade the Greeks to agree to Latin ideas. Many theologians throughout Church history (i.e., Anselm, Moltmann) have attempted various "compromises," but none have proved satisfactory to both sides. Congar, a *filioquist*, asserts instead that the two formulas are complementary, as seen in the fact that the Fathers of the Church held both formulas in communion.[86] Likewise, when we examine the *Filioque* debate in medieval theology, we seem to find complementary evidence as well.

Before attempting to "resolve" this debate exegetically (in chapter 3), we may make an initial comparison of these two views along two lines—historical (i.e., the impact of the respective positions upon history), and theological (i.e., the strengths and the weaknesses of the theological positions themselves). First, in our historical analysis, we notice two related

---

idea is described well by Hryniewicz, "The early Church often appropriated to itself the conviction that she was controlled by the Holy Spirit, and for this reason the identity and continuity of her sacramental nature was preserved. The Holy Spirit, which takes effect in the community of believers, was the highest authority for the early Church and the only real security. Very early on, conscious decision was affirmed in the conviction: 'the Holy Spirit and us' (Acts 15:28). . . . The authority and rule of the Holy Spirit in the early Church, however, was placed far ahead of all individualism and subjectivism" (Hryniewicz, "Der Pneumatologishe Aspekt der Kirche aus Orthodoxer Sicht," 137–38).

86. Congar, *I Believe in the Holy Spirit*, 1:188.

themes regarding the Eastern Church: (1) it never completely broke from the handcuffs of imperialism, and (2) it did not recognize the authority of Christ over the Holy Spirit in ecclesiastical and soteriological issues to the same degree as the West. While granting "monarchical" authority to the Father as divine source, the "working out" of this authority in the context of humanity tends to escape into mysticism. Berman notices that this tendency is revealed in Eastern art:

> Eastern Christian art has reflected the theology of the Eastern Church, and also the theology of the West between the sixth and tenth centuries, in its emphasis on transcendence (or "otherworldliness," as it is called in the West). This is a theology centered in heaven, in man's "ascent to the infinite," in man's deification. The emphasis is on God the Father, the Creator. Christ has shown mankind the way to him. The icons reflect this.[87]

The Western Church, on the other hand, and Western culture as well seem to exemplify some strong benefits in association with of the *Filioque*. The clause was ratified by Popes who, in general, attempted to insure that the Church would not be mastered by the State but would be subject to Christ alone. Christ is King; the Pope is "vicar." The results of their "incarnational" focus seem non-coincidental in at least two ways—the rapid development of the Catholic faith, and the progress of Western culture and the Western legal system. Berman provides the logic needed for such a conclusion:

> But Western theology of the eleventh and twelfth centuries shifted the emphasis to the second person of the Trinity, to the incarnation of God in this world, to God the redeemer. God's humanity in Christ took the center of the stage. This was reflected in the papal amendment of the Nicene Creed by the proclamation that the Holy Spirit "proceeds" not only "from the Father" but also "from the Son" (Filioque). God the Father, representing the whole of creation, the cosmic order, was incarnate in God the Son, who represents mankind. By the Filioque clause, God the Holy Spirit, who is identified in the Nicene Creed with the Church, was said to have his source not only in the First Person but also the Second

---

87. Berman, *Law and Revolution*, 176–77.

> Person of the Trinity—not only in creation but also in incarnation and redemption.
>
> Thus the Church came to be seen less as the communion of saints in heaven and more as the community of sinners on earth. Rationalism itself was an expression of the believing in the incarnation of divine mysteries in human concepts and theories. God was seen to be not only transcendent but also immanent. . . . It was not transcendence as such, and not immanence as such, that was linked with the rationalization and systematization of law and legality in the West, but rather incarnation, which was understood as the process by which the transcendent becomes immanent. It is no accident that Christianity, Judaism, and Islam, all three of which postulate both a radical separation and a radical interconnection between God and man, also postulate that God is a judge and lawgiver and that man is governed by divine laws. Nevertheless, the distinctive features of the Western concepts of human law that emerged in the eleventh and twelfth centuries—as contrasted not only with Judaic and Islamic concepts but also with those of Eastern Christianity—are related to the greater Western emphasis on incarnation as the central reality of the universe. This released an enormous energy for the redemption of the world; yet it split the legal from the spiritual, the political from the ideological.[88]

Though the data provided by cultural and legal improvements as witnessed in the West do not provide *conclusive* evidence with respect to the *Filioque* debate, we may safely infer from Berman's analysis that such improvements may well be linked to the Spirit's unique role in Western theology—not as one that places a specific focus upon the Spirit himself, but because in the *Filioque* the Spirit has been recognized as one who possesses "executorial authority" to magnify Christ and to dispense Christ's salvation. The Spirit is seen as the one who executes Christ's authority (including Christ's legal authority) in time and space in order to bring glory to Christ. *Filioque* Christology thus displays the heart of medieval theology—that Christ is to be honored in all respects: theology, law, culture, art, politics, et cetera. Berman's argument is that almost all modern liberties, as promoted through the legal and civic institutions of the West, and our modern understanding of "local autonomy" are related to what happened

---

88. Ibid., 178.

during this time (though many of its benefits will not be completely seen until the Protestant Reformation and after). From this we can safely infer that, because of the imperial authority possessed by the State, such liberties could not have developed in the East.

In evaluating the theological strengths and weaknesses of these two positions, it seems that the logic of Augustinian thought regarding procession (and particularly with respect to Augustine's conception of "relational opposition") is fairly convincing. Applying such logic to the doctrine of the Spirit's authority with respect to the divine economy in the Church age, we can deduce that the authority of the Son and the authority of the Spirit can only be distinguished (and understood to be non-conflictory) if the Spirit is "under" the authority of Christ.

This outstanding strength, however, is coupled with a considerable weakness. Colin Gunton has noticed a common complaint among many contemporary theologians that Augustine's *persona* of the Spirit—identified as God's love and gift to the world—does not adequately distinguish the Spirit from the Son, who "might equally, perhaps with more justification, be described as the Father's love and gift to the world."[89] Such a lack of distinction is understandable when we remember that Augustine owes much to Platonic thought, as evidenced in his analogy of the immanent Trinity to the threefold structure of the human mind, with the Spirit being compared to the will. As with Plato, who said that knowledge consists in the recollection of the Forms known before one's temporal existence, Augustine views the will as that which relates memory to knowledge by bringing the contents of memory into conscious reasoning. Likewise, the function of the Spirit in the Trinity is to bring the Father and the Son unto relationship—a unitive function that neglects many other features of the Spirit's actions and can easily lead to a subordination of the Spirit to the Son, even within the immanent Trinity.[90] The effect may well be a neglect of the Spirit's nature as a divine *Person* in his own right. This is essentially ratified in Augustine's description of the Father as *auctoritas* and the Spirit as *communitas*. The Spirit seems to possess an executorial role in the economic Trinity but not the personal authority to carry it out.

89. Gunton, *Theology through the Theologians*, 109.
90. Ibid., 110.

Jenson holds that Augustine's three "persons" are functionally indistinguishable. "Augustine could no longer conceptualize the saving relation between God and creatures by saying that the Father and the Son are transformingly present in the Spirit, as the Greek originators of trinitarianism had done."[91] Thus, the work of the Spirit can be easily thought of as an impersonal process whereby God acts upon us. Since (as we have seen) authority always resides in *persons*, this conception of the Spirit diminishes or eliminates the Spirit's authority and implies that the Spirit is simply a *function* of Christ. Inch, a Western theologian who remains strongly in favor of *Filioque*, summarizes the effect of this weakness upon the Western Church:

> Herein lies one of the fundamental errors in the Western Church, according to their Eastern counterpart: it presumes to know the secret working of the Spirit in others. It does not respect the sanctity of life expressed in the diversity of the Spirit's work. Thus, this understanding of the way of the Spirit proves too narrow. But the problem lies more deeply in that the West presumes to understand what escapes us all. *By attempting to bring divine truths down to human forms, it loses the mystical quality of faith and the transcendent character of the Spirit as being present within us.*[92]

Such criticisms, while valid, do not pose a death sentence upon *Filioque* or the notion of the Spirit's executorial authority. We must realize that the Eastern view has gaping weaknesses as well (and that in discerning the Spirit's *authority to act* we must take contributions from both views into consideration). Gunton charges that, like the charismatic movement, Eastern Orthodox theology tends to develop an insufficient relationship between Christ and the Spirit. As Barth has stated, this suggests a mystical assent to the Father without the mediation of the Son.[93] Such a lack of theological development gives the impression that the Church can stand under the authority of the Spirit alone. This can be sensed in Hryniewicz' description of the Spirit's "authority" with respect to Orthodox Church bishops.

---

91. Jensen, *The Holy Spirit*, 2:126–27.
92. Inch, *Saga of the Spirit*, 224 (emphasis mine).
93. Barth, *Church Dogmatics*, 1/1:481.

The Authority of the Holy Spirit and Historical Theology: Assessing Historical Debates

> In light of the orthodox tradition, the function of the bishops does not emerge out of the personal legal delegation, which is given to him individually through Christ; it is instead the work of the Holy Spirit in the entire community. . . . *The general consensus of all bishops became the expression of the highest authority in the Church as the indication of the presence and the work of the Holy Spirit.*[94]

Kasper points out another weakness in Greek pneumatology. Not only is the Eastern tradition, in its dogmatic creedal formulas, almost completely silent about the relation of the Spirit to the Son, but there is also no relation drawn between the economy of salvation (the economic Trinity) and the inner life of the Trinity (the immanent Trinity). According to Kasper, if the Son has a share in the sending of the Spirit in the history of salvation (which he obviously does), then he cannot fail to have a share into the intra-trinitarian procession of the Spirit.[95]

Protestant Theology

The Catholic-Protestant controversy battled in two arenas—the nature of authority and the basic doctrines of the faith—that became interwoven through the notion that "correct" doctrine is ultimately determined by the authority one accepts regarding the interpretation of Scripture. Such an "interpretative authority" was presumed by both parties to be possessed primarily by the author of the text. In this section, we will examine the nature of "interpretive authority"[96] as well as the Holy Spirit's possession or delegation of such an authority. Western Medieval theology, which developed a general framework for understanding the Spirit's role as authoritative "Executor" of Christ's will on earth, had not yet worked out precisely *how* the Spirit fulfills this role in the world, particularly in relation to the interpretation of Scripture. Thus, in the development of a "post-medieval" pneumatology, the issue of scriptural interpretation was naturally the first

---

94. Hryniewicz, "Der Pneumatologishe Aspekt Der Kirche," 137–38 (emphasis mine).

95. Kasper, *The God of Jesus Christ*, 218.

96. Ramm sees this as an aspect of "veracious authority." In connection with the Church, Ramm defines "veracious authority" as the authority to determine the truths of revelation (Ramm, *The Pattern of Authority*, 56). As the "source" of truth, the Holy Spirit is the one who possesses the *veracious authority* necessary to claim a legitimate and ultimate "interpretive authority" (12).

"executorial" question to arise. It is "prolegomena" in that, before the Church can develop a systematic set of doctrines, she must first determine her interpretive methods.

The Reformers sought to establish a *pneumatological* method of interpretation that could guide their subsequent theologizing. Before the Reformation began, however, *interpretive authority* was essentially equated with Roman Catholic authority. The Roman Church claimed that she possessed two key ingredients necessary for interpretive authority: (1) the proper source of truth—the Bible, and (2) the proper hermeneutical tools for interpreting the source of truth—Tradition. God, who was considered final authority, had expressed his authority in revelation and continues to express his authority in and through the Church. This led to the doctrine of the Church's "infallibility." Several factors led to the eventual mistrust of Roman Catholic hermeneutics from the perspective of the "Protestants." The Protestant rallying cry, "sola scriptura," did not mean that scriptural authority excludes all other means of knowing God's will (i.e., Tradition, reason), but that Scripture provides the norm for the other means as the "final court of appeal." Luther, for example, held to the primacy and all-sufficiency of the *sensus literalis* of Scripture, thus countering the four-fold hermeneutical approach of medieval theology (which included analogical [logical], allegorical [mystical], and anagogical [moral] approaches). The cultural changes that resulted from the Reformation did not come about by any attempt toward social revolution—the "revolutionary" aspect of the Reformation era was its new emphasis on the Word of God. This emphasis coincided with the rise in literacy, the invention of the printing press, and the rediscovery of Greek and Roman classics within the culture of Renaissance humanism. All of these changes resulted in an interest in returning to "sources."

> The Reformation of the sixteenth century was a *modern* movement that drew inspiration from the general culture and learning of the time. It is no accident, therefore, that the earliest heroes of the Reformation were, when all is said and done, not visionaries or social revolutionaries or even religious mystics, but scholars and Bible translators.[97]

---

97. Badcock, *Light of Truth and Fire of Love*, 87.

The Reformation also coincided with the breakdown of ecclesiastic unity, cultural unity and denominational unity. Without an emperor or Pope as their ecclesial authority, the Protestant's authority became individualized or denominationalized. The Bible, as interpreted by the individual believer or the denomination, could once again become the foundation of societal authority.

Martin Luther and John Calvin

The debate over the nature of the Spirit's role in biblical interpretation is exemplified at the Diet of Worms, where Martin Luther cried, "It is written!" and the Church replied with excommunication. While many theologians recognize Luther's role in the development of the Western world's understanding of the nature of authority, few however, have understood Luther's perspective regarding the authority of the Spirit. For Luther, the Spirit has his own existence in God's eternal glory, apart from the Word and apart from the physical world, and thus cannot be controlled by us. The Spirit is the "sphere" of revelation where Christ is present and the Word is alive. Luther remarks,

> For Christian holiness, or the holiness common to Christendom, is found where the Holy Spirit gives people faith in Christ and thus sanctifies them, Acts 15[:9], that is, he renews heart, soul, body, work, and conduct, inscribing the commandments of God not on tables of stone, but in hearts of flesh, II Corinthians 3[:3].[98]

Luther also proclaims, "In the whole of Scripture there is none but Christ, either in plain words or in involved words."[99] Instead of adopting the Augustinian view of the Spirit as the gift of grace mediated primarily through the Church, Luther connected the Spirit once again with the authority of Christ and the authority of the Word of God—and thus gave us grounding for our pattern of authority. As a result, Luther's pneumatology is best understood as the Spirit of Christ working through the channel of the Word of God. This became a major theme of Reformation theology, representing a shift away from the earlier concern for precise definitions of

---

98. Luther, "On the Councils," 145.
99. Luther, *The Works of Martin Luther*, 11:223.

the Spirit's nature and toward the doctrine of the *work* of the Spirit in terms of the subjective appropriation of the gospel by the believer.

In Luther's theology, the Spirit's work continues in the Christo-centric theme of Western medieval theology, but takes on a new role—that of securing or mediating the incorporation of the believer into Christ through the Word of God. This Word reaches the heart and leads the believer to genuine faith through the inward work of the Spirit. As the instrument of the Spirit, the Word is connected to the Spirit through the resurrection of Christ. How does this occur? By placing the power of the resurrection into the context of the gospel, the Spirit causes the risen Christ to live His risen life in our midst through the message of the Word. Luther thereby holds that the work of the Holy Spirit is always a logical outworking of the *Filioque* clause, in that the Spirit serves as a mediator of the experience of Christ, and thus "reveals every relation to Christ which is not experience, which does not rest on the mediating, real and redeeming presence of Christ."[100] All other talk about the presence of Christ outside this sphere is either spiritualistic mysticism or moralistic imitation of Christ. Indeed, the only Spirit Luther knows is the Spirit of Christ. Luther tells us that the main work of the Spirit is not to authorize or justify the actions of the magisterium, but rather to create faith within those who believe—and specifically, faith in the historical Christ.

Although John Calvin is frequently acknowledged as "the theologian of the Holy Spirit" among the sixteenth century reformers, the doctrine of the Spirit's *authority* may be the most overlooked aspect of Calvin's pneumatology as well. According to John Hesselink, "an important aspect of his doctrine of the Holy Spirit has been neglected, namely, how the Holy Spirit leads, guides, governs, and rules in the life of the believers."[101] Calvin at times allows the Spirit a certain freedom *over* the Word and the inspiration of the Word (even more so than Luther) without ever speaking of the Spirit as disconnected from Christ. This is alluded to in his statement, "Our mind must be illuminated, and our heart established by some exterior power, in order for the Word of God to obtain full credit with us."[102] At other times,

---

100. Prenter, *Spiritus Creator*, 61.
101. Hesselink, "Governed and Guided by the Spirit," 161.
102. Calvin, *Institutes*, III.ii.7.

The Authority of the Holy Spirit and Historical Theology: Assessing Historical Debates

however, Calvin *subordinates* the Spirit to the Word of God (both the Word of God in the Person of Christ and the written Word) and in such thinking we can discern an *executorial authority* of the Spirit.[103] This latter aspect is evident in Calvin's *criterion* (German, *kriterion*[104]), which was utilized by the reformers to designate a functional authority, and in his *discremin*, which is a set of related criterion. Johnson explains how such a *criterion* was applied to the office of the Spirit as He speaks through the Word:

> The word *discremin*, which is used frequently, is intended to designate a configuration of criteria that are in some way organically related to one another as reciprocal coefficients. Calvin's doctrine of the Word and Spirit may be cited as a classic example of the theological *discremin*. It requires the *testimonium Spiritus Sancti*, or that the Holy Spirit "attests" the written Word of Scripture, in order for it to be authoritative and useful for theological purposes. It also reassures that the Word of Scripture be utilized to "test" the Holy Spirit, or to "test the spirits to see whether they are of God" (1 John 4:1). Within this doctrine both the Scripture and the testimony of the Holy Spirit are criteria, but they are inseparably related as reciprocal coefficients.[105]

Calvin illustrates the nature of this *discremin* when arguing that the Spirit is only being consistent with himself when he uses that Word which he has previously revealed:

> By a kind of mutual bond the Lord has joined together the certainty of his Word and of his Spirit, so that the perfect religion of the Word may abide in our minds when the Spirit, who causes us to contemplate God's face, shines; and that we in turn may embrace

---

103. This subordination occurs in a different way, though, than in Augustine's formulation. Whereas in Augustine's theology believers are seen as justified by the Spirit's *caritas*, in Calvin's theology the Spirit comes through other means, in particular the Word and the Sacraments. Calvin sees the Spirit's role in salvation as quite distinct (though not completely independent) from the role of Christ, and this distinction clarifies the nature of the Spirit's *executorial authority* in almost all subsequent evangelical theology.

104. Reformers first used this word to describe the role of the judge who presided over and passed sentences in a court of law. Such an authority was understood to be resident in one's office, commission, or status—not in the person.

105. Johnson, *Authority in Protestant Theology*, 15.

> the Spirit with no fear of being deceived when we recognize him in his own image, namely, in the Word.[106]

Oosterhaven finds Calvin's concept of order in the background of all Calvin's theology. Calvin was educated in Stoic philosophy, which identified God with order and held that the unity of the world was maintained by Reason.[107] The Spirit is seen in this model of God as the archetype and controller of order through reason. The Spirit is to be understood as active in creation, demonstrating authority in and through his bestowal of "beauty and order." As a result, Calvin gave Protestant theology and doctrine a hermeneutic that reflects his concept of order and that is derived from his *discremin*.

> If we . . . look only to Calvin, we are forced to take with total seriousness his reiteration that the Word and the Spirit are inseparable in constituting the *discremin* that must reign over Christian doctrine. It was the development of this second noetic office of the Spirit which gave Protestantism a systematic doctrine of theological authority. . . . It was this same Calvin, who emphasized and re-emphasized, more than any of the other Reformers, that the Word becomes authoritative as, and *only as*, it is joined with the *testimonium Spiritus Sancti*.[108]

The Roman Catholic Magisterium

The authority of the Spirit, according to the counter-Reformation, is evident in the "infallibility" of the Roman Catholic Church. According to Congar,

> The Spirit is guaranteed to pastors insofar as they are pastors of the *Church*, recognized by the Church as having the grace that dwells in it and as appointed or given by God Himself. This guarantee of faithfulness, of which the Spirit is the principle, is given to the *Church*. It is such a firm guarantee that to admit that the Church is capable of error is to impute a failure on the part of the Spirit.[109]

---

106. Calvin, *Institutes of the Christian Religion*, I:ix.3.
107. Osterhaven, "John Calvin," 25.
108. Johnson, *Authority in Protestant Theology*, 54.
109. Congar, *I Believe in the Holy Spirit*, 1:151.

The Catholic Church's faithfulness, according to counter-reformation Catholic theologians, was radically and yet erroneously questioned by the Reformers. John Fisher exemplifies this attitude by arguing that the promise of the Spirit was not made simply to the apostles but to the Church until the end of the age. As a result, the Spirit provides *the* hermeneutical principle for determining truth.

> The universal Church cannot fall into error, being led by the Spirit of truth dwelling in it for ever. Christ will remain with the Church until the end of the world.... [The Church] is taught by the same one Spirit to determine what is required by the changing circumstances of the times.[110]

Such an "interpretive authority" was made an institutional standard via the Council of Trent. Catholic theologians at Trent appealed to the continual activity of the Spirit throughout the Church age as a primary justification for the handing down of the apostolic traditions and for the trust that should be placed in those traditions. This, however, is not distinguished from the trust we are to have in the canonical Scriptures. What the Reformers attributed to the Holy Spirit (that is, the authentic interpretation of the Scriptures) the theologians of Trent ascribed to "the Church," the body of Christ where the Spirit was living in the form of a living gospel.

This lead to the doctrine of the Church's "infallibility,"[111] by which the Roman Church claims to be the authoritative interpreter of written revelation.[112] Since Christ is the Head of the Church and the Church is His body, the authority of the Roman Church becomes the authority of the indwelling Christ. This is witnessed in the statement declared at the

---

110. Fisher, *La Documentation Catholique*, 942, col. 481.

111. Küng says that "infallibility" means that "the Church is not deceiving or deceived, because she has a share in the truth of God himself, 'who can neither deceive nor be deceived' (Vatican I: *Deus revelans, qui ned falli nec fallere potest*, D 1783)"; also that "a fundamental remaining in the truth, which is not disturbed by individual errors" (Küng, *The Church*, 342). Kung cites John 14:16–17 as God's promise of infallibility to the Church.

112. Ramm holds, "The Roman Catholic Church traditionally believes that it is graced with infallibility when it teaches and interprets revelation (in her case, oral and written). Her interpretations and teachings are therefore as authoritative as the revelation she interprets" (Ramm, *The Pattern of Authority*, 56). Ramm later adds, "The Church is, therefore, the supreme interpretive authority in all matters of faith and morals, and under certain stipulations speaks with infallibility" (64).

Council of Trent (Fourth Session), that all interpretation was to be in accord with the "holy mother Church—whose role is to judge the true sense and interpretation of the Holy Scriptures." In a sense this seems to amount to an elevation of the Church's interpretation of the Bible over the Bible itself. This is admitted openly in traditional Catholic doctrine, as seen in the introduction to *A Catholic Commentary on Holy Scriptures*:

> Nevertheless . . . the Church is superior to the Bible in the sense that she is the Living Voice of Christ and therefore the sole infallible interpreter of the inspired Word, whenever an authoritative interpretation is required.[113]

The teaching magisterium of the Roman Catholic Church refers to the Holy Spirit as the guarantor of its teachings and decisions. The magisterium is not the same as the theologian, who has an inherent pastoral dimension and aims to build up ecclesiastical communities. The magisterium, however, "teaches in light of a gift of the Holy Spirit and passes authoritative judgment on 'new teachings and on considerations proposed by theology.'"[114] The World Council of Churches has given a very positive definition of the nature and role of the magisterium:

> [The magisterium] is the guarantee that the salvific Word of Christ will be really addressed to the concrete situation of the given age. Hence it does not replace the work and rule of the Spirit. In fact, the "magisterium" lives through the Spirit and is always subject to its guidance. The "magisterium" is the concert form in which the guidance of the Spirit maintains historical continuity with Jesus Christ. . . . The charismatic structure of the Church ensures that the Holy Spirit imparts impulses to the Church in other ways besides through official hierarchical organs of the Church. This means also when it is applied to the relationship between the Pope and the Bishops, that individual bishops can be channels for the impulses of the Holy Spirit.[115]

The vital connection of the magisterium with the authority of the Spirit is examined in John Wright's article, "Authority in the Church today:

---

113. Orchard, *A Catholic Commentary on the Holy Scriptures*, 2.
114. Richard, "The Enigma of Theologians," 331.
115. *Authority, Conscience, and Dissent*, 125–26.

A Theological Reflection."[116] Wright attempts to clarify that the authority transferred from the Holy Spirit to Roman Church leaders is not exercised *above* the Church but from *within* the Church by respecting the rights conferred by the Spirit to each believer.[117] According to Wright,

> [I]t is the Holy Spirit vivifying the whole Church who is the source of their authority, not simply the will and consent of the members of the Church; for all parts of the Church receive the Holy Spirit for their particular tasks as a gift given by the risen Lord to the whole Church and through the whole Church, especially through the Word and Sacrament. This interrelationship of the Holy Spirit, the whole Church, and authorities within the Church solidifies both the mode in which authority is to be exercised in the Church and also the scope of its exercise.[118]

This structure, however, reflects the inner reality of the Church, which is essentially the Spirit. There is therefore a direct correlation between the "magisterium" and the Holy Spirit—the One who provides the internal reality of authority. According to Inch, "This stance [held by the Roman Church] likened the structural and pneumatic aspects of the Church to body and soul, so that one might not be viewed apart from the other."[119]

Congar, however, admits that the tendency of the counter-Reformation was to "give an absolute value to the Church as an institution by endowing its magisterium with an almost unconditional guarantee of guidance by the Holy Spirit."[120] Biblical references in some of its decisions (i.e., the Mariological dogmas of 1854 and 1950) have been "quite remote," and basis for such decisions was essentially based on faith in the Church itself, "animated by the Spirit."[121]

---

116. Wright, "Authority in the Church," 364–82.
117. Ibid., 364–82.
118. Ibid., 373–74.
119. Inch, *Saga of the Spirit*, 230.
120. Congar, *I Believe in the Holy Spirit*, 1:151–57.
121. Ibid.

The "Interpretive Authority" of the Spirit—Definition and Storyline

The central debate within this theological period has to do with the relationship between the authority of the Spirit and the authority of Scripture. As an integral part of the Pattern of divine authority, the nature of this relationship is crucial for both Protestant and Roman Catholic theologies in their respective understandings of the Spirit's interpretive authority.

The Catholic version of "interpretive authority" essentially reduces to their understanding of "Tradition," which Congar refers to as a single apostolic tradition handed down in the Church through written Scripture as well as through teaching, discipline, and rites.[122] Vatican II described Scripture and Tradition as forming a unity through which the faithful are brought to a full knowledge of God's truth.[123] Such understandings of Tradition place the Spirit-inspired writings and decrees of the teaching magisterium (i.e., councils and bishops) essentially on par with Scripture. One indeed wonders whether the Spirit is actually placed *over* the magisterium, is *replaced* by the magisterium, or is *conjoined with* the magisterium. Eno admits that, "in practice, a juridical criterion like Roman approval, while secondary, becomes the *operative* norm."[124] While the Spirit has "interpretive authority" to speak "through" the Word as interpreter of the Word, the Roman magisterium, in essence, assumes the role of "mediator" between the Spirit and the Word.

Protestants, on the other hand, claim that the recognition of this Spirit/Word relationship, as stated in terms of their theological *discremin*, is probably *the* reason for the success of the Protestant Reformation. Davison traces the roots of Reformation theology back to medieval theology in order to show how earlier attention to this relationship laid the necessary groundwork.

> During the long night of the Middle Ages the teaching of the New Testament was obscured by the huge shadow of the Church, a building which, intending to point men heavenwards, gradually blocked

---

122. A synthesis of Congar's thoughts regarding Roman Catholic Tradition can be found in Congar, *I Believe in the Holy Spirit*, vol. 3.

123. Van Engen, "Tradition," 1106.

124. Eno, "Pope and Council," 210.

out from view the sun in its splendour and the azure of the sky. Reformers before the Reformation and the great leaders in the sixteenth century did much to clear the air and bring men face to face with God in Christ.... In vindication the authority of the Scriptures against the encroachments of the Churches were [sic] helping to prepare the way for the complete supremacy of the Spirit.[125]

Bolich points out that the genius of the Reformation was not that the doctrine of the Spirit's witness provides a "principal thesis from which other doctrines were to be systematically deduced," but rather that the Reformers began with the text of Holy Scripture and made the witness of the Spirit integral to their entire doctrinal system, so that the witness of the Holy Spirit was inextricably bound up with the Scriptures.[126]

In Luther's theology, the Spirit is not to be seen as some "doctrine" creating an unquestionable rational theory but as a living presence *over* the world, one that reveals Christ *in* the world.[127] Christ is revealed through the Spirit, who is ultimately the interpreter of the Word, so that the written Word becomes a "living Word" through the Spirit. The crux of the Spirit's "executorial authority" in Luther is thus the *contemporaniety* of the Word. The "Word of the Spirit" becomes an "inward Word" when the outward (written or preached) Word penetrates the heart. In this action the Spirit is authoritative with respect to the believer or the one who is being saved. Luther, however, refuses to bind the Spirit *in* the Word, allowing his theology (unlike many theologians who followed him) to retain the authority of the Spirit *over* the Word. In opposition to Roman theology, Luther's model does not allow for a delegation of the Spirit's own infallibility to any human person or institution, but only to the Scriptures. In this way, *"interpretive authority" is retained as a property of the Spirit.*

Calvin's pneumatology and particularly his "internal testimony of the Spirit" teach us that the foundation of the Spirit's interpretive authority can only be what Ramm refers to as *veracious authority*. The Spirit has the authority to testify biblical truth to the individual, thus giving the Spirit authority *over* the individual believer. While believers are utterly destitute of the light of truth, they are not ignorant that this Word is the instrument

---

125. Davison, "The Person and Work of the Holy Spirit," 211.
126. Bolich, *Authority and the Church*, 65.
127. See Prenter, *Spiritus Creator*, 201.

of the Spirit's illumination.[128] Calvin's emphasis is always on the work or agency of the *Spirit of Truth* whereby the Spirit serves as the source of internal or spiritual interpretation within the believer. This implies an interpretive authority of the Spirit that is essentially instrumental—the Spirit is the instrument through which Christ speaks his Word in the human heart. While Calvin essentially limited the Spirit's work to that of salvation and sanctification, the Spirit is attributed with a certain *veracious authority* to restore order to humankind and "seal our minds" in truth.[129]

As a result, Luther and Calvin portray the Spirit as possessing an interpretive, veracious authority, which is in turn an expression of the Spirit's "executorial authority." This authority is enacted with respect to Scripture and within the Church. This illuminating Spirit, in other words, authoritatively resides *over* the Church and yet executes his authority *under* Christ, speaking *through* the Word. Because the Word is a product of the Spirit and because the Spirit continues to speak this Word in contemporary confirmation, the witness of the Holy Spirit is seen as the *interpretive* authority established for man by God. For the Reformers the Spirit is not bound to the Word but always speaks through the Word or in accordance with the Word, thus remaining consistent with himself.

Ramm strongly asserts that the "Protestant Principle of Authority"—the Holy Spirit speaking in the Scriptures—is the only means for avoiding the imposition of the erring voice of man upon the authoritative Word of God. His convincing logic runs as follows:

> The truer Protestant principle is that there is an *external* principle (the *inspired* Scripture) and an *internal* principle (the witness of the Holy Spirit). It is the principle of an objective *divine* revelation, with an interior *divine* witness. These two principles must always be held together, so that it may be said either that (1) our authority is the Holy Spirit speaking in the Scriptures, or, (2) our authority is the Scriptures sealed to us by the Holy Spirit.[130]

As a result, the "storyline" development of the Spirit's authority has now reached a level of practical objectivity. In other words, Protestants

---

128. Calvin, *Institutes of the Christian Religion*, I.ix.3.
129. Ibid., ix.1–2.
130. Ramm, *The Pattern of Authority*, 29.

could begin to see Scripture as an *objectification* of the Spirit's authority, and thereby begin to grasp God's character and will with much more significant detail than ever before.

Modern Theology

Since precise limitations of the Spirit's authority with respect to the Word were not yet well-defined within Protestant theology, a door was left open for followers to either limit the Spirit's authority to the Word alone (resulting in various forms of Christian rationalism), or to overreact to this thinking by separating the Spirit from the Word (often resulting in various forms of Christian "enthusiasm"). Either way, Prenter contends that after the Reformation the work of the Spirit was narrowed to the *individual,* especially with respect to the work of sanctification, regeneration, and the interpretation of Scripture. Several other related activities (i.e. the Spirit's work in creation, providence, history, Church governance, and mission) were given little or no attention.[131]

On top of this, rapid changes in European intellectual and social culture during the seventeenth, eighteenth, and nineteenth centuries—particularly in the natural sciences, philosophy, and literature—elevated modern confidence in human reason as well as skepticism regarding "traditional authority" or "Spirit."[132] Hume challenged religious "authority"

---

131. Commenting on Prenter, Carlson says that this has opened the door to a philosophical / "substantial" concept of God's Spirit, which regards the Spirit as a divine energy that can be infused and appropriated. With the help of this "energy" man is able to produce the "fruits of the Spirit." Thus he will grow in grace and holiness, as he follows the example of Jesus Christ. "Prenter contends that when you do that to Luther's theology, you distort it by trying to compress his thought within the molds of mediaeval scholasticism, against which Luther himself rebelled. Luther held a much more dynamic view, which can be summarized by saying that the work of the Holy Spirit is to conform man to Christ. This is accomplished by conforming man to Christ's death and resurrection. This whole concept of conformity to Christ must be set over against the scholastic concept of imitation of Christ" (Carlson, "Luther and the Doctrine of the Holy Spirit," 137).

132. Newton's mathematical physics, for example, presented nature as a rational, unified order where there were no "hidden purposes" (of God) to discover. "As a result of Newton's work, 'God' was no longer needed as the hypothesis to authorize the world; 'God' became a projection of nature. . . . This shift led to a heightened stress on reason as a primary authority for interpreting all human experience. It meant as well that traditions (as promoted by the Church) or supernatural appeals to the 'Spirit' were suspect" (McKim, "Authority," 47).

by attacking the validity of making empirically demonstrable statements about God. Kant was helpful to the Christian concept of authority in some ways, but his argument that theology must be based only upon moral laws meant for the "modern man" that God could be known only through rational means, if at all. As a result, many groups throughout the modern period "hungered" for a new sense of the Spirit and decried that almost all traditional approaches left them only half full. Anabaptists, for example, believed themselves to "possess" the Spirit and sought a more pronounced doctrine of the Spirit's interpretive authority (thereby rejecting Lutheran and Reformed teaching regarding authority). Quakers held that the "authority" of Church and Scripture must yield to the Spirit's "inner light" of immediate revelation as the final authority for Christian theology and life. Pentecostal and charismatic groups at times disconnected the Spirit from the Word completely, looking for an experience that lay beyond the teaching of Scripture. This modern landscape was often shaped by a shift in the notion of "the priesthood of the believer," which now meant that the individual was no longer bound by an authoritarian Church and was free to use his or her own intellectual and spiritual capacities for discerning truth. According to Livingston, the "modern age" brought a renewed awareness and trust in each person's own capacities.

> Reason supersedes revelation as the supreme court of appeal. As a result, theology faced a choice of either adjusting itself to the advances in modern science and philosophy and, in so doing, risking accommodation to secularization, or resisting all influences from culture and becoming largely reactionary and ineffectual in meeting the challenges of life in the modern world.[133]

Modern theology therefore emerged through an accommodation to human subjectivism, and took the form of both experientialism (which often seemed to replace the Spirit with human morality) and rationalism (which replaced it with human reason).[134] These two approaches are represented by the theologies of Schleiermacher and Henry. For our purposes,

---

133. Livingston, *Modern Christian Thought*, 2.
134. Erickson defines "Modern Theology" as simply the "Theology of the nineteenth and twentieth centuries, beginning particularly with reaction to the thought of Immanuel Kant" (Erickson, *Concise Dictionary of Christian Theology*, 107).

the essential debate had to do with the final "authority" or method one could rely upon when interpreting Scripture.

Friedrich Schleiermacher

Friedrich Schleiermacher, often referred to as "the father of modern theology," defines the Spirit as "the union of the divine essence with human nature in the form of the common Spirit which animates the corporate life of believers."[135] Schleiermacher's "liberal theology" does not give the Spirit a metaphysical status apart from this union. The Spirit confirms the notion of an immanent deity, which seems to be best understood as emerging "from below" as the presence of God in the Church. This presence is defined in terms of a "feeling of absolute dependence." The operation of the Spirit is to be recognized primarily with regard to the humanization of the individual, so that one can be released from external sanctions and enjoy the positivistic (scientific) character of modernity. Schleiermacher asserts, "Without being knowledge, [religion] recognizes knowledge and science. In itself it is an affection, a revelation of the Infinite in the finite, God being seen in it and it in God."[136]

As a result, all doctrine is to be derived from an experiential foundation. The interpretation of the Bible in the establishment of doctrine does not proceed on grounds of rational objectivity, but as a function of the Christian Church wrestling with questions of personal faith, piety, and ethics. Each witnessing community possesses an "interpretative authority" in that each views the Holy Spirit as the one who works to form and define that particular community of believers.[137] "The Spirit for Schleiermacher is effectively the spiritual influence left behind by Jesus that gives coherence to the life of the Church as a spiritual entity, and therefore to the life of the Christian faith."[138] Within this paradigm the Spirit is freed from the Catholic/Protestant approach to pneumatology (which to the "liberals" limited the Spirit to a role of preservation of life through specific method-

---

135. Schleiermacher, *The Christian Faith*, 123.
136. Schleiermacher, *On Religion*, 36.
137. Badcock, *Light of Truth and Fire of Love*, 112.
138. Ibid., 112.

ologies) and given "authority" to meet new challenges with fresh insights and unique results.[139]

Following in the steps of Schleiermacher, nineteenth-century liberal theologians portray the Christian faith, and particularly Jesus' life and teaching, as the fulfillment of humanity's highest religious or moral aspirations. Such aspirations are thought to be embryonically implanted in universal human nature. Sabatier, for example, interprets Schleiermacher psychologically, and holds his "feeling of absolute dependency" to be an "emotional experience" that is prompted by the *internal testimonium Spiritus Sancti* and that becomes the sole authority over Christian theology. The Bible and the Church are historical and experiential "consequences and effects" of such an authority, and since neither is a "first cause," neither can play a role in the theological *discremin*.[140]

CARL HENRY

Carl Henry's pneumatology has attempted to combat liberal and neo-orthodox notions of "authority" and in doing so has served to define the Spirit's role in the inspiration and illumination of authoritative Scripture more precisely. For Henry, the Spirit's establishment of biblical authority must precede the Spirit's own interpretive activity. This was one of the main points established in his classic work *God, Revelation, and Authority*. Henry's key hermeneutical principle is that the Spirit's work in the inspiration of biblical propositions must be distinguished "from the Spirit's present function as authoritative interpreter in the believer's comprehension of the scripturally given revelation."[141] Henry is concerned that the Holy Spirit is given a rightful place in the transference of authority from Christ to Scriptures, thus avoiding the development of the sort of "dualism" between Christ and Scripture that we see in Barth, liberal theologians, and others. Henry explains how this duality develops:

> Because the prophetic witness anticipates Christ as its climax and the apostolic testimony exalts Jesus as the promised son of God to whom all authority is given, Scripture has sometimes been ad-

139. Inch, *Saga of the Spirit*, 241.
140. Johnson, *Authority in Protestant Theology*, 78.
141. Henry, *God, Revelation, and Authority*, 2:13.

versely contrasted with Jesus Christ or with the Spirit of God as the sovereign authority. This contrast has been prompted during the past two centuries by champions of higher critical views of Christ. But the critical assumptions governing negative theory of Scripture inevitably carry over also into other spheres, such as Christology and pneumatology, so that any attempt to seal off the authority of Christ or of the Spirit from the fate of Scripture is vain.[142]

Henry posits that the Holy Spirit stands between Christ and Scripture and thereby confers to the Scripture a corresponding authority.[143] Though he is concerned that evangelicals have forgotten the Spirit's role in conferring such an authority, Henry refuses the corrections offered by many "neo-Barthians" (i.e., Leowen, Pinnock, Kelsey),[144] arguing that they always move toward communal or functional hermeneutics. Instead, Henry asserts that "the Spirit of God—not any private interpreter (2 Pet. 1:20), evangelical or nonevangelical—is the authoritative illuminator of the scripturally given Word."[145] Henry's pneumatology is best expressed by Leonard Champion: "The testimony of Scripture possesses the authority of the Spirit and every believer, guided by what Calvin calls 'the testimony of the Spirit within,' will recognize and respond to its truth."[146]

Henry's evangelical approach, however, does tend to incorporate a classic scholastic approach to theology, as witnessed in his assertion that the sole foundation of theology rests on the presupposition that the Bible, as God's self-disclosure, presents the truth of God in propositional form, and that the theological task is simply "to exhibit the content of biblical revelation as an orderly whole."[147] Such an approach to doctrinal development adopts a modern or scientific hermeneutic in that it excludes the possibility of any interference from (or need to reference) tradition or culture. Indeed

---

142. Ibid., 4:35.

143. Ibid., 4:256–68.

144. For example, Henry states that "[Howard J. Loewen's] implication that 'the authority of the Bible can . . . be . . . truly demonstrated only in the context of the presence and activity of the Holy Spirit who is essential to the personal appropriation of the Word of Scripture' is highly questionable, if this means that inner personal experience establishes the truth and/or the authority of the Bible" (Henry, *God, Revelation, and Authority*, 4:268).

145. Henry, *God, Revelation, and Authority*, 4:289.

146. Champion, "The Baptist Doctrine of the Church," 38.

147. Henry, *God, Revelation, and Authority*, 1:244.

the theologian can interpret Scripture and develop a doctrinal system in isolation from such influences. Henry's thinking, in a real sense, mirrors that of modern philosophers Descartes and Kant with respect to their confidence in the mind's ability to know truth and to make rational decisions without needing to recognize the influence of tradition. The Spirit, as a result, can aid the systematic theologian in the correct interpretation of Scripture through the use of rational exegetical methods alone.

OTHER CONTRIBUTORS

Karl Barth's view of the Spirit departs from many of the evangelical theologians of his day, particularly those who attempt to precisely define the Spirit's nature. According to Barth,

> Spirit . . . is neither a divine nor a created something, but an *action and attitude* of the Creator in relation to his Creation. We cannot say what Spirit is, but that he takes place as the divine basis of this relation and fellowship. Spirit is thus the powerful and exclusive *meeting* initiated by God between Creator and creature.[148]

Barth's "relational" pneumatology is essentially a response to attacks from "liberals" on the Spirit's divine sovereignty. Barth viewed the Spirit as having a sovereignty of action that, once encountered, makes us "free for God."[149] Barth's pneumatology does not limit the Spirit's function in divine revelation to the giving and recording of the Word of God, but instead reasserts the Spirit's lordship in the event of revelation.[150] According to Barth,

---

148. Barth, *Church Dogmatics*, III/2:356 (emphasis mine). In agreeing with Barth's idea that the Holy Spirit "seems to be behind a wall" and hidden from humanity, Pentecostal theologian Burton Janes asserts that, for believers, "our actions can either enlarge or destroy the barrier, revealing the Spirit for all to see" (Janes, "Taking a Step Toward Pentecost," 24). Janes particularly finds comfort in Barth's three cautions regarding the Spirit in revelation: (1) Barth holds that subjective revelation must never override the objective. Here Janes quotes Barth, "Subjective revelation is not the addition of a second revelation to objective revelation"; (2) Barth cautions against specifying the precise way man experiences the Holy Spirit. Barth says that we can never express or state that which lies behind our experiences of the Holy Spirit because it is not revealed to us, because it is revelation itself; (3) Barth steers clear of sectarianism, which perceives the testimony of the Spirit in terms of an immediate spiritual inspiration and bypasses the Word (26).

149. Barth, *Church Dogmatics*, I/1:536–39.

150. Barth's pneumatology "elevated the long-neglected role of the Holy Spirit to new

> The Holy Spirit is the Lord (acting upon us in revelation as the Redeemer) who makes us really free, really children of God, who really gives His Church utterance to speak the Word of God. . . . [the Spirit] is really the hidden essence of God Himself, and therefore the Lord in the most unrestricted sense of the concept, who—in His utter unsearchableness—becomes manifest in revelation in this respect also.[151]

Barth's pneumatology also seems to be a reaction against modern conceptions of truth, particularly against the modern idea that the human subject may determine truth through rational or experimental methodologies. According to Rosato, "The strict Christological framework in which Barth situates his pneumatology in the Church Dogmatics is proof enough the he is struggling against subjectivism with as much force as he can assemble."[152]

Barth's theological method presents Jesus Christ as the "objective" executor of revelation and the Holy Spirit as the "subjective" executor, though it is this subjective aspect that becomes the primary determinate. God's grace is manifested both in the objective revelation of God in Christ and man's subjective appropriation of this revelation through the Spirit.[153] For Barth, the Spirit as revealer always remains the Lord and interpreter of the truth of God as well. Scripture is the "Word of God" because by the Holy Spirit it became and will become to the church a "witness" to divine revel-

---

significance in its exposition of divine revelation" (Henry, *God, Revelation, and Authority*, 4:256).

151. Barth, *Church Dogmatics*, I/1:536–39.

152. Rosato, *The Spirit as Lord*, 84. Barth's response to the "subjectivism" of Schleiermacher is particularly penetrating: "Were the Spirit, the mediator of revelation to the subject, a creature or a creaturely force, we would be asserting and maintaining that, in virtue of his presence with God and over against God, man in his own way is also a lord in revelation" (Barth, *The Doctrine of the Word of God*, 535).

153. As a result, Barth becomes not only one of the greatest defenders of Filioque in modern times, but he also links this doctrine with divine revelation by making Christ the true revealer of the Word. In this way the Spirit, not the human subject, is the authoritative interpreter of the Word. Rosato explains, "By welding pneumatology to Christology, Barth removes even from the subjective appropriation of the Christ-event by the believer every trace of subjectivism. Thus, the existential experiences of Christian consciousness, which are the direct result of the Spirit's presence, are ultimately rooted in the objective election of Jesus Christ, which alone lends their noetic quality ontic significance" (Rosato, *The Spirit as Lord*, 84).

tion. This witness is not identical to the revelation; rather, God's revelation occurs in our encounter with the Spirit and enlightenment by the Spirit to a knowledge of God's Word. Thus, the outpouring of the Spirit is God's revelation, and in this reality we are free to be God's children and to know, love, and praise him in his revelation.[154]

Barth says that the verification of God's truth is provided by the Holy Spirit alone (not by reason, the individual, or the Church itself). Thus, interpretation of Scripture is a function of the Spirit's work in shaping the Church, and is a very practical endeavor.

> With his insistence on the concept of *theopneustia* Barth nullifies any purely philosophical hermeneutics. Pneumatology is from now on to afford him a specifically Christian tool of interpretation which corresponds to his trinitarian teaching and to his Christology.[155]

THE VERACIOUS AUTHORITY OF THE SPIRIT—DEFINITION AND STORYLINE

In response to enlightenment humanism, which granted supreme authority to the human intellect and moral conscience, modern theologians began searching for ways to define and establish a Christian understanding of authority, to establish that Christianity was indeed the highest form of rationality or the most rational system, and to determine the ultimate methodology in the determination of truth. Though many theologians attempted to employ the doctrine of the Spirit in their methodologies, they often became victims of "modern" reductionism. In particular, the Spirit's *veracious authority*—his work with respect to the determination of truth—seems to be essentially reduced to a work of humanization (Schleiermacher), human or enlightened rationality (Henry), or personal encounter (Barth). Borrowing from Kantian philosophy—which divides the "noumenal" realm of spiritual knowledge from the "phenomenal" realm of experiential knowledge—Schleiermacher reduces the Spirit's work to religious experiences, and particularly to the role of interpreter of religious experiences within the Christian community. The Spirit has authority only in that he

---

154. See Barth, *Evangelical Theology*, 53ff.

155. Rosato adds that, in doing so, the Spirit "continually fashions the Church into the contours of the incarnate Word" (Rosato, *The Spirit as Lord*, 80–81).

helps the interpreter to get behind the printed words to the author's wider social context, and then relate to that context as a manifestation of universal life. The Spirit's veracious authority to inspire the written Word of God as a historical document, however, begins to be questioned. Schleiermacher's "liberal" followers reduced the Spirit to humanity's highest religious or moral aspirations and the Spirit's authority to a *moral authority* that allows believers to enter the Church community and function as moral beings.

Barth is certainly to be complimented on his fresh attempt to portray the Spirit's transcendence in the midst of modern reductionism. It is questionable, however, that this authority is indeed *immanent*, in that Barth seems to reduce the Spirit's work to a merely noetic function, "pointing back to its role in the Trinity rather than forward to its work in the world."[156] Barth, as a result, seems reluctant to grant the Spirit a firm place in the "pattern of authority." His tendency to blur the distinction between Spirit and Word makes the truth of the Bible seem dependent on encountering or hearing the Spirit's voice speaking through it, and makes the Word seem as transcendent as Barth's portrayal of the Spirit.[157] The Spirit is granted a *functional* authority (to cause the Word to function as revelation for today) rather than a *veracious* authority (to inspire an historical, authoritative Word).

Unlike Barth, Henry refuses to make the authority and infallibility of Scripture conditioned on human response. Though Barth denounced bibliolatry and professed to exalt the Spirit, Henry accuses Barth's "functional reinterpretation of inspiration" of promoting a "broken biblicism" in that Barth wants to "detach discussion of the doctrine [of inspiration] from any correlation of it with a cognitively valid and infallible text."[158] While Henry coincides closely with Barth's emphasis on the Spirit's sovereignty in relation to the Word of God, Henry also finds in the Spirit a veracious authority to inspire the historical Word.

> The transcendent Spirit of God therefore remains no less active in the relation to the authority and the interpretation of Scripture than

---

156. Thompson, *The Holy Spirit in the Theology of Karl Barth*, 198.

157. Indeed Barth has been criticized by many evangelicals for promoting a "transcendent" Spirit that seems remote, abstract, and divorced from history and humanity.

158. Henry, *God, Revelation, and Authority*, 4:258.

in its original inspiration. Prophetic-apostolic inspiration stands in the larger context of the whole process of divine relation involving the communication activity of the Spirit of God.[159]

Henry, however, seems to have *reduced* the Spirit's authority to the authority of the Word of God. Henry is typical of "modern" evangelical theologians who tend to bypass the discussion of theological method—and the Spirit's place in that discussion—and move directly to the task of constructing theological systems (as though the process of moving from the ancient biblical text to the contemporary affirmation of doctrine and theology was self-evident). According to Grenz and Franke,

> Although [evangelical systematics] are written from a variety of different theological perspectives (Reformed, Wesleyan, Baptist, dispensationalist, charismatic, etc.) and arrive at strikingly different conclusions about issues of central importance in theology, on the question of method they are remarkably similar. For the most part these evangelical systematic theologies make use of a decidedly rationalist approach to theological method.[160]

Such an approach seems to look back to Charles Hodge, who derived his "propositional" approach from post-reformation Protestant orthodoxy and its rationalism. The Protestant reaction to the counter-reformation led second-generation reformers to adopt the methods of their adversaries, in essence trying to "prove the authority of the Bible using the same Aristotelian-Thomistic arguments which Roman Catholics used to prove the authority of the Church."[161] Thus, a significant shift in theological method occurred from the neo-platonic Augustinianism of Luther and Calvin to the neo-aristotelian-thomistism of their immediate followers—a shift that obviously led to a de-emphasis on the Spirit's witness.

Whereas Schleiermacher neglects the Spirit's *inspiration* of the Word, Henry reduces the need for the Spirit's *illumination* of the Word. Such erroneous tendencies tend to neglect the history of theology as well as the Spirit's role as *teacher* with respect to the Word of God and the histori-

---

159. Ibid., 258.
160. Grenz and Franke, *Beyond Foundationalism*, 13.
161. Rogers, *Biblical Authority*, 29.

cal Church. Ramm's pattern of authority, once again, provides the needed balance:

> If Christ has founded a Church and given it His word; if the Holy Spirit is the Teacher of the faithful; if the Church is "the house of God . . . the pillar and ground of the truth" (1 Tim. 3:15); then *every generation of Christian theologians must be prepared to take seriously the history of theology (broadly interpreted to include symbols, councils, theologians, treatises) as possessing manifestations of the teaching ministry of the Holy Spirit.*[162]

Ramm holds that "veracious authority" is spoken "not only of the one who possesses truth but also of one who aids in the determination of truth," and makes a vital link between the Spirit and such an authority:

> Here is the Spirit who is veracious within himself; and in his ministry he ministers the truth. . . . Here in the ministry of the Spirit is the ultimate credibility of the New Testament; here is the sufficient and necessary cause for the writing of the New Testament; here is the authority of the divine Scriptures traced to their executor; and here is the real source of our own inward certainty of the Christian faith. And the *testimonium* is an integral element in the teaching ministry of the Holy Spirit.[163]

The veracious authority of the Spirit, therefore, is demonstrated in both the inspiration and illumination of Scripture. Since a person possesses veracious authority on a given subject when "he would be more likely to possess the truth about the subject than most other men,"[164] we can extrapolate this principle to the omniscient Holy Spirit, inferring that the Spirit of God possesses ultimate veracious authority.

In the history of theology, our pattern of divine authority is repeatedly demonstrated in terms of adherence to a veracious authority granted to the Word of God by the veracious Spirit. The New Testament carries the authority which Jesus delegated to his apostles and which the Holy Spirit held over the inspired writers.

---

162. Ramm, *The Pattern of Authority*, 57 (emphasis his).
163. Ramm, *The Witness of the Spirit*, 57.
164. Ramm, *The Pattern of Authority*, 12.

> Here as elsewhere, the mode of delegation of authority in the New Testament is by the Holy Spirit. It is the Spirit who inspired the New Testament, it is the Spirit who witnesses to Christ in the heart, and it is the Spirit who quickens the heart to see the truth of God in the pages of the New Testament.[165]

While the Spirit's veracious authority is primarily witnessed through inspiration and illumination, the Spirit may also grant *secondary authority* to theologians, Churches, persons, creeds, symbols, councils and treatises—but only for the purpose of Christ's ministry and government. The quality of their work or words must be judged by its adherence to the pattern of authority. The Spirit, however, always retains primary veracious authority that cannot be equated with any of these mediums.

Postmodern and Contemporary Theology

Our study of the first four periods of theological history has allowed us to discern provisional definitions of the Spirit's authority in relation to the Triune God (an authority over the world), to Christ (an authority to execute Christ's will), and to the Scriptures (an authority to inspire and illuminate them). We have seen in Church history initial argumentation for the Spirit's place in the "principle" and "pattern" of authority.

Now, as we survey postmodern and contemporary theology, we find that the concern in pneumatology shifts to the relation between the doctrine of the Holy Spirit and the doctrine of the Church. In searching for a renewal of the Spirit's *power* in the Church, we find postmodern theology often proceeding from a different starting point than previous theologies. According to Bloesch, "Many theologies today encourage us to seek a doctrine of the Spirit 'from below'—beginning with the impact of the Spirit in human life—rather than one 'from above,' in which we begin with the doctrine of the immanent Trinity."[166] Contemporary theology does not usually begin with transcendent ideas that the Church should adopt but with ideas that stem from the various needs of the Church. The question in this section is therefore, "Does the Holy Spirit possess authority in or over

---

165. Ibid., 55.
166. Bloesch, *The Holy Spirit*, 49.

the Church?" In other words, does the Spirit function as *governing authority* within the Church, and if so, what is the nature of such an authority?

Perhaps the simplest definition of postmodernism is *that philosophy which comes after modernism, usually as a response to the deficiencies of modernism.* Postmodernists, of course, would remind us that there is no *single* postmodern philosophy or theology and that postmodernism is as varied as the responses themselves. What are some of the contemporary responses being given to "modern" understandings of pneumatology? To answer this, a brief survey and comparison of five "postmodern" theologians will be conducted in order to initially discern various contemporary understandings of the relationship between the Spirit and the Church. In doing so, however, we must keep a larger goal in mind. Since the ultimate goal of this entire work has to do with the recovery of a biblical conception of the Holy Spirit's authority in and over the Church—one that might confront contemporary misconceptions of "Spirit")—these five theologians should also be investigated for the purpose of further dialogue (and indeed will serve as such in chapters three and four)

Evangelical "Postmodern" Theologies of the Spirit

According to Veith, "One response to the end of modernism is to recover what was of value in the premodern era and to apply old worldviews in new creative ways to our contemporary times."[167] This seems to be the response of a few evangelical and Catholic theologians. A recent Catholic/Methodist joint summit, for example, observed that, "encouraging signs of the activity of the Holy Spirit" in the Church today include "a growing hunger for truth now clearly unsatisfied by the achievements and claims of science and technology."[168] They also see a revitalization of the Spirit's role in the mediation of authority in the Church to be based on Scripture and Church history:

> Christ's authority is mediated through the Spirit, who is Love, and hence all authority that flows from this source is part of God's good gift. . . . But this mediation is not static; it is not a matter of endless repetition or formulae. The Spirit moves the Church to constant

---

167. Veith, "Out-Clintoning Clinton," 21.
168. Roman Catholic-World Methodist Council Joint Commission, "The Holy Spirit, Christian Experience, and Authority," 226.

reflection on the Scriptures which he himself inspired and on their traditional interpretation.[169]

This "postmodern" approach recognizes once again the essential community basis for the discovery of truth and spiritual life, but seems to retain the Spirit's place in the pattern of divine authority. Oden, for example, speaks of a "postmodern paleoorthodoxy" which calls theologians to assess all texts from the historic Church that allege to be consensual Christian teaching, listening continually to the centrist interpreters of the received traditions. According to Oden, we will recognize heresy not by pure rational analysis, but "only by first knowing and sharing deeply in the language, worship, ethics and ethos of the ecumenical testimony of many cross-cultural generations of apostolic testimony."[170] The result of such a "paleoorthodox" approach seems to be a renewed focus on an experience of the Spirit within the Church that coincides with a general (though perhaps not total) respect for the pattern of divine authority. Two recent whole-book treatises on the theology of the Holy Spirit that attempt such an approach from an "evangelical" perspective include Clark Pinnock's *Flame of Love* and Gary Badcock's *Light of Truth and Fire of Love*.

Clark Pinnock's *Flame of Love*

Pinnock's opening concern is with the work that remains to be done regarding the recovery of "a more experiential basis for the doctrine of Spirit."[171] Pinnock asks us to view the Church from the standpoint of the Spirit, rather than as an institution or sacrament, because "this is the natural way to regard a community that was created by the Spirit on the day of Pentecost."[172] The effectiveness of the Church is thus due to God's power rather than human competence. "The Church rides the wind of God's Spirit like a hawk endlessly and effortlessly circling and gliding in the summer sky. . . . The main rationale of the Church is to activate all the implications of the baptism of the Spirit."[173] Pinnock adds,

169. Ibid., 231.
170. Oden, *Life in the Spirit*, 474.
171. Pinnock, *Flame of Love*, 10.
172. Ibid., 113.
173. Ibid., 114.

> My concern here is to try and recover the two-dimensionality of charism and sacrament original to Christianity. . . . The Spirit comes in power through sacrament and charism to enable the Church to participate in God's mission of mending creation and making all things new.[174]

While Pinnock claims to be an evangelical theologian, his focus seems to be on the *experience* of the Spirit rather than on any sort of *authority* of the Spirit. One of Pinnock's main concerns is to clarify the nature of the relationship between Christ and the Spirit. Pinnock tends to grant the Spirit a mission that is distinct from the mission of Christ (and thereby tend toward a "universalistic" understanding of salvation). What might we conclude about his assessment of the Spirit's authority in relation to Christ's authority? In chapter three we will investigate this question in light of our pattern of authority.

Gary Badcock's *Light of Truth and Fire of Love*

Badcock vigorously argues that the experience of God—which is for him the primary issue in all discussion regarding the Spirit—"has not always been integrated in any meaningful way into systems of theology."[175] His concern is thus with the Spirit's role in the spiritual life as it is experienced within the Church. According to Badcock, "one of the central arguments that will be developed in what follows is that there is a more subtle, reciprocal relationship between . . . Spirit and Church, than is generally allowed."[176] Badcock hopes that such a reformulation of the Spirit/Church relationship will mean that pneumatology might be linked to ecclesiology without necessarily being dominated by it.

Badcock provides a penetrating analysis of the history of pneumatology. In particular, he notes that Western theology seems unable or unwilling to integrate the work of the Spirit into theological thought. Badcock demonstrates that when such deficiencies exist the first result is an impoverished Church life. The Church's theology "hardens into intellectual

---

174. Ibid., 119–20, 142.
175. Badcock, *Light of Truth and Fire of Love*, 1.
176. Ibid., 2.

or moral Puritanism"[177] and "ceases to be really related to the God who is the source of life."[178] Nevertheless, Badcock's model gives the Spirit a somewhat "mystical" role in relation to the Church, a role that provokes spiritual experience. Can we discern any notion of the Spirit's authority from this model? If so, what sort of authority does the Spirit possess in light of the pattern of authority? We will investigate this further in chapter four.

Communitarian "Postmodern" Theologies of the Spirit

Veith adds that, "The other response to the end of modern rationalism is to take the next step and deny rationalism altogether. These postmodernists maintain that truth claims and moral absolutes are nothing more than a personal or social construction."[179] This might be thought of as a strictly "communitarian postmodernism." In this model, the denial of modern rationalism seems to coincide with a general dismissal of the need to place primary reliance on traditional sources of "authority" that emerged before the modern era (i.e., the authoritative Word of God and, secondarily, orthodox theologians and Church creeds). While these sources may be respected, the primary focus seems to be on *the experience of "Spirit" (i.e., as God's power, liberation, or presence) in the context of the Church community*. Three contemporary whole-book treatises that attempt to construct theologies of the Spirit on such a "communitarian" perspective include Michael Welker's *God the Spirit*, Jürgen Moltmann's *The Spirit of Life*, and Peter Hodgson's *Winds of Spirit*.

Jürgen Moltmann's *The Spirit of Life*

Moltmann attempts to provide a "Universal Affirmation" of the Holy Spirit that can serve as "a new paradigm in pneumatology" appropriate for our time.[180] Our problem, according to Moltmann, is one of experience, and particularly "the false alternative between Divine Revelation and human experience of the Holy Spirit"[181] provided by dialectical

177. Ibid., 4.
178. Ibid.
179. Veith, "Out-Clintoning Clinton," 21.
180. Moltmann, *The Spirit of Life*, back cover endorsement by Peter C. Hodgson.
181. Ibid., 5.

theology (i.e., Barth, Brunner, Bultmann). The modern antithesis between revelation and experience only results in "revelations that cannot be experienced, and experiences without revelation."[182] Such theology presents God as "Wholly Other" and the Spirit as the "being-revealed" of God's self-revelation. Moltmann resolves this tension in his doctrine of the Church, extolling that, as "the fellowship (κοινωνία) of the Holy Spirit" (2 Cor 13:13), the Spirit "draws [believers] into *his* fellowship . . . into the [Trinitarian] community he shares with the Father and the Son."[183] Moltmann characterizes his worldview as "panentheism," which begins with "the world in God and God in the world."[184] In his vision of the Church, this worldview translates into a breakdown of the distinction between the fellowship amongst the trinitarian Persons and fellowship amongst believers. Moltmann thus defines the Spirit in terms of God's presence "as community."[185]

> God the Spirit evidently enters into a relationship of reciprocity and mutuality with the people concerned and—in line with this— allows these people to exert an influence on him, just as he exerted an influence on them.[186]

Since, for Moltmann, the Spirit amongst believers "becomes their fellowship,"[187] we must ask whether the Spirit in this model possesses any sort of "authority" with respect to the Church. This will be discussed further in chapters three and four.

---

182. Ibid., 7.

183. Ibid., 217.

184. Ibid., 98, 103. Moltmann admits, "We can find in many [mystical theologians] a pantheistic vision of the world in God and God in the world. . . . This history of the Holy Spirit that is poured out upon all flesh, and this new world that is glorified in God, are what the mystical theologians mean with their neoplatonic-sounding doctrine" (Moltmann, "Theology of Mystical Experience," 517–19).

185. Moltmann, *The Spirit of Life*, 217.

186. Ibid., 218.

187. Ibid.

The Lord Is the Spirit

Peter Hodgson's *Winds of Spirit*

Hodgson develops this book by first saying that "theology is drawn and driven by winds of the Spirit,"[188] and then by building an entire "constructive Christian theology" around his postmodern understanding of the Spirit. For Hodgson, "God is not an isolated supreme being over against the world. Rather, embodied by the world, incarnate in the shapes of Christ, God becomes a concrete, living, relational God, 'Spirit.'"[189] Borrowing from Tillich, Hodgson's God is not a Being (which to Hodgson is a term developed by modern metaphysics) but a *power of being* by which all *beings* are. Amazingly, Hodgson's modified Trinity includes *God, the world, and Spirit*, and this Spirit is "not something that exists in advance as a supernatural person of the Godhead."[190] Rather, the Spirit is seen as a panentheistic "primal energy" that "takes on the shape of many created spirits; not just the spirits of living persons but of ancestors and animals as well as plants, trees, rivers . . ."[191]

Emerging from this understanding of the Spirit is Hodgson's idea of "ecclesial community," whereby the very purpose of the Church as a liberating experience of God comes forth. "My proposal is that [constructive theology] makes the direct object of its concern neither the practice of faith nor the texts of faith but the experience that gives rise to faith—a *revelatory* experience having its source and referent in *God*."[192] Using Hegel's ecclesiology, Hodgson expands on Augustine's idea that the Holy Spirit is the "bond of love" and as such the "soul" that indwells and quickens the mystical body. The Spiritual community is "transfigured intersubjectivity," distinguishable from all other forms of human love and friendship. As a result, what sort of authority does Hodgson's model grant to "Spirit?" We shall investigate Hodgson's views further in chapters three and four.

---

188. Hodgson, *Winds of the Spirit*, xii.
189. Ibid., xii.
190. Ibid., 282.
191. Ibid., 284.
192. Ibid., 35.

Michael Welker's *God the Spirit*

Welker's book is an explication of a postmodern pneumatology that emerges from the Holy Spirit's "pluralism." A theology of the Spirit is best developed against the background of "postmodern sensitivities," which abandon the assumption of a "unity of reality" and instead "assume a reality that consists of a plurality of structural patterns of life and of interconnected events."[193] Upon this grounding a "realistic theology" is birthed, one that allows us to gain a recognizable reality of the Spirit and theological access to the Spirit without sliding back to the problematic thinking associated with modernity—namely that a single system of reference could put God and God's power at our disposal. According to Bloesch, "[Welker] theologizes in a postmodern way, avoiding totalistic metaphysics and respecting differences in cultural ethos," and this makes his pneumatology essentially a "Spiritology from below" that begins with human experience.[194] What results is a postmodern ecclesiology, one in which the Spirit's main work is to reveal God's power in the formation of pluralistic communities.[195]

> The Spirit reveals God's power by simultaneously illumining different people and groups of people and enabling them to become not only recipients, but also bearers of God's revelation. The Spirit reveals the power of God in strong, upbuilding, pluralistic structures. This pluralism is not a disintegrative, Babel-like pluralism, but constitutes enriching, invigorating force fields. It is not bound

---

193. Welker, *God the Spirit*, 37–38. Here Welker looks to the postmodern theology of Mark Taylor, whose "trilemma of postmodern theology" asks us "to acknowledge tradition, to celebrate plurality, and to resist domination" (footnote on M. Taylor, in Welker, *God the Spirit*, 21); also to the postmodern philosophy of J. F. Lyotard as developed in his *The Postmodern Condition: A Report on Knowledge*.

194. Bloesch, *The Holy Spirit*, 260.

195. In this intersubjective work, Welker concludes that "the Spirit of God, not the communion of the sanctified itself, is the power that recognizes, enlivens, and maintains the body of Christ in constantly new ways" (Welker, *God the Spirit*, 312). An example of such "concrete manifestations" of the pluralistic Holy Spirit is the charismatic movement—where the abundance and diversity of the gifts of the Spirit are taken seriously and the separation between community leaders and laity is broken down. Welker asserts that "speaking in tongues," for example, was a privilege given by the Holy Spirit for healthy, pluralistic reasons: it works against abstract individualism (such as we witness in modernity), it gives rise to concrete attestations to the presence of the Spirit, and it prevents collapse into a disintegrative pluralism and relativism.

up with an abstract, uniform individualism that reduces everything to an unrealistic, abstract quality, reducing everything to "the ego," the subject, the decision-maker, the consumer, or the payee.[196]

Welker finds most theologies of the Spirit yield to the tendency to "jump immediately to 'the whole' [and thus remain] stuck in the realm of the numinous, the conjuration of merely mystical experience, and in global moral appeals."[197] The pluralism of the Spirit, on the other hand, is more "realistic" because the promises of the outpouring of the Spirit give witness to a specific sensitivity to differences. Unity of the Spirit continues to exist within such pluralism, but "becomes a reality not by imposing an illusory homogeneity, but by cultivating creaturely differences and by removing unrighteous differences."[198] In this way the Church is depicted by Welker, first and foremost, as a pluralistic society of believers. Still, the Spirit's work in the Church seems to only possess a *functional authority*. Does the Spirit truly retain any sort of "governing authority" with respect to the Church? We shall investigate this further in chapter four.

Other Contributors: "Practical" Theologies of the Spirit

Since this work also has to do with the Spirit's authority *in practice*, I will also briefly examine the works of several other contemporary theologians that wrestle with *practical issues in the Church* from the perspective of the Holy Spirit's work therein. These theologians and their recent works include: Stephen Fowl's *Engaging Scripture* and Stanley Grenz and John Franke's *Beyond Foundationalism* (on hermeneutics); Richard Hütter's *Suffering Divine Things* and Grenz and Franke's *Beyond Foundationalism* (on the practices of the Church); James Buckley and David Yeago's *Knowing the Triune God* and Gregory Jones and James Buckley's *Spirituality and Social Embodiment* (on Christian spirituality). These contemporary theologians will in turn become ideal "dialogue partners" for chapters five, six, and seven.

---

196. Welker, *God the Spirit*, 21–22.
197. Ibid., x.
198. Ibid., 25.

Stephen Fowl's *Engaging Scripture*

Fowl builds his hermeneutics on a specific view of authority, placing primary emphasis upon the Spirit's work within the Church. Fowl begins his "essay in the theological interpretation of Scripture" by saying that, "for Christians, Scripture is authoritative."[199] As his thesis develops, it becomes clear that, for Fowl, authority is essentially *ecclesial,* in that it "recognizes that the Spirit has been and still is at work in the lives of Christians and Christian community."[200] The Spirit seems to possess ultimate authority in hermeneutics, an authority to assist local church communities to reach crucial theological decisions based on "communal consensus."[201]

For Fowl, the Spirit seems to display some sort of "hermeneutical authority" with respect to the community. What sort of authority might this be? We will investigate this further in chapter five.

Stanley Grenz and John Franke's *Beyond Foundationalism*

Grenz and Franke present a hermeneutical model that understands the Church to be a "socially constructed" reality through the Spirit's work of "world construction." As individual members of society deem their knowledge about the world to be "objective," so religion involves a legitimization of the socially-constructed world that places a society within a sacred and cosmic frame of reference and gives participants a sense of being connected to ultimate reality. This "world construction" today does not lie in the text itself but in the Spirit as he speaks through the biblical texts and, in doing so, "performs the perlocutionary act of creating a *world*"[202]—which is precisely the eschatological world in the Church, the world God intends for creation as disclosed in the text.

For Grenz and Franke, this Spirit who constructs the Church community seems to display some sort of "authority" in the construction process. What sort of authority is this? We will pick up this discussion in chapters five and six.

---

199. Fowl, *Engaging Scripture*, 2–3.
200. Ibid., 203.
201. Ibid.
202. Grenz and Franke, *Beyond Foundationalism*, 77 (emphasis theirs).

THE LORD IS THE SPIRIT

Reinhard Hütter's *Suffering Divine Things*

A contemporary doctrine of practical ecclesiology that seems to grant the Spirit some sort of "authority" is found in Hütter's ecclesiology. Reminiscent of Luther, Hütter aligns the Spirit with the doctrines and practices of the Church. The Church begins with a trinitarian conception of "communio–ecclesiology," where the Church is the fellowship of participation in the communion of the Father with the Son in the Spirit. Hütter's concern is that the Church see herself rightly, as "a glad recipient" of God's saving work, but also as a body that understands how this "receiving" takes place. "This receiving embodied in practices is precisely the way in and through which the Holy Spirit works the saving knowledge of God."[203] In this paradigm, Church doctrine and practice become the "mediate forms" through which the Spirit guides the Church to truth, and these truths become the "binding authority" of the Church.[204] Since Hütter describes the Spirit's actions as the "*poimata*" of the "Spiritus Creator," the Spirit seems to possess a sort of "poetic authority" with respect to the local church. How might such an authority of the Spirit be discerned in light of our pattern of divine authority? We shall investigate this further in chapter six.

James Buckley and David Yeago's *Knowing the Triune God*

Buckley and Yeago seek to construct an "evangelical Catholicity" that is "deeply embedded in the Luther tradition."[205] Like Hütter, who seeks to discover the Spirit's work in the practices of the Church, these editors attempt to understand the Spirit's work in the Church's practice of *spirituality*—they "hope to *know* the triune God by the gift of the Spirit in the practices of the Church."[206] They want to re-focus on the Spirit's work as that which goes beyond the modern "dividing line between the inner and the outer" (which aligned the Spirit with inward subjectively and posited the Spirit against outward practices). Instead, all aspects of spirituality must begin from "one

---

203. Hütter, "The Church," 23.

204. Hütter, *Suffering Divine Things*, 128. Hütter adds, "As paradoxical as it may sound, the core Church practices and Church doctrine, precisely in their binding nature, are essential if the Holy Spirit is to lead the Church to perfect truth and teach it new things by perpetually reminding it of Jesus Christ" (128).

205. Buckley and Yeago, *Knowing the Triune God*, 2.

206. Ibid., 6 (emphasis theirs).

single starting point: in the Spirit, beginning with God's action and beginning with the Church and its practices are *one* beginning, in a unity in which the divine and the human are neither divided nor confused."[207] Because of the Spirit's intimate role in the *practices* of spirituality, we must ask Buckley and Yeago whether the Spirit has a specific authority with respect to spirituality. We shall investigate this further in chapter seven.

Gregory Jones and James Buckley's *Spirituality and Social Embodiment*

Jones and Buckley's goal is to confront modern "spirituality," which only "takes us out of the socially embodied world into a more inward (mystical) space." A "socially-embodied spirituality," on the other hand, "calls us beyond our selves to more material realities."[208] Jones develops this spirituality by looking at Bernard of Clairveaux, and concludes that,

> Christian living involves a journey of learning to know oneself precisely as one who is known by God. This journey of self-knowing requires awareness of both our absence from God . . . [and] our being renewed in the divine image by God's Spirit learned through such practices as prayer and almsgiving.[209]

Yeago builds on this initial approach to spirituality by showing its actualization *in the Church*. "The mature Luther" described the Church as "the gathered people" which believes in Christ and has the Holy Spirit: "The inward is given through the outward: it is by virtue of its divine character *as* a bodily, public assembly that this community is endowed with these inward, spiritual blessings."[210] The Spirit is thereby the one who distributes Christ's salvation "through the Christian Church and through the forgiveness of sins imparted in the Church."[211] The Spirit incorporates believers into the Church so that one's private spirituality can find expression in adherence to the Church.[212] Since such a view seems to elevate the practices of the Church to a place of paramount importance in the development of

---

207. Ibid., 17–18 (emphasis theirs).
208. Jones and Buckley, *Spirituality and Social Embodiment*, 1.
209. Jones, "A Thirst for God or Consumer Spirituality," 6.
210. Yeago, "A Christian, Holy People," 108.
211. Ibid., 115.
212. Ibid., 116.

the believer's spirituality, we will need to ask Jones and Buckley whether the Spirit retains "authority" with respect to this development. We shall investigate this further in chapter seven.

The Governing Authority of the Spirit—Definition and Storyline

Now that we have observed several contemporary approaches to the Spirit/Church relationship (both theoretical and practical approaches) we are able to examine them in search of a provisional definition of the Spirit's *governing authority*, and then pose initial questions for each approach regarding its alignment with the provisional definitions discerned earlier. These questions will be further addressed in chapter three and four as well.

In discerning the "authority" of the Spirit in relationship to the Church, it seems that these various "communitarian" and "paleoorthodox" perspectives might be categorized in terms of "functional power" and "governing authority," respectively. A *function* is the ability or power to perform specific duties, but does not imply any delegation of authority from one person to another[213] (and in this sense it is not an "authority" at all, since it is not essentially *personal)*. In the "communitarian" approaches to ecclesiology presented by Welker, Moltmann, and Hodgson, the Spirit only seems to possess the *functional power* to perform a specific task within communities (i.e., creating pluralistic communities within our human experience, experiencing the Spirit "as community," or invoking liberating experiences, respectively). The Spirit's "authority" seems to be reduced to his "power" to create an experience of God in the context of the Church community, but without due concern for the pattern of authority.

"Governing authority," on the other hand, incorporates the authority inherent in one's own person along with a delegated authority to work or function as "governor" (we might think of a "governor" who is granted the authority to rule locally under the auspices of a President or King). Such a "governing authority" of the Spirit seems to coincide with Oden's "paleoorthodox" understanding of the doctrine of the Spirit (which generally respects the pattern of authority) while listening to the "postmodern" desire

---

213. "Function" can be defined as "the occupation of an office. By the performance of its duties, the officer is said to fill his function" (*Black's Law Dictionary*, "Function," 606).

for a renewed focus on the experience of the Spirit within the Church. In this scenario, the body of Christ, having a temporary status until Christ returns with his eschatological Kingdom, is created and administered by the "governing authority" of the Holy Spirit.

Whereas a "functional power" of the Spirit is not necessarily associated with the other aspects of the Spirit's authority already discussed, the Spirit's "governing authority" implies a vital connection to these aspects. If the Spirit's authority or power is not related to the other elements in our pattern of authority, what will this do to our understanding of the Spirit's "authority"?

As a result, initial questions can be asked regarding each of the abovementioned "whole book" theologies of the Holy Spirit. For instance, in their concern for the experience of the Spirit, have these theologians left behind various aspects of our pattern of authority in the developing their models? What does this do to the notion of the "governing authority of the Spirit"? In particular, we will need to ask:

1. Does Moltmann's "panentheism" depreciate the Spirit's authority as a divine Person?
2. Does Pinnock's "universalism" or Hodgson's "modified trinitarianism" nullify the Spirit's executorial authority?
3. Does Welker's "pluralism" reduce the Spirit's veracious authority with respect to inspiration, and does Badcock's attention to spiritual experience reduce the Spirit's veracious authority with respect to illumination?
4. Precisely what effects do any deficiencies in Moltmann's, Hodgson's, and Welker's models have on a development of a biblical understanding of the Spirit's "governing authority"?

Conclusion

In chapters three and four I will attempt to confirm the above definitions of the Spirit's authority through the exegesis of Scripture and through Biblical/Systematic theology. If it can be demonstrated in Scripture that the Spirit indeed has an "authority" in keeping with each of the definitions proposed in this chapter, we would then be able to speak of the Spirit as possessing *plenipotentiary authority*.[214] This is an authority that incorporates and activates all aspects of authority discussed thus far (i.e., authority *over the world*, authority to execute Christ's will, authority to execute Christ's will *in accordance with Scripture*, and the authority to execute Christ's will *as governor of the Church*).

We have surveyed theological history and uncovered a story that reflects the doctrinal development of the Spirit's authority within the context of the pattern of authority. We began with a study of the patristic writers and inferred that the Fathers of the early Church recognized the Holy Spirit's divine authority as a divine Person. We then examined the traumatic debate in medieval theology regarding *Filioque* and concluded that Augustine's model seems to grant the Spirit an "executorial authority" to act under the authority of Christ. We studied the Protestant debate regarding the "interpretive authority" of the Spirit and discovered that the reformers did not allow such an authority to be delegated to any human institution. We briefly surveyed the landscape of modern theology and found that evangelicals have affirmed that the "veracious authority" of the Spirit is allied with the inspired text rather that with human reason or experience. Finally, we surveyed several "postmodern" theologians and discovered that "paleoorthodox" theologians point toward the Spirit's "governing authority" within the Church.

---

214. "Plenipotentiary authority" is possessed by "one who has full power to do a thing; a person fully commissioned to act for another" (*Black's Law Dictionary*, "Plenipotentiary," 1176). Oxford English Dictionary has "Invested with full power; esp. as the deputy, representative, or envoy of a sovereign ruler; exercising absolute power or authority (*The Compact Oxford English Dictionary*, 1365). Such an authority goes beyond that of an *ambassador*, who simply acts on behalf of another, but includes a full authority to govern as well.

3

The Authority of the Holy Spirit and Systematic Theology: Part I

❈ THE PRIMARY GOAL of chapters three and four is to develop a biblical/theological model that describes the nature of the Holy Spirit's authority along with the various "realms"[1] of authority possessed by the Spirit, thereby displaying the Spirit's place within the "principle" and "pattern" of divine authority.

Methodology

I will attempt to do build this model by exegeting several passages of Scripture, many of which lie at the heart of the theological debates reviewed in chapter two. Regarding our *principle* of authority, we inferred from Patristic theology that the Spirit should be thought of as a divine Person who reveals *divine authority* in the world. In this chapter, we shall investigate Scriptures and theological concepts in an attempt to confirm and describe the nature of the Spirit's divine Personhood, specifically as a Person who possesses and reveals divine authority.

Regarding our *pattern* of authority, we discovered in chapter two that the "filioque theology" of the medieval Church allows us to infer the notion of the Spirit's *executorial authority*—an authority to act under Christ's authority. In this chapter we shall examine Scriptures and theological concepts in an attempt to confirm and describe this executorial authority. In

---

1. "Realm" will be defined as a general sphere or territory where authority can be displayed at will.

the next chapter we shall examine two predominant realms where the Spirit seems to act with executorial authority.

Hermeneutical Goals and Assumptions

In this chapter and the next I will employ a grammatical-historical and "critical realism"[2] approach to the exegetical task. First, in my exegesis of Scripture I will study specific words and particularly "speech acts" of Scripture in search of evidence for the authority of the Spirit, and will attempt to keep in mind any historical issues that may influence my exegesis (those that emerged from the biblical culture or the theological debates discussed in chapter two).

Second, I will attempt to employ "critical realism" in my exegesis as a way of making us more "humble observers" of the text. Critical realism instructs us to approach the text from a perspective of *realism* (an interpretive philosophy that affirms a reality independent of our own minds), while taking a *critical* stance toward our own observational powers—knowing that we too have been influenced by our own culture, personal biases, and hermeneutical communities. Many of these communities have a rather "narrowing" effect on systematic theology and on the interpretation of Scripture. Critical realism is especially helpful in such a study that, as we have seen, has been so debated and divisive throughout theological history. Therefore, I will attempt to approach my exegesis with an appropriate self-criticism, at times examining interpretations that disagree with my own.

In addition, I will attempt to set these passages within the larger context of biblical theology and systematic theology as presented in the procedure that follows.

Procedure for Exegetical and Theological Analysis: Moving from Scripture to Theology

An outline of the exegetical/theological "flow" through chapters three and four will proceed as follows:

Chapter Three

A. The Divine Authority of the Spirit

---

2. See Vanhoozer, *Is There A Meaning in This Text?*, 300–302.

1. with respect to created life (Ps 104:29–30)
2. as confirmed by divine access and revelation (1 Cor 2:10–13)

B. The Executorial Authority of the Spirit
   1. in relation to the present authority of Christ (John 15:26)
   2. with respect to the present revelation of Christ (John 16:12–15)

Chapter Four

C. The Veracious Authority of the Spirit
   1. with respect to the inspiration of Scripture (John 14:16–17, 26)
   2. with respect to the illumination of Scripture (2 Pet 1:20–21)
D. The Governing Authority of the Spirit in the Church
   1. with respect to the eschatological and immediate "realm" of authority in the Church (Isa 11:2; Isa 32:15–16; Acts 1:5–8)
   2. with respect to the immediate "effects" of this realm in establishing and governing the Church
      a. Democratization (Isa 59:21)
      b. Liberation (Rom 8:2)
      c. Transformation (2 Cor 3:17–18)

The flow of the four sections in chapters three and four, and the main aspects of authority to be discussed, will parallel the sections of historical theology in chapter two. The only variation from the sequence of chapter two is that the discussion of the Spirit's "interpretive authority" (from the Reformation period) will be woven into the discussion of the Spirit's "veracious authority" (which is the broader term).

Relying upon Scripture as final authority, each of the four sections above (A, B, C and D) will follow a procedure involving four "steps" from exegesis to theology: Introduction to the section, Exegesis of passages, Biblical Theology, and Systematic Theology.[3]

---

3. While Carson exhorts exegetes to be "critical realists" regarding their own theological assumptions, he also thinks systematic theology can indeed flow from exegesis to systematic theology. "It is absurd to deny that one's systematic theology does not [sic] affect one's exegesis. Nevertheless, the line of final control is the straight one from exegesis right through biblical and historical theology to systematic theology. The final authority is the Scriptures, the Scriptures alone. For this reason exegesis, though affected by systematic theology, is not shackled by it" (Carson, *Scripture and Truth*, 92).

THE LORD IS THE SPIRIT

INTRODUCTION

In each section I will begin by restating the provisional "definition" that emerged from chapter two. Then I will proceed by asking a specific question regarding that particular "aspect"[4] of the Spirit's authority—a question I will attempt to answer by the end of that section. With this question in mind, I will then suggest specific passages that seem to provide initial evidence pertaining to the question.

EXEGETICAL SECTIONS

This step involves the exegesis of those passages of Scripture most critical to the discussion at hand. I will use targeted studies of each passage to discern their meaning with respect to the Holy Spirit and his authority. I will look for solid clues in each passage regarding the nature of this authority, pointing them out as they emerge.

BIBLICAL THEOLOGY

This step will be an attempt to place the passages I have exegeted into the broader context of the whole of Scripture and progressive revelation. In doing so I will look for broad scriptural themes that emerge with respect to the Spirit's authority.

SYSTEMATIC THEOLOGY

In this final step, the systematic theology findings of each section will build on the findings of the previous sections. I will seek to discern "descriptions" of the Spirit's authority that result in specific parameters (i.e., limitations) for all subsequent sections.[5] In developing these descriptions of the

---

4. For sake of introducing and categorizing the various definitions of the Spirit's authority, I will occasionally speak in terms of the various "aspects" of the Spirit's authority. By "aspects" I do not mean separate "parts" of the Spirit's authority but the varying "perspectives" or "angles" from which the Spirit's authority might be examined.

5. As a preview, the first section—"The Divine Authority of the Spirit"—will provide the first and most general "parameter," that is, the essential "who" of the Spirit's authority (and once again reflects our "principle" of divine authority). The other three sections will provide specific parameters in conjunction with our "pattern of divine authority"—"how"

Spirit's authority for systematic theology, I will first "dialogue" with various contemporary theologians who have written "whole book" treatises on the Holy Spirit (those we touched on in the sections in chapter two entitled "Evangelical 'Postmodern' Theologies of the Spirit" and "Contemporary 'Postmodern' Theologies of the Spirit"). I will attempt to "listen to" the main contribution of each book for our discussion.

Second, I will utilize my exegesis and biblical theology to respond to each author. Having discerned from Scripture various clues and patterns regarding the authority of the Holy Spirit, I will now use Scripture to assess whether this author affirms or denies a biblical notion of the Spirit's authority.

Finally, I will discuss this aspect of the Spirit's authority in light of systematic theology and specifically within the broader scope of our principle and pattern of divine authority, looking to confirm a biblical/systematic notion of the Spirit's authority within the entire pattern.[6] I will attempt to provide a formal description of this authority that will clarify its precise nature and identify specific "titles" for the Spirit that represent each description. This description, of course, will be far more definitive than the "provisional" summary statement gleaned from historical theology (in chapter two).

Exegetical and Theological Analysis

We now begin our exegetical and theological analysis of the four critical "aspects" of the Holy Spirit's authority as discerned in our study of historical theology.

---

and "where" the Spirit's divine authority is revealed with respect to specific "aspects" of authority. These aspects can be found in relation to Christ, the Scriptures (truth), and the Church (God's people). While these various aspects of the Spirit's authority can be generally *distinguished*, we shall discover that they cannot be *separated* (as if the Spirit were to demonstrate authority in only one "aspect" at a time).

6. However, since there are no formal theological definitions of "The Authority of the Spirit" at this time in systematic theology, the insights from theologians with respect to pneumatology may well only provide "parameters" for such definitions.

The Divine Authority of the Spirit

In our study of historical theology we discovered that various patristic theologians (i.e., Athanasius, the Cappadocians) attempted to "prove" the Spirit's divinity by demonstrating such attributes as the Spirit's *Lordship* and *transcendence* (as well as his immutability, supremacy, eternality shared divinity, and involvement in certain activities).[7]

INTRODUCTION

The essential question now has to do with our *principle* of authority: "How might we confirm the divine *nature* of the Spirit as a Person of the Triune God, and how might we understand the divine *authority* of the Spirit with respect to the world and with respect to divine self-revelation *in* the world?" While only a few passages make a direct assertion of the Spirit's divinity, several passages of Scripture imply the Spirit's authority as a Person who is transcendent *over* the world and as such reveals God *in* the world. The passages to be investigated in this section are Ps 104:29–30 (which demonstrates the Spirit's divine transcendence and rightful dominion with respect to creation) and 1 Cor 2:10–13 (which Athanasius used to demonstrate that the Spirit is not created but emerges directly from God, and which shows the Spirit's unique access to God with respect to divine revelation).

EXEGESIS OF PASSAGES

In my exegesis of these passages, I will attempt to isolate specific attributes that confirm the Spirit's divine Personhood and authority, including divine transcendence, rightful dominion, divine access, and divine "revealedness."

---

7. As seen in chapter one, *Lordship* centers in control, authority, and presence. According to Frame, "As controller and authority, God is 'absolute,' that is, his power and wisdom are beyond any possibility of successful challenge. Thus God is eternal, infinite, omniscient, omnipotent, and so on" (Frame, *The Doctrine of the Knowledge of God*, 17). Frame also points out, "Divine transcendence in Scripture seems to center on the concepts of control and authority" (15).

The Authority of the Holy Spirit and Systematic Theology: Part I

Divine Transcendence of the Spirit with Respect to Created Life— Exegesis of Psalm 104:29–30

Psalm 104 is a "nature Psalm"[8] that portrays Yahweh as Creator and Ruler throughout all features of the "cosmos." Genesis 1 serves as a model for this Psalm in that its seven stanzas parallel the seven days of creation.[9] Yahweh's rule is described both poetically (i.e., v. 12) and eschatologically (vv. 31–34). Many commentators see this Psalm (especially vv. 19–24) as having been strongly influenced by the "Hymn to the Sun" (the Sun of the pagan god, Akhenaten[10]). The immediate framework for our passage is vv. 24–28, which portrays the notion of the *dependency* of all things upon Yahweh. He created the entire array of creatures upon the earth (v. 24) that depend upon him for food and look to his hand for all good things (vv. 27–28). Here, in contrast to the royal imagery of vv. 1–4, the Lord is pictured as a farmer who goes out to feed his animals and who provides from his crops in due season. This theme of providence is expounded in vv. 29–30, where God acts on behalf of his creation and the Spirit is sovereign over life and death, over creation and "re-creation." A chiastic arrangement leads the reader from the face of God to the face of creation.[11]

> You hide your face (פָּנֶיךָ) . . .
> You take away their spirit (רוּחָם) . . .
> You send forth your Spirit (רוּחֲךָ) . . .
> You renew the face (פְּנֵי) of the earth.

Two prominent theological themes—God as Creator and God as Ruler—intersect in vv. 29–30 so as to demonstrate the *transcendent* nature of Yahweh's divine authority. Throughout the Psalm, God's rule is shown to

---

8. Anderson, *Psalm 100–150*, 717. Anderson adds, "This Psalm is usually defined as 'a hymn in which the central theme is the works of God in creation'" (717).
9. Deissler, "The Theology of Psalm 104," 32.
10. Pritchard, *Ancient Near Eastern Texts Relation to the Old Testament*, 371a.
11. See Montague, *Holy Spirit: Growth of a Biblical Tradition*, 71.

The Lord Is the Spirit

be providential,[12] redemptive, and authoritative, and yet this is so because God himself is indeed transcendent.[13]

29[14] תַּסְתִּיר פָּנֶיךָ יִבָּהֵלוּן תֹּסֵף רוּחָם יִגְוָעוּן וְאֶל־עֲפָרָם יְשׁוּבוּן׃

29 Thou dost hide Thy face, they are dismayed; Thou dost take away their spirit, they expire, and return to their dust.

Specific words in this passage are so vivid that they require special attention. The word תַּסְתִּיר (hiphil imperfect, 2d person, masc., sing.) here implies more than "you hide" but rather "withdraw one's favor or providential care."[15] This verb begins a string of four imperfect verbs, giving the psalm a sense of God as the continuous actor as well as director of the activity. The word פָּנֶיךָ ("your faces," 2d person plural) refers to the "face" (or "faces") of the Lord, which is not actually hidden but, in this sense, *turned away*.[16] The result is יִבָּהֵלוּן ("they are dismayed," niphil imperfect, 3d person plural), meaning, "be disturbed, dismayed, terrified" (cf. Ps 83:18). The farmer imagery in vv. 27–28 helps us understand why, in 29a, when God hides his face "they are dismayed." They are dismayed simply because they are very hungry!

In 29b, however, the Lord is portrayed as much more than their food supplier—he is their very life support system. The word תֹּסֵף ("you take away," qal imperfect, 2d person singular) means to remove or withdraw, and is used in Ps 85:4 in terms of God removing his wrath. The word רוּחָם ("their breath") is literally "their spirits," and refers to the vital principle of life imparted by the Spirit of God (cf. Gen 2:7; Job 12:10).[17] Because the plural

---

12. According to Deissler, the theme of *creatio prima* (continuous creation, or providence) begins in the third stanza with participles that convey a durative function (104:10, 13, 14) and portrays both nature and all human life as continuing works of God (Deissler, "Theology of Psalm 104," 35).

13. The Lord is described as "very great" and "clothed with splendor and majesty" (v. 1); he "makes the clouds His chariot" (v. 3); He made all things "in wisdom" (v. 24); all living things "wait for You" (v. 27); the earth "trembles" before him (v. 32).

14. Hebrew passages will be taken from the BHS, 4th ed.

15. Anderson, *Psalms 100–150*, 724.

16. See van Rooy "פָּנִים," 3:638–39. See Lev 17:10, 20:5; Deut 31:17; Ezek 7:22.

17. Dahood, however, understands "spirit" in this verse to be the actual "Spirit of God" imparted. "That 'your spirit' is intended appears from the balance with *paneka*, 'your face' . . . adding that the men in Qumran altered מהור to הכהור" (Dahood, *Psalm III*, 46). This,

form does not distinguish between humans and other creatures, Limburg rightly argues that this psalm is *geocentric* rather than *anthropocentric* (the word "earth" occurs seven times, while humans appear hardly at all), and that this psalm utilizes an "integration model" that emphasizes humanity's commonality with other creatures (as portrayed in Gen 2:7–9, 19).[18] Thus Yahweh's dominion, not man's, is at the forefront in Psalm 104.

The word עֲפָרָם ("their dust") is specified as the material of the human body (cf. Gen 2:7; 3:19). This is their own native dust from which they sprang forth and to which they shall יְשׁוּבוּן ("return," "turn back"). This verb (qal perfect, 3ms) refers in this context to dying and essentially indicates that they never "rise above" the level of the material, but always find themselves "under" the Spirit who grants their very breath.

30 תְּשַׁלַּח רוּחֲךָ יִבָּרֵאוּן וּתְחַדֵּשׁ פְּנֵי אֲדָמָה׃

30 Thou dost send forth Thy Spirit, they are created; And Thou dost renew the face of the ground.

The word תְּשַׁלַּח ("you send," qal imperfect, 3ms) is often used with the prophets (i.e., Jer 7:25), while רוּחֲךָ ("your Spirit" or "your breath") is the same word as used in verse 29 (except here in the singular case). Here, as in Isa 63:11–14, the Spirit signifies God's personal, active presence as well as his sovereignty and Lordship.[19] The intent of the Psalmist is clear: the spirit of every living thing depends on God's *Spirit*. According to Kidner, this comparison of the divine Spirit to the human spirit, "so far from implicating Him in our misdeeds, deepens our accountability, since we handle only what is His."[20] The Spirit is not simply presented here as a divine agent. Rather, in this passage we indeed find one of the clearest expressions in

---

however, is not likely because of the above chiasm, and because of obvious parallelism to Gen 2:7, which many major commentators (i.e., Anderson, Alexander, Deissler) agree. Alexander, for example, asserts, "Their breath [is] the vital principle [of life] imparted by the Spirit of God (Gen 2:7), which is the God of the spirits of all flesh, i.e. the author of all life whatsoever" (Alexander, *The Psalms*, 427).

18. This model also stands in opposition to the "dominion model" of Genesis 1. See Limburg, "Down to Earth Theology," 344–45.

19. A "sovereign" is defined as "one that exercises supreme authority within a limited sphere" (*Webster's New Universal Unabridged Dictionary*, "Sovereign"). The Spirit's sovereignty is evidenced in all aspects of creation (see Biblical Theology section below).

20. Kidner, *Psalm 100–150*, 372.

the OT of the Spirit's divine *transcendence*. As in Gen 1:2, רוּחַ seems to be used as a metaphor for God's sovereignty (and specifically the sovereignty of אֱלֹהִים) over creation.

The word יִבָּרֵאוּן ("they are created") alludes to the continual process of "re-creation" (or *divine providence*).[21] The idea conveyed with this word seems to be in specific reflection to Genesis 1, where God's power is demonstrated in *creation ex nihilo* ("out of nothing"). This verse, however, goes beyond such a reflection, in that the Spirit is portrayed as *necessary* with respect to life. Alexander holds that, in this passage, "The absolute power of God over the life of his creatures is expressed by representing him as annihilating and creating the whole race at his pleasure, by a breath."[22] Thus in this passage we can infer more than simply divine *power* in relation to the Spirit. Because of the contrast between vv. 29 and 30, this passage also indicates the *pre-eminence* of the Spirit with respect to physical life. The Spirit is portrayed as the necessary cause of the creature's life, which thereby sets up a relationship involving dependency on the part of the creature (rather than a dependency *upon* the creature in any sort of way). The Spirit is given a place of dominion; since he is portrayed as a life-giving Creator, however, the Spirit should be seen as possessing *rightful* dominion.[23]

---

21. Oden asserts that the Spirit's work with respect to creation and divine providence might be thought of as "general operations" that are shared with the Father and the Son and that display divine sovereignty. The Spirit, for example, enables political order and restrains the capacity for humanity to destroy itself. The Spirit's "general operations" also include, "the offering of life, supporting of life newly given, nurturing continuing life, strengthening life nurtured, and guiding life strengthened. This applies to all forms of life, whether plant, animal, or human. . . . By the Spirit the enormous diversity of creation is brought into a single meaningful whole. Even the sins of the fallen, for which God is not responsible, are in time made serviceable to the whole" (Oden, *Life in the Spirit*, 34–35). See also Job 33:4, 34:14, 15.

22. Alexander, *The Psalms*, 427.

23. Frame links the act of creation to covenant Lordship, which is then related to divine transcendence and authority. "In a broad sense, all of God's dealings with creation are covenantal in character. . . . During the creation week, all things, plants, animals, and persons are appointed to be covenant servants, to obey God's awl, and to be instruments (positively or negatively) of His gracious purpose. Thus everything and everybody is in covenant with God (cf. Isa 24:5: all the 'inhabitants of the earth' have broth the 'everlasting covenant'). The Creator-creature relation is a covenant relation, a Lord-servant relation. . . . If God is covenant *head*, then His is exalted above His people; His is transcendent. If He is *covenant* head, then His is deeply involved with them; His is immanent" (Frame, *The Doctrine of*

The word וּתְחַדֵּשׁ ("you renew," piel imperfect, 2ms) means "bring back," implying that all earthly life is also renewed by the Spirit. The term פְּנֵי ("the faces of the earth") refers to the "surface" of the ground (cf. Gen 2:6, 4:14, 7:4) and may have been written with the flood in mind. "There is evident allusion to the renovation of the earth desolated by the flood, and the joyous change of its face or aspect when re-peopled."[24]

Divine Authority of the Spirit as Confirmed by Divine Access and Revelation—Exegesis of 1 Cor 2:10–13

While it has received varied interpretations,[25] this passage certainly exposes the Spirit's *divine transcendence* in terms of divine revelation. According to Thiselton, this passage provides "a thorough appreciation of the nature of God as Other who is not to be transposed into an instrument for self-esteem and self-affirmation (v. 12a), [or an] appreciation of God's revelation of himself as sheer gift (v. 12b)."[26] This passage was most widely used by the Patristics (particularly Athanasius) in defending the Spirit's divinity against the Arians.

10 ἡμῖν δὲ ἀπεκάλυψεν ὁ θεὸς διὰ τοῦ πνεύματος· τὸ γὰρ πνεῦμα πάντα ἐραυνᾷ, καὶ τὰ βάθη τοῦ θεοῦ.[27]

---

the Knowledge of God, 12–13 [italics his]). And, as we have seen, Frame asserts that "divine transcendence in Scripture seems to center on the concepts of control and authority" (15). Frame also explains the nature of covenant: "*Covenant* may refer to a contract or agreement among equals or to a type of relation between a lord and his servants. Divine-human covenants in Scripture, of course, are of the latter type. In the most prominent ones, God as covenant lord selects a certain people from along all the nations of thee earth to be His own. He rules over them by His law, in terms of which all who obey are blessed and all who disobey are cursed" (12, italics his). What Frame seems to be describing here is that of a *rightful dominion* (or *authoritative dominion)*, and when correlated with God—and the Spirit—as the Creator, we can then extrapolate such a *dominion* in relation to all living creatures.

24. Alexander, *The Psalms*, 427.

25. Origen used this passage not to demonstrate the Spirit's divinity but to show that the Spirit is the one who illumines the obscure passages of Scripture, uncovering the source of the "deeper" doctrines of God. Athanasius sees this passage, however, as proof for the Spirit's deity (See Haykin, "The Spirit of God," 513–28).

26. Thiselton, *The First Epistle to the Corinthians*, 252.

27. Greek passages will be taken from the *Nestle-Aland Greek New Testament*, 27th ed.

>10 but unto us God revealed *them* through his own Spirit, for the Spirit all things searches, even the depths of God.[28]

The word ἡμῖν (dative pronoun, "to us") refers back to "those who love him" (v. 9), not to some inner circle within the church. Its emphatic position stresses the privileged position of the recipients of God's revelation as well as Paul's recognition of God's *free choice* in revealing these things through the Spirit. Thus we gain an initial hint of God's "non-derivative" authority.[29] The verb ἀπεκάλυψεν (aorist, passive, of ἀποκαλύπτω)[30] in this context demonstrates that,

> [This word] is not confined in Paul to the foundational message of Christ. . . . For the Spirit who guides the disciples into all truth opens up the understanding of revelation which is given them in the word of Jesus and of the Apostles (cf. Eph 2:18).[31]

The rulers of this age (v. 8), and particularly their lack of knowledge regarding the mystery of God's wisdom (v. 7), is countered in this passage by what God has revealed by his Spirit "to us." The contrast lies not so much between "us" and "them" but between the reasons why they could not, but we can, understand the things God has prepared for his people (v. 9).[32] Verse 10, therefore, along with 11–13, emphasizes the authoritative *means* of revelation—the transcendent Spirit—not the recipients themselves.

Paul was always aware that he was a bearer of divine revelation (1 Cor 15:9–11) based on the revelation he received in his encounter with the resurrected Lord (1 Cor 15:8). Paul had always viewed *Jesus* as the author of divine revelation, as witnessed in his attack on the Galatian heresy (Gal 1:1–12) and in this context as well (1 Cor 1:30—2:2). But

---

28. English passages will be taken from the *New American Standard Bible* (NAB), 1995 ed., unless otherwise indicated.

29. "Non-derivative" authority can be defined as supreme or undelegated authority (i.e. possessed only by divinity).

30. The word carries the idea of "revealed," "disclosed," or "brought to light" and is particularly used for the divine revelation of certain supernatural secrets (Bauer, "ἀποκαλύπτω," 112). It is also used with respect to the prophets in 1 Pet 1:12 and Christ in Matt 11:25, 16:17, and Phil. 3:15.

31. Brown, "Revelation," 3:315.

32. Fee, *God's Empowering Presence*, 99.

now Paul presents the *Spirit* as the agent of this revealing activity[33] (διὰ τοῦ πνεύματος—"through his Spirit"—is a genitive prepositional phrase indicating agency). This agency is not like a human agent, which simply represents another human, but indicates full possession by God and identity with God[34] (as is confirmed by the genitive article τοῦ, "his own"). In this verse, "The Holy Spirit is the agent of this definitive revelation of grace, a revelation with a definite beginning or advent (constantive aorist), an unveiling by the Spirit where 'human ability and research would not have sufficed.'"[35] It is easy to see why Athanasius chose this passage for defending the Spirit's "transcendence."

Paul's main argument begins in 10b, particularly with ἐραυνᾷ (present, indicative, active), which in this context indicates a "search for knowledge of that which is still hidden in the depths of God."[36] There is a sort of inseparability between this verb and the previous one, which Barrett picks up in his translation ("searches out"), explaining that this spelling does not mean *search to discover* but refers to the activity of exploring God's purposes thoroughly in order to *reveal* them.[37] The word was typically used in a professional researcher's report—the work of one who thoroughly searches out all details available. Paul uses these common Gnostic words to highlight the Spirit's unique searching activity and to counter those who supposed that they could find God by their own searching.[38]

The Spirit is able to reveal God's wisdom "to us" because the Spirit searches πάντα ("all things"). As a direct object of the verb, πάντα clarifies "not that [the Spirit] conducts searches with a view to obtaining informa-

---

33. The key word in this entire passage, of course, is πνεῦμα. Paul has already referred to the Spirit in conjunction with power (2:4), and now inundates the passage with seven reference to πνεῦμα and πνεύματος (vv. 10–14, meaning either "Spirit" or "spirit"), three references to the adjective, πνευματικοῖς (vv. 13, 15) and one to the adverb, πνευματικῶς (v. 14).

34. The article is probably used here as a demonstrative (or possessive) pronoun (i.e., "who belongs to"). See Dana and Mantey, *A Manual Grammar of the Greek New Testament*, 147.

35. Fee, *The First Epistle to the Corinthians*, 86.

36. Seitz, "Seek," 3:533. This word can also indicate "examine," "investigate," "illuminate" (Bauer, "ἐραυνάω," 306) or "explore" (NRSV, NIV).

37. Barrett, *The First Epistle to the Corinthians*, 74.

38. See Barrett, *The First Epistle to the Corinthians*, 74, 188–89.

tion, but that he penetrates *all things.*"³⁹ This includes τὰ βάθη τοῦ θεοῦ ("the depths of God"). The phrase τὰ βάθη literally means "of a well" and figuratively refers to hidden depths (i.e., of Satan in Rev 2:24); here it designates God's essence, as well as his attributes, volitions, and plans.⁴⁰ This expression is similar to Rom 11:33, where Paul expounds on the profound greatness of God (which carries over from His Jewish and apocalyptic thought). The Spirit has a glorious task that reflects his glorious nature; Athanasius found this searching activity to be proof of the Spirit's divinity.

> Would it not be evil speech to call the Spirit who is in God (ἐν τῷ θεῷ) a creature, him who searches even the depths of God? For from this the speaker will learn to say that the spirit of man is outside himself, and that the Word of God, who is in the Father (ἐν τῷ πατρὶ) is a creature.⁴¹

This verse reveals perhaps the most foundational attribute of the Spirit's divine Personhood—full access to the divinity. A subordinate cannot go into the bedroom of the superior; only one with authority has full access to the master's inner chambers. The Spirit as a divine Person has full access to the Triune God, eternal authority to enter into the very depths of God.

Such an authority, however, can never be disconnected from the intimately-connected result of this searching activity: the revelation of these depths *to us*. Hodge states,

> What was undiscoverable by human reason, God hath revealed by his Spirit . . . for he alone is competent to make it; for he alone searches the depths of God. . . . this passage proves at once the *personality* and *divinity* of the Holy Ghost. His personality, because intelligent activity is ascribed to him; he searches; his divinity, because omniscience is ascribed to him; he knows all that God knows.⁴²

What is the Spirit revealing to us? If we connect this verse back to vv. 2–8 we discover that the Spirit has searched the depths of God and revealed to us *wisdom*, a wisdom found only in context with the mystery

---

39. Morris, *The First Epistle to the Corinthians*, 56.

40. Wolff refers to this as *Unergründliche*—God is grounded in nothing but His own selfhood (Wolff, *Der erste Brief des Paulus an die Korinther*, 58).

41. Athanasius, "First Letter to Serapion," 22.121.

42. Hodge, *An Exposition of the First Epistle to the Corinthians*, 38 (emphasis mine).

of the cross. Fee summarizes: "Redemption through the cross comes from the profound depths of God's own wisdom, which his Spirit, given to those who love him, has searched out and revealed to us."[43]

> 11 τίς γὰρ οἶδεν ἀνθρώπων τὰ τοῦ ἀνθρώπου εἰ μὴ τὸ πνεῦμα τοῦ ἀνθρώπου τὸ ἐν αὐτῷ; οὕτως καὶ τὰ τοῦ θεοῦ οὐδεὶς ἔγνωκεν εἰ μὴ τὸ πνεῦμα τοῦ θεοῦ.
>
> 11 for who knows of men the things of man except the spirit of the man which [is] in him, so also the things of God no one knows except the Spirit of God.

The explanatory γὰρ ("for") introduces an analogy for explaining verse 10. Because the Spirit searches out the depths of God, the Spirit *alone* knows the things of God. Paul employs the principle of "like is known by like"; in this case influenced by the OT motif that no one has ever seen God.[44] The Spirit's knowledge is "continuous" (since οἶδεν is a defective perfect of οἶδα, indicating a continual knowledge of "the thoughts of God"). The analogy is that the only person who knows what is inside one's mind is oneself.

> This sentence is *not* trying to make a definitive pneumatological statement. It is analogy, pure and simple. And the analogy does not have to do with the constituents of personality; rather, it has to do with our common experience of personal reality. . . . God's Spirit, therefore, who as God knows the mind of God, becomes the link to our knowing him also, because as v. 12 goes on to affirm, "we have received the Spirit of God."[45]

Neither is Paul intending to provide anthropological insight. The idea is that *only* the Spirit of God has authority to enter the inner chambers of God. While Barrett thinks this comparison lies in the usage of the word πνεῦμα, Thiselton finds it in the *role* of πνεῦμα.

> The point of the analogy does *not* turn on human spirit within/ divine spirit within, but on the possession of an *exclusive initiative to reveal one's thoughts, counsels, stance, attitudes, intentions*, or what-

43. Fee, *God's Empowering Presence*, 100.
44. Fee, *The First Epistle to the Corinthians*, 111.
45. Ibid., 111–12.

The Lord Is the Spirit

ever else is "within" *in the sense of hidden from the public domain, not in the sense of location.*⁴⁶

This verse therefore sets up a discontinuity between the limited knowledge of humankind and the transcendent Spirit, who knows the mind of God.⁴⁷ Athanasius states the obvious implication of 11b: "What kinship could there be, judging by the above, between the Spirit and the creatures? For the creatures were not; but God is being (ᾧ ἐστιν) and the Spirit is from him."⁴⁸ Paul uses Gnostic words to demonstrate this profound disparagement, and the implied distinction between πνεῦμα in reference to the Holy Spirit (11b) and πνεῦμα in reference to the "spirit" of man (11a) is obvious. The Spirit's authority to enter the depths of God is an *exclusive* one.

> 12 ἡμεῖς δὲ οὐ τὸ πνεῦμα τοῦ κόσμου ἐλάβομεν ἀλλὰ τὸ πνεῦμα τὸ ἐκ τοῦ θεοῦ, ἵνα εἰδῶμεν τὰ ὑπὸ τοῦ θεοῦ χαρισθέντα ἡμῖν·
>
> 12 Now we have received, not the spirit of the world, but the Spirit who is from God, that we might know the things freely given to us by God.

The discontinuity established in v. 11 only finds re-connection in the Holy Spirit. The phrase τοῦ κόσμου ("of the world") is a qualitative

---

46. Thiselton, *The First Epistle to the Corinthians*, 258 (emphasis his). Thiselton holds that Paul is using spatial language with respect to the human person in order to indicate modes or aspects of being.

47. The issue of "discontinuity" will be taken up again in the systematic theology portion of this section. Here it is important to note that some commentators see only a natural *continuity* between God's Spirit and the human spirit. Ryle, for example, holds that Paul is arguing as if the word πνεῦμα—used in relation to both ἀνθρώπου and θεοῦ—embodies a natural continuity between human spirit/human person and divine Spirit/God (Ryle, *The Concept of Mind*, ch. 1). Thiselton points out that "as numerous writers over the last 50 years have rightly urged," this view is "simply false" (See Thiselton, *The First Epistle to the Corinthians*, 258). "The logic of Paul's thought is that if, by analogy, one person cannot know the least accessible aspect of another human being unless that person is willing to place them in the public domain, even so we cannot expect that God's own thoughts, God's own purposes, God's own qualities, God's own self could be open to scrutiny unless his spirit makes them accessible by an act of unveiling them" (Thiselton, *The First Epistle to the Corinthians*, 258–59).

48. Haykin, "The Spirit of God," 521.

genitive, demonstrating not the place this "spirit" is found but what sort of "spirit" this is. The Stoics thought of God as a world-spirit or an animating world-soul.⁴⁹ This notion is reflected in postmodern thought as well.⁵⁰ Paul speaks of such a spirit in Rom 8:15 and 2 Cor 11:4 as a spiritual force opposed to God. Because of the pervasiveness of this force, "conversion meant to pass from its authority to God."⁵¹ Such a force is contrasted with the Spirit that is ἐκ τοῦ θεοῦ ("from God"). Since ἐκ in this case conveys more than a simple genitive (*from* or *out of*), appropriate translations include "sent by God," "issues from God," or "comes from God." Obvious comparison can be made with John 15:26 (which speaks of the Spirit's "procession," and will be taken up in section 3). Here Paul is making a special effort to point out the Spirit's divine origin and transcendence. Fee proclaims,

> With this sentence and the next we come to the central issue in the paragraph. . . . Since "like is known by like," the Spirit of God becomes the link on the human side for our knowing the ways of God. As in vv. 6–9 Paul makes that point by way of antithesis to those of the present age. He thus reminds the Corinthians that they belong to a different world order, a different age, and therefore must not do as they are now doing—pursue or think in terms of merely human σοφια. In receiving the Spirit, it was not "the spirit of the

---

49. The Stoics envisioned πνεῦμα to be like fire in that it could pass into whatever it willed, assimilating other entities to itself. Rather than embracing the biblical notion of God as a transcendent "consuming fire" however, the Stoics envisioned "God" with the extreme immanence of a world-spirit (see Thiselton, *The First Epistle to the Corinthians*, 260). This is, of course, in opposition to the NT sense of divine πνεῦμα. Even Bultmann admits that Paul uses πνεῦμα most often as "divine power that stands in contrast to all that is human, not 'spirit' in the sense of the inner self of Platonic dualism" (Bultmann, *Theology of the New Testament*, 1:1530.

50. As we saw in chapter two, much of postmodern theology has strains of inherent *Panentheism*, which, like the πνεῦμα τοῦ κόσμου spoken of here, involves a God who "knows the world—a world in which change, process, and freedom are real elements." Hartshorne, one of its chief proponents, holds that a perfect knower (i.e., God) includes the world within himself. The concrete God is the God who knows, includes, and is changed by the world. This, according to Hartshorne, is the God who loves the world and who shares the joys and sorrows of each creature in the world (see Hartshorne and Reese, *Philosophers Speak of God*).

51. See Fee, *God's Empowering Presence*, 75. The "spirit of the world" repeats the idea of "the wisdom of this age" (v. 6), which suggests a self-regarding wisdom, a man-centered planning in which man provides for his own interests.

world" that "we have received." By this Paul is not suggesting that there is a "spirit" of the world comparable to the Holy Spirit; neither is he referring to demonic "spirits." He is rather saying something about the Holy Spirit. The Spirit whom was have received is not "of this world"; he neither comes from this world nor belongs to this world. Rather he is "the Spirit who is from God."[52]

The contrast resides in the source (κόσμου vs. θεοῦ) and in the results: the "spirit of the world" finds expression in the wisdom of this present world order while the Holy Spirit reveals God's wisdom (as demonstrated in the cross of Christ, vv. 1–8).

Since ἐλάβομεν (aorist, active, ind., "have received") indicates a whole, completed action, this reception of the Spirit can be seen as a covenant gift to believers. The repetition here is key: "the Spirit of God (v. 11); . . . the Spirit [which is] of God (v. 12)." The Spirit who knows the depths of God is the same Spirit we have received. The "ἵνα clause" indicates purpose—we have received this transcendent Spirit "*that* we might know the things freely given by God" (rather than the things of this world). The word εἰδῶμεν (perfect, active, first person plural subjunctive of the defective perfect οἶδα) indicates an active knowing, a state of being involving constant learning, particularly with respect to "the things freely given to us by God." Also, in this context, χαρισθέντα (aorist, passive part.; χαρίζομαι) indicates that the Spirit freely and graciously "leads to the knowledge of what God has bestowed."[53] The force of this verse, therefore, is not only that the Spirit of God is the means by which the knowledge from God is freely bestowed, but also that this Spirit retains his transcendent origination in God when he is "received" and when this knowledge is "freely given." It is interesting

---

52. Fee, *God's Empowering Presence*, 102. This stands in contrast to some who say that this passage primarily has to do with apostolic inscripturation. Kaiser, for example, asserts that "Paul is not talking about the Spirit that animates believers, but about the Holy Spirit's operation in delivering the Scriptures to the apostle (Kaiser, "A Neglected Text in Bibliology Discussions," 315). However, "receive . . . the Spirit" is a common phrase in Paul's letters (i.e., 2 Cor 11:4; Gal 3:2, 14; Rom 8:15) and "refers primarily to Christian conversion" (Fee, *God's Empowering Presence*, 102).

53. Esser, "Grace," 2:123. The aorist tense indicates that in this passage, Paul is speaking not only of the future but also of the present life of Christians (See Barrett, *The First Epistle to the Corinthians*, 75). This word can also refer to "give as a gift of grace" or "give graciously as a favor" (Bauer, "χαρίζομαι," 1078).

The Authority of the Holy Spirit and Systematic Theology: Part I

to note that the Spirit is not specifically described here as the revealer but as the one who allows access to divine revelation. The Spirit's authority is portrayed here with respect to the human ability to know God in his self-revelation.

> 13 ἃ καὶ λαλοῦμεν οὐκ ἐν διδακτοῖς ἀνθρωπίνης σοφίας λόγοις ἀλλ' ἐν διδακτοῖς πνεύματος, πνευματικοῖς πνευματικὰ συγκρίνοντες.
>
> 13 which things we also speak, not in words taught by human wisdom, but in those taught by the Spirit, combining spiritual *thoughts* with spiritual *words*.

Here we find that the Spirit not only reveals God's truths but also provides language that makes conversation about these truths possible. Paul returns to his theme of preaching (started in 2:1–7), making the Spirit central to this activity. His spoken words are indeed διδακτοῖς (passive verbal adjective, "taught"), once again, by the agency of the Spirit (πνεύματος parallels v. 10). Paul sets up a contrast here between the origins of the λόγοις ("words") that are spoken—not from a ἀνθρωπίνης ("human") origin (which implies "lateral" communication) but from the Spirit (which, by comparison and parallelism with v. 10, implies transcendent origination).

Thus, the Spirit's *transcendence* and revelatory *agency* are linked once again, here in the context of the Spirit's *teaching* (which includes the inspiration of Paul's words). Divine revelation is provided only as the *transcendent* Spirit demonstrates his rightful place with respect to spiritual teaching. The Spirit teaches Paul how to "combine spiritual thoughts" (that emerge only from the transcendent mind of God) with the immanence of "spiritual words"—thus displaying a certain divine authority in and through these words.

Biblical Theology

In these passages we have discovered several attributes of the Spirit that confirm his divinity and Personhood, including *transcendence*, rightful dominion, and divine access. Other exclusively divine attributes are portrayed in the OT, where the Spirit is described as omnipresent (Ps 139:7) and the

The Lord Is the Spirit

Spirit of judgment (Isa 4:4). In the NT he is the "Spirit of holiness" (Rom 1:4) and the "eternal Spirit" (Heb 9:14).

The Spirit's transcendence over creation and over life itself, as portrayed in Ps 104:29–30, is indeed a progressive theme in Scripture. Transcendence "seems to center on the concepts of control and authority"[54] and translates into authority when developed in the context of our pattern of divine authority.[55] It is first established in Gen 1:1–2 (which, as we have seen, is the obvious basis for Psalm 104:30). Waltke convincingly demonstrates that Gen 1:1 is a summary statement (or formal introduction) "which is epexegeted in the rest of the narrative" and that Gen 1:2 is best interpreted according to a "precreation" model (i.e., "creation" occurs when that which is "formless and void" takes form).[56] The two phrases פְּנֵי תְהוֹם ("the face of the deep") and פְּנֵי הַמָּיִם ("the face of the waters") are often believed to have the same meaning, both describing what is *over* this surface—"darkness" and the "Spirit of God."[57] "Darkness" is not presented as a *power* but as a *dominion*. The "Spirit of God" who מְרַחֶפֶת ("hovered over" or "moved upon") the surface, however, is given a place of creative—or rightful—dominion (since אֱלֹהִים is repeated from v. 1). This word only occurs again in Deut 32:11, referring to an eagle "fluttering over" her young in her nest as she cares for them.[58] Waltke asserts that this can only be "the creative, life giving Spirit of God waiting for the proper moment to begin history

---

54. Frame, *The Doctrine of the Knowledge of God*, 15.

55. Frame explains, "over and over, the covenant Lord stresses how his servants must obey his commands (Exod. 3:13–18, 20:2; Lev. 18:2–5, 30, 19:37; Deut. 6:4–9)" (Frame, *The Doctrine of the Knowledge of God*, 16).

56. Waltke holds that the literary pattern follows that of Gen 2:4–7. Genesis 1:2 is thereby to be seen as a circumstantial clause to the main clause of v. 3, one that has the pattern ו + NOUN + VERB (as in וְהָאָרֶץ הָיְתָה) and describes the negative state of the "earth" before "creation" (Waltke, *Creation and Chaos*, 31–34). Levinson agrees with this model, asserting that God is working on inert matter. "Rather than *creatio ex nihilo*, 'creation without opposition' is the more accurate nutshell statement of the theology underlying our passage" (Levinson, *Creation and the Persistence of Evil*, 1988).

57 See Westermann, *Genesis 1–11*, 106.

58. Though the Talmudic tradition interprets וְרוּחַ in this context as an actual wind or moving air (an entity created by God on the first day), it would be inappropriate to translate וְרוּחַ אֱלֹהִים impersonally—as in "mighty wind"—because אֱלֹהִים is always designated "God" in this chapter. See Levinson, *Creation and the Persistence of Evil*, 24; also Sarna, *Genesis*, 6.

by the creation of heaven and earth through the Word."⁵⁹ As a result, this passage can only be interpreted through a conception of the Spirit's *rightful dominion*:

> When we come to the origin of those things which are contrary to God we are caught in a dilemma. A good God characterized by light could not, in consistency with His nature, create evil, disorder and darkness. On the other hand, it cannot be eternally outside of Him for that would limit His sovereignty. The Bible resolves the problem not by explaining its origin but by assuring us that it was under the dominion of the Spirit of God.⁶⁰

Evidence of the Spirit's sovereignty and transcendence with respect to creation continues in the OT: in "re-creation" after the flood (Gen 8:1), at the creation of the people of Israel (Exod 14:19–20, 15:10), in the breath of life (Job 33:4), in the creation of heavenly hosts (Ps 33:6), and regarding his *understanding* of the created order (Isa 40:13).

The Spirit's transcendence, rightful dominion, and divine authority extend into the discussion of moral authority and accountability. Exodus chapters 25–40, for example, depict the Spirit's moral transcendence as displayed through the tabernacle in such a way as to create maximum impact immanently.⁶¹ In Exod 34:34 the Spirit is referred to as "the Lord's presence," in 40:34 as "the glory of the Lord" (that filled the tabernacle, so that not even Moses could enter), and in 40:38 as "the cloud of the Lord"

---

59. Waltke, *Creation and Chaos*, 52.

60. Ibid., 52. Likewise, Calvin holds this passage to declare the Spirit's eternality: "The Spirit is introduced (in Genesis 1), not as a shadow, but as the essential power of God, when Moses tells that the as yet formless mass was itself sustained in him (Gen 1:2). Therefore, it has become clear that the eternal Spirit has always been in God, while with tender care he supported the confused matter of heaven and earth, until beauty and order were added" (Calvin, *Institutes*, I:xiii.22).

61. In such descriptions, the transcendent nature of the Spirit is not lost when God's "glory" or "presence" becomes immanent. In fact, such imagery seems to magnify the Sprit's divine authority. Isa 63:10 speaks of "his Holy Spirit" and Eph 4:30 of "the Holy Spirit of God"—references to the Spirit's conjoined transcendence and immanence. "Here the full ascription is not just a form of solemn speech, calling special attention to the role the Spirit in ethical life, but also an emphatic description that the *Holy* Spirit is none other then the Spirit *of God*. . . . Both of these aspects—the Spirit as the presence of God and the Spirit's relationship to the ethical life—need closer examination" (Fee, *God's Empowering Presence*, 714).

and "fire" (on the tabernacle by day and in it by night").[62] The tabernacle (and of the temple that appears later) demonstrated the Spirit's moral authority, first, in that it was to be constructed with such precise dimensions and specifications. The Lord told Moses, "Make this tabernacle and all its furnishings exactly like the pattern I will show you" (Exod 25:9).[63] Some of these instructions, if disobeyed, were punishable by expulsion or death (Exod 28:2, 43; 30:34–38). Second, the Spirit's authority as moral sanctifier (pointed out by Basil) is depicted through the water-cleansing rituals performed in the consecration of priests (Num 19:1–10) and the purification of men (Lev 15:13; 2 Kgs 5:10–13).

This early depiction of the "Holy" Spirit is picked up later by Paul in 1 Cor 3:16–17. Here Paul refers to the Church as a "temple" where the Spirit dwells as a divine Person with moral authority: "Do you not know that you are a temple of God and that the Spirit of God dwells in you?" (3:16). Paul continues, "If any man destroys the temple of God, God will destroy him, for the temple of God is holy, and that is what you are" (3:17). Such severe consequences for dishonoring the Spirit bring out the ethical nature of his authority,[64] while "holy" brings forth the entire temple imagery as a place set apart for God and not to be desecrated in any way. What once stood for ritual holiness now stands for a moral-ethical holiness that should depict the new "temple" where the Spirit "dwells."[65]

---

62. This presence of God was eventually understood to be the Spirit of the Lord (see Isa 63:9–14). "In many of the contexts where God's presence is manifested, the Spirit of God is signified (Exod 40:34ff).... In fact, the glory-cloud may be depicted as a 'Spirit-temple' out of which the Spirit moves to affect the will of God.... Throughout the OT, the Spirit is present in some form during all sacred construction projects, be it in the creation of Eden, the Mosaic tabernacle, or the Solomonic or exile temple" (Hildebrandt, *An Old Testament Theology of the Spirit of God*, 46–47).

63. According to Chen, "These seemingly cumbersome rules were not intended to burden the people, but to show God's unquestionable authority and holiness, and emphasize that people could only come to God on God's terms, not on their own. They had to obey reverently not only in the construction of the tabernacle, but also in the way they worshipped. Any irreverence or ritual uncleanness could result from an individual being cut off from his people or in death" (Chen, "The Tabernacle: What is it?"; par. 6).

64. "Destroy" likely refers to the fearful judgment of God in the last day (Fee, *God's Empowering Presence*, 117).

65. According to Fee, this passage presents us with "a remarkable metaphor to depict the nature of the local church and offers the strongest warning in the NT against those who

In addition, whereas the OT often portrays the Spirit as an impersonal force or dominion, the NT often points to the Spirit as possessing a divine authority centered in his *divine Personhood*. This is clearly portrayed in Acts 5:3–10. In 5:3 we understand that only a person can understand the complexity of the sort of financial "lie" portrayed here. That this Spirit has the same authority as "God" (v. 4) is demonstrated by the deaths of Ananias and Sapphira (vv. 5, 10). The Spirit's divine Personhood is also displayed in our ability to "grieve" (Eph 4:30) or "blaspheme" (Matt 12:31–32) him through disobedience or hardness of heart.

Systematic Theology

In developing a "formal description" of the sort of divine authority proper to the Holy Spirit's divine Personhood, I shall first investigate Moltmann's pneumatology, and then respond to Moltmann with my exegetical findings.

Jürgen Moltmann's *Spirit of Life* and the Divine Authority of the Spirit

As seen in chapter two, Moltmann presents a "panentheistic" worldview that strongly influences his understanding of the Church.[66] This connection is further seen in his view of the Church as the usual (but not only) vehicle of transformation, moving forward in the power of the Spirit in accordance with its eschatological vision. Underlying this transformation is *evolution*, a cosmologically internal process by which the Holy Sprit executes God's continuing creation. Such a "process" is decipherable in *God in Creation*, "The Spirit is the principle of creativity on all levels of matter and life. She creates new possibilities and in these anticipates new designs

---

would take the local church lightly" (Fee, *God's Empowering Presence*, 113).

66. Moltmann's cry is "let us come back once more to the foundation and justification for the panentheist vision of the world in God" (Moltmann, *The Spirit of Life*, 212). His panentheism grants Lordship to the Son (for the purpose of freedom) but not to the Spirit (See Moltmann, *The Trinity and the Kingdom*, 88–90). His model is also "postmodern" in that it is critical of modern notions of Trinity that begin with God as "absolute subject" (which is based in anthropological thinking), and particularly of Western Christianity (which is "monotheistic" in much of its experience and practice).

and blueprints for material and living organisms. In this sense, the Spirit is the principle of evolution."[67]

Moltmann's "panentheistic" vision of creation theology leads him to draft a vital connection between the Spirit's work in creation and in redemption. While Moltmann argues for the Hebrew view of the Spirit as the principle of vitality in creation, he actually goes beyond this Hebrew vision by making the doctrine of the Spirit's creative work the core to all theology. Badcock comments on Moltmann's thought:

> Only when one has recognized [the Spirit's place in creation] is it possible to move on to posit a continuity between this aspect of the Spirit's work and the Spirit's presence in the history of Israel, in the life and work of Jesus, and the birth of the Church, and in the experience of the saints.[68]

Moltmann relies often on Hegelian thinking regarding "Spirit-consciousness" as seen in his claim that "the creative and life-giving Spirit therefore arrives at consciousness of itself in the human consciousness."[69] This is also witnessed in his description of the Spirit as an integral "characteristic" of the material world.

> The history of the creative Spirit embraces human history and natural history, and to that extent is to be understood in dialectical-materialist terms as "the movement," "the urge," "the spirit of life," "the tension," and "the torment" which—as Marx said with Jacob Bohme—is matter's pre-eminent characteristic.[70]

---

67. Moltmann, *God in Creation*, 100.

68. Badcock, *Light of Truth and Fire of Love*, 131.

69. Moltmann, *The Spirit of Life*, 228–29. Hegel indeed sees all human consciousness as forms of Spirit-consciousness, stating, "Spirit is thus self-supporting, absolute real being [*Wesen*]. All previous shapes of consciousness are abstract forms of it; they result from spirit analyzing itself, distinguishing its moments, and dwelling for awhile with each . . . Spirit, then is consciousness in general which embraces sense-certainty, perception, and the Understanding . . . [it] is that type of consciousness which has Reason" (Hegel, *Phenomenology of Spirit*, 264–65). Similarly, Moltmann proclaims that Spirit-consciousness inevitably links human cultural systems with "the natural ecosystems of the earth" and "re-shapes the self-isolating consciousness which rules over itself and nature, into consciousness of the Spirit which creates life and community" (Moltmann, *The Spirit of Life*, 229).

70. Moltmann, *The Church in the Life of the Spirit*, 34.

As a result, Moltmann sees the Spirit working in and through nature religions, which remind us of "nature's cycles and rhythms" and the need for "harmony with the earth and with the moon." The Spirit, in the traditional paradigm, "remains for us just as inexperiencable, hidden and 'other' as God himself," and results in "a permanent discontinuity between God's Spirit and the spirit of human beings."[71] A "religion of the earth," however, "will emerge out of the world religions that will teach us the spirituality of the earth in order that we may recognize ourselves as 'children of the earth.'"[72] We can conclude that Moltmann's attempt to overcome this discontinuity, along with his panentheistic vision of "creation theology," goes to the heart of the discussion of the Spirit's divine Personhood and divine authority.

Response

Moltmann's panentheism seems to deny that the Spirit is a divine Person *distinct from* and *transcendent over* the world.[73] Our study of Ps 104:29–30,

71. Moltmann, *The Spirit of Life*, 5. Moltmann explains that in this situation "the Holy Spirit is not a modality of our experience of God; it is a modality of God's revelation to us. If the Spirit is a modality of our own experience, then human experience of God is the foundation of human theology. But this can be at the cost of the qualitative difference between God and human beings. If the Spirit is viewed as a modality of the divine relation, then the foundation of theology is God's revelation of himself. But in this case the qualitative difference between God and human beings makes every immediate relation of human beings to God impossible. And so there can be no natural human theology either" (5).

72. Moltmann, "Christianity in the Third Millennium," 88.

73. Panentheism sees God as distinct from the world in some sense, but only as the "supreme effect." God's reality or purpose (for goodness) is not destroyed as he comes to know the world (he remains the *supreme* effect). However, since a perfect knower includes within himself the object which is known, God must be affected and changed by everything that happens in the world (i.e., his knowledge changes). Franklin attempts to describe the panentheist understanding of God: "There must be some element in God which remains the same regardless of what happens in the world—i.e. an element that is not affected by any particular event in the world. This element, since it is not changed by any event, is eternal. It is also abstract. Since God's eternal, abstract self-identify is presupposed by any state of affairs whatsoever, it follows that God is the universal and supreme cause. . . . But that which is eternal and abstract is deficient in actuality and can exist only as an element in a larger whole which is temporal and concrete. Thus God's eternal, abstract, essential self-identity exists only as an element in the temporal, concrete, complex reality which is God in his completeness" (Franklin, "Panentheism," 819). Franklin adds, "As the world grows, God grows. God becomes" (819). Thus panentheism threatens divine transcendence, which, as seen in chapter one, has traditionally been a watershed attribute for "theism."

1 Cor 2:10–15, and other passages, however, confirm a definitive *discontinuity* between the Holy Spirit and the world.[74] In Ps 104:29–30, God is revealed as the supplier, supporter, and sustainer of both physical life and the human spirit, in such a way that his divine *necessity* is starkly contrasted with human *dependence* (as a contingent person). Through his Spirit, Yahweh is transcendent over all creation (v. 29) as well as "re-creation" (v. 30). The probable comparison drawn between the Spirit and Akhenaten's "Hymn To The Sun" ("when thou hast risen they live, when thou settest they die"[75]) seems to confirm that the Psalmist grants Yahweh's Spirit supreme authority over life and death.

We have seen that this passage indicates continuous divine action in the world. Can such a notion coincide with the Hebrew impression of the Spirit's relative independence *from* the world? Deissler holds that this Psalm resolves this dilemma:

> [The Psalmist's] view of God's created world is obviously dialectical: God is omnipotent, but his limitless power and wisdom (v. 24) liberate his creation in such a way that dependence and independence do not negate each other. . . . This act of creation . . . is accomplished through his *ruach* . . . [indicating that] life and death "correspond" to the sovereign order of the omnipotent God.[76]

Psalm 104:29–30 thus depicts human "spirits" as utterly dependent on Yahweh's continued creative activity. Eichrodt summarizes the tone of "authority" in this passage:

> Hence every living thing in the world is dependent on God's continually letting his breath of life go forth to renew the created order; and when its vital spirit from God is withdrawn every creature must sink down in death. Thus, *ruach* is at all times plainly superior to

---

74. Frame claims to find twelve "discontinuities" in Scripture between God's thought and ours. One of these is that God's thoughts are "self-validating", serving as their own criteria of truth. "God's thoughts are true simply because they are His. . . . This is the lordship attribute of authority in the area of knowledge" (Frame, *The Doctrine of the Knowledge of God*, 22).

75. Pritchard, *Ancient Near Eastern Texts*, 371a.

76. Deissler, "Theology of Psalm 104," 36–37.

Man, a divine power within his mortal body subject to the rule of God alone.[77]

First Corinthians 2:10–13 presents several other discontinuities that demonstrate the transcendent source of revelation. The Spirit, who is completely transcendent *in God* and has full access *to God*, sharply contrasts the recipients of the Spirit's revelations, who by definition are dependent upon the Spirit for divine knowledge (v. 10). As seen earlier, reception of the Spirit's revelations is essentially equated with submission to the Sprit's authority. As Hodge states,

> As the things which the Holy Ghost has revealed address themselves not only to the intellect as true but to the conscience as obligatory and to the affects as excellent and lovely, not to receive them is not to receive, in our inward experience, their truth, their authority, and their excellence.[78]

Only the Spirit possesses the exclusive right to *reveal* God's thoughts, which are otherwise hidden from public domain (vv. 10, 11). Only the Spirit knows the mind of God, as opposed to "the spirit of the man" which only knows "the things of man" (v.11). The Spirit, who is uniquely "of God," is starkly contrasted with the "spirit of the world" (v. 12). This results in quite disparate "wisdoms" ("words taught by human wisdom" vs. "words taught by the Spirit") (v. 13). Panentheists, however, do not tend to recognize such "discontinuities," but instead speak in terms of the Spirit's "immanence," "emanations," "mediation," et cetera. Moltmann refers to the Spirit not as a pre-existing person but as "the name given to the experienced presence of God."[79] Other "panentheist" theologians follow suit. Hodgson, for example, states:

> Far from being dualistic, then, spirit is a mediating term: it is the ideal manifested in the real, the unity of reason and nature, soul and body, male and female, God and world. It overreaches all these dichotomizing distinctions and levels the hierarchy between them. . . . God is "Spirit" insofar as God is present to, active in, embodied by that which is other than God namely, the natural and

---

77. Eichrodt, *Theology of the Old Testament*, 2.47–48.
78. Hodge, *An Exposition of the First Epistle to the Corinthians*, 43.
79. Moltmann, *The Spirit of Life*, 120.

human worlds. Thus in Scripture "Spirit" refers to that modality of divine activity whereby God indwells and empowers the forces of nature, the people of Israel, the ecclesial community, and individual persons.[80]

Welker refers to the Spirit more often as a "force field" than as a person; the Spirit is described in terms of God's "activity," liberator, fullness, knowledge, pouring out, power, presence, and "selflessness."[81] As we shall see in chapter four, the Spirit for Welker is only a "public person" found within "a structured social environment and in exchange with that environment" (one that turns a self-relating center of personal authority into an actual person).[82] As Christ's public "domain of resonance" within the world, Welker says that the Holy Spirit is to be understood as "a pluriform unity of perspectives on Jesus Christ, of relations to Christ, and of the spoken and lived testimonies to Christ," and adds, "In this respect the Spirit is a unity in which we participate, a unity that we help to constitute."[83] Obviously, this does not lend itself to a traditional understanding of the Spirit as a distinct "Person" of God. According to Gregory of Nazianzus, if the Holy Spirit is not a Person of God but only an activity or function of God, then, "He will be effected, but will not effect, and will cease to exist as soon as He has been effected, for this is the nature of an activity."[84]

Panentheism tends to re-define the Trinity according to a purely social model that depends upon human participation. Moltmann begins with the social Trinity and moves toward divine unity amongst the Persons and with the world. Thiselton warns, however, of the temptation to opt for a "social" Trinity in order to "legitimate an egalitarian view of society," one that easily results in "manipulation in the service of power-interests and ceases to be

---

80. Hodgson, *God in History*, 111.

81. Welker's "de-personification" of the Spirit seems to be an overreaction to "modern" versions of authority that tend toward totalitarianism (i.e., "authoritarianism," see chapter one). He accuses Kung, for example, of complying with a modern understanding of "transcendent authority" and "absolute authority" by "invoking autonomy as a criterion for distinguishing between religiosity which forms experience and religiosity which deforms it" (Welker, "God's Power and Powerlessness," 45–46.

82. Welker, "Der Heilege Geist," 139 (author's translation from German text).

83. Welker, *God the Spirit*, 314.

84. Gregory of Nazianzen, "On the Holy Spirit," VII:319.

a quest for theological truth."⁸⁵ It seems somewhat contradictory to try to reconstruct theology in process terms—as Moltmann's panentheism apparently does—and yet to assert belief in "an immanent Trinity in which God is simply by himself, with the love which communicates salvation."⁸⁶ Like today's liberation theologians, Moltmann often interprets the Spirit's transcendence in strictly historical terms, especially with reference to the *future*. For Moltmann, "the Spirit is 'transcendent' only in the way the future transcends the present. The Spirit is not *over* but *ahead*."⁸⁷

Barth responds to Moltmann by asking him, "Would it not be wise to accept the doctrine of the immanent Trinity of God?"⁸⁸ Whereas Moltmann surrenders the traditional distinction between the immanent and economic Trinity, Barth retains this distinction in a way that protects the Spirit's Lordship. "The Holy Spirit, in distinction from all created spirits, is the Spirit who is and remains and always becomes anew transcendent over man even when immanent in him."⁸⁹ Barth's trinitarianism thus preserves the traditional idea that "the immanent and economic trinity could not be identified or confused but distinguished and united in a way analogous to the Incarnate Logos."⁹⁰

Gunton claims that Moltmann joins many others today who "explicitly or implicitly appear to be replacing [the immanent Trinity] with some form of emanationism. While Moltmann claims to avoid Neoplatonic forms, there is plentiful use, at various crucial stages of the argument, of the language of emanation."⁹¹ Gunton adds,

> Thus, in place of Augustine's Neoplatonist construction of the inner Trinity, we have one of the relation of God to the world. But, I believe, that is worse; for by blurring the boundaries between God and the world, it endangers the distinctive reality of both. Despite

---

85. Thiselton, *Interpreting God and the Postmodern Self*, 157.
86. Moltmann, *The Trinity and the Kingdom*, 151.
87. See Moltmann, *Theology of Hope*.
88. Barth, *Karl Barth Letters 1961–1968*, 175.
89. Barth, *Church Dogmatics*, vol. I/1, 488.
90. Molnar, "The Function of the Immanent Trinity," 369–70.
91. Gunton, review of *The Spirit of Life*, 789.

all the disavowals, there are clear tendencies on many parts of [Moltmann's] work of a divinization of the cosmos.[92]

While Moltmann's understanding of the Spirit rightly avoids the conception of a completely *independent* personhood, the Spirit "appears to lose his *particular* personhood."[93] This is especially seen in Moltmann's dependency upon Hegelian thought.[94] In the end, Moltmann admits, "[the Spirit] himself is nothing other than the efficacy of the Son and Father. The Spirit is gift, not giver."[95] Moltmann's great concern is the restoration of the "experience of the Spirit" as exhibited through "immanent transcendence" ("God in all things").[96] Moltmann, however, "fails to explain why

---

92. Ibid., 789–90.

93. Ibid., 790.

94. Hegel turns out to be behind many contemporary pneumatologists who rely on his view of a dynamic world "Spirit." First, it should be noted that there is certainly something "right" about Hegelian thinking. According to Gunton, for Hegel, "Spirit is that which at once unifies and gives meaning to what happens in the human cultural enterprise. It is a dynamic force, at once cosmic and human, individual and social. Hegel's cultural programme was to take quite seriously that which pre-modern culture, and particularly that of Christendom, had achieved" (Gunton, *The One, The Three and the Many*, 147). However, "The problem with Hegel is the way in which his Trinity is conceived"—i.e., it is modalist, and in its pantheistic tendencies it leads to the swallowing up of history in God (148). Schner adds further insight, "Hegel attempts to engage the chief characteristics of modernity: the turn to the subject, the loss of transcendence, the relativization of truth, the absolutization of human freedom, and the secularization of the sacred. To do so he transforms the Christian doctrine of the Holy Spirit into the Absolute Spirit, while preserving God as "the transcendent factor of the creative process without ever coinciding with it. . . . A merely infinite God is a pure abstraction, and a merely immanent force within the dynamic unfolding of reality is no God either. The all-encompassing philosophy which results, despite its efforts to hold the transcendent in a paradoxical relation with both the finite and the infinite, seems inevitably to fail in two important ways: on the one hand, its transformation of the Holy Spirit into the Absolute Spirit rebounds back upon Christian thought and practice in a fashion which results in the very secularization of belief Hegel wished to challenge; and on the other hand, that same transformation only functions as a legitimation of modernity to the extent that it can be 'practiced' in an irreligious manner" (Schner, "Louis Dupre's Philosophy of Religion," 261–62).

95. Moltmann, *The Spirit of Life*, 291.

96. See Moltmann, *The Spirit of Life*, chapters 1–3. Hansen interprets "immanent transcendence" as the experience of God's Spirit that is "in principle, a reality graspable in, with, and beneath all things, preceding—and making possible—the phenomena of experience as such" (Hansen, review of *The Spirit of Life*, 220).

The Authority of the Holy Spirit and Systematic Theology: Part I

this experience is necessarily a transcendental one, and even more critically, a salutary one."[97]

The evidence of discontinuity provided in 1 Cor 2:10–15, however, does not *prohibit* the possibility of intimate communion and communication with God. Within the very context of discontinuity we discover the possibility not only of the reception of God's revelation and wisdom but also of God's *own Spirit*. The purpose of this reception is very clear: so that "we may understand what God has freely given us" (v. 12), which includes (at some level) a personal knowledge of "the depths of God" (v. 10). The nature of the Spirit's divine "theistic"[98] authority, unlike panentheism, provides a basis for true and intimate relationship and communication between distinct "persons."

Further Discussion and Formal Description

As introduced in chapter one, the Spirit possesses divine authority because (1) he is *Divine* (and therefore transcendent), and (2) he is a *Person* (and thereby able to reveal God's mind to other persons). The evidence gathered in this section confirms and distinguishes the Spirit's authority as a divine Person, and can thereby be summarized along similar lines: (1) divine *transcendence*—rightful dominion over created life, and (2) *personal, divine access to the Father*—by which God's will is revealed and all things are judged.[99] Because of these characteristics, the Spirit indeed has the right to

---

97. Hansen, review of *The Spirit of Life*, 220.

98. Theism, defined in the Judeo-Christian sense, refers to the belief in "God as creator and sustainer of the universe" (Feinberg, "Theism," 1082). This definition necessarily implies *self-existence*, that God is the *first cause* for all created things and therefore cannot be in any way reduced or dependent upon creation (see Pss 48:14; 29:10; 102:25–27; James 1:17; Num 23:19). "The incomparable divine transcendence involves a radical dualism between God and the world that ought not be blurred by a resurgent monism and pantheism. Although made like God and in the divine image, mankind is not (like Christ) begotten of God or an emanation from God of the same divine nature. The ultimate goal of salvation is not reabsorption into the being God but unbroken fellowship with God" (Lewis, "God, Attributes of," 459).

99. As mentioned in chapter one, divine transcendence can be witnessed in God's intellectual attributes (omniscience, faithfulness, wisdom), ethical attributes (holiness, righteousness), and existential attributes (freedom, authenticity). We must particularly remember that as the *Holy* Spirit he possesses transcendence with respect to moral purity, goodness, and righteousness. The Hebrew word קׇדְשְׁךָ carries a trace of transcendence in

command obedience *from* all human beings and the right to reveal divine authority *to* human beings.

The Spirit's authority as a divine Person can therefore be understood in relation to both the *Trinity* and the *world*. This concurs with the foundation laid in chapter one—our "principle of authority" (the triune God in self-revelation) and our definition of "divine authority" (as the supreme, transcendent right to command obedience to reveal God's authority *in* the world). Regarding the Spirit's relation to the Trinity, 1 Cor 2:10–13 provides considerable light, affirming a complete "indwelling" of the Spirit in the Father and in the Son through the notion of the Spirit's eternal access into the depths of God (2:10–11). This passage exemplifies the patristic idea of "perichoresis" or mutual interpenetration of the divine persons within each other (also known as the "circuminsession," "mutual indwelling," or "inexistence" of the three persons). The Council of Florence gave the following formula:

> Because of this unity [of nature] the Father is completely in the Son and completely in the Holy Spirit; the Son completely in the Father, completely in the Holy Spirit; the Holy Spirit completely in the Father, completely in the Son.

Regarding the Spirit's transcendence over created life, both Ps 104:29–30 and 1 Cor 2:12–13 provide substantial confirmation. The classic theological notion of the "royal metaphor" can be established on such passages, portraying the transcendent rule of God in terms of a monarchy that incorporates both divine unity and divine sovereignty. The French theologian Widmert portrays this aptly:

> The divine monarchy, God in his unity and his simplicity, is the bond of this mutual presence of the Father, the Son and the Holy Spirit. Indissolubly complementary presences, they live in constant exchange of love. They render themselves present to the world in their common and perpetual, sovereign, and merciful action. There is no confusion between them, no separation among them, they are neither confused with their creation nor separated from it.
>
> The communion of the divine presences at the heart of the one and simple monarchy is always renewed and never exhausted.

---

that it not has "holy" but also "separated" or "ordained" within its semantic field (Averbeck, "Holy," 3:687–89.

Communion that realizes the establishment of the Kingdom of God (the reign of God), actually active in the life of believers, in the witness and liturgy of the Church, rendering them present to a world that is idolatrous or without God, this communion is all that, under a form still veiled, exercising its attraction on the world because it is eternally the communion of the presences of the Father, the Son and the Holy Spirit in their indefectible harmony.[100]

While such monarchical language is reflected in several of the early Church councils, the roles of the Son and the Spirit are often diminished (with respect to the Father) in their confessions. The idea that "monarchy" only refers to the Father is now being challenged by many contemporary Trinitarian theologians. Torrance, for example, asserts that the divine monarchy is shared by all three person of the Godhead, since in his mind the one being (*mia ousia*) of God is identical with the Trinity. The Son, for example, "ought not to be thought of as proceeding from the *Person* of the Father . . . but from the *Being* of the Father."[101] The same holds for the Spirit. Whereas Orthodox theology prescribes *underived* and *derived* deity, Torrance holds that causality and subordination within the intra-divine relations is "quite unacceptable" and agrees with Gregory that "to subordinate any of the three Divine Persons is to overthrow the Trinity."[102] From this we can infer that the divine transcendence, Lordship, and the authority associated with the *divine monarchy* can be attributed to the Son and to the Spirit as well as to the Father. Torrance's trinitarianism also retains a vital re-connection between the immanent Trinity and the economic Trinity—a connection that was basically severed in scholastic, and particularly Thomistic, theology.[103]

100. Widmert, *Gloire au Pere, au Fils et au Saint-Esprit*, 64–65.

101. Torrance, *The Christian Doctrine of God*, 141. Orthodox theologian Zizioulas agrees with the First Council of Constantinople (381), which changed the Nicaean wording to simply *ek tou patros* (Zizioulas, "The Doctrine of the Holy Trinity," 51–52). Torrance, however, holds to the original wording of the Nicene Creed: *ek tes ousias tou Patros* ("from the essence of the Father").

102. Torrance, *The Christian Doctrine of God*, 179.

103. O'Donnell explains that Augustine's theory of persons as "subsistent relations" paved the way for this division: "The Augustinian emphasis on the divine essence led eventually to the split in Aquinas between the tracts *De Deo Uno* (the unity of God) and *De Deo Trino* (the trinity of God). . . . Furthermore as the doctrine of the Trinity became more metaphysical, it also become more abstract and divorced from the trinitarian experience of God in the saving events of history" (O'Donnell, *Trinity and Temporality*, 44).

The Lord Is the Spirit

In the OT, "Yahweh" always retains a notion of transcendence. The built-in limitation and immanence of matter seems to be behind God's warnings to the Israelites not to put him into the same category with physical creatures, let alone with false gods conceived of in material forms (Deut 4:12, 15–18). God's commandment in Exod 20:4 ("You shall not make for yourself an idol or any likeness of what is in heaven above or on the earth beneath or in the water under the earth") is not only a prohibition against idolatry, but also against the tendency "to make any image which in their minds might capture the essence even of the true God."[104] Idolatry breaks down the distinction between Spirit and spirit, which is what the writer of Psalm 104 denounced (thus creating the hunger for God he speaks of). This distinction, of course, is essential with respect to the Spirit's divine transcendence, and seems to be in Isaiah's mind when he states,

> Who has directed the Spirit of the LORD, Or as His counselor has informed Him? With whom did He consult and *who* gave Him understanding? And *who* taught Him in the path of justice and taught Him knowledge and informed Him of the way of understanding? (Isaiah 40:13–14)

Some metaphors used for "Spirit" in Scripture are described with a sense of transcendence: the origin and destiny of "wind" is beyond human knowledge (John 3:8) and "living water" is superior to well water (John 4:9–11). Such metaphors often portray the Spirit as possessing a *mysterious* quality that disallows the breakdown of Spirit and spirit. Kasper warns that, in light of the Spirit's "mysterious" nature,

> The basis of a theology of the Holy Spirit is not to be found in analogies from the life of the human spirit. The Latin tradition in particular has been accustomed to such analogies ever since Augustine; in them the Son is correlated with knowledge through the interior word and the Spirit with the will and the loving union of Father and Son. Such analogies can indeed shed some light as supplementary aids to understanding; the starting point and foundation, however, even in Augustine, is the testimony of faith to the action of the Spirit in the history of salvation.[105]

---

104. Cottrell, *What the Bible Says about God the Creator*, 227.
105. Kasper, *The God of Jesus Christ*, 223.

Barth's understanding of the Spirit within the Trinity is somewhat like Torrance's. Saying that the economic Trinity is the way to the Immanent Trinity, Barth works within the framework of a God who is sovereign Lord of all. Barth thereby exalts the Spirit as Lord (which is manifest most overtly in his role in creation[106]) and as Revealer: "the Holy Ghost is God and Lord in the fullness of Deity, in the total sovereignty and condescension, in the complete hiddenness and revealedness of God."[107]

In developing a "formal description" of the Spirit's authority as a divine Person, we can accept contributions from a "social" Trinity (i.e., *perichoresis*), a "monarchical" Trinity, and a Barthian approach. Certain aspects of these models do reflect the biblical evidence describing the Spirit's divine authority, specifically with respect to divine access (the social Trinity; 1 Cor 2:10b), divine "transcendence" (the monarchical Trinity; Ps 104:29–30; 1 Cor 2:10a), and divine revelation "to us" (a Barthian approach; 1 Cor 2:10a).

As a divine Person of the Trinity, the Spirit thereby possesses "divine authority" in his *very nature*. Because of this, such an authority can and will serve as a foundational parameter for investigating the Spirit's *work*. The Spirit will not only retain this divine authority in everything he does, but every aspect of the Spirit's authority examined subsequently will indeed be marked by his divine authority. This divine authority is retained as the Spirit "goes to work" in the world, ensuring that the Spirit's work *in* the world is never reduced to an immanent force, energy, process, or function *of* the world or of the church community.

Executorial Authority of the Spirit

In our study of historical theology we also discovered that certain medieval church theologians (i.e., Augustine, Anselm) argued for the Spirit's "procession" from the Father and the Son, thus implying an "executorial authority" on the part of the Spirit. One key passage that lies at the center of the medieval debate over the *Filioque* clause is John 15:26—16:15.

---

106. See Thompson, *The Holy Spirit in the Theology of Karl Barth*, 22.
107. Barth, *The Holy Ghost and the Christian Life*, 11.

Introduction

The primary question to be discussed in this section is, "How does the authority of the Spirit relate to the authority of Jesus Christ and to the authority of the Father?" We will proceed to exegete John 15:26 and 16:12–15 as the foundational study for understanding the Spirit's executorial authority. Then, in the next chapter we will be able to use these findings in discussing two crucial "realms" of the Spirit's executorial authority: veracious authority and governing authority.

Exegesis of Passages

The Executorial Authority of the Spirit with respect to the Present Authority of Christ—Exegesis of John 15:26

> Ὅταν ἔλθῃ ὁ παράκλητος ὃν ἐγὼ πέμψω ὑμῖν παρὰ τοῦ πατρός, τὸ πνεῦμα τῆς ἀληθείας ὃ παρὰ τοῦ πατρὸς ἐκπορεύεται, ἐκεῖνος μαρτυρήσει περὶ ἐμοῦ·
>
> When the Helper comes, whom I will send to you from the Father, *that is* the Spirit of truth who proceeds from the Father, He will bear witness of Me.

Jesus' statement is found in a larger discussion of his description regarding the sort of relationship the disciples are to have with the world (15:18–27). "If the world hates you" Jesus proclaims, "you know that it has hated me before it hated you" (v. 18), and "He who hates me hates my Father also" (v. 23). Even so, the disciples "will bear witness" of Jesus (v. 27). This verse (15:26) tells the disciples that it is ultimately the Spirit who bears this witness of Jesus. In saying this, Jesus provides three clues for understanding the nature of the relationship between Jesus and the Spirit, and between their respective "authorities."

First, Jesus discloses that he will be the one to πέμψω (aor., "send") the Spirit from the Father. This future tense, active verb tells us that the sending of the Spirit will occur at a specific time and as a specific action initiated by Jesus himself. The Spirit will be "sent like a messenger."[108] This verse must be correlated with John 14:16, where Jesus revealed that the

---

108. Bauer, "πέμψω," 794. This word can indicate "to dispatch someone, whether a human or transcendent being, usually for the purposes of communication" (ibid.).

Father would "give" the Spirit (in response to Jesus' prayer), and especially with 14:26, where Jesus says that the Father would πέμψει the Spirit ἐν τῷ ὀνόματί μου ("in my name"). According to Barrett, the idea behind "in my name" is "to act in relation to me, in my place, with my authority."[109] Not only are both the Father and the Son partners in the "sending" of the Spirit, but the Father's act of sending the Spirit "in my (Jesus') name" equates with sending him "with Jesus authority." This confirms the idea that the Spirit comes with Jesus' authority as executor of Jesus' will. According to Beasley-Murray:

> The Spirit is to be "sent" by the Father "in the name of Jesus," a remarkable declaration which binds the Spirit closely to Jesus. Constantly in this Gospel Jesus is represented as the Sent One of God, having his origin in God, a mission from God, and an authority from God (cf., e.g., 4:34; 5:23, 24, 30, 37; 6:38–40; 7:16; 8:16, 18, 26; 12:44–49); that the Spirit is *sent* by the Father carries similar implications.[110]

The sending of the Holy Spirit thereby includes the impartation of Jesus' own authority as a very part of the sending activity. Now, in 15:26, Jesus instructs us that he will do the sending *himself*. In saying that he himself would send the Spirit from the Father, "it is plain the Spirit is regarded as connected in the most intimate fashion with both the Father and the Son."[111] In correlating these two verses, we can conclude that, since Jesus and his Father are one (10:30), the "sending" of the Spirit cannot be attributed to one without the other.

Second, the Spirit ἐκπορεύεται ("proceeds") from the Father. This is an indicative verb as well, but, being in the present tense and middle deponent voice, it simply indicates "go out" or "go forth."[112] Whereas the *sending* of the Spirit does not create controversy, the *procession* of the Spirit, as we have seen in chapter 2, is perhaps the *most* controversial doctrine in pneumatology. Bruce claims that this word "has probably no metaphysi-

109. Barrett, *The Gospel according to St. John*, 390.
110. Beasley-Murray, *John*, 261.
111. Morris, *The Gospel According to John*, 606.
112. The word ἐκπορεύεται is also used by John in Rev 22:1 for the river of the water of life that comes forth from the throne of God *and from the lamb*. This is quite significant in that, for John, *water* is often a term used for the Spirit.

cal significance; it is another way of saying that the Spirit is sent by the Father."[113] This may be an easy way to attempt a resolution, but *procession* appears to be different from the activity of sending. The difference between πέμψω and ἐκπορεύεται is found in tense (future vs. present), voice (active vs. middle), and the fact that πέμψω (unlike ἐκπορεύεται) is neither preceded nor followed by a preposition. Still, since "whom I will send to you from the Father" is set in "synonymous parallelism" with "who proceeds from the Father," we can conclude from the context that ἐκπορεύεται refers here to the *mission* of the Spirit (as opposed to some ontological "procession" or even to the nature of the relationship of the Spirit to the Father).[114] This is further shown in the phrase "he will bear witness of me" (particularly with the use of the masculine pronoun ἐκεῖνος[115]), which tells us that the procession of the Spirit amounts to the mission of the Spirit as one who in certain respects replaces the Son. Carson presents the logic of *filioque* that emerges from this verse:

> [Thus, the Spirit] belongs to the godhead every bit as much as the Son. In short, the elements of a full-blown doctrine of the Trinity crop up readily in the Fourth Gospel; and the early creedal statement, complete with the *filioque* phrase, is eminently defensible, once we allow that this clause in 15:26 does not itself specify a certain ontological stature, but joins with the matrix of Johannine Christology and pneumatology to presuppose it.[116]

Finally, the Spirit μαρτυρήσει (future, indicative, active; "will witness") of the Son and is sent περί ("on behalf of") the Son. The word μαρτυρήσει actually refers us back to παράκλητος ("advocate" or "counselor"), which is the verbal adjective of παρακαλέω (literally, "to

---

113. Bruce, *The Gospel of John*, 316. With ἐκπορεύεται we might well expect the preposition ἐκ (typically, "out from") rather than παρα·. In fact, the Greek Fathers change παρα· to ἐοκ in this passage in order to support the doctrine of the Procession. But John often uses this preposition to express what comes from God (seventeen times), particularly with respect to the Son (1:4; 6:46; 7:29, etc.).

114. Carson, *The Gospel According to John*, 529.

115. 0Ἐκεῖνος ("he will") breaks with the neuter status of the preceding relative pronoun; thus, "the Spirit is thought of in personal terms" (Barrett, *The Gospel according to St. John*, 482).

116. Carson, *The Gospel According to John*, 529.

The Authority of the Holy Spirit and Systematic Theology: Part I

call alongside") and which must be thought of in legal terms, as an authorized representative or advocate.[117] The Spirit is thereby sent *under* Christ's authority. This advocacy, however, is primarily *on behalf of Christ* rather than us. "The Spirit, so to speak, conducts Christ's case for him before the world."[118] The Spirit "comes" (16:8) with the full legal authority of Jesus, and with the same ultimate goal as Jesus—the redemption of the world.

The implication of these truths is that Jesus Christ, in his full authority and mission, is continually "with us" in the Holy Spirit. This truth will be fleshed out further in the next passage.

The Executorial Authority of the Spirit with respect to the Present Revelation of Christ—Exegesis of John 16:12–15

> 12 Ετι πολλὰ ἔχω ὑμῖν λέγειν, ἀλλ' οὐ δύνασθε βαστάζειν ἄρτι
>
> 12 I have many more things to say to you, but you cannot bear them now.

John 16:12–15 is the fifth and last of Jesus' "Paraclete passages." Verse 12 informs us that Jesus' speaking ministry is not complete even after his resurrection and ascension. Since the NT continually confirms that Jesus' is God's *supreme act* of revelation (i.e., Col 1:15–23; Heb 1:1–4), we must conclude with Carson that,

> Jesus is the nodal point of revelation, God's culminating self-disclosure. . . . That does not mean he himself provides all the details his followers will need; it does mean that "extra" bits the Holy Spirit provides after he is sent by Christ Jesus, consequent upon Jesus' death/exaltation, are nothing more than the filling out of the revelation nodally present in Jesus himself.[119]

The "more things" Jesus has to tell his disciples seem to be determined in v. 13.

---

117. The legal tones associated with παράκλητος are sharpest in John 16:7–11, where the Paraclete serves more as a prosecuting attorney rather than as counsel for the defense

118. Morris, *The Gospel according to John*, 607. "The passive form does not rule out the possibility that the Paraclete may be an active speaker on behalf of someone before someone else" (Carson, *The Gospel according to John*, 499).

119. Carson, "The Gospel According to John," 539.

13 ὅταν δὲ ἔλθῃ ἐκεῖνος, τὸ πνεῦμα τῆς ἀληθείας, ὁδηγήσει ὑμᾶς ἐν τῇ ἀληθείᾳ πάσῃ· οὐ γὰρ λαλήσει ἀφ' ἑαυτοῦ, ἀλλ' ὅσα ἀκούσει λαλήσει καὶ τὰ ἐρχόμενα ἀναγγελεῖ ὑμῖν.

13 But when He, the Spirit of truth, comes, He will guide you into all the truth; for He will not speak on His own initiative, but whatever He hears, He will speak; and He will disclose to you what is to come.

While τὸ πνεῦμα τῆς ἀληθείας ("the Spirit of truth") will be discussed in depth in the next section (regarding the Spirit's *veracious authority*), we should say here that the action of the Spirit of Truth—"the great Giver and revealer of the truth of God"[120]—is once again placed at the very heart of revelation. It is this Spirit that will ὁδηγήσει ("guide") Jesus' disciples into all truth. This verb is indicative, future, active, and a "gradual unfolding, as happens when one is led along a path."[121] It begins a series of eight future tense verbs (found in vv. 13–14), which demonstrate the solemn emphasis of Jesus' promise of the Spirit. This verb may reflect the idea that Jesus is the ὁδός ("the way") as well as "the truth" toward which the Spirit "guides" (John 14:6). The Spirit as guide appears in several OT texts (i.e., Isa 63:14; Ps 143:10). The same verb is used in Rev 7:17 for the Lamb who guides the saints to the spring of life-giving water.

The difficulty of v. 13 lies with ἐν τῇ ἀληθείᾳ πάσῃ ("in all truth"). The preposition has the alternate reading εἰς ("into").[122] Barrett asserts that John knew of the LXX tendency to place ἐν before τῇ ἀληθείᾳ and that, while ἐν suggests guidance in the whole sphere of truth, the difference between the two readings is slight.[123] Carson also holds ἐν to be the best reading, and figures that this preposition suggests an exploration of truth already principally disclosed (as opposed to εἰς, which hints of truth not yet discovered).[124]

---

120. Bullinger, *Word Studies on the Holy Spirit*, 81.
121. Montague, *The Holy Spirit*, 360.
122. The alternative reading receives little support in the Nestle-Aland text.
123. Barrett, *The Gospel according to St. John*, 489.
124. Carson, *The Gospel according to John*, 539.

Jesus himself is the truth (14:6), now the Spirit of truth leads the disciples into all the implications of the truth, the revelation, intrinsically bound up with Jesus Christ. There is no other locus of truth; this is *all truth*. The notion of "guidance" . . . [has to do] with understanding God as he has revealed himself, and with obeying the revelation—as the occurrence of this verb in the Psalms makes clear (e.g. Ps 25:4–5 [LXX 24:4–5]; 143:10 [142:10]).[125]

Specifically, the Spirit will guide them in πάση truth, or all the implications of the truth of Jesus himself. This complements the idea that there are things they cannot bear now (v. 12). The phrase οὐ γὰρ λαλήσει ἀφ' ἑαυτου ("for he will not speak from himself") seems to mean that the Spirit "has no message over and above that which is implicit in the incarnate Word; it is his function to make that message explicit."[126] John is not saying here that the Spirit does not take personal initiative, but rather that the Spirit is presented as a speaking agent with a very important qualification: ὅσα ἀκούσει λαλήσει ("whatever he hears, he speaks"). This implies that the Spirit speaks not in verbatim but rather always in complete accordance with that which he hears from the Father and from the Son.[127] As Jesus received his message and directions from the Father (see 3:34–35; 5:19–20; 7:16–18; 8:26–29, 42–43; 12:47–50; and 14:10), so the Spirit receives from Jesus what he imparts to the disciples. However, there is an essential difference in their respective tasks: "Jesus brings the truth, and makes it present through his coming into the world; the Spirit-Paraclete opens up this truth and creates the entrance into it for the believers."[128]

> 14 ἐκεῖνος ἐμὲ δοξάσει, ὅτι ἐκ τοῦ ἐμοῦ λήμψεται καὶ ἀναγγελεῖ ὑμῖν
>
> 14 He shall glorify me; for He shall take of Mine, and shall disclose it to you.

---

125. Ibid., 539–40.

126. Bruce, *The Gospel of John*, 320.

127. Morris states, "It is not said whether He hears them from the Father or the Son, but the point is probably not material. The emphasis in these verses is on the Spirit rather than on either of the other Persons. This expression will indicate His harmony with Them. He is not originating something radically new, but leading men in accordance with the teaching already given from the Father and the Son" (Morris, *The Gospel according to John*, 700).

128. Beasley-Murray, *John*, 300.

In v. 14 we go "behind the scenes" to discover *why* and *how* the Spirit is doing these things. The Spirit's goal is to glorify Jesus and to complete Jesus' revelatory mission by disclosing to the disciples that which the Father has given to Jesus. The word δοξάσει ("will glorify") is the active, future tense of the verb δοχάζω ("praise," "glorify").[129] The emphasis is on appearance; "the manifestation of a person, with special stress on the impression this creates on others."[130] As the Son glorified the Father by submitting to the Father's authority and doing his work on earth (John 7:18; 17:4), so the Spirit in his coming will submit to Jesus' authority and glorify him. According to Beasley-Murray:

> [This] suggests that the revelatory work of the Spirit, described as "he shall glorify me," has a special relation to the *redemptive* work of Jesus, wherein the revelation of God in Christ reaches it apex. In the Spirit's unfolding of that revelation the glorification of Jesus in his death and exaltation continues.[131]

The rest of the verse tells us *how* the Spirit will glorify Christ. The Spirit shall ἐκ τοῦ ἐμοῦ λήμψεται ("take what is already mine") and then shall ἀναγγελεῖ ὑμῖν ("disclose it to you"). Ἀναγγελει ("report," "announce," "proclaim") indicates a reannouncement of what has been communicated before.[132] This is a Christological application and limitation of the truth of 1 Cor 2:10–12, where we discovered that the Spirit is not to be seen as one having an independent speaking authority but rather an authority to search out the depths of God and reveal God's thoughts to us.

What is the Spirit "taking from" Christ and "disclosing" to us? Carson points out that "*taking from what is mine and making it known to you* does

---

129. Though δόξα meant "opinion" or "conjecture" in classical Greek, it was transformed in the LXX to refer to the honor brought/given by God or the expression of God's glory and power (Ps 24:7; 29:3; Isa 42:8). See Aalen, "Glory," 44–46.

130. Aalen, "Glory," 45.

131. Beasley-Murray, *John*, 284.

132. John 4:25 uses this verb in reference to the *Messiah's* reporting ("he will report to you all things"). The fact that both are future, aorist, active strengthens the notion that "he [the Spirit] will take what is mine and disclose it to you" is a *preannouncement*. "In these passages it is not so much a matter of a proclamation which will bring about its own fulfillment in the shape of an event . . . as the revealing, the *reporting* of that 'which was from the beginning' (1 Jn 1:1)" (Becker and Muller, "Proclamation," 2:44–46).

not simply mean that the Paraclete passes on what Jesus declares, but that all the revelation bound up in Jesus' person and mission are pressed home on the disciples."[133] The Spirit brings the weight of Jesus' character and revelation, and most notably his authority, to bear on humanity. In doing so, the Spirit takes on the role of *executor* in such a way as to bring glory to Jesus.

> 15 πάντα ὅσα ἔχει ὁ πατὴρ ἐμά ἐστιν· διὰ τοῦτο εἶπον ὅτι ἐκ τοῦ ἐμοῦ λαμβάνει καὶ ἀναγγελεῖ ὑμῖν
>
> 15 All things that the Father has are Mine; therefore I said that He takes of Mine and will disclose *it* to you.

Verse 15 reiterates the last phrase of v. 14, but adds a crucial presupposition: "all things that the Father has are mine." Jesus tells us that this is the underlying *reason* the Spirit "takes of what is mine." This verse demonstrates that the completeness of revelation—bound up in the Father, Son, and Holy Spirit—is now to be disclosed by the Spirit. This stark portrayal of the "economic Trinity" implies *economic authority*. The Spirit, who is both "under" Jesus' authority and speaks *with* Jesus' authority, reveals the Father who is revealed in the Son.[134] There is no diminishing of the Father's authority—or Jesus'—in the words spoken by the Spirit.

BIBLICAL THEOLOGY

Early portrayals of the relationship between Christ and the Spirit are seen in Isa 11:2 and 61:1, where the Spirit is given to the Messiah as an anointing for ministry. This is confirmed in Luke 3:22 ("and the Holy Spirit descended upon Him in bodily form like a dove"). For Luke, this anointing opens the door to a new understanding of the Messiah's ministry, essentially making the Spirit dominant in Christ's conception (Luke 1:35), temptation (Luke 4:1–13), return from temptation to Galilee (Luke 4:14), etc.

However, once the Spirit is poured out by Christ (Acts 1:5; 2:4), Paul begins to refer to the Spirit as "the Spirit of Christ" or "the Spirit of the Son" (Rom 8:2, 9; 2 Cor 3:17; Gal 4:6; Phil 1:19). As we have seen, John refers to the Spirit as the One who is "sent by" Christ (John 15:26). John confirms

---

133. Carson, *The Gospel according to John*, 541.
134. Bruce, *The Gospel of John*, 321.

this notion in Rev 22:1, referring to the Spirit as the water of life that "ἐκπορευόμενον ('flows') from the throne of God and of the Lamb."

As a result, after Pentecost the Spirit's authority becomes specifically *executorial*—his mission is Christologically focused. His ultimate goal is to glorify Christ, explain Christ's truth, and continue Christ's mission. While the Son uses his authority to glorify the Father (John 17:1), the Spirit now uses his authority to glorify the Son (John 16:13–14). Whereas the Son is the agent of God's redemption (2 Cor 5:18), meriting access to the Father and working *for* us; the Spirit is now the authoritative agent of God in the administration of redemption (2 Cor 3:6–11), enabling access to the Father by working *in* us (Eph 2:8). While the Father has authority to judge sin and the Son to forgive sin, the Spirit is portrayed as the one who has the authority to "convict the world concerning sin" (John 16:8). The Spirit's executorial authority can be distinguished from the executive authority of the Son in several NT passages (i.e. Luke 1:35; 3:22; 12:10). According to Oden, "The power to bring into being proceeds from the Father. The power to mediate the saving act belongs to the Son. The power to consummate and realize God's saving work belongs to the Spirit."[135]

Systematic Theology

In developing a "formal description" of the Holy Spirit's "executorial authority," I shall first investigate the pneumatologies of Pinnock and Hodgson and then respond to these pneumatologies with my exegetical findings.

Clark Pinnock's *Flame of Love* and Peter Hodgson's *Winds of the Spirit*

As mentioned in chapter two, one of Pinnock's main concerns is that we clarify the nature of the relationship between Christ and the Spirit. Pinnock does not speak of the Spirit's "authority" per se, but instead explains that the Spirit's mission in creating the Church is complementary but not subordinate to the Son's mission. The "danger of subordination of the Spirit to the Son" with respect to ecclesiology is that "the church is seen as the body

---

135. Oden, *Life in the Spirit*, 23.

of Christ to which the Spirit is added as a helper."[136] Pinnock adds, "the mission of one is not subordinated to the mission of the other—there is a mutual and reciprocal relationship between them. Neither Son nor Spirit ought to be subordinated to the other."[137] Instead, we need to include a modified "Spirit Christology" in our theology (while avoiding "adoptionism"). Pinnock makes a strong case for this, demonstrating that Jesus' life (being led by the Spirit) recapitulated human history (through his entire life, death, and resurrection), that his earthly ministry was empowered by the Spirit, that his baptism and anointing were in the Spirit, that he relied upon the Spirit in overcoming temptation, and that his resurrection by the Spirit is the missing piece in modern soteriology (thereby giving back to the Spirit his rightful role in the work of atonement).[138] Like Moltmann, however, Pinnock advocates the elimination of the *filioque* clause in the Nicene Creed,[139] along with any idea of subordination within the economic Trinity. The *filioque*, according to Pinnock, "diminishes the role of the Spirit and gives the impression that he has no mission *of his own*."[140]

Hodgson presents a quite different alignment of the Christ-Spirit relationship. As seen in chapter two, behind Hodgson's understanding of the "liberating Church" lies a relational God who has meaning for us only in *revelatory experience*. God is "ideal but not yet real, rich in potential but not actual" when viewed apart from the world. It is in and through relationship with the world that God *becomes* "Spirit."[141] Bloesch surmises that "Spirit"

---

136. Pinnock, *Flame of Love*, 115.

137. Ibid., 92. Pinnock adds, "whereas Jesus bespeaks particularity, Spirit bespeaks universality."

138. Ibid., 85–102.

139. He is "indebted to Eastern Orthodox theology, which has always maintained that Western traditions have diminished the role of the Spirit by giving the Son an ontic role and the Spirit only a noetic one" (Pinnock, *Flame of Love*, 92). Cross points out, however, that Pinnock aligns Luther "too closely" with Anselm (with respect to his atonement theory), citing Gustaf Aulen's *Christus Victor* in crediting Luther's return to the classical view. Cross also defends Luther's centralization of justification in theology, stressing that Pinnock provides "too much of a corrective" in saying that "Christ did not appease divine anger—his death and resurrection constitute the saving event into which we are being drawn" (Cross, review of *Flame of Love*, 18–20).

140. Pinnock, *Flame of Love*, 187 (emphasis mine).

141. Hodgson, *Winds of the Spirit*, 49.

becomes "the dominant category in [Hodgson's] doctrine of God."[142] The Spirit seems to hold a place of highest "authority" regarding the divine hierarchy: "Spirit encompasses the whole, God and world together."[143] The Spirit is seen as active in all religions, and Jesus, while the greatest, is only one of the great sages of history through whom the Spirit is preeminently manifested. According to one reviewer, Hodgson's theology "seeks access to the mystery of the being and action of the triune God though pneumatology rather than Christology."[144]

Hodgson's "panentheistic" pneumatology essentially leads him to deny the independence of the Spirit of the Lord from the spirit of the world and to find unity in postmodern diversity by embracing "Spirit." For Hodgson, the Spirit of God becomes almost equated with Hegel's "objective Spirit" of the social matrix, a world-dependent spirit that provides a "community of freedom."[145] Hodgson thereby completely redefines the traditional concept of the "personhood" of the Spirit. Hodgson's concept of the Trinity has been redefined as well—the "Trinity" is *God-World-Spirit* (with the person of Christ being replaced by the world!)[146] Hogdson also views the relationship between Christ and the Spirit as a "reciprocal" one, holding that we must guard against "the dangers of subordinationism (of the Spirit to Christ) and supersessionism (of Christ by the Spirit)." For Hodgson,

> The challenge is to work out a theology of the Spirit that embraces and empowers the *Christ-gestalt* without superseding it. The *figure of Christ*, we have said, represents the turn from the second to the third moment of the divine life, from worldly difference to spiritual mediation. The *figure of Christ*, for Christians, lends definition to both God-in-the-world and God-as-Spirit; thus Christ is essential to both but is not as inclusive as either of these moments.[147]

Since "Christ" is redefined as the *form* ("gestalt") of God in the world, the Spirit becomes the one who helps us discern (or interpret) these forms.

---

142. Bloesch, *The Holy Spirit*, 260.
143. Hogdson, *Winds of the Spirit*, 155.
144. Guthrie, review of *Winds of the Spirit*, 379–80.
145. See Hegel, *Phenomenology of Spirit*, 263–409.
146. See Hodgson, *Winds of the Spirit*, chapter on "The Triune Figuration of God."
147. Hodgson, *Winds of the Spirit*, 289 (emphasis mine).

"It is the complex interplay of Christ and Spirit that enables Christians to always make ambiguous and relative judgments in history."[148] Hodgson's theology, as a result, trends to shun the notion of the Spirit's authority.

> There is no absolute guarantee against illusion and self-deception, no sacred authority to which to appeal, but rather a constant struggle of interpretation. The Spirit is our companion in that struggle, but how we use the Spirit is up to us. It behooves us to use it critically, suspicious of all claims to authority, rather than in a state of uncritical enthusiasm, whether for Christ or for nation.[149]

Response

The most crucial issue for our discussion of Pinnock is how we are to understand his statement that the *filioque* clause "gives the impression that the Spirit has no mission *of his own*."[150] Our exegesis and biblical theology demonstrate that the Spirit does indeed have a unique mission when compared to the mission of the Son. The Spirit's mission, however, is not "of his own" in the sense of having an authority to act independently of Christ's authority in any way. Herein lies Pinnock's subtle error. As we see in our exegesis of John 15:26 and 16:12–15, Jesus sends the Spirit "in my name" (or, "in my place," "with my authority"), and spells this out by saying he will send the Spirit to "testify of me" (15:26), to "guide you into all truth" (16:13), to "not speak on his own initiative," to "glorify me" (16:13), and to "take of Mine, and . . . disclose it to you" (16:15).

Because it essentially disassociates the Spirit's authority from Christ's, Pinnock's model leads to disastrous results when we assess a closely related issue: the sufficiency of Christ for salvation. In his chapter entitled "Spirit and Universality," for example, Pinnock challenges "restrictivist thinking," which holds that "there is no salvation outside Christianity."[151] His basis for

---

148. Ibid., 290.

149. Ibid., 290. Hodgson adds, "it is naïve to think that this Christ, supposedly revealed in an authoritative Scripture, provides an absolute criterion by which to judge history, for Christ is known and interpreted only through the witness of the Spirit in concrete situations" (290).

150. Pinnock, *Flame of Love*, 187 (emphasis mine).

151. Ibid., 188. Pinnock feels that "universalism is perhaps less of a threat (than restrictivism), because a number of biblical texts indicate plainly that person are free to accept or reject salvation" (190).

this is that "the Spirit is under nobody's control" and, like the wind, "blows wherever it pleases (John 3:8)."[152] Indeed some of Pinnock's goals are quite positive—to develop "a sense of the dynamic movement of the Spirit and of rejoicing and celebration in his presence" and to depict "a Spirit who deeply attracts, his saving grace extended wide, wide as the ocean of the world."[153] Nevertheless, his understanding of the Spirit in other religions goes beyond traditional evangelical understanding (namely, that Christian truths may be embedded in other religions) to say that the "Spirit is present and may be experienced" in them.[154] He clarifies his position in his chapter in *Four Views on Salvation in a Pluralistic World*, arguing that "the centerpiece of modal inclusivism is belief in the Spirit as everywhere active, even in the context of the religious life."[155] Of course we must ask Pinnock if this would include non-Christian, pagan, and satanic religions.

Pinnock's inclusivism is grounded in his view of the Spirit, in that the Spirit's work with respect to the economy of salvation has been essentially aligned with the Spirit's work with respect to creation.[156] As a result, the biblical evidence for the Spirit's *executorial authority* (and the parameter provided therein) is somewhat dismissed.

Hodgson goes a step beyond Pinnock, essentially making the Spirit the dominant partner to Christ by diminishing the actually *deity of Christ* to that of "world forms." Hodgson then, in effect, equates the Spirit with the community's interpretation of these forms. Hodgson's "panentheism" sounds much like Moltmann's, in that the Spirit seems to be essentially

---

152. Ibid., 104.

153. Williams, review of *Flame of Love*, 36.

154. Pinnock, *Flame of Love*, 204. Pinnock also claims that "wherever people love one another, care for the sick, make peace not war, wherever there is beauty and concord, generosity and forgiveness, the cup of cold water, we know the Spirit of Jesus is present" (210).

155. Pinnock, *Flame of Love*, 204.

156. This subtle confusion is demonstrated in such statements as: "the cosmic breadth of Spirit activity (in the universe) can help us conceptualize the universality of God's grace," and "there is no general revelation or natural knowledge of God that is not at the same time gracious revelation and a potentially saving knowledge" (Pinnock, *Flame of Love*, 187). Pinnock also sets up a false dichotomy between an almost complete "continuity" of creation/redemption and "neo-Marcionites" who "deny that criterion is a work of grace and that God is reaching out to people everywhere" (198). He further adds, "we refuse to drive a wedge between what God does in creation and in redemption, because the Spirit is Lord and Life-giver in both spheres" (Pinnock, "An Inclusivist View," 106).

The Authority of the Holy Spirit and Systematic Theology: Part I

reduced to an activity of the community (but actually goes beyond Moltmann in diminishing Christ's deity). As a result, biblical evidence for the Spirit's executorial authority as the "Spirit of Christ" is mostly ignored—the Spirit does not come to fulfill Christ's will *with Christ's authority* because Christ's authority has been essentially obliterated.[157] Since Hodgson's vision of a "liberated world" with "liberated communities" emerges so far outside both the "divine" and "executorial" notions of the Spirit's authority, can this model even be considered "Christian?"

In order to respond to both Hodgson and Pinnock, we need to develop a more precise biblical understanding of the sort of "authority" related to *Filioque*. We can do this by developing a model that accounts for both the Spirit's apparent "authority over" Jesus during the Messiah's earthly ministry and for Jesus' obvious "authority over" the Spirit after Pentecost.

In chapter two we discussed specific strengths and weaknesses of the Eastern and Western perspectives, and concluded that the real issue at stake is indeed one of *authority*. *Filioque* seems to support the position that the Spirit obtains his *authority to act* (i.e., executorial authority) from the Son as well as from the Father, and this seems to be the concern of many contemporary theologians as they revisit *filioque*. Hendry, for example, holds that the denial of *filioque* opens the way to a sort of dual authority structure that may easily neglect Christ's present-day authority, "as if the mission of the Son and that of the Spirit were two separate and distinct movements sent forth from God to men."[158] Kasper sees evidence of *filioque* in the vital connection between the immanent and economic Trinities.

> But if the economy of salvation and the theology of the inner life of the Trinity should not diverge but rather correspond, and if the Son

---

157. Hodgson states: "The Spirit is . . . the means by which the Christ-gestalt fans and flames out to embrace the world. 'Christ' is no longer incarnate in the individual body of Jesus of Nazareth but rather is infused into the world by the Spirit, which shapes corporate bodies of redemptive praxis. . . . The Spirit is dependent on Christ in one fundamental sense: The Spirit known by the Christian community of faith is not any spirit or a multiplicity of spirits but the Spirit defined, profiled, discerned, interpreted (see 1 Cor 2:13–14) by the concrete configuration of the Christ-gestalt in Jesus of Nazareth" (Hogdson, *Winds of the Spirit*, 288). Hogdson appears to say here that the ontological nature of Christ has been reduced to world-forms and that the Spirit is now to be understood (and "interpreted") in terms of these "forms" of Christ in the world.

158. Hendry, *The Holy Spirit in Christian Theology*, 46.

> has a share in the sending of the Spirit in the history of salvation, then he cannot fail to have a share in the intra-trinitarian procession of the Spirit.[159]

Bray makes the point even more succinctly. "The real question is one of authority," he tells us, and explains this in terms of Christ's relationship with his Father:

> Does Christ have all power in heaven and earth, or is he dependent on the Father in some way? If the Holy Spirit does not proceed from him, does this mean that he must rely on the Father to send the Spirit? . . . we must ask whether Christ sends the Spirit by divine right or only by divine permission. This takes us back to the whole question of Arianism, which is where the debate originally began. If Christ sends the Spirit only by permission, then there is a sense in which he is not fully and ultimately God.[160]

Further Discussion and Formal Description

This leads us to the conclusion that the Spirit's *divine authority* is revealed to us as an essentially *executorial authority*. How is this "executorial authority" to be understood? While the Spirit's divine Personhood creates parameters for comprehending the Spirit's *nature,* the biblical evidence has shown us a critical parameter for understanding this divine authority. The Spirit's executorial authority in fact *qualifies* his divine authority. Indeed, the Spirit's activity is that of a *divine Person* rather than that of a "force-field" or "primal energy." Nevertheless, this divine Person does not possess just any sort of divine authority, but rather an *executorial* divine authority.

In attempting to present a convincing argument for the Spirit's "executorial authority" in theology, we will first need to determine the nature of the Spirit as a "divine agent" (i.e., is his agency authoritative?) and then determine if this agency is "independent" of Christ's authority or "under" his authority (i.e., is his agency *executorial?*)

---

159. Kasper, *The God of Jesus Christ*, 8.
160. Bray, "The Double Procession of the Holy Spirit," 425–26.

Divine Agency and Executorial Authority

First, Breck has developed a fascinating study of the growth and development of the Johannine concept of the "Spirit of Truth" in ancient Hebrew thought. According to Breck, most studies on the Spirit "tend to overlook the significant development that took place in Israel's religious consciousness, and specifically in the understanding and presentation of Spirit, which occurred during the period from the earliest historical writings to the oracles of the post-exilic prophets."[161] A significant turning-point in OT development of *ruach* is noted in Num 27:18–23. Here Joshua is singled out as one in whom the Lord's Spirit is already present and active.

> By this indwelling of the Spirit, [Joshua] is recognized as a charismatic leader, possessing the qualifications necessary to assume the divine commission laid upon him. Here *ruach* is no longer conceived as an agent or instrument used by God; it appears rather as Yahweh's own power at work within His chosen human vessel.[162]

This demonstrates that Israel's religious consciousness has matured "from an understanding of *ruach* as an objective instrument of the divine will towards a view of the Spirit of the Lord as a *mode of divine activity.* Spirit is 'God in action.'"[163] The Spirit in Numbers 27 represents the immanent expression of God's *presence* and total *person,* which would certainly include God's *authority.* Breck points out that this tradition becomes even clearer in Ezekiel and the post-exilic prophets.

> *Ruach* (especially in prophetic tradition) signified divinity itself, the presence in history of the transcendent holy God.... [It] gradually developed from a capricious inspirational *dynamic* or *charismatic power* in primitive Hebrew thought into the indwelling bearer of the divine Word. Thus ruach became a virtual synonym for Yahweh in His act of self-disclosure.[164]

The NT πνεῦμα stands in the tradition of this latter understanding of *ruach*, and is applied by Paul and John as the self-disclosure of Christ

---

161. Breck, *The Spirit of Truth*, 6.
162. Ibid., 10–11.
163. Ibid., 11 (emphasis mine).
164. Ibid., 160.

after his resurrection. Though Paul speaks of the "Spirit of Christ" and the "Spirit of the Son," the relation between Christ and the Spirit in the Synoptic gospels (as seen in our study of Biblical Theology) is not presented this way.

> [The synoptics] describe the Spirit as having divine priority over against Jesus and Jesus as the bearer of the Spirit. This description is in accordance with the prophecies that the Spirit will rest on the Messiah. That is why he is called Messiah, the Anointed One, because the Lord has anointed him with his Spirit.[165]

Dunn attempts to integrate these various perspectives. He outlines a "three-fold pattern of salvation history" in Luke/Acts that includes (1) the period of the old covenant, where Jesus is the creation of the Spirit (Luke 1:35), (2) at Jordan, where Jesus becomes the uniquely anointed Man of the Spirit, the "first fruits" (according to Paul) of the new age and covenant (Luke 3:22), and (3) at Jesus' exaltation he becomes Lord of the Spirit and baptizer in the Spirit (Acts 2:33).[166] Dunn concludes that, during Jesus' earthly ministry (the intermediate stage), "the Spirit is the dominant partner."[167] However, while there is evidence that the Spirit did possess a certain authority over Jesus in his earthly ministry, this evidence is not played up by any of the NT writers. Instead, Jesus seems to have been granted an obvious authority *over* the Spirit in John, Acts, and Paul's writings.

> For both Paul and John the unitary event of crucifixion, resurrection, ascension was a decisive turning point in the relation between Jesus and the Spirit; describing the transition, they took care to show Jesus the exalted one no longer dependent on the Spirit but now Lord of the Spirit indeed.[168]

Such subordination is not only apparent in John 15:26 and 16:12–15 (Jesus "sending" the Spirit; the Spirit disclosing Jesus), but in Acts we also find the Spirit acting as Christ's *agent*—administering Christ's Kingdom (1:1–5) and executing Christ's will (2:33–38). First Corinthians 15:45

---

165. Berkhof, *The Doctrine of the Holy Spirit*, 16.
166. Dunn, *Jesus and the Spirit*, 138.
167. Ibid.,139.
168. Dunn, *The Christ and the Spirit*, 340.

The Authority of the Holy Spirit and Systematic Theology: Part I

provides an example of the Pauline depiction, which demonstrates that, as the πνεῦμα ζῳοποιοῦν ("life-giving Spirit"), the Spirit fulfills a representative capacity. Indeed the Spirit acts as Christ's agent so as to enable the mission of the Son—the reconciliation of humanity with the Father.[169] Dunn points out the intimate connection being drawn here by Paul between Christ and the Spirit.

> Paul identifies the exalted Jesus with the Spirit—not with a spiritual being (πνεῦμα ζων) or a spiritual dimension or sphere (pneumatikon), but with the Spirit, the Holy Spirit (πνεῦμα ζῳοποιοῦν). Immanent Christology is for Paul pneumatology; in the believer's experience there is no distinction between Christ and Spirit. This does not mean of course that Paul makes *no* distinction between Christ and Spirit. But it does mean that later Trinitarian dogma cannot readily look to Paul for support at this point.[170]

Paul's abundant use of the phrase ἐν πνεύματι or simply πνεύματι (forty-four times in the NT) is also crucial in understanding the Spirit as God's agent (i.e., Rom 1:9, 2:29, 8:13, 14, 16, 9:1, 12:11, 14:17, 15:16). Easley explains Paul's usage of this phrase in Rom 15:16.

> The significance of ἐν πνεύματι in Romans 15:16 changes considerably from the meaning in 9:1. The apostle speaks of the offering collected for the Jerusalem church, that it might be sanctified by the Holy Spirit. [In 15:16] the Spirit is considered the agent who sets apart (sanctifies) this particular historical offering.[171]

Thus, the exalted Jesus is not so much the bearer of the Spirit as he is the sender of the Spirit. Likewise, as Jesus' personal ambassador or agent, the Spirit is portrayed throughout the NT (with the exception of the synoptics) as Jesus' *divine agent*—one who acts under the authority of Christ to creatively execute Christ's will. As an *agent* the Spirit has the ability to act in the world in a literal and intentional way so as to fulfill Christ's mission; as a *divine* agent he carries into this activity the divine authority of God.

---

169. For further clarification of the subordination of the Spirit, see Hilary, "On the Trinity," VIII:19; IX.
170. Dunn, "1 Corinthians 15:45," 139.
171. Easley, "The Pauline usage of πνεύματι," 305.

How is the Spirit's agency related to his authority? Here it must first be remembered that, at his ascension, Jesus Christ is granted "all authority in heaven and on earth" (Matt 28:18). This does not mean that Jesus did not possess full authority before his ascension (or his incarnation), but that the *execution* of divine authority in the world *now begins in Christ*. Therefore, the revelation of our pattern of divine authority is now, in essence, *the continuing revelation of Jesus*. As a result, the Spirit's post-resurrection "divine authority" (discussed in section A) may now only be understood as an *executorial* divine authority. Since John 15:26 and 16:12–15 demonstrate that the Spirit is given authority as Christ's *agent*,[172] divine authority in today's world is *only* witnessed as the Spirit creatively executes Christ's will. According to Clarke, "As Christ is represented as the ambassador of the Father, so the Holy Spirit is represented as the ambassador of the Son, coming vested with his authority, as the interpreter and executor of his will."[173]

While our exegetical conclusions provide great assistance in discerning the nature of the Spirit's authoritative agency, further discernment regarding the nature of agency is required. First, an "agent" might be defined as "a person authorized by another to act for him, one entrusted with another's business, . . . one who acts for or in place of another by authority from him."[174] From this definition we can conclude that an agent must (1) be a "personal" agent (who acts in an intentional way, and has the potential or capacity for acting in a literal sense); (2) act "in place of another," which implies distinction from the being or personhood of the one represented; and (3) possess authority granted by the one represented to act "for him" and with respect to his "business." The result is that the agent will possess the authority to act in accordance with the will of the one in ultimate authority (an authority retained via relationship with the one in ultimate authority).[175]

---

172. The Spirit is described by John as a Person (given the personal pronoun "he" in John 16:13) who will have the capacity to act (Jesus utilizes the future tense, "he will"). Acting "under" the Son while retaining His relationship with the Father and the Son (16:15), the Spirit, being Holy, stands in marked distinction from a world which needs conviction (see 16:8–11).

173. Clarke, *Christian Theology*, 157.

174. *Black's Law Dictionary*, "Agent," 64.

175. One might say that the incarnation was not an act which retained a sense of God's

At this point we need to assess several theological models of divine agency to see if they align with both the above definition and our exegetical conclusions.[176] Owen Thomas surveys the problems and issues that have recently confronted traditional theological conceptions of divine agency in his *God's Activity in the World: the Contemporary Problem*. Thomas presents a compilation of essays from several theological perspectives. By briefly examining these perspectives, we can discern today's theological landscape with respect to divine agency, and assess the impact of these models upon the Spirit's authoritative agency.

1. G. Ernest Wright presents a "traditional" neo-orthodox approach to divine agency. His central thesis is that biblical theology is the recital of God's mighty acts, and that "biblical faith . . . is first and foremost a confessional recital of the gracious and redemptive acts of God."[177] Though Wright's approach boldly affirms God's historic activity, it has been rightly criticized by Gilkey and others that it so emphasizes the *interpretation* of historical events that it denies a *literal* sense of divine activity.[178]

2. Frank Dilley's understanding of divine agency rests on Bultmann's demythologized view of the NT, interpreting God's action as that

---

authority, but was instead one of submission (Phil 2:6–8). Authority is retained in this act, though, in that Christ's relationship with the Father was not disrupted in His salvific work. "God was in Christ, reconciling the world to Himself . . . " (2 Cor 5:19).

176. These models should also be evaluated in light of a theistic understanding of authority as assumed in the definition of divine ἐξουσία which would include "the power to give orders" as well as "right of action" (Betz, "Might," 606, 608). This "right" assumes an authority to act in some way while retaining a separate identity from the person upon which or sphere within which one is acting. A theistic understanding of authority simply involves the idea of a God who exists, who created the world, whose identity is to be distinguished from the world, and who acts in and through the world.

177. Wright, in Thomas, *God's Activity in the World*, 120.

178. This translates into a mystical version of the Spirit's activity in the world, easily reduces to pantheistic versions of "miracles," and no longer allows us to speak of the Spirit as possessing an authority to *literally* act as God's agent in the world. Gilkey comments, "When we ask (Wright): 'All right, what has (God actually) done?' No answer can apparently be given. Most of the acts recorded in Scripture turn out to be 'interpretations by Hebrew faith,' and we are sure that they, like the miracles of the Buddha, did not really happen at all" (Thomas, *God's Activity in the World*, 37).

which occurs only within finite events and visible to the eye of faith. God's agency is observed within an existential "paradox of faith," one that "understands as God's action here and now an event which is completely intelligible in the natural or historical connection of events."[179] Thus, the Spirit's action in the world is not to be understood in terms of literal events, but only within the context of the analogy of personal relations. Dilley's primary weakness is seen in his confusion of supernatural "miracles" with personal encounters or natural phenomena, thus missing the traditional distinctions between primary and secondary causes.[180] This results in a blurring of the traditional distinction between the Spirit and the world as well.

3. David Griffin follows Whitehead's conception of divine events, attempting to develop a closer unity between divine and non-divine causes. His "process theology" approach attributes several influences as explanations of events (including previous events, the purposes of God, and the event's own self-determination). Griffin insists that extraordinary acts of God do occur, "although these events in no way involve an interruption of the normal course of events."[181] These acts may even occur in the form of a "revelation," which "involves a present action of God (as Holy Spirit) on the believer."[182] Such actions of the Spirit may be influenced by historical figures (such as Christ) or historical events (as found in Scripture), but any "necessary" connections as such are denied. As a result, the Spirit is easily reduced to a world process.[183] Such a model, more than any

---

179. Thomas, *God's Activity in the World*, 65.

180. Primary and secondary causes are understood in relation to one another—"the relation between two events or states of affairs where the first is necessary or sufficient or both for the occurrence of the second" (Piggin, "Cause," 200).

181. Thomas, *God's Activity in the World*, 129.

182. Ibid.

183. Hodgson takes a similar approach, following Whitehead's and Harris' theories of "holism" (Hodgson, *Winds of the Spirit*, 185), but refers to his model as "postmodern science." In this model, "the creative presence in the universe results from the interplay of chance and regularity" (191) and the Spirit is referred to as a "Creative and Alluring Cosmic Eros" (194). "God's love for the world is erotic in the sense that God creates, designs, and allures the world in its vitality and materiality, while at the same time transfiguring that materiality into relationships of spirituality, that is, of inwardness, recognition, mutuality, self-giving" (194).

other, is now shaping contemporary understandings of the Spirit's agency. Burrell, for example, explains the mentality driving the "postmodern" redefinition.

> The problem is that the polarities so often experienced in our lives as opposites—individual/society, mystical/revolutionary, contemplative/active—incline us all too easily to adapt the gospel to one pole or another. This very fact, however, may suggest a redefinition of the Spirit as that power which permits us to hope for what history has shown humankind so incapable of realizing: the reconciliation of these very opposites.[184]

We must conclude that, since "process" versions of the Spirit's activity in the world do not retain a distinction between the Spirit and the world, such a model does not serve well in explaining the biblical data with respect to the Spirit as an authoritative divine agent (as gathered in the exegesis of John 15:26 and 16:12–15).

4. Austin Farrer's Reformed approach aligns much better with our definition of "agent" and our biblical criteria for understanding the nature of the Spirit's authoritative agency. First, in Farrer's thought there is no breakdown between primary and secondary causes. "God acts through creaturely agencies without either forcing them or competing with them. But it is neither necessary nor possible to understand or conceive the 'causal joint' between finite and infinite action."[185] Agents are personal and thus free in the use of their will. Farrer sees one of the primary actions of the Spirit as that of opening blocked channels in the unconverted. How does the Spirit do this without violating the will of the individual?

> He forces upon us conditions in our creaturely environment which challenge our voluntary response, and, when the response is unworthy, show it up for what it is. So Christ bears upon mankind, and his crucifixion shows us what we are.

---

184. Burrell, "The Spirit and the Christian life," 322.
185. Austin Farrer, in Thomas, *God's Activity in the World*, 12.

> And it is by continued association with Christ that we are opened to the action of the Holy Ghost.[186]

Here is where an understanding of the Spirit's "executorial authority" comes to fruition. Farrer's model does meet the conditions defined earlier, thus allowing for an authoritative agency of the Holy Spirit. In the Reformed tradition, "the Spirit has, as its task, to apply the salvation obtained by Christ to mankind,"[187] and this is certainly reflected in John 16:13–14. The Reformed tradition demonstrates that the Spirit's activity is primarily an instrumental work aimed at awakening faith in Christ. John Calvin summarized one of his major sections on the work of the Spirit by saying that "the Holy Spirit is the bond by which Christ effectually unites us to himself."[188]

Nevertheless, Farrer's discussion of the Holy Spirit (like the classical Reformed perspective) tends to place the Spirit into such strict subjection to the historic Christ that it approaches "modalism" (i.e., it reduces the "Persons" of the Trinity to three "modes" of God's appearance or activity). While the Reformed model does retain *one* sense of the Spirit's authority to act as Christ's executor in the world, it does not always seem to cover the entire range of the Spirit's executorial activity. According to Berkhof, in Reformed theology, "the Spirit is customarily treated in noetical, applicative, subjective terms . . . the Spirit is a second reality beside Christ . . . serving in the application of his atoning work, in the realization of justification by faith."[189] Still, we can utilize this model as a foundation for our development of the Spirit's authority to act as Christ's authoritative agent in the world. By evaluating such activities we can develop a broad perspective regarding the Holy Spirit's agency as it relates to his executorial authority. We might think of the Spirit's executorial authority in a way that nearly parallels Phil 2:6–11 (the *kenosis* passage): The Holy Spirit, who, being in very nature God, and who does not consider equality with God something to be grasped, takes the role of a servant—Christ's servant. At

---

186. Farrer, *Saving Belief*, 125.
187. Berkhof, *The Doctrine of the Holy Spirit*, 21.
188. Calvin, *Institutes*, I:337–38.
189. Berkhof, *The Doctrine of the Holy Spirit*, 23.

Pentecost Christ grants the Holy Spirit the authority necessary to fulfill Christ's will in the world.

The Spirit's "Own" Authority?

Second, in assessing the strengths and weaknesses of "eastern" and "western" pneumatologies (chapter 2), we recognize the need to seek a theological "balance" between (1) an approach that *separates* the person (and authority) of Christ from the person (and authority) of the Spirit and (2) one that *subordinates* the Spirit to Christ in such a way that the Spirit loses his "own" personhood (and authority). According to our exegesis, the Spirit's executorial authority runs counter to the idea that the Spirit can act completely on his "own" initiative, as Pinnock and eastern orthodox theology seem to imply. As we have seen, Protestant reformers intentionally developed a pattern of authority, with Christ, the Spirit, and the Scriptures forming an inseparable unity. The Spirit's authority within this pattern is thereby a derivative one, deputized by the Lord Jesus. This is the point of John 16:13. Such an understanding of the Spirit's place in relation to Jesus, according to Kasper, was a vital aspect of the early Church's theology:

> The Church's pneumatology was therefore inspired chiefly by the intention of safeguarding the unity of the history of salvation and of understanding the Holy Spirit as the Spirit of Jesus Christ, the Spirit who is inseparably connected with the person and work of Jesus and whose task it is to make the person and work of Jesus present in the church and the individual Christian and thus brings them to their completion. The new thing which the Spirit brings is that he constantly makes Jesus Christ present and renews his eschatological newness.[190]

This being said, it must be added that the Spirit retains his divine Personhood in his agency *under* Jesus' authority. If the Holy Spirit has divine transcendence *over* creation (Ps 104:29–30), then his agency as actor *within* creation must carry divine transcendence into that immanent action. There can be no "blurring" of the Spirit's Personhood with human persons. Second, when Christ specifies the nature of the Spirit as his Executor, he describes the Spirit as a divine Person with divine authority. In John 14:26

---

190. Kasper, *The God of Jesus Christ*, 209–10.

The Lord Is the Spirit

Jesus says he will send the Spirit "in my name," or essentially "with my authority." Also, by saying that the Spirit will "take of Mine and will disclose *it* to you," Jesus implies in John 16:14 that the Spirit will be the sort of Executor who is "free" to bring the weight of Jesus' revelation and authority to bear on humanity. Kasper expresses the Spirit's personhood in terms of "the freedom of the Spirit."

> According to the New Testament, it is the task of the Spirit to give a universal presence to the person and work of Jesus Christ and to make these real in the individual human being. The task is carried out, however, not mechanically but in the freedom of the Spirit. For "where the Spirit of the Lord is, there is freedom" (2 Cor 3:17). . . . The freedom of the Spirit is incompatible with the Spirit being simply an impersonal principle, a medium or dimension; rather, the freedom of the Spirit presupposes the relative independence of the Spirit. . . . The explicit acknowledgement of the independent personality of the Spirit is therefore anything but speculative indulgence; at issue in it is the reality of Christian salvation: the Christian freedom that is based on the freedom of God's gift and grace.[191]

Freedom of the Spirit means that the Spirit has the executorial authority to instill freedom *in the world*. The Spirit's executorial authority is an authority to act *immanently* without losing *transcendence,* and thereby to impact the world by displaying divine authority *in* the world. Such an immanent divine authority was present in OT times in the form of the tabernacle, the temple, and David's messianic throne. It was also present in Jesus' earthly ministry as he *speaks with authority* (Luke 4:32) and casts out demons with divine authority (Mark 1:27). Recognizing the need for the continuation of an immanent divine authority after his departure, Jesus sends his Spirit upon all flesh.

> The Spirit is far more than an instrumental entity, the subjective reverse of Christ's work. His coming to us is a great new event in the series of God's saving acts. He creates a world of his own, a world of conversion, experience, sanctification; of tongues, prophecy, and miracles; of mission; of upbuilding and guiding the Church, etc. He appoints ministers; he organizes; he illumines, inspires, and sustains; he intercedes for the saints and helps them in their weak-

---

191. Ibid., 211.

nesses; he searches everything, even the depths of God; he guides into all truth; he grants a variety of gifts; he convinces the world; he declares the things that are to come.[192]

In referring to Jesus as "the Lord of the Spirit," Dunn seeks to find the sort of "balance" that allows for an intimate relationship between Jesus and the Spirit while retaining their distinction:

> There is thus both a fusion and a continuing distinction between Jesus and the Spirit. So far as divine revelation from heaven is concerned we do not have distinct channels, Jesus and the Spirit, but one—Jesus through the Spirit, or even Jesus as the Spirit. So far as the believer's experience of Jesus is concerned, the Spirit and Christ are one. And yet there is still a distinctive position for Jesus in heaven; the Spirit still cries, "Jesus is Lord" (1 Cor 12:3).[193]

Gunton proposes a complementary "balance" that confirms the Spirit's executorial authority as well.

> Any attempt to identify the Spirit must show that there is a way of God's action towards us and his world which is not *separable* from his action in Christ, but not *reducible* to it either. . . . On such a basis there can be a legitimate attempt to identify the Spirit both as a trinitarian person and in relation to the other persons of the Godhead.[194]

Gunton holds that, in the authoritative structure of the divine economy, the transcendent Son is characterized by immanence *in* the economy (becoming flesh and redeeming the world) while the immanent Spirit is characterized by transcendence *over* the economy. Thus, the Spirit acts *under* (or, on behalf of) Christ's "transcendent immanence." Both Son and Spirit possess immanence but manifest it differently: "The Son *becomes* flesh; the Spirit acts *towards* and *in* the world."[195] Such a structure does not contradict John 15:26 (the fact that the crucified, risen, and ascended Christ is the mediator of the Spirit to those who believe), nor John 16:12–15 (the fact that, in the Church age, the Spirit is described in terms that place

---

192. Berkhof, *The Doctrine of the Holy Spirit*, 23.
193. Dunn, *The Christ and the Spirit*, 1:339–40.
194. Gunton, *Theology through the Theologians*, 112.
195. Ibid., 112.

him *under* the authority of the Son—particularly when it comes to "speaking"). While this might seem to imply that the Spirit has no authority in the divine economy, *executorial authority*, properly conceived, satisfies the economic paradigm of John 15 and 16 without compromising the Spirit's divine Personhood.

This conception of the Spirit is somewhat different than the one implied by Augustine (as the immanent possession of Jesus). Ironically, the Augustinian conception of the Spirit may pose a real danger with respect to the Spirit's executorial authority. Bray rightly holds that, "if the Holy Spirit really is a person in his own right, we ought to avoid language that calls him the 'bond of love' between the Father and the Son, even if there is a sense in which this is truth, because the language itself has a depersonalizing effect." Bray also provides a corrective to this Augustinian conception of the Spirit by applying one aspect of the "eastern" perspective on the Trinity, namely that "personal relationships must be freely established between responsible agents and not be the byproduct of some other relationship or process."[196] If we fail to give the Holy Spirit the kind of personal identity or particularity that is required when we identify his action in the world, severe problems develop in our pneumatology.

> We shall identify his work *apart from the work of the Father and the Son*, and in terms of what we happen to find attractive or appealing at the present time. . . . The reason is that if we cannot conceive of the Spirit as the free Lord, then *we may succumb to the temptation of identifying him with some immanent causal force*: with our ecclesiastical or political institutions, or with some private experiences and beliefs.[197]

The Spirit is to be conceived "as God's free and life-giving activity in and towards the world as he maintains and empowers the human activity of the incarnate Son."[198] As the agent of Christ's resurrection, the Spirit is the giver of Christ's resurrection life; as the agent of Christ's humanity, the Spirit is the giver of Christ's human intimacy. From this we may conclude

---

196. Bray, "The Double Procession of the Holy Spirit," 423.
197. Gunton, *Theology through the Theologians*, 189 (emphases mine).
198. Ibid., 116.

that any denial or reduction of the Spirit's divinity or of his personhood will result in a diminishing of the Spirit's executorial authority as well.

We can now conclude: (1) *The Spirit's executorial authority places strict christological boundaries upon the activity of the Holy Spirit today.* The Spirit indeed acts "under Christ's authority." "Universalists" (such as Pinnock) and "postmodernists" (such as Hodgson) seem to react to such boundaries, seemingly because these boundaries run counter to the notions that the Spirit can act "independently" or as a "world-spirit." (2) Under Jesus' authority, *the Spirit retains divine Personhood and authority in his execution of Jesus' will. In other words, the Spirit is the unique divine Executor with respect to the fulfillment of Jesus' mission today.*

The Spirit thus possesses an *executorial* divine authority—an *executorial authority* to act on behalf of Christ in the world while retaining the *divine authority* associated with his divine Personhood. As we shall see in the next chapter, this divine Executor has been given the authority to fulfill Jesus' mission in two crucial realms: (a) as divine Teacher who possesses "veracious authority" with respect to divine truth, and (b) as divine Governor who possesses "governing authority" within the Church.

4

The Authority of the Holy Spirit and Systematic Theology: Part 2

Exegetical and Theological Analysis: Two Realms of the Spirit's Executorial Authority

❋ IN CHAPTER THREE we examined the essential "nature" of the Spirit's authority—specifically, the Spirit possesses a "divine authority" grounded in his divine Personhood and an "executorial authority" to execute Christ's will. Now we will examine two "realms" wherein the Spirit displays this executorial authority with respect to the Church.

The Veracious Authority of the Spirit

In chapter two we discovered that Protestant theologians in essence defended the Spirit's "veracious authority" by arguing for the Spirit's rightful place in the *illumination of Scripture*. We also learned that Evangelical theologians, who debated "liberals" in the modern period, defended such an authority with respect to the *inspiration of Scripture*.

INTRODUCTION

The primary question at hand in this section is, "How should we define the nature of the Spirit/Scripture relationship?" The Spirit's place within the pattern of divine authority also requires us to investigate: "How does the Spirit display his '*executorial* divine authority' in the realm of *Truth*?"

Specifically, we need to ask, "How is this authority related to the Spirit's act of 'speaking' truth in and through written Scripture?" as well as "What sort of 'authority' does the Spirit possess in performing such an act?" I shall proceed by investigating two passages that both Henry and Barth viewed as crucial in the verification of truth, and that speak of the Spirit's authoritative role in the inspiration and illumination of Scripture—John 14:16–17, 26 and 2 Pet 1:20–21. In this section I shall thereby attempt to show that the Spirit's *veracious authority* is an extension of his *executorial authority*—that the Spirit "speaks" on behalf of Christ and "executes" the will of Christ through the inspiration and illumination of Scripture.

Exegesis of Passages

In chapter two we concluded that modern theology's debate has to the with the Holy Spirit's place in "the inspiration of Scripture." John 14:16–17, 26 perhaps deals more directly with this question than any other.

The Veracious Authority of the Spirit with Respect to the Inspiration of Scripture—John 14:16–17, 26

> 16 κἀγὼ ἐρωτήσω τὸν πατέρα καὶ ἄλλον παράκλητον δώσει ὑμῖν, ἵνα μεθ' ὑμῶν εἰς τὸν αἰῶνα ᾖ
>
> 16 And I will ask the Father, and He will give you another Helper, that He may be with you forever.

The context of this passage is provided in v. 15, where Jesus tells his disciples, "If you love Me, you will keep My commandments." Beasley-Murray holds that since "my commands" is interchanged with "my word" and "my words" in vv. 21, 23, 24, "'my commands' include the full range of the revelation from the Father, not simply ethical instructions."[1] Jesus is telling us that the one who loves him will live within the light of divine revelation in all respects.

Now, in John 14:16, Jesus begins to explain how the Spirit will bring the truth of revelation into all aspects of practical reality and morality. As in 16:7, the Spirit is given the title παράκλητον, which here has the sense of an "advocate" or "legal counselor" (rather than that of a prosecuting at-

1. Beasley-Murray, *John*, 256.

torney).² The conjunction ἄλλον ("another") is important in linking Jesus' ministry with the Spirit's—they are both παράκλητον, both advocates. The idea is that of a "tag team"—since Jesus is "going away" (John 16:7), this new παράκλητον will be "with you forever." Jesus will be as "present" in the Spirit as he was his incarnation. This "presence" will be especially noticed with respect to Jesus guidance and authority. How is it that the Spirit will authoritatively guide Jesus' disciples?

> 17 τὸ πνεῦμα τῆς ἀληθείας, ὃ ὁ κόσμος οὐ δύναται λαβεῖν, ὅτι οὐ θεωρεῖ αὐτὸ οὐδὲ γινώσκει· ὑμεῖς γινώσκετε αὐτό, ὅτι παρ' ὑμῖν μένει καὶ ἐν ὑμῖν ἔσται.
>
> 17 *that is* the Spirit of Truth, whom the world cannot receive, because it does not behold Him or know Him, but you know Him because He abides with you, and will be in you.

The identity of this "other" Paraclete is made clear in v. 17: he is "the Spirit of Truth." The three uses of this title in chapters 14–16 provide a capstone to John's sustained treatment of the Spirit in previous chapters (i.e. 1:32–33; 3:5–8; 4:23–24; 6:63; 7:37–39). The "executorial" aspect of this title is noted by Carson: "Coming so soon after 14:6, where Jesus claims to be the truth, 'the Spirit of Truth' may in part define the Paraclete as the Spirit who bears witness to the truth, i.e. to the truth that Jesus is."³

Breck outlines the Semitic and pagan background and the dualistic nature of "Spirit of Truth" in contrast to a "Spirit of Perversity."⁴ While Carson holds that such a dualistic force is not found in John, and Barrett believes it is irrelevant for this Gospel, Beasley-Murray rightly points out that the obvious correlation of such a Spirit-dualism with "Prince of Light" and "Angel of Darkness" in Qumran texts "seems to demand a personal dualism here."⁵ The contrast in this verse between Spirit of Truth and

---

2. It is interesting to consider the Holy Spirit's role as "advocate" who defends us (and as "Spirit of Truth" [v. 17] who helps us to know and speak truth) in contrast to the devil's role as "prosecuting attorney" (and as "Father of lies" [John 8:44] who attacks the Church with accusations and deceptions).

3. Carson, *The Gospel according to John*, 500.

4. See my engagement with Breck's *Spirit of Truth* in my subsequent discussion of Systematic Theology.

5. Carson, *The Gospel according to John*, 500; Barrett, *The Gospel of John*, 463; Beasley-Murray, *John*, 257.

ὁ κόσμος ("the world") provides an initial clue for such a dualism. This Spirit of Truth that "abides in you" is the Spirit "who bears witness to the truth *which is Jesus* (14:6)."[6] The Jesus who will reign with all authority (after his resurrection and ascension) is the Jesus who will send this Spirit of Truth to reign over the *revelation* of divine truth so that believers might "know Him [the Spirit]."

The phrase δύναται λαβεῖν, ὅτι οὐ θεωρεῖ αὐτὸ οὐδὲ γινώσκει approaches the very heart of the Spirit's veracious authority *in the world*. In John, λαβεῖν, θεωρεῖ, and γινώσκει are faith-related terms, requiring believers to humbly "receive" the truth of revelation and "behold" and "know" the Spirit of Truth. The verb λαβεῖν (aorist active infinitive of λαμβάνω) implies the results of receiving the "Spirit of Truth," namely, an active submission to the Spirit's truth and to the Spirit himself.[7] The verb γινώσκει connotes an intimate personal relationship with the Spirit. The Spirit's *veracious authority* is also exposed in the world's inability to receive such truth (since it is in essence "above" the world) or to know God through such a reception.

> 26 ὁ δὲ παράκλητος, τὸ πνεῦμα τὸ ἅγιον ὃ πέμψει ὁ πατὴρ ἐν τῷ ὀνόματί μου, ἐκεῖνος ὑμᾶς διδάξει πάντα καὶ ὑπομνήσει ὑμᾶς πάντα ἃ εἶπον ὑμῖν [ἐγώ].
>
> 26 But the Helper, the Holy Spirit, whom the Father will send in My name, He will teach you all things, and bring to your remembrance all that I said to you.

As we saw in the last section, "in my name" provides strong evidence that the Paraclete's mission is invested with Jesus' authority (John 15:26). Now, in 14:26, we learn that this authoritative mission involves διδάξει ("teaching") and ὑπομνήσει ("reminding"). These two complementary activities demonstrate the Spirit's continuation of Jesus' message and logically imply a future inscription of the disciples' "remembrance." The word ὑπομνήσει is only found here in the NT, but μιμνῄσκω is used in John 2:17, 22 and in 12:16 when the disciples remembered Jesus' pre-passion

---

6. Beasley-Murray, *John*, 257 (emphasis his).

7. This context seems to indicate the notion of receiving someone "up" or "into" (i.e., one's life), as in John 1:12, where the sense it: "receive someone in the sense of recognizing the other's authority" (Bauer, Λαμβάνω, 584).

teachings—immediately after Jesus' resurrection and after the coming of the Spirit, respectively. These incidents illustrate that the Spirit's "teaching" includes and yet goes beyond literally "reminding" the disciples of what Jesus said (in John 12:16 their remembrance includes additional "understanding"). "He not only enables them to *recall* these things but to precise their significance, and so he teaches the disciples to grasp the revelation of God brought by Jesus in its richness and profundity."[8] This "grasp" of revelation is then used by the Spirit to produce the entire NT. By assuring the disciples that the authority of his own truth will continue after his death and resurrection, Jesus recognizes the Spirit's veracious authority with respect to future revelation. The Spirit will even be granted the right to expand and explain Jesus' teachings within the *Sitze im Leben* of the various local Church and historical settings found in the NT epistles.

The Veracious Authority of the Spirit with Respect to the Illumination of Scripture—2 Peter 1:20–21

As we saw in chapter two, Protestant theology brought forth a critical debate regarding the Spirit's veracious authority with respect to the interpretation of Scripture—specifically, whether such an authority is ever fully delegated to a particular body of believers, or whether it is retained by the Spirit as the one who speaks in the Scriptures. Thus, while both Protestant and Catholic theologians refer to the Spirit as the one who aids in the human interpretation of Scripture, the question that divides them has to do with the sort of "interpretive authority" possessed by the Spirit. This question can be further investigated by exegeting 2 Pet 1:20–21.

> 20 τοῦτο πρῶτον γινώσκοντες ὅτι πᾶσα προφητεία γραφῆς ἰδίας ἐπιλύσεως οὐ γίνεται·
>
> 20 But know this first of all, that no prophecy of Scripture is [a matter] of one's own interpretation.

The OT background of this verse is very important. The word προφητεία ("prophecy") refers back to specific prophetic passages of the OT (emphasizing their authoritative proclamation), while γραφή

---

8. Beasley-Murray, *John*, 261.

("Scripture") denotes the OT Scripture as a whole (John 20:9; Acts 8:32).[9] The noun ἐπιλύσεως ("interpretation") is found only in this verse, though it occurs in verbal form in Mark 4:34 and Acts 19:39 ("explain" or "unravel a problem"). While several scholars have tried to find a meaning for ἐπιλύσεως (i.e., "revealment, "setting forth," "inspiration") other than "interpretation," Curran convincingly demonstrates that the semantic and metaphorical range of this word remains within the bounds of the "explanation" or "interpretation" of puzzling or mysterious statements (including omens, dreams, and visions).[10]

When ἐπιλύσεως is used in this passage with ἰδίας ("of its own"), we must ask whether this is referring to the prophet's (i.e., the original author's) *own* interpretation of the divine revelation or to a *private* interpretation of historic revelation (according to a Church or contemporary exegete). While the second view prevails today in most modern English translations (with the exception of the NIV), Bauckham concludes after a lengthy investigation that the evidence leans toward the idea that this verse rejects a charge by Peter's opponents that OT prophecy is only the prophet's own human interpretation of divine visions.[11] Kelly, however, argues (1)

---

9. Γραφη could refer simply to "writing," but its uniform NT usage is always in reference to Scripture (i.e., the Old Testament). See Guthrie, *The Pastoral Epistles*, 175. A debate ensues regarding whether this word means Scripture as a whole or separate passages within Scripture. Many translations and commentators (including AV, NAS, RSV, Moffat) hold that this must refer to "all Scripture" since the Apostle is clearly thinking of the OT in its entirety here, and since this is the sense in other Pauline writings (i.e., Gal 3:8; Rom 11:1). Kelly, though, translates it as "every Scripture" for (1) grammatical reasons (". . . there is no definite article in the Greek, and where pas is used with a noun in the singular without the article it usually means 'every' rather than 'whole' or 'all'" [Kelly, *A Commentary on the Pastoral Epistles*, 202]), and (2) lexical reasons: "Having spoken generally of the sacred writings, Paul may now be anxious to emphasize their usefulness in all the individual passages which make up the whole" (202–3). At any rate, whether the reference is to the whole body of Scripture or to the sum of its individual passages, it seems that the Scriptures are being referred to here as an entire unit.

10. Curran, "The Teaching of II Peter 1:20," 351–52.

11. Bauckham, *Jude, 2 Peter*, 229–34. Likewise, Green holds that both the grammar and sense of the passage seem to go not with the following passage but with the preceding one (vv. 16–19) where Peter is talking not about interpretation but authentication. It also seems to correspond with Peter's statements about false teachers (2:1; 3:16). The same God whom the apostles heard speak in the transfiguration spoke also through the prophets. The argument in vv. 10–21 is a consistent and indeed necessary conclusion to the preceding

that this would simply make verse 21 a repetition of verse 20 rather that a reason for it, and (2) that ἰδίας as a reference to the prophet's own interpretation seems grammatically awkward, since a prophet has not actually been mentioned.[12] Baukham admits to the possibility "that v. 20 rejects the opponents' charge that Old Testament prophecy is thoroughly ambiguous, so that anyone can interpret it any way he likes and no one can say which way is correct."[13]

> 21 οὐ γὰρ θελήματι ἀνθρώπου ἠνέχθη προφητεία ποτέ, ἀλλὰ ὑπὸ πνεύματος ἁγίου φερόμενοι ἐλάλησαν ἀπὸ θεοῦ ἄνθρωποι.
>
> 21 for no prophecy was ever made by an act of human will, but men moved by the Holy Spirit spoke from God.

Since a definitive conclusion to the above debate seems to be adrift, we must ask whether the issue makes a significant difference for our purposes here. Indeed it does not, because Peter's purpose for this passage is to demonstrate the true source of prophecy. Verse 21 reveals this source: literally, "not by the will of man was prophecy born at any time, but, being born by the Holy Spirit, men spoke from God." The last part of this phrase hinges on the word φερόμενοι (present, passive participle of φέρειν, lit. "to bear").[14] The apostle's use of this word in conjunction with "Holy Spirit" informs us that the prophets of Scripture were "being carried along/upheld/born by the Holy Spirit." This participle is actually a maritime metaphor, and this same word is used in Acts 27:15, 17 of a ship carried along by the

---

paragraph. Thus, we can rely on the apostolic account of the transfiguration because God spoke. And we can rely on Scripture because behind its human authors God spoke (Green, "2 Peter and Jude," 101). While Green's explanation does not seem to fit as well with the semantic range of ἐπιλύσεως, one is able to find support for his view in the OT, where false prophets are characterized as ones who "speak visions from their own minds, not from the mouth of the Lord" (Jer 23:16). In this case, Peter would be informing us that true prophecy came only from God (v. 21).

12. Kelly, *A Commentary on the Epistles of Peter and Jude*, 324.

13. Bauckham, *2 Peter, Jude*, 232. In such a case v. 21 would inform us that Scripture must have the meaning God intended because it is inspired by God. This also correlates well with v. 19a, "a more sure word of prophecy."

14. The usage here recalls the pagan Greek Θεοφορος ("born by a god"), and its usage with πνεύματος (the LXX πνευματοφορος) as found in Hos 9:7 and Zeph 3:4 to describe prophets (See Bauckham, *2 Peter, Jude*, 233).

wind. "The prophets raised their sail, so to speak (they were obedient and receptive), and the Holy Spirit filled them and carried their craft along in the direction he wished."¹⁵ In contrast, the word also appears in Eph 4:14 regarding those "carried by winds of false doctrine." In this passage, Peter's view of inspiration "is the nearest the New Testament approaches to the more typically Greek ideas of inspiration as a complete surrender of mind and will to the overpowering Spirit."¹⁶ This γὰρ ("for") clause clearly speaks of the Spirit's authority to inspire scripture, and becomes the basis for the truth of v. 20.

As a result, we can conclude that *the Spirit's inspiration must be seen as the sure basis for the Spirit's illumination.* Verse 21 tells us why scriptural prophecy cannot be interpreted by anyone other than God (neither the prophet nor the contemporary exegete)—because prophecy has a *divine origin.* Kelly concludes, "The inference that consequently a correct understanding of Scripture depends upon the aid of the Spirit is implicit but clear."¹⁷ The Spirit as Divine Interpreter displays veracious authority not only when inspiring the Scripture but also when providing contemporary illumination of that scriptural record.

Biblical Theology

Several other passages demonstrate that a progressive revelation of the Spirit's veracious authority can be discerned, including Job 32:8, 1 Cor 2:14–15 and 2 Tim 3:16, 17. Together, these Scriptures will help us develop within Scripture a rich conception of the "Spirit of Truth."

In Job 32:8 ("But it is a spirit in man, and the breath of the Almighty gives them understanding"), the נְשָׁמַת ("breath") of the Almighty is directly associated with the רוּחַ ("spirit") of man,¹⁸ allowing man to בִּין, ("understand") wisdom.¹⁹ This reflects the entire book of Job, where Wisdom

---

15. Green, *The Second General Epistle of Peter and the General Epistle of Jude*, 102.
16. Dunn, "Pneuma," 705.
17. Kelly, *A Commentary on the Epistles of Peter and Jude*, 325.
18. וְנִשְׁמַת is from נְשָׁמָה which usually means "breath," but here is usually translated "inspiration" (see KJV, NASB).
19. תְּבִינֵם is from the root בִּין (Qal pf.), which means "understand" or "understanding," and here takes the idea of perception, insight, or discernment.

is portrayed a divine gift, is personified as one who reveals herself to the just man, and appears as the principle of right order within the cosmos (e.g., 28:20–28). Through these metaphors the interrelationship between Spirit, Word, and Wisdom is vividly shown. In Job 33:3–14, for example, Elihu speaks words of wisdom which (according to the LXX) are "taught by the Spirit."[20] Breck asserts that this interrelationship provides an initial foundation for a NT understanding of "Spirit of Truth." The Spirit is also portrayed in Job 4:12, 15 and 26:3 åas the teacher of truth and director of the human development of "understanding." Since Job's personification was so strongly evidenced in intertestamental literature (i.e., the Wisdom of Solomon), Breck concludes that the Spirit "was projected into Israel's future as an eschatological figure."[21] In that literature it becomes clear that Job's portrayal, and the ethical dualism inherent in his metaphor, demonstrate the fact that "the functions of the Spirit of Wisdom presage those of the Spirit of Truth.[22] Breck concludes,

> In the Hebrew Wisdom writings . . . the Holy Spirit as sanctifier and revealer of Truth re-emerged as the most adequate theological expression of God's loving and saving presence among humankind. Although Jesus is depicted as Wisdom in the Gospel of Matthew and other New Testament writings, He is chiefly characterized as the incarnation of Spirit and Word, the revealer and embodiment of divine Truth.[23]

In Paul's writings this Spirit of Truth motif is worked out in the context of the Trinity and in the Church. In 1 Cor 2:1–8 we find the association once again between Spirit, Word, and Wisdom, but this time in the context of the knowledge of Christ (see 2:2, 16). This passage confirms that the Spirit's veracious authority is both ministerial and executorial—he ministers the truth of Jesus Christ, not just truth in general terms or truth independent from Christ. We should not miss the crucial connection drawn in this passage between the Spirit's revelatory *transcendence* and

---

20. Job 32:8 also seems to express a certain Hebrew dualism, which "is rooted, however, in the ancient near-eastern traditions that identify the human life-principle with the divine breath or spirit" (Breck, *Spirit of Truth*, 85).

21. Breck, *Spirit of Truth*, 86.

22. Ibid., 90.

23. Ibid., 93.

his revelatory *agency*, a connection that confers *authoritative agency* to the Spirit with respect to revelation.

In chapter 3 we discovered that 1 Cor 2:10–13 creates an intimate association between the Spirit's divine authority and his role in revelation. Verses 14–15, however, continue this Spirit of Truth theme by comparing ψυχικὸς ἄνθρωπος ("natural man") with πνευματικὸς ("the spiritual man"). The things of God are μωρία ("foolish") to the "natural man" and thus rejected. "To see [the cross] as foolishness means to stand over against God and his ways—and to stand *under his judgment* as without his Spirit and therefore apart from 'what he has freely given us.'"[24] Also, without the Spirit he lacks the ability to discern. Pearson states that "Paul rejects Philo's view that man has within him—breathed into him by God—the capacity for knowing God and the higher truths of the universe. The wisdom of God comes only through the Holy Spirit."[25] In sum, the Spirit's revelation is primarily that of spiritual *truth*, a truth that displays the Spirit's veracious authority.

As for the Spirit of Truth in the Church, 2 Tim 3:16–17 speaks of Scripture's "profitability" in the Church for teaching, reproof, correction, and training in righteousness. This profitability, however, is *based on* Scripture's pneumatological character—"every Scripture is θεόπνευστος," literally "breathed into by God."[26] Grudem, in assessing πνεο ("breathe out"), concludes that, for the OT, "this breathing must be understood as a metaphor for speaking,"[27] This passage thus reveals the intimate association between the authority of the Spirit and the authority of Scripture. Since the Spirit's "speaking" produces *profitable* Scripture,[28] the Spirit must retain

---

24. Fee, *God's Empowering Presence*, 106 (emphasis mine).

25. Pearson, "The Pneumatikos-Psychikos Terminology in 1 Corinthians," 39.

26. This is the rendering in pre-Christian Greek literature (reflecting the first century Hebrew view of inspiration) (cf. Josephus, C. Ap. I. 37ff.; Philo, Spec. leg. I. 65; iv. 49). Also, θεόπνευστος can be understood here predicatively ("every Scripture [is] inspired by God and profitable . . ."), or adjectivally ("every God-inspired Scripture is also profitable . . ."). The predicative construction is preferred since the same two adjectives are also used predicatively by Paul in 1Tim 4:4, and since this seems to be the natural reading here in the absence of a verb.

27. Grudem, "Scripture's Self-Attestation," 39.

28. "Timothy is not therefore being informed of the inspiration of Scripture, for this was a doctrine commonly admitted by Jews, but he is being reminded that the basis of its profitableness lies in its inspired character" (Guthrie, "The Pastoral Epistles," 176).

an authority *over* Scripture even after it is written—thus giving the Spirit privileged authority to *use* these Scriptures in the act and process of divine illumination.

Systematic Theology

Now I shall attempt to develop a systematic understanding of the Spirit's veracious authority—first examining the Spirit's authority with respect to the inspiration of Scripture, and then with respect to the illumination of Scripture.

Veracious Authority of the Spirit and the Inspiration of Scripture

In building a "formal description" of the Spirit's veracious authority, I shall first investigate Welker's pneumatology with respect to the "inspiration" of Scripture and respond to Welker with my exegetical findings.

Welker's "Pluralism of the Spirit"

As seen in chapter two, Welker understands postmodern ecclesiology primarily in terms of the Spirit's revelation of God's power in the formation of pluralistic communities. Welker's model sees inspiration as a function of the emerging cooperative efforts of those in multi-faceted, "pluralistic" partnership. This partnership develops within the context of the "outpouring of the Spirit" (as described in Joel's vision and experienced at Pentecost).

> Within a partnership that is both multi-faceted and appropriately named "pluralistic," and within emerging cooperative efforts, people impacted by the outpouring of the Spirit open up reality and the future for one another. Within this polycentric diversity the fullness of the presence of God becomes experientially present as it is manifest by the Spirit. Whether people are distinguished and divided by language, race, gender, age, and social status, this pouring out "from heaven" signifies that these people—dismantling unjust differences and cultivating natural, creative differences—establish with one another and for one another a fully representative intimacy with God's will. Mediated through this intimacy, they establish a fully

representative intimacy in and with the world, one that they are not able to attain in their natural-finite perspectives.[29]

Such partnership, which involves intimacy with both God and the world, provides the context for the plurality of testimonies that we find in the Bible. These testimonies reflect the fullness of God's presence. Welker adds that "upon this acknowledged basis it does not appear only to be correct and sensible, but also objectively necessary to say that *Scripture is inspired*."[30] How exactly does this inspiration occur?

> It is the Spirit who produces through the text a charged field of experiences. . . . Certainly in many cases (these experiences) are conflicting and sometimes they are simply not compatible with one another. But this is not a weakness of the Scripture, as a narrow-sighted rationality might think. It is rather a unique strength. Because in this way *the biblical texts become clearly subordinated to the reality to which they refer and to which they testify*.[31]

Welker also presents a concern over a reductionistic view of Scripture, particularly to any theory of inspiration that attempts to locate the authority of Scripture autonomously in itself or even in the human writer. Such views neglect the Spirit who utilizes Scripture in the spiritual liberation of persons within Christian communities. One reviewer thinks Welker constructs his doctrine of inspiration "from the 'bottom up' data of creaturely experience of the Spirit" in that "the Spirit is attuned and sensitive to difference, creatively woven by natural and spirited processes into a rich and complex unity."[32]

Welker's postmodern solution to "the problem of the inspiration of Scripture" reflects his "realistic theology" proposed earlier in the book. The Holy Spirit works in and through reality by allowing the biblical testimo-

---

29. Welker, *Gottes Geist*, 255 (author's translation from the German text).

30. Ibid., 255 (author's translation from the German text). Welker thereby understands the authors of Scripture to be inspired but not necessarily the words. The idea that the Holy Spirit "dictated every word" is a model "exemplary of the Protestant scholasticism of the 16th and 17th centuries" (253; author's translation from the German text). This model "produces a simplistic and reductionistic conception of the Spirit and of inspiration" (254; author's translation from the German text).

31. Welker, *Gottes Geist*, 256 (italics his; author's translation from the German text).

32. Larson, review of *God the Spirit*, 70.

The Authority of the Holy Spirit and Systematic Theology: Part 2

nies—concrete, partial, fragmentary, and even conflicting testimonies—to point to the presence and reality of God. Thus, Scripture seems to be the biblical writer's testimony that emerges from the community's experience with the Spirit. This is emphasized in Welker's use of *Spannungsfeld* ("charged field"), which is an extension of his previously and frequently used term *Kraftfeld* ("force field"). This latter term appears to be a metaphor borrowed from the physics of magnetism.

Response

The question that must be raised is whether the above terms serve well in developing a "realistic" theology, let alone a biblical one. Does Welker's theology reflect a biblical notion of the Spirit's "personhood" and specifically of the "Spirit of Truth?"

First, while the Spirit's subordination to Christ is affirmed, Welker does not make any effort to show the implications of such a subordination, leaving the Spirit essentially stripped of his *executorial* authority to reveal the truth of Christ.[33] Welker's exclusive reliance on a social Trinity indeed leaves the reader thinking that the Spirit may act on his own authority. Since, as seen in chapter three, the Holy Spirit is Christ's public domain of resonance within the world, the unity of Christ and the Spirit is socially-constructed within the world. Welker understands the Holy Spirit to be "a unity of perspectives on Jesus Christ," one we actually help to constitute. Such a view clearly slashes at the notion of the Spirit's divine Personhood. According to Dallavalle, "one might ask how Welker allows for the tran-

---

33. Welker argues that the NT evidence goes beyond a simple "representational model" of the Holy Spirit as the Spirit of Christ (e.g., Romans 8), as the One who simply glorifies Christ and declares His truth (John 16:13–14). Such a reductionistic model understands a person to be a "center of action," and this understanding must now be supplemented by one that incorporates a "domain of resonance" within which such a center of action becomes a person. This means that personhood is formed only within a structured, diverse web of relationships. Welker says, "An individual center of action, even when it self-referentially governed and develops a self-consciousness, does not yet form a person. Only through a structured social environment and in exchange with that environment does an individual, self-conscious center of action become a person. One can go so far as to say that what turns a self-relating center of personal authority into an actual person is the unity of that structured social sphere" (Welker, "Der Heilege Geist," 139 (author's translation from German text). Welker holds that the Spirit is actually Christ's *Resonanzbereich* ("domain of resonance")(140).

scendence of this very public and concrete Spirit, particularly in his assertion that the Spirit brings the gift of the 'clear knowledge of God.'"[34]

Second, Welker's doctrine of inspiration seems to be verbally affirmed and yet subtly reinvented. The "Spirit of Truth" as presented in John 14–16 should be our main source for evaluating contemporary perspectives on "inspiration." These chapters inform theology of the correct association of Spirit and Scripture, thus reflecting the pattern of divine authority. This pattern is fulfilled in the Spirit's ministry as he "aids in the determination of truth" (i.e., expresses veracious authority). The Spirit's veracious authority, as we have seen, is a matter of "executing" (inspiring, illuminating) the truth of Jesus Christ, the Word of God. Jesus, who is "the truth" (John 14:6) and who pleads with the Father to "sanctify them (his disciples) in the truth" (John 17:17), sends the Spirit of Truth to "guide you into all truth" (John 16:13). While this "sending" of the Spirit is a vital aspect of the Spirit's executorial authority, it also provides a foundation for the development of a theology of the Spirit's veracious authority in that the Spirit now "stands between" the Word of God incarnate and the Word of God written. The Spirit himself authoritatively deposits Jesus' truth in the text by *speaking* in that text. Rather than opting for a communally-based understanding of inspiration, this doctrine must begin with the Spirit of Truth, who retains divine, revelatory authority in the act of inspiration and who acts with executorial authority by interpreting Jesus' past teachings so as to bring forth a "fuller" explication in association with the Spirit's outpouring. As Ramm has discerned, our pattern of authority requires that we first ensure that vital connection is kept between Christ and Spirit when developing a biblical understanding of the inspiration of Scripture. Oden reminds us that,

> The Spirit does not speak independently of the triune God as if functioning as an autonomous authority, but always speaks and recalls so as to enable the mission of the Son—the reconciliation of humanity with the Father.[35]

The "Spirit of Truth" thereby "inscribes" divine truth (i.e., the Father's truth as interpreted by the Son) in the form of the biblical text, thus pro-

---

34. Dallavalle, review of *God the Spirit*, 796.
35. Oden, *Life in the Spirit*, 53

viding authority to the text. When Paul tells Timothy that "all Scripture is God-breathed" (2 Tim 3:16), we understand that Scripture is breathed out by God as the product of His Word or speech. Welker's problem is that he seems to have replaced the Spirit's authority as a distinct Person and as "Spirit of Truth" with the Spirit's work in the community of believers. "Truth" is no longer linked with the Spirit as *speaker* but to the Spirit as he is *heard*. If the inspiration of Scripture by the Spirit is simply a product of the human authors or a by-product of the experiences of the Spirit within the community, the Spirit ultimately loses His authority in speaking for God.[36]

Further Discussion and Formal Description

Further background regarding the concept of "Spirit of Truth" is provided by Breck, who explains how the Spirit's ministry of "remembering" and "teaching" (John 14:26) becomes critical for "completing" Jesus' revelation in the early Church.

> In these early apostolic writings, fulfillment of the promise of an eschatological outpouring of the Spirit occurs after Jesus' glorification, when the Spirit of Truth comes to dwell within the believing community and incorporates to its members full knowledge and understanding of Jesus' teachings.[37]

It follows that a veracious authority of "Spirit of Truth" is an extension of the Spirit's executorial authority.

> This text [John 14:26] focuses on how valuable the Spirit-energized Scriptures are. The Church, in short, came to confess the inspiration of Scripture because they experienced through these writings the power and truth of the Spirit of God. These documents were, they knew, "animated with the Spirit of Christ."[38]

---

36. See Oden, *Life in the Spirit*, 67–69. Oden explains the "theandric analogy," which views Scripture as truly human, analogous to the humanity of Christ, in that it is "fleshed out" in human language and human lives within historical settings. Such a functional view of Scripture surfaces in Welker's approach. According to Oden, classical exegetes were cautious with such an analogy. More often, they viewed the Spirit as the author of Scripture, with the personality of the writers becoming fittingly adapted instruments of the divine address.

37. Breck, *Spirit of Truth*, 163.

38. Grenz, *Revisioning Evangelical Theology*, 120–21.

The Lord Is the Spirit

Breck reveals that the Johannine understanding of "Spirit of Truth" has its roots in several sources, most notably the Hebrew prophets and the Qumran Community. The pre-exilic prophets present the Spirit as the imparter of two kinds of knowledge: cultic knowledge with its consequent legal demands, and moral knowledge as expressed by the term אֱמֶת. This word denotes "truth" of an ethical character, is central to the sort of moral knowledge acquired by hearing (and *heeding*) the Word of God, and is the essential message uttered by the Spirit though the mouth of the prophet. Such a "Spirit of Truth" is revealed through the lips of David in Ps 51:6.

> Like divine Wisdom, אֱמֶת evokes on the part of the human spirit a response to God's revelation (cf. Isa. 29:24). To possess such knowledge is to renounce the "spirit of harlotry" and to walk in the ways of the Lord (Hosea 14:9). "Knowledge," therefore, is fundamentally an ethical rather than an intellectual category. It is obtained by the discernment of the human spirit, which responds in faithful obedience to the Lord as He reveals Himself through Spirit-inspired prophetic utterance.[39]

Such "truth" therefore entails obedience to authority. The Qumran tradition, however, is even more revealing with regard to the Spirit's authority. 1QS 3:8—4:26 outlines the Qumran teaching on the "two Spirits" as a critical section in the "Rule of the Community." This passage speaks of the initiatory rite for entering the Covenant, along with regulations for purification through required rituals and inner repentance. This purification, however, is only accomplished through the sanctifying action of the Spirit (3:8–9). According to Breck, this early understanding of the Spirit of Truth "forms the thematic center of the penitential Psalm 50/51:10–12."[40] The Qumran passage ends with the description of a spirit-dualism that is quite similar to the rabbinic teaching on the two "inclinations" (*yezer*) that inhabit unequal portions of the hearts of men (4:15-26).

It is the middle section (3:17b–21a), however, that most overtly depicts the Spirit in terms of authority.

---

39. Breck, *The Spirit of Truth*, 21.
40. Ibid., 127. 1QS 4:20–21, for example, reads, "He will cleanse him of all wicked deeds with the Spirit of Holiness; like purifying waters He will shed [sprinkle] upon him the Spirit of Truth to cleanse him of all abomination and falsehood."

> He has created man to govern the world, and has allotted unto man two Spirits that he should walk in them until the time of His visitation: they are the Spirits of Truth and Perversity.... Dominion over all the sons of righteousness is in the hand of the Prince of Light [= the Spirit of Truth]; they walk in the ways of light. All dominion over the sons of perversity is in the hand of the Angel of Darkness [= the Spirit of Perversity]; they walk in the ways of darkness.

What we discover in this passage is the Qumran mindset that runs throughout their theology: The Spirit of Truth and the Spirit of Perversity each have a dominion over separate classes of men,[41] thus resulting in two radically distinctive "revelations." While Breck's weakness is his de-emphasis on the relationship between the Spirit's revelation and the Lordship of Christ, his view of the Spirit as the one who reigns over God's people in truth helps us understand biblical revelation in a new light. Those who receive the Spirit's truth within this revelation are places *under* the Spirit's authority in doing so. As mentioned earlier, Qumran strongly influenced Johannine theology, as reflected in John's "Spirit of Truth" emphasis (John 14–16), and in his continuous "dualism" between light and darkness. Paul picked up such a dualism in Romans, particularly in Rom 8:2–17 (see exegesis of Rom 8:2 in next section).

This sets in motion a theory of inspiration that places the authority of Scripture "under" the authority of the Spirit. Grenz calls for a non-foundational "revisioning" of the Spirit/Scripture relationship where the two are neither torn asunder nor collapsed together. According to Grenz, the theological methodology of Protestant systematic theology has tended to separate bibliology from pneumatology. "Consequently, the reestablishment of the integral link between Spirit and Scripture must begin methodologically through the reorientation of the doctrine of Scripture under

---

41. Breck demonstrates the strong influence of Iranian/Zoroastrian thought in shaping this Jewish Spirit-dualism (i.e. as well as many other Jewish themes, such as their apocalyptic speculation). Whereas Greek thought tended to subsume ethics under cosmology, Iranian dualistic religion introduced to the Qumran community the songs and Zoroastrian teachings of Zarathustra, which is essentially ethical. Such teaching presents both Holy and Evil Spirits, which divide mankind into two opposing camps Iranian dualism contrasts those under the dominion of the Holy Spirit, who walk according to the Truth and manifest righteousness, with those under the evil Spirit, who are followers of the Lie and practice unrighteousness" (Breck, *The Spirit of Truth*, 113).

the doctrine of the Holy Spirit."[42] Grenz rightly calls for a return to the paradigm of the ancient Church, which, grounded in the Apostles' Creed, employed a simple trinitarian structure for their theology. Thus bibliology was placed under the broader discussion of pneumatology, ensuring that the Bible was the "book of the Spirit." Such a model provides a needed correction to the classical Reformed approach.

> Many Reformed theologians treat bibliology as the central dimension of the discussion of revelation that is placed as prolegomenon to the development of systematic theology. . . . Transformed in this manner into a book of doctrine, the Bible is easily robbed of its dynamic character. Separating the doctrine of Scripture from its natural embedding in the doctrine of the Holy Spirit conceptually separates Scripture from the Spirit, whose vehicle of operation it is.[43]

Vanhoozer takes such a re-structuring even further. He has distilled J. L. Austin's contributions to linguistics in a way that seems to "open up" the Spirit's revelatory action.[44] For Austin, a speaker's "illocutionary act" (or "force") is that which the speaker accomplishes in saying something (i.e., promising, commanding). Using Austin's theory, Vanhoozer delineates the contributions of the author, presenting four factors that comprise the semantics of biblical literature: proposition (what the statement is about), purpose (the intent of the author), presence (the incarnation of the author in a literary form) and power (the "illocution" that depends upon proposition, purpose, and presence).[45] It is the "presence" of the author—specifically the author's *voice*—that provides authority to a statement. Vanhoozer also points to the "multi-faceted" authority of Scripture (in the forms of assertives, directives, etc.) that together demonstrate the Spirit's authority to speak "truth" in and through an astounding array of canonical/linguistic vehicles of the Scriptures (i.e., narratives, propositions, poetry, prophecy, etc.).[46] These ideas help us to conceive of the Spirit's

---

42. Grenz, *Revisioning Evangelical Theology*, 114.
43. Ibid., 114–15.
44. Vanhoozer, "The Semantics of Biblical Literature," 86–103.
45. Ibid., 91–92.
46. Ibid., 92.

authority as something present *within* the text—in both its inspiration and illumination.

Veracious Authority of the Spirit with Respect to the Illumination of Scripture

In building a "formal description" of the Spirit's veracious authority, I shall also investigate Badcock's "spirituality" with respect to the "illumination" of Scripture and respond to Badcock with my exegetical findings.

Badcock's "Spirituality"

As seen in chapter two, Badcock's primary concern is with the Spirit's work and with the Spirit's role in the spiritual life. Due to the deficiencies of Western pneumatology (i.e., its lack of integration of the Spirit's work into theological thought), "life itself is robbed of theological depth."[47] Such "shallowness" has particularly occurred in Protestantism.

> In the Protestant tradition, where the Spirit tends to be seen as an adjunct of the Word, there is a degenerate tendency to restrict the work of the Spirit to the gift of faith in the Word. . . . What is especially lacking here is an awareness of the Spirit's presence, not merely in the sacraments and the fellowship of the Church, and where love is found, but also in darkness and doubt, and in the difficult carrying of the cross.[48]

Badcock also sides with Moltmann's argument for a view of the Spirit as the principle of vitality in creation so that, with Moltmann, we might "remain open to the wind of the Spirit, where it is found."[49] In his concluding chapter he asserts that "the real theme of the doctrine of the Holy Spirit is that of human life and glory in relation to God," and then seeks to reestablish pneumatology on the grounds of its *humanizing* effects (rather than in terms of "moral inwardness").

---

47. Badcock, *Light of Truth and Fire of Love*, 4–5.
48. Ibid.
49. Ibid., 131.

Response

While Badcock makes other excellent critiques as well, he may run into troubled waters when his desire for a renewed mysticism seems to lead to a bifurcation of spirituality and rationality. For example, in challenging the notion of the doctrine of the *pneumatology,* Badcock wants to disassociate *logos* and *pneuma* (as he does later, subtly, with Christ and Spirit). "Can one speak rightly of a *logos* of *pneuma,* or might we perhaps better speak in our theology of the Spirit in terms of love, and so, for example, of a love of the Spirit, a *pneumatophilia.*"[50]

Though Badcock proclaims, "the question of discernment is always central in all claims to experience of the Spirit," he does not venture into the nature or source of such discernment, particularly with respect to his emerging "mysticism." While Badcock is somewhat successful in his attempt to reestablish pneumatology on the grounds of its *humanizing* effects, this approach not only neglects any mention of the illumination of Scripture in the "humanizing" process, but also ignores the parameters and authority invoked by the "Spirit of Truth," that is, the Spirit's veracious authority to speak through the Word in association with spiritual experience.[51] The Spirit's veracious authority is conspicuous by its absence, in that his pneumatology is not "grounded" in the Spirit/Scripture relationship. Indeed, while Badcock is listening closely to the theological pulse of our day, there is little evidence that Badcock has "listened" to the illuminating Spirit in providing his own points. According to one reviewer, "The author feels the freedom to rest his theological case in rather selectively broad theological principles. Badcock surely conceives the theological task too abstractly."[52]

---

50. Ibid., 5.

51. Badcock holds that, for the Reformers, "pneumatology is subordinate to the Word of God" (Badcock, *Light of Truth and Fire of Love,* 94). While this is somewhat accurate, it only led to a deficient pneumatology in Reformed theology. Badcock seems to misrepresent the Reformers, who at least in part honored the Spirit's veracious authority: "Although the Reformers wish to distance themselves from the idea that the Holy Spirit's authority is mediated through the leaders in the Church, rather than through the Word of God as contained in Holy Scripture, they are not entirely successful in their claims" (94).

52. Williams, "Pneumatologies Have Consequences," 36.

The Authority of the Holy Spirit and Systematic Theology: Part 2

Further Discussion and Formal Description

As seen in chapter two, the doctrine of the Spirit's "illumination" was popularized by John Calvin. Calvin distinguished illumination from pure biblical "knowledge," which is an essential but not central element of faith. In his commentary on 1 Cor 2:15 he asks:

> Did [Christ] not descend to earth in order to manifest the will of the Father? And did he not faithfully fulfill that mission? He did. But his preaching accomplishes nothing unless the Spirit, the inner teacher, opens up the way to the mind. [53]

As Dowey points out in his commentary on Calvin, "Knowledge never becomes a criterion by which the faithful can be distinguished from the unfaithful, because God has enlightened some of the reprobate with true knowledge of the gospel to deepen their inexcusability" (and cites Saul and Judas as prime examples).[54] Illumination, however, is a special activity of the Spirit that enables the darkened mind to comprehend objective knowledge clearly communicated by God. Calvin grants the Spirit a certain "axiological" (or moral) authority to illuminate the truth of Scripture in the mind and heart of the believer.

> Therefore, none come to him but those who have heard and learned from the Father. And what is the nature of this hearing and learning? It is when the Spirit by a wonderful and special power forms the ears to hear and the mind to understand. We must understand therefore that no one can enter the kingdom of God except he whose mind has been renewed by the illumination of the Holy Spirit.[55]

As we saw in chapter 2, the Reformers sought to correct Rome's dogma of Church tradition as the guarantor of correct scriptural interpretation. For the Reformers, the Spirit's assistance in the correct interpretation of Scripture was a central aspect of *sola scriptura*. Both Luther and Calvin placed the Spirit over Scripture—Luther emphasizing the Spirit's work *through* the Word in preaching, the sacraments, and salvation; Calvin, the Spirit's inspiration and subjective illumination. The Quakers of the seventeenth century

---

53. Calvin, *Institutes* III.ii.20; Calvin, *Commentary on 1 Corinthians 2:15*, XLIX:344c.
54. Dowey, Jr., *The Knowledge of God in Calvin's Theology*, 172.
55. Calvin, *Institutes* III.ii.20; Calvin, *Commentary on 1 Corinthians 2:15*, XLIX:344c.

began to distort this delicate Spirit/Word formulation by making the subjective *experience* of the Spirit (over against Scripture) the primary source of knowledge for faith and practice. Seventeenth century "enlightenment," on the other hand, promoted the use of *reason* in interpretation. While eighteenth century Methodism expressed a more balanced approach, the Pietism of the nineteenth century bifurcated the Spirit and Word again by elevating personal sanctification (in the Spirit) over "secular" activities. In the twentieth century this division only increased as Pentecostals separated "the baptism of the Holy Spirit" from the initial reception of the Word of the Gospel, and as "biblicists" stripped Spirit-baptism of its experiential component and elevated "scientific" interpretative methods over the Spirit's illumination. Thus, Protestant circles have also experienced serious confusion regarding the Spirit's authority in relation to Scripture.

While most of the above traditions remain fully alive today, the variable landscape had led postmodernity to a certain skepticism regarding the authority of "tradition." This may inadvertently be helping the Church to re-emphasize the *Spirit's* authority to illuminate Scripture. Such an authority must now be seen in terms of revealing the Father (through the Son) *inwardly* but not completely *subjectively*. This epistemological distinction is pointed out by contrasting θειότης (in Rom 1:20 refers to the "deity" that can only be known visibly, particularly through nature) with θεότητος (in Col 2:9 means "divinity" or "Godhead"). This latter concept specifies the fullness of the trinitarian God who dwells in Christ and can be known personally, concretely, and revelationally in him. Our pattern of divine authority tells us that truth is ontologically grounded in God the Father but now focused on Jesus, who reveals the truth by providing incarnational interpretation of the Father's truth (John 14:16, 17, 26). Jesus' truth is then recorded in the Scriptures. Only the Spirit, however, can provide contemporary interpretation of this truth *to me*. This basic pattern of divine authority with respect to revelation is sometimes unrecognized in classical evangelicalism. The Spirit has been given a *veracious authority* to reveal God's truth *by the Father* (being "sent" by the Father), and yet the Spirit performs this revelation in and through the authority *of Jesus* (coming "in my name"). The Spirit of Truth is not the ultimate source of truth; instead, he is the executor of the truth, "opening up" God's truth so that it can be *known* by believers and have authority *in and over believers*.

As a result, we can say that, without the Spirit's execution and contemporary interpretation of this truth, there can be no true authority in the world. However, this leads us to questions regarding epistemology—how we can actually *recognize* divine authority in this world. This is addressed by Jesus' word "abides" (John 14:17). The abiding Spirit prevents a humanistic, rationalistic understanding of truth. The Spirit of Truth is never to be reduced to a dead letter, but must always remain centrally focused as the revealer and interpreter of the *living God*, that is, the person of the Father through the Son. The Spirit thus retains a revelatory *purpose* in his inspiration and illumination of the written word of God. It must be admitted that many evangelicals have missed this central purpose of the Spirit in settling for a "dead letter." As the Spirit "speaks" again through the Scriptures into the contemporary church, he shapes the community by providing wisdom, moral guidance, doctrine, et cetera. The Spirit authoritatively leads God's people in the present by illuminating and applying these God-inspired, authoritative speech acts with respect to their present context.

In conclusion, the Spirit of Truth (1) displays veracious authority as a central realm of his executorial authority (the realm of truth), (2) executes this authority by inspiring "speech acts" in the form of written revelation, by illuminating this revelation, and by appropriating its truth in application, and (3) is to be honored as the divine Teacher who provides תְּבִינֵם ("understanding," Job 32:8) in terms of wisdom and guidance.

Thus, the "Spirit of Truth" has not only been given an executorial authority to execute Christ's will and speak on Christ's behalf but also a veracious authority to inspire and illuminate Scripture. We have also begun to discover a biblical framework for understanding the Spirit's role in establishing the kingdom of God in the world, a framework to be filled out in the next section.

The Governing Authority of the Spirit

In chapter two (the section entitled "Postmodern and Contemporary Theology") we surveyed several theologians who share a common concern for attempting to understand the Spirit's relationship to the Church. Now we shall use Scriptures and theology in search of a model that will address some of the most serious questions and issues facing contemporary churches.

The Lord Is the Spirit

Introduction

Whereas contemporary postmodern theologians generally seek to illuminate the Spirit's *power* or *function* in the Church, we also observed that some evangelical "postmodern" theologians seem to grant the Spirit a certain "governing authority" with respect to the Church. Since we have determined that the Spirit's authority as Christ's Executor (an "*executorial* divine authority") incorporates a veracious authority as "Spirit of Truth," we can now seek to discern how all these aspects of the Spirit's authority are activated with respect to the Church. The question at hand is therefore, "How should we understand the Spirit's authority with respect to God's work in creating and governing the Church?" With this question we seek to understand the *administration* and *execution* of the rule of Christ through the Spirit in the Church.[56]

The following passages demonstrate that the Spirit establishes and governs the Church by defining and creating a christological/veracious/eschatological/person-oriented *realm of authority* (with respect to God's people) in our present time and space. This realm represents the authority of the messianic, eschatological kingdom coming to us in the Church through the "Spirit of Restoration."[57] The idea is that of the "blueprint" of the future kingdom now impeding on the present through the Spirit. The Spirit's realm (1) demonstrates the governing authority of the Spirit in terms of specific eschatological *qualities* within our immediate Church reality, and (2) comes to bear with respect to people through specific, powerful *effects* that allow God's people to actually participate in the Spirit's governing activity through specific church "practices."

The Spirit's realm of governing authority must therefore be investigated on these two interrelated "levels" of effective government.[58] The

---

56. The notion of "governing authority," for our purposes, will be discussed not so much in terms of rulership but administration. Christ will be considered ruler or King while the Spirit serves as his governor or administrator.

57. Oswalt observes that this restoration theme in the OT points to the Spirit's government, one that "results in righteous lives and just dealings" (Oswalt, *The Book of Isaiah*, 587). See Isa 32:15–16 below. The Hebrew concept of "shalom" embodies such an eschatological vision.

58. The interrelationship between these two "levels" of investigation can be seen in the fact that each passage (while speaking primarily to one particular aspect of the Spirit's governing authority), indeed addresses both levels.

first ("general") level describes the *nature* of this eschatological, immediate "realm" of authority in the Church. Crucial passages to be examined include Isa 11:2 and 32:15–16 (which describe specific *restorative qualities* possessed by the messianic King and in turn by the Spirit) and Acts 1:5–8 (which demonstrates the *immediate presence* of this eschatological Spirit in the present Church age).[59]

The second ("specific") level of discussion—inseparable from the first—has to do with the immediate "effects" of the Spirit, demonstrated within the Spirit's realm, through which the Spirit establishes and governs the Church. These effects are presented in Isa 59:21 (which demonstrates the *democratization* of God's Spirit amongst God's people), Rom 8:2 (which delineates the *liberation* of God's people), and 2 Cor 3:17–18 (which reveals the Spirit's Lordship in the *transformation* of God's people into the image of Christ).

Exegesis of Passages—The Nature (Qualities and Presence) of the Spirit's Governing Authority in the Church

The Spirit's "realm" of authority creates an eschatological "structure" for the Church. This structure can be discerned by examining its qualities and its "presence" in the creation of the Church.

The Eschatological Qualities of the Spirit in the Church—Exegesis of Isaiah 11:2

Isaiah presents a pneumatological framework where the Spirit's executorial authority can be initially understood in terms of eschatological qualities. In making direct references to the Messianic Spirit, Isaiah grants the Spirit specific governing qualities. While Isaiah thought of Israel's future salvation in terms of a Messianic King who would sit on the throne of David, he

---

59. Basil used the Isaiah passages in his defense of the Spirit's divinity, and by Moltmann in his explication of the Spirit's role in the kingdom of God. Welker uses Acts 1 to demonstrate the Spirit's "action of liberation and of overcoming the world" (Welker, *God the Spirit*, 228–39).

introduces the Spirit as the instigator of the Messiah's benevolent rulership. Such an eschatological hope becomes the theme of Isaiah 11.[60]

Isaiah depicts the King as Yahweh's "servant," his official representative authorized to carry out divine rule upon earth, and the Spirit as God's power that will rest on this servant, allowing him to carry out his future ministry. Isaiah 42:1–9, for example, is a "servant song" that particularly relates Yahweh's servant to the Spirit. In Isa 11:2, the Spirit of Yahweh is the one who provides ruling qualities to the Messiah.

וְנָחָה עָלָיו רוּחַ יְהוָה רוּחַ חָכְמָה וּבִינָה רוּחַ עֵצָה וּגְבוּרָה רוּחַ דַּעַת וְיִרְאַת יהוה

The Spirit of the LORD will rest on Him, The Spirit of wisdom and understanding, The Spirit of counsel and strength, The Spirit of knowledge and the fear of the LORD.

First, the Spirit וְנָחָה ("will rest" or "will settle down and remain") on this Messiah.[61] This is an allusion to divine anointing. The initial fulfillment of this prophecy is seen in Matt 3:16 when the Spirit comes to rest on Jesus in the form of a dove, anointing him for his ministry.

Isaiah 11:2 portrays a *messianic* Spirit: of judgment, rulership, justice, wisdom, strength, knowledge, and fear of God.[62] This Spirit provides an anointing that "gives the king the abilities necessary to carry out the demands of his office."[63] Since the Spirit is the chief element transmitted through this kingly anointing (see 1 Sam 16:13), this King in fact gains his authority by the anointing of the Spirit. According to Bock, "Isaiah 11:2 notes that the Spirit of God will rest on this King (cf. Luke 3:21–22) and

---

60. "In [Isaiah] 11:1–16 the messianic hope which began to be expressed in 7:14 and which was amplified in 8:23—9:5 comes to full flower. The Messiah is not merely promised or announced but is depicted as ruling. In place of the craven and petty house of David or the arrogant and oppressive empire of Assyria, here is a king in whose hands the concerns of the weakest will be safe. He will usher in a reign of safety and security to which the weary exiles may come streaming in return" (Oswalt, *The Book of Isaiah*, 277).

61. See Oswalt, "נוח," 3:56–57.

62. Many NT commentators think these "seven Spirits" of the Messiah's reign show up again in Rev 3:1 and Rev 2:7, 11, 17, 29, 3:6, 13, 23. Such an eschatological framework provides tangible evidence of the Spirit's structuring work that demonstrates the Spirit's governing authority under the Messiah's rule.

63. Wildberger, *Isaiah 1–12*, 471. Also, from 1 Sam 16:13 we learn that the Spirit is the chief element transmitted through this kingly anointing. There is a real sense implied that this King in fact gains his authority by the anointing of the Spirit.

that He will bring wisdom and understanding (cf. Luke 11:29–32). Isaiah 11:2 is the probable link to Jesus as the regal Bearer of the Spirit."[64] The King's ruling qualities are described here as gifts of the Spirit, including חָכְמָה ("wisdom," skill or intellectual understanding), בִּינָה ("understanding," insight or discernment), עֵצָה ("counsel," used of Messiah, "he who is planning something wonderful"), and גְּבוּרָה ("strength," refers to ultimate power or sovereign rule).[65] Such gifts are placed into the context of וְיִרְאַת יהוה ("the fear of the Lord").[66] According to Wildberger, "וְיִרְאַת does not refer to fear before God (since it is presented as a gift from God) but is essentially a guarantee that the Messiah is authentic, that he respects and upholds God's will utterly."[67] These Spirit-endowed qualities provide the Messiah with a unique governing authority necessary to execute God's will. In Isa 32:15–18 and Acts 1:5–8 we shall see that this same Spirit is sent by the Messiah to execute *his* will in the Church age.[68]

Christ appears in this verse as the sovereign king who rules with compassion and as divine judge who interprets God's laws through mercy. The Spirit himself established the Messiah's "realm" of authority. Since this passage is ultimately eschatological, the Spirit must be understood here to be a "Spirit of Restoration," having the authority to bring the Messiah's government to full authority in the eschaton. According to VanGemeren,

> The Spirit of God is particularly associated with the messianic age. David was endowed by the Spirit of God (2 Sam. 23:2; cf. 1 Kings 3:5–15). Kingship in Israel was a sacral office because the Davidic

---

64. Bock, "The Son of David and the Saints' Task," 452.

65. See Wilson, "חכם," 2:133; Fretheim, "בין," 1:652–53.

66. This is emphasized by the gloss that appears at the end of the verse, as a result of the dittography in v. 3a.

67. Wildberger, *Isaiah 1–12*, 473. This form of ירא appears forty-five times in the OT, meaning fear, terror, reverence, piety. "Generally this term depicts terrors of everyday life. . . . In a special sense, the fear of God is characteristic of some in the OT who God has endowed with the Spirit in order that they might fairly rule the people of God" (Van Pelt and Kaiser, ירא, 2:533). This is true of David (2 Sam 23:3) and here of the coming Messiah.

68. The Spirit himself—and the Spirit's qualities—establish the Messiah's "realm" of authority. Since this passage is ultimately eschatological, the Spirit must be understood here to be a "Spirit of restoration," having the authority to bring the Messiah's government to full authority in the eschaton (this notion will be explored further in the section on "governing authority").

king was an extension of Yahweh's rule on earth. The Messiah, too, was invested with special authority by the presence of the Spirit (Isa. 11:2). The Lord Jesus was empowered by the Spirit at baptism (Matt. 3: 16), when the Father confirmed his messianic mission (see Isa. 11:1; 61:1). The Spirit of God is evident in miraculous healing and in the casting out of demons, the sign of the intrusion of the eschaton: "If I drive out demons by the Spirit of God, then the kingdom of God has come upon you" (Matt. 12:28). The Holy Spirit is the eschatological sign of the presence of the messianic age, characterized by "the Holy Spirit and fire" (Luke 3:16).[69]

Calvin points out that, "[Isaiah] shows that [these gifts] dwell in Christ, in order that they may be communicated to us."[70] In this passage, therefore, we see a glimpse of the Spirit's "qualities" in the anointing of the Messiah that are now available to those who are "in Christ" (Rom 8:9–11; Eph 1:3, 17).

The Eschatological Realm of the Spirit of Restoration—Exegesis of Isaiah 32:15–16

This passage points to the Spirit as the governor of kingdom restoration according to a specific eschatological blueprint. The eschatological qualities associated with the Spirit—righteousness, justice, and peace—follow closely after severe divine judgment (vv. 9–13), leading to the abandonment of the land and the city (v. 14). This passage marks Isaiah's first reference to the Spirit being "poured out" from on high in the sense of salvation. This will result in fertile land (vv. 15–16), works of righteousness (vv. 16–17), and peaceful habitation (v. 18).

15 עַד־יֵעָרֶה עָלֵינוּ רוּחַ מִמָּרוֹם וְהָיָה מִדְבָּר לַכַּרְמֶל (וְכַרְמֶל) וְהַכַּרְמֶל לַיַּעַר יֵחָשֵׁב

15 Until the Spirit is poured out upon us from on high, and the wilderness becomes a fertile field, and the fertile field is considered as a forest.

The judgment and emptiness of vv. 9–14 will not cease עַד ("until") the Spirit is יֵעָרֶה (niphal impf, "poured out"). In this context, the preposition does not indicate that the Spirit's work is completely delayed until his

---

69. VanGemeren, *The Progress of Redemption*, 459.
70. Calvin, *Commentary on the Prophet Isaiah*, 1:376.

The Authority of the Holy Spirit and Systematic Theology: Part 2

outpouring; rather that the Spirit being depicted here as acting up until that time. In this verse the Spirit is "the agent of restoration, by whom the Lord renews all things to a state of blessing and *shalom*."⁷¹ While Isa 32:11 warns the people to וְעֹרָה ("make [themselves] bare"), here the Spirit will be "poured out" after judgment in order to clothe the wilderness with abundance and God's people with "righteousness" and "justice." Such an outpouring brings about "a reversal of the present condition, a renewal that is, indeed, revolutionary, the very opposite of the condition described [earlier]."⁷²

Isaiah 44:3 repeats this imagery, vividly portraying the יֵעָרֶה ("pouring out") of the Spirit upon "your offspring" (i.e., the Lord's remnant people). In Isa 30:28 the image of a stream is used in reference to the judgment coming upon Assyria. Here it is a portrayal of a sovereign Lordship, one that is reflected in an ever-increasing agricultural bounty: from a wilderness to a fertile field to a forest.

> In any case, the outpouring of the Spirit becomes a central facet of the Old Testament hope. If God's people were ever to share his character, an outcome devoutly to be hoped for, then it would have to come about through an infusion of God's Spirit into human beings. This development relates fundamentally to a crisis of Lordship. God cannot fill where he does not rule.⁷³

With all this in mind, we can conclude that the Spirit possesses such an eschatological, restorative Lordship that incorporates God's people into the restoration process (even though full restoration will not be realized until the land/kingdom is completely restored). The eschatological benefits of the Spirit's outpouring are described in the next verse.

16 וְשָׁכַן בַּמִּדְבָּר מִשְׁפָּט וּצְדָקָה בַּכַּרְמֶל תֵּשֵׁב

16 Then justice will dwell in the wilderness and righteousness will abide in the fertile field.

Here the Spirit administers the moral structures of the eschatological kingdom, resulting in a kingdom environment energized by moral and

---

71. VanGemeren, *Interpreting the Prophetic Word*, 459.
72. Young, *The Book of Isaiah*, 2:399. See also Seevers, "ערה," 3:528.
73. Oswalt, *The Book of Isaiah*, 587.

spiritual vitality. Whereas v. 15 focuses in on the land that receives eschatological renewal at the outpouring of the Spirit (a very significant renewal in itself), v. 16 spells out the eschatological governing qualities possessed and provided by the *Spirit of Restoration*. The Spirit establishes and governs the kingdom in terms of his own וּצְדָקָה ("righteousness," which is basically a respect for God's laws and results in divine order) and מִשְׁפָּט ("justice," respect for the rights of others and results in fair judgment).[74] The Spirit provides a *dynamic righteousness* so that lawful order might be established[75] and *social justice* so that the needy and oppressed might be defended. The Spirit will govern the Messianic, eschatological kingdom, as well as its restorative process, by means of the "moral authority" encapsulated in these distinct qualities. In this way the Spirit creates a realm of authority for the *people* who inhabit the renewed land (this is made plain by the words שָׁכַן ["dwell," "abide"] and תֵּשֵׁב ["abide," "remain"]).

In vv. 17–18 we find another essential quality of the Spirit—שָׁלוֹם ("peace"). As a "work of righteousness" (v. 17), this concept is listed in relationship to justice and righteousness, as another quality of the Spirit in association with the eschatological Kingdom. The Spirit's "*shalom*" is the quintessential kingdom longing. Whereas Isaiah's history is filled with violence and turbulence, the Spirit allows for "quietness," "confidence forever," "secure dwellings," and "undisturbed resting places" (vv. 17–18).

---

74. For specific definitions see Leupold, *Exposition of Isaiah*, 505. Righteousness in the prophets is often described in terms of God's eschatological rule, and specifically "that perfect quality whereby God relates to his creation and brings about a wise, harmonious, and blessed order. It is a dynamic and relational term for the kingdom that embraces the beginning, process, and goal of redemptive history. God rules over his creation, sustains it, and transforms it to bring everything into conformity to his will. In his righteous rule he reestablishes peace, harmony, and goodness" (VanGemeren, *Interpreting the Prophetic Word*, 363). "Justice" is a ruling quality whereby God "acts without discrimination or recrimination and with wisdom and equity. His just rule brings favor and joy to all who seek him because the ruthless, legalist, opportunist, and oppressor will be removed from his presence" (364 [italics his]).

75. VanGemeren points out that God's righteousness is dynamic because "all his acts work together harmoniously in creating a better world, a world of shalom.... The godly responds by doing righteous acts. They, too, cultivate relations that reflect God's righteousness by dispensing mercy, giving to the needy, caring for the poor, and advancing God's righteous rule" (VanGemeren, *Interpreting the Prophetic Word*, 363).

The Authority of the Holy Spirit and Systematic Theology: Part 2

This passage thereby defines the eschatological, immediate Kingdom of God in terms of qualities of the Spirit. These qualities that define the Spirit's "realm" of authority are also associated with the eschatological salvation of God's people.[76] Isaiah no longer treats the Spirit as one who *brings* judgment or salvation—now the Spirit *is* their salvation, a "downpayment" of the coming eschatological salvation and of the *righteousness, justice,* and *peace* that will later appear in totality.[77]

> This is the first clear and positive association of the Spirit of the Lord with the new eschatological life that is part of the coming salvation.... [H]ere the Spirit *is* the eschatological ethical salvation itself, not merely wind of judgment but water of life.[78]

These qualities thereby provide the essential eschatological structure by which the Spirit rules in and through the community of God. The effects of this rule, as we shall see below, include democratization, liberation, and transformation. These effects will allow God's people to participate in the church and her government by means of specific "practices."

The Immediate Realm of the Spirit—Exegesis of Acts 1:5–8

In this passage we receive a sense of the "immediate" connection that Jesus wishes to portray between the Spirit and the present Kingdom of God.[79] The chapter begins with a reference to the vital link between the Spirit and Jesus' choice of the twelve Apostles (v. 2). Since the Apostles represent for Luke the authentic Church that will manifest herself to the world, apostolic authority is thereby tied directly to the Holy Spirit. Montague comments:

> Luke wants to underline their authority by relating it both to Jesus and to the Holy Spirit. Though the twelve had not yet been en-

---

76. This realm might be considered a domain or sphere of influence in the world that is established and realized in history on the basis of particular attributes of the Holy Spirit, such as justice and righteousness. This "realm" is also seen as developing throughout salvation history as the Spirit sharpens and increases his governmental influence.

77. See Montague, *Holy Spirit*, 40.

78. Montague, *Holy Spirit*, 40. See Rev 22:17, where the Spirit as true water of life flows as a river (Rev 22:1) in John's eschatological vision, one that provides "salvation" for the nations by producing fruit for the healing of nations.

79. "Immediate" in this context might be defined as "present" in time and space.

dowed by the Spirit, they have been chosen by Jesus himself in an act that was Spirit-inspired.[80]

This choosing lays the foundation for the NT connection between the future eschatological kingdom and the "immediacy" of the Spirit, as first described by Jesus in Acts 1:3–5. The highlight of Jesus' teaching about the Kingdom of God (v. 3) is expressed in his "promise" (v. 4) that "in a few days you will be baptized in the Holy Spirit" (v. 5). This Kingdom/Spirit connection is further amplified by Jesus' mandate to wait for the Spirit "in Jerusalem" (v. 4)—the political center of the eschatological kingdom—rather than returning to their homeland (Galilee).

5 ὅτι Ἰωάννης μὲν ἐβάπτισεν ὕδατι, ὑμεῖς δὲ ἐν πνεύματι βαπτισθήσεσθε ἁγίῳ οὐ μετὰ πολλὰς ταύτας ἡμέρας

5 for John baptized with water, but you shall be baptized with the Holy Spirit not many days from now."

In this "promise," first prophesied in Isa 32:15 and Joel 2:28–32, were the "last words" of Jesus before his ascension. The verb ἐβάπτισεν ("baptized") literally means "immersed in water" (usually as a means of cleansing). Here it is associated with cleansing from sin (see Acts 2:38). The term "baptized with the Holy Spirit," according to Marshall, "is considerably widened in its metaphorical use, and no one synonym can do justice to its range of meaning as a Christian technical term for the reception of the Spirit."[81] In this context it seems to be an allusion to Jesus' "kingdom authority"[82] in that it is compared by Jesus to John's "baptism unto repentance," which was performed because "the kingdom of God is at hand" (Matt 3:2).[83] We can infer that, at the coming of the Spirit (in Acts 2), the

---

80. See Montague, *Holy Spirit*, 272. Some commentators link "through the Holy Spirit" with the commandment (i.e., Bruce; Arrington), but it probably belongs with the following verb construct, thus reading, "to the apostles whom he had chosen through the Holy Spirit" (see also NAB; Marshall, *The Acts of the Apostles*, 57n).

81. Marshall, *The Acts of the Apostles*, 58.

82. "Kingdom authority" might be defined as the authority possessed by the Messiah in the eschatological kingdom or delegated by the Messiah to one that represents the Messiah's eschatological agenda.

83. This has usually been missed in the contemporary debate regarding the baptism of the Holy Spirit. Certainly there is a strong experiential element in this baptism (See Dunn, *The Christ and the Spirit*, 2:233–38).

eschatological kingdom (and the immediate authority displayed therein) is still "at hand." The initial fulfillment of Jesus' "kingdom authority" on earth is revealed in Acts 2:38, as Peter tells the Jews observing Pentecost that they too can have the gift of the Spirit if they will "repent and be baptized in the name of Jesus" (i.e., the *authority* of Jesus). The Spirit's authority is therefore seen here as a matter of "executing" the kingdom rule of Jesus Christ in human lives. As the first "downpayment" of the fulfillment of Joel 2:28–32, the Spirit's "baptism" is a predecessor of the final eschatological outpouring that will occur with physical earthly changes as well. Whereas the government of the Spirit is presented in the OT in broad, qualitative parameters (i.e., Isa 11:2 and 32:15–16), the Spirit's governing authority is now to be understood in terms of an immanent experience.

> 6 Οἱ μὲν οὖν συνελθόντες ἠρώτων αὐτὸν λέγοντες, Κύριε, εἰ ἐν τῷ χρόνῳ τούτῳ ἀποκαθιστάνεις τὴν βασιλείαν τῷ Ἰσραήλ;
>
> 6 And so when they had come together, they were asking Him, saying, "Lord, is it at this time You are restoring the kingdom to Israel?"

The Spirit/Kingdom connection develops even more pointedly in vv. 6–8. The disciples' question in v. 6 reflects the sentiments of every pious Jew (described in Sir 48:10 as the "restoration of the twelve tribes of Israel"). The Jews understood that the fullness of the Spirit was to be equated with the fullness of kingdom authority and messianic reign.[84] The disciples' question also shows their expectation of an *immediate* fulfillment, and Jesus seems to address this desire for immediacy in vv. 7–8.

> 7 εἶπεν δὲ πρὸς αὐτούς, Οὐχ ὑμῶν ἐστιν γνῶναι χρόνους ἢ καιροὺς οὓς ὁ πατὴρ ἔθετο ἐν τῇ ἰδίᾳ ἐξουσίᾳ, 8 ἀλλὰ λήμψεσθε δύναμιν ἐπελθόντος τοῦ ἁγίου πνεύματος ἐφ' ὑμᾶς καὶ ἔσεσθέ μου μάρτυρες ἔν τε Ἰερουσαλὴμ καὶ [ἐν] πάσῃ τῇ Ἰουδαίᾳ καὶ Σαμαρείᾳ καὶ ἕως ἐσχάτου τῆς γῆς.
>
> 7 He said to them, "It is not for you to know times or epochs which the Father has fixed by His own authority; 8 but you shall receive power when the Holy Spirit has come upon you; and you shall be

---

84. See Montague, *Holy Spirit*, 271–73.

The Lord Is the Spirit

> My witnesses both in Jerusalem, and in all Judea and Samaria, and even to the remotest part of the earth."

Jesus rebukes their concern with the precise *timing* of the kingdom's fulfillment, but not the *fact* of its fulfillment. He answers their question by presenting ἁγίου πνεύματος (v. 8) as the vital substitute for βασιλείαν (v. 6). While χρόνους refers to the time of the Kingdom's establishment, "καιροὺς [refers] to the critical events accompanying its establishment."[85] The word ἀλλά ("however") is a "superordinating conjunction," indicating that it is more important for the disciples to receive the Spirit than to know the timing of the Kingdom. The Holy Spirit will be present as a δύναμιν ("power") that begins the kingdom's fulfillment. We must not miss the fact, however, that in this passage (as in the gospels and particularly in Christ's encounters with demons) δύναμιν is closely connected with ἐξουσία! The Father's ἐξουσία (verse 7) determines the fullness of καιροὺς (see Eph 1:10), which is immediately and climactically related with the δύναμιν and fullness of God's Spirit, so that δύναμιν becomes a definitive demonstration of ἐξουσία.[86] Rather than being given the ἐξουσία themselves to "know the times or epochs" of the kingdom's restoration, they shall possess the Spirit's δύναμιν as a present expression of God's ἐξουσία. This is made clear in verse 8b—the Spirit will provide the δύναμιν necessary for the disciples to embark on their mission to the world, and this mission will be an expression of Christ's new messianic authority (Matt 28:18).[87] The Spirit creates an immediate "realm" of the Kingdom that coincides with the disciples' witness to the death and resurrection of the Lord Jesus Christ. In this passage, and its "playing out" in the book of Acts, the governing role of the Spirit is demonstrated in terms of *immanence* and *space*—geography is "conquered" through the power of the Spirit activated in the spreading of the gospel. It is also demonstrated in the *redemptive* nature of the Spirit's government, which will extend "to the ends of the earth" (Acts 2:5–9).

---

85. Bruce, *The Acts of the Apostles*, 70.

86. As seen in chapter one, "ἐξουσία belongs to a state of effectiveness which lies behind δύναμις" (Barrett, *The Holy Spirit and the Gospel Tradition*, 78).

87. See Robertson, *Word Pictures in the New Testament*, 4-6.

The Authority of the Holy Spirit and Systematic Theology: Part 2

EXEGESIS OF PASSAGES—THE EFFECTS OF THE SPIRIT'S GOVERNING AUTHORITY IN THE CHURCH

The following three passages demonstrate specific *effects* of the governing Spirit with respect to God's people—democratization, liberation, and transformation. In other words, they move us from the governing *qualities* of the Spirit to the *impact* of the Spirit upon the church community.

Democratization—Exegesis of Isaiah 59:21

Isaiah 59:21 is the central announcement in OT Scripture of God's "Covenant of the Spirit" with His remnant people. This is an unconditional covenant, ensuring them of their eternal possession of his Spirit. It not only continues in the eschatological tone of Isa 11:2 and 32:15–17 (placing the Spirit in close association with the Messianic King and his eschatological kingdom), but now the Spirit is presented as the main *actor* in that Kingdom. This covenant therefore has strong implications for our understanding of the Spirit's place in executing the benefits of the New Covenant.

וַאֲנִי זֹאת בְּרִיתִי אוֹתָם אָמַר יְהוָֹה רוּחִי אֲשֶׁר עָלֶיךָ וּדְבָרַי אֲשֶׁר־שַׂמְתִּי בְּפִיךָ לֹא־יָמוּשׁוּ מִפִּיךָ וּמִפִּי זַרְעֲךָ וּמִפִּי זֶרַע זַרְעֲךָ אָמַר יְהוָֹה מֵעַתָּה וְעַד־עוֹלָם:

"And as for Me, this is My covenant with them," says the LORD: "My Spirit which is upon you, and My words which I have put in your mouth, shall not depart from your mouth, nor from the mouth of your offspring, nor from the mouth of your offspring's offspring," says the LORD, "from now and forever."

This verse is structured to make a profound impact on the "post-exilic" Jewish reader looking for security in a time of intense trial. It immediately follows a vivid description of the Messiah's judgment and deliverance that will result in eternal eschatological security (59:18–20). This verse also serves as an introduction to chapter sixty, paving the way for a fullness of salvation to be experienced in Zion, "the City of the Lord, Zion of the Holy One of Israel" (60:14).[88]

---

88. Such a well-placed passage is typical in the writings of Isaiah. According to Merrill, Isaiah provides theological "summaries" that connect Israel's history with her future. "[Isaiah] makes of the present a culminating explanation of the past, that is, its logical and theological outcome, but he also uses the present as a launching pad for the projectile of eschatological hope and expectation" (Merrill, "Old Testament History," 79).

The noun בְּרִיתִי ("my covenant") must be understood in light of Isaiah's theology of divine covenants, which is established on Yahweh's glory and faithfulness to his "remnant people" (e.g., Isa 54:10 and 55:3–5).[89] The concept of divine covenant in the prophets is often used "as a divine constitution or ordinance with signs or pledges."[90] Here the "constitution" is God's "pledge" to bless His true followers with two gifts—his רוּחִי ("Spirit") and his דְבָרַי ("Word"). The context of this passage makes this first gift appear to be the "Spirit of Restoration" in that the Spirit is involved in the application of God's redemption (in regeneration and sanctification) and in prophetic expectation.[91] In this context רוּחִי also refers to the "prophetic Spirit"[92] that comes on the people as a whole, empowering them to speak his Word. Such a Spirit is presently עָלֶיךָ ("upon you"), that is, his remnant people.[93] Since the majority of such references to the Spirit until this time were for the prophets (i.e., Moses in Num 11:17; David in 1 Sam 16:13), it would be astounding news that the Spirit would now be permanently residing "upon" the entire believing community.[94] This covenant thus marks

---

89. Isaiah 59:19–20 refers directly to the "remnant" of Israel. The antecedent of the plural preposition אוֹתָם ("with them") in 59:21 must therefore be the remnant mentioned in these two previous verses. Isaiah 42:6 and 49:6–8 speaks of the fact that God has chosen His Servant/Redeemer as a Covenant to "the people," which must be the remnant of Israel, those who have remained faithful to God and humble before Him. Isaiah 42:6 "suggests that God's purpose of salvation would finally extend to the whole world and not just to one race" (McConville, "ברית," 1:752). With these proclamations, the context of covenant blessing is now limited to the "remnant" of Israel. This is further confirmed in 56:4–6, which speaks of those who "hold fast My covenant."

90. Brown, Driver, and Briggs, "ברית," 137.

91. See VanGemeren, "The Spirit of Restoration," 97.

92. This follows the pattern of Num 11:29 (which also includes the Spirit and the word of prophecy). Examples of "the prophetic Spirit" are numerous: 2 Chron 15:1, 20:14, 24:20; Isa 48:16, 61:1; Zech 7:12; Neh 9:30. When the Spirit of God comes or falls on those divinely chosen and commissioned for the work of God, it is almost always given to selected individuals or groups (i.e., the seventy elders of Num 11:17, 25; Saul in 1 Sam 10:6, 10).

93. The present tense, implied linking verb "is" would be expected here because אֲשֶׁר עָלֶיךָ is immediately surrounded by qal perfect verbs. In opposition to Whybray, who holds this action to be future (see Whybray, "Isaiah 40–66"), most commentators agree the Spirit is depicted here as already residing "upon" the post-exilic remnant. See also comments by Ma, in *Until the Spirit Come*; also by Oswalt (*The Book of Isaiah*) and Eichrodt (*Theology of the Old Testament*).

94. Traditionally the prophetic Spirit has been seen as that which impels a prophet

the initial *effect* of the Spirit's action upon the community—"democratization."[95] Implied here to a limited degree, this initial provision of the Spirit is yet "far from what Joel envisions in 3:1–2."[96] Accompanying this "democratization" is the Spirit's internalization of divine revelation so that God's people might live in submission to God's will. This is clearly depicted in another closely related covenant—Jer 31:33: "This is the covenant I will make with the house of Israel after that time," declares the Lord. "I will put my law in their minds and write it on their hearts. I will be their God, and they will be my people." In Isa 59:21 the prophet ensures believers that the Spirit will also transforms their offspring, thus "assuring the continuity of the new community from generation to generation."[97] As the Executor of the New Covenant, the Spirit's role is to manifest God *in* the community, allowing this community to remain hopeful in a time of eschatological tension. Such a role is described well by Eichrodt:

> In Isaiah we find a prophet who keeps tension between the consummation of world-history and the present condition of the Jews. The Spirit is at work in both. Thus the Spirit is seen as both the Spirit of judgment and destruction preparing the redeemed in Israel for the visible dwelling of God among them (Isa. 4:4), and the sign of the everlasting covenant Yahweh has made with Israel (Isa. 59:21).[98]

of God to utter instruction or warning, to know and speak the Word of God. With Joel, though, the prophetic gift is transformed. Rather than a single individual or select group possessing the Spirit, the Spirit will be shared by all those within the Community of the Spirit. In Isaiah 59:21 this sharing is not only anticipated, it is spoken of as present reality.

95. "Democratization," which is most clearly specified in Joel 2:28–32, is "a special endowment of the Spirit in every member of the people of God. . . . The assurance of the Spirit is given to all—regardless of sex, social standing, or age—who find refuge in the Lord alone" (VanGemeren, *Interpreting the Prophetic Word*, 125).

96. Ma, *Until the Spirit Comes*, 198. While Joel 2 provides a vision of the completion of the Spirit's restoration in terms of community democratization, we must recognize also that "the Holy Spirit is God's eschatological gift to the new community before the Day of the Lord (2:28–32)" (VanGemeren, *Interpreting the Prophetic Word*, 124). Along with Isaiah and Ezekiel, Joel foresaw a time when God would pour out his Holy Spirit on His people in unprecedented fashion. This eschatological imagery occurs four times in the OT: Isa 32:15, 44:3–4; Ezek. 9:29; Joel 2:28. The promise of the Spirit "gives hope to the godly who live in a world filled with tension between curse and blessing" (VanGemeren, "The Spirit of Restoration," 90).

97. VanGemeren, *Interpreting the Prophetic Word*, 359.

98. Eichrodt, *Theology of the Old Testament*, 62.

The Lord Is the Spirit

The other gift is דְּבָרַי ("the word"), which is a clear reference to God's covenantal "Word of Promise." To the believing Jews, the Word came to be seen as a priceless legacy, the guarantee of future covenantal blessings. It is depicted here as the key instrument in the Spirit's restoration activity. Since both "Spirit" and "word" share the verb לֹא־יָמוּשׁוּ ("shall not depart"), this verse declares an inseparability between the two.[99] Such a correlation presents to us not a dead letter but a Word that is alive, "living and active and sharper than any two-edged sword" (Heb 4:12). Eichrodt comments on this verse:

> The effect of the Spirit was to make the word from the past live, and to bring it into contact with the present in binding immediacy. . . . Side by side with the Spirit which God causes to rest upon his people the words which he has put into their mouth form the context of the everlasting covenant linking Israel with its God.[100]

The Spirit's governing authority is thereby asserted in association with this Word. According to Eichrodt, this association,

> was another way of asserting the sovereignty of the divine Lord over the dominant forces of Nature. The inner homogeneity of the two concepts was already suggested by the primary concrete meaning of the idiom which enabled the same expression to be used to designate both the spirit of God as the breath of life going forth from him and the word of God as the breath of his mouth.[101]

The rest of this verse explicates the Spirit's governing authority for the remnant community. The verb לֹא־יָמוּשׁוּ (Qal impf, 3d pers. pl, "shall not

---

99. For "the presence of the Spirit assures that the promises declared up to v. 20 will come true" (Ma, *Until the Spirit Comes*, 135. As the religious tradition of Israel developed we discover the proclamation of the word of Yahweh to be the most predominant activity of the Spirit (Whybray, *Isaiah 40–66*, 229). These "men of the Spirit" (Hos 9:7) were mediators of the word, and their words were the decisive determiners of the pattern of religious thought, and the signs that accompanied their words were indicators of the authority of the covenant God. In this covenant we find a perfect coincidence of "Spirit" and "Word," along with its perpetual endurance (Montague, *Holy Spirit*, 60). This mindset is clearly communicated in Ezek 36:27, "And I will put my Spirit in you and move you to follow my decrees and be careful to keep my laws."

100. Eichrodt, *Theology of the Old Testament*, 64.

101. Ibid., 49.

depart") is mostly used with inanimate things (in Josh 1:8 it is associated with "book of the law" and "your mouth"). The clever contrast (created by a simple change in preposition) between בְּפִיךָ ("in your mouth") and מִפִּיךָ ("out of your mouth") demonstrates the faithfulness and surety of this covenant to God's remnant people. Such a security is expanded in the final phrase, "or from the mouths of your seed, or from the mouths of your seed's seed, says the Lord, henceforth and forever." This phrase echoes several prophetic Scriptures, such as 2 Sam 23:2; Jer 1:9; Isa 51:16; Ezek 36:26–27; Jer 31:33–34—each demonstrates the notion of the perpetual eschatological presence of the "Spirit of Restoration," particularly in association with the Word of Promise. Also, זַרְעֶךָ ("your seed") does not necessarily refer to those of biological descendancy, but specifically those who will serve the living God. Ma thereby holds that this passage suggests a gradual expression of the prophetic Spirit to a wider group of people.[102] The power of the Word is ensured to remain with them as an intimate aspect of the Spirit's endowment.

Isaiah 59:21 therefore speaks of the Spirit's governing authority in terms of *covenantal effects* of the *Spirit of Restoration*—specifically, *democratization and internalization*. The fulfillment of such covenantal action in the Church is further specified in the following passages in terms of the Spirit's *liberation* and *transformation*.

Liberation—Exegesis of Romans 8:2

This verse seems to extend Christ's authority to proclaim liberty and favor upon God's people (see Isa 61:1 and Luke 4:18). The word πνεῦμα appears twenty-one times in Romans 8, far more than any other chapter in Holy Scripture. Romans 8:1–13 presents the Spirit as the key to spiritual life, with the antithesis between flesh and Spirit setting the stage for the Spirit's authority within the Church to be explicated. Romans 8:1–2, however, presents the critical framework for the entire chapter in terms of the Spirit's *liberation* from condemnation.

> ὁ γὰρ νόμος τοῦ πνεύματος τῆς ζωῆς ἐν Χριστῷ Ἰησοῦ ἠλευθέρωσέν σε ἀπὸ τοῦ νόμου τῆς ἁμαρτίας καὶ τοῦ θανάτου.

---

102. Ma, *Until the Spirit Comes*, 8.

> For the law of the Spirit of life in Christ Jesus has set you free from the law of sin and of death.

Verse 2 explains that the grounds of "no condemnation" (v. 1) is found in the νόμος ("law") of the Spirit of life. What sort of "law" could this be? Moo surveys some popular interpretations of νόμος in this context. For some commentators it refers to the Mosaic Law, as an instrument of righteousness leading to life (cf. 7:10). Others render it to be the "law written on the heart" (cf. Jer 31:31–34). According to Moo, these answers force Paul to contradict himself (with 8:3 and 3:27, respectively). Also, neither answer fits the context well. Instead, the word in this context must mean "principle" or more likely "binding authority" as to a master (where "binding" might be roughly thought of as "controlling" or "subjecting").[103] The immediate context (7:21–25) confirms the idea of νόμος as a "binding authority," while the genitives that follow νόμος (i.e., "of sin" or "of the Spirit") specify that authority. Thus, the "binding authority" of sin and death is contrasted here with the "binding authority" of the Spirit. In this way "sin," like the Spirit, is personified. Keck comments on the nature of "sin" in Romans chapters 7 and 8:

> Sin is not something that one does, a transgression; rather, sin is something that does something to the doer. The coming of the commandment stimulated sin, until then inert ("dead," 7:8), so that it came to life and the self "died"—became subject to death.[104]

Thus, sin appears in Rom 8:2 as an "authority" that one inevitably obeys. Against this authority the Spirit's authority is contrasted. "Over against this structure of enslaving power, liberation has occurred by means of a superior power—the Spirit. . . . The Spirit too is a 'law'—a moral structure which governs life because one 'obeys' it."[105] Several commentators see this verse as a "play on words"—specifically, on the "νόμος" of the Spirit. Moo unabashedly credits the Spirit with authority, one that results in liberation.

---

103. See Moo, *The Epistle to the Romans*, 474–75.
104. Keck, "The Law and 'The Law of Sin and Death,'" 48.
105. Ibid., 49.

The actor in the situation is, then, the Spirit himself. It is God's Spirit, coming to the believer with power and authority, who brings liberation from the powers of the old age and from the condemnation that is the lot of all who are imprisoned by those powers.[106]

The "law of the Spirit" is a law τῆς ζωῆς ("of life") as well. The Spirit confers a liberated life as an integral part of his authority. In this verse we see a strong connection between an *effect* of the Spirit and his governing *realm*. Because they are under the Spirit's "law," those within this realm experience the Spirit's liberation. This liberation theme of 8:2 was previously announced in 6:18–22; now it serves as the answer to the "imprisonment" of 7:23–24. Paul wants believers to know that the Spirit's authority has acted *for* them, conferring *to* them an authentic *liberation* at the very height of their experience of bondage to the tyranny of sin. Fee expands on this sort of "freedom."

> In contrast to the use of "freedom" language in Galatians, where it referred exclusively to the freedom of God's children vis-à-vis their former "enslavement" to Torah observance (and by extension to "the elemental spirits of the universe"), in this letter "freedom" language refers predominantly to "deliverance" from the tyranny of sin. . . . The freedom from this "law" of sin and death comes from "the law" of the life-giving Spirit who, after Christ has effectively dealt with sin on the cross, now indwells" the believer in the very place sin once lived.[107]

Paul goes on to develop chapter 8 around this "law of the Spirit" theme, expanding on and describing the "glorious freedom" (v. 21) of God's children who live under the Spirit's governing authority. According to Keck, the γὰρ ("for") in v. 3 suggests that v. 2 "functions as a topic sentence, and that vv. 3–30 are its exposition."[108] Verses 3 and 4 reiterate the insoluble link between Christ and the Spirit with respect to the liberation of the believer. In coordination with the Son's redemption (v. 3), the Spirit's "freedom" is demonstrated vis-à-vis the believer's freedom to obey (v. 4). Verses 6–11 describe the eschatological ordering of the lives of believers "in

---

106. Moo, *The Epistle to the Romans*, 475–76.
107. Fee, *God's Empowering Presence*, 526.
108. Keck, "The Law and 'The Law of Sin and Death,'" 48.

the Spirit." Verses 12–17 instruct the believer in terms of one's "obligation" to put fleshly deeds to death "by the Spirit" (vv. 12–13) and provides a secure basis for being "led by the Spirit" through the testimony of the "Spirit of sonship" (vv. 14–17). The main point of the chapter is simply this: Paul is bringing the eschatological reign of the Spirit into the overall reality of Christian experience so that believers will recognize the Spirit's *liberty*. The Spirit of Restoration thus goes far beyond internalization, liberating believers from spiritual bondage.

Transformation—Exegesis of 2 Corinthians 3:17–18

In 2 Cor 3:6–18, Paul contrasts Moses' ministry with "the surpassing glory" of the New Covenant of the Spirit. Paul tells us in v. 7 that, whereas the "ministry of death" was glorious, the ministry of the Spirit "shall be even more glorious." This verse explains v. 6 ("the letter kills, but the Spirit gives life") and begins an elaborate set of contrasts (four of them in vv. 7–16) that culminates in vv. 17–18. The *a fortiori* argument employed here exemplifies a comparative increase. The tense of ἔσται ("shall be") in v. 8 is that of a logical (rather than chronological) future, pointing to the presently operative "ministry of the Spirit" as well as to the Parousia. Martin holds the eschatological dimension in this passage to be predominant, "since for Paul the future has already begun in the age of the Spirit, of which believers have a foretaste."[109]

The reason the ministry of the Spirit is more glorious than Moses' ministry is answered in vv. 16–18. Verse 16 seems to be a "citation" of Exod 34:34: "whenever Moses went in before the LORD to speak with Him, he would take off the veil . . ." It serves as a transition from the argument of vv. 12–15 to the conclusion in vv. 17–18 (the implied "he" means "they," the ones in the New Covenant). Paul makes a few crucial changes to the Exodus text (LXX) that allows him to interpret it as he intends in vv. 17–18.

> 17 ὁ δὲ κύριος τὸ πνεῦμά ἐστιν· οὗ δὲ τὸ πνεῦμα κυρίου, ἐλευθερία.
>
> Now the Lord is the Spirit; and where the Spirit of the Lord is, there is liberty.

---

109. Martin, "2 Corinthians," 63. Martin points out that this eschatological Spirit is also found in 2 Cor 1:22 and 5:5.

The Authority of the Holy Spirit and Systematic Theology: Part 2

This verse appears as an interpretation of the newly transformed "citation" of Exod 34:34. This is made certain by the introductory formula, ὁ δὲ κύριος.[110] Paul essentially explains for his readers the meaning of יהוה in the Exodus passage: "'the Lord' *refers to* 'the Spirit.'"[111] Observation of this literary devise clears up the debate over whether "the Lord" is referring to God, Christ, or the Spirit, because Paul is interpreting the Exodus text in light of the present argument.[112] Fee's explanation resolves the debate:

> The Lord in that text is now to be understood (not literally but in an analogical way) as referring to the Spirit—not because this is the proper identification of the Lord in the Exodus text but because in this argument that is the proper way to understand what happens to those who, as Moses, now "turn to the Lord."[113]

The idea that κύριος means "Spirit" rather than the resurrected Christ is confirmed by the following clause: "the Spirit of the Lord." Paul seems to want to remove any potential misunderstanding regarding the previous clause. The Spirit *is* the Lord. Commenting on 2 Cor 3:17, Fee also points out that the Spirit is Lord in the New Covenant.

> The Lord to whom Moses turned is the one whose "Presence" tabernacled in the midst of his people Israel. By removing the "veil"

---

110. This phrase occurs regularly throughout Jewish literature as a formula for interpreting words from a text that has just been cited. Galatians 4:25 is nearly identical, when Paul picks up a word from a previous sentience and elaborates on its meaning.

111. Paul had previously told the Galatians that he was interpreting the Sarah and Hagar stories allegorically: "These things are allegorized; for there are two covenants, one from Mount Sinai, begotten for slavery, which is Hagar. Now 'Hagar' stands for Mount Sinai in Arabia" (Gal 4:24–25a). Similarly, this passage might be translated, "Now 'The Lord' stands for 'the Spirit'" (See Fee, *God's Empowering Presence*, 311–12).

112. Both Greenwood and Ferguson indeed hold that "the Lord" refers to Christ, but neither interacts with Exodus 34 (Greenwood, "The Lord Is the Spirit" 467–72; Ferguson, *The Holy Spirit*, 55). Thus, these arguments only stand if Paul is not referring to Exodus 34, but this is a fact upon which most commentators agree (i.e. Garland, *2 Corinthians*, 196; Fee, *God's Empowering Presence*, 312–13; Barrett, *The Second Epistle to the Corinthians*, 123). Hafemann holds, rather, that "Paul is not identifying Christ and the Spirit, but making it clear that Moses' experience of YHWH in the tent of meeting is equivalent to the current experience of the Spirit in Paul's ministry, even as Paul could refer in 3:3 to the Spirit unleashed in his ministry as the 'Spirit of the living God'" (Hafemann, *Paul, Moses, and the History of Israel*, 399).

113. Fee, *God's Empowering Presence*, 313.

of the old covenant, Christ has ushered in the New Covenant. The "Lord" to whom God's newly constituted people turn, whose "Presence" is now in their hearts, is none other than the life-giving Spirit of the living God.[114]

The Spirit is the "Lord" who removes the veil from the hardened heart so that God's people might experience liberty from death. Frame views divine lordship as "covenant headship," in that all created things "are appointed to be covenant servants, to obey God's law, and to be instruments of His gracious purpose."[115] The Spirit can thereby be said to have "headship" (authority) over the New Covenant. As Fee points out, however, this Lordship implies "presence" as well. The Spirit thereby connects God's authoritative Lordship with his divine, personal presence.[116]

In turning to the Lord, believers enter into the ἐλευθερία of the Spirit, the "liberty" that comes at the end of the dominance of the written law.[117] Though this word has been both debated and abused, here it refers primarily to the freedom from "the veil" as interpreted in v. 15. It is a freedom from the old covenant, from the "covenant of the letter" that leads to condemnation and death. The emphasis in this verse is less on freedom from the old covenant and more on freedom to boldly enter God's presence and behold his glory. Such a freedom is protected and controlled by the Spirit.

18 ἡμεῖς δὲ πάντες ἀνακεκαλυμμένῳ προσώπῳ τὴν δόξαν κυρίου κατοπτριζόμενοι τὴν αὐτὴν εἰκόνα μεταμορφούμεθα ἀπὸ δόξης εἰς δόξαν καθάπερ ἀπὸ κυρίου πνεύματος.

18 But we all, with unveiled faces beholding as in a mirror the glory of the Lord, are being transformed into the same image from glory to glory, just as from the Lord, the Spirit.

Here Paul returns to the beginning of his argument and includes the Corinthians in the experience of the Spirit's glory. The word δὲ ("but")

---

114. Ibid., 313.

115. Frame, *The Doctrine of the Knowledge of God*, 13.

116. Authority relates to presence, "for God is never present apart from His Word" (Frame, *The Doctrine of the Knowledge of God*, 18).

117. Barrett, *The Second Epistle to the Corinthians*, 123.

contrasts the Corinthians with those whose hearts are veiled (vv. 14–15).[118] The imagery in this verse shifts to the ἀνακεκαλυμμένῳ ("unveiled") faces of those who have experienced the freedom of the Spirit. This participle describes an attribute of "faces," and, being in the perfect tense, indicates here a continual state resulting from a previous action. Once lifted, the veil remains lifted.

In such a state they are κατοπτριζόμενοι ("beholding as in a mirror") the glory of the Lord. This modal participle describes the manner in which the main verb, μεταμορφούμεθα ("are being transformed"), is accomplished.[119] Being in the present tense, this verb also demonstrates that the "beholding" is continuous, free from interruption, and an integral part of the transformation process. Transformation occurs by continually "beholding" Christ,[120] and involves a process: ἀπὸ δόξης εἰς δόξαν ("from glory to glory"). This phrase goes back to the motif of v. 11, and emphasizes "the non-fading reality and ever-increasing dimension of the glory that is now ours through the ministry of the Spirit—as we continually behold Christ and are being constantly renewed into his likeness."[121] While the old covenant was glorious but temporary, the glory of the New Covenant will remain forever.

The final phrase, καθάπερ ἀπὸ κυρίου πνεύματος, is the most difficult of all. It could mean "just as from the Lord, the Spirit" or "from the Spirit of the Lord." The first option seems preferable because in most cases word order should prevail, and because when two adjacent anarthrous

---

118. Though some hold that the contrast is between Paul and Moses (v. 13), Fee correctly finds the above option more convincing, based on (1) ἡμεῖς πάντες ("we all"); (2) the flow or argument, beginning with v. 14b, intentionally moved from Moses to contemporary Jews (those who have "veiled hearts" because they continue in the old covenant); (3) 4:1–6, where Paul returns to the theme of his ministry and its recipients; and (4) the mirror imagery of v. 18 (See Fee, *God's Empowering Presence*, 315–16).

119. The idea of this verb is "to change the inward reality to something else" (Trench, *Synonyms*, 264; TDNT).

120. Rather than the active voice (i.e., "produce a reflection" or "to reflect as a mirror"), κατοπτριζόμενοι takes the middle voice, resulting in imagery that means "to look at something in a mirror" (i.e. ,to contemplate). The normal meaning of κατοπτριζόμενοι is "look into a mirror," and the application of the imagery in 4:3–6 is clearly referring to those who do not see the glory of God vs. those who do see God's glory in the face of Jesus Christ, who is the likeness of God.

121. Fee, *God's Empowering Presence*, 318.

nouns are ambiguously in the same case, the best solution is usually the contextual one. The point of the whole argument has been the role of the Spirit in Paul's ministry—that of a New Covenant—and the fact that the Spirit in the lives of the Corinthians validates the glory of that ministry. This takes us back to v. 17 (the interpretation of v. 16)—"the 'Lord' stands for the Spirit"—and restates it with anarthrous simplicity.

> This is a literary moment, pure and simple, in which all that has proceeded is neatly rounded off. We already know from v. 17b that the Spirit in any case is the "Spirit of the Lord." The Spirit, we are now reminded, is the key to our experience of the presence of God.[122]

Biblical Theology

Many of the passages analyzed above allude to the nature of the Spirit's governing authority as the "Spirit of Restoration." As Governor of the future "eschatological kingdom" (Isa 11:2; 32:15–16), the Spirit of Restoration can be seen moving through biblical history from beginning to end, demonstrating progression according to an eschatological blueprint. Now, as Governor of Christ's "immediate" Church era (Acts 1:5–8), the Spirit progressively generates *realms* of authority in the world that reveal Christ's kingdom authority along with the Spirit's eschatological, restorative *qualities*. In doing so, the Spirit also progressively brings forth specific *effects* in the context of the Church that demonstrate this authority and promote ecclesial restoration with respect to God's people.

Biblical history confirms that the progression accomplished by the Spirit of Restoration can be generally understood along the lines of the "progress of redemption"—the story of salvation history whereby "the Bible reveals the progression of God's plan for his people."[123] While the Spirit of Restoration is, of course, an integral part of this grand story, his place in the story is often overlooked. The Spirit's qualities of *righteousness* and *justice*, for example, are usually made present in unlikely situations involving suffering, oppression, weakness, hopelessness, fear, doubt, etc. (see Num

---

122. Ibid., 319.
123. VanGemeren, *The Progress of Redemption*, 15.

11:17; Isa 34:16; 44:3; 59:18–21; 61:1; 63:11; Hag 2:5; Rom 8:2, 26; Phil 1:9; 1 Thess 1:6). In such passages an integration of the Spirit's qualities and effects upon people occurs. Such an integration insures that the divine authority of the Spirit remains intact in his governing activities. God's people are thus authorized for the service of ministry. In other words, as the authoritative Spirit dwells within God's people and within communities of believers, *he "becomes" their authority*—retaining authoritative qualities while employing them in the restoration process, granting to them a certain authority to participate in his work and to execute his will.

How does this integration play out in Scripture? The Spirit first appears in Gen 1:2, showing himself to be intimately involved in the design of the world. We may assume that the creation of Adam (1:26–28) included a fullness of Spirit that allowed for complete fellowship with God (Gen 2:7). After Adam sinned, something changed in an absolute and spiritual sense—the text tells us that he "died" (Gen 2:17; 3:6)—this fullness was now lost and the effect was felt in all aspects of creation (Gen 3:14–19; Rom 8:19–22). God now begins his plan for redemption through the Spirit's restorative work, one that develops slowly but progressively, particularly through the divine covenants. Through the covenants "the Israelite people recognized afresh the irruption of God's transcendental life into the paltry patchwork of this world."[124] Though they witnessed this covenant development through specially authorized human instruments (i.e., Moses, David), "They could find no other way of grasping the astounding force which radiated from these leaders, and gave them the capacity for their task, than to designate it the living breath or Spirit of God."[125]

Central to this progressive restoration theme is the notion of the authoritative "dwelling" of the Spirit, first seen in the OT tabernacle/temple and later in the NT Church. In the last chapter we discovered the Spirit's divine/moral authority in such "dwellings." The Spirit's governing authority is also depicted when the Spirit "dwells" among God's people in the physical tabernacle (i.e., Lev 8:3–5). The tabernacle was first a project intended to help the Israelite learn to work with others and later a place where God

---

124. Eichrodt, *Theology of the Old Testament*, 50.
125. Ibid., 50.

would continually manifest His presence.[126] In such imagery, God's presence "dwells" in such a way as to provide political rulership, revelation, blessing, and guidance, and protection for Israel.[127]

In post-exilic Israel the Spirit moves beyond simply dwelling to *resting* upon the believing remnant. "Democratization" of the Spirit, prophesied by Moses (Num 11:29) and prophesied as a covenant blessing (Isa 59:21) will be fulfilled by the "pouring out" of the Spirit (Jer 31:31–33; Joel 2:28–31). For post-exilic Jews, this New Covenant outpouring would mean a new governance of the Spirit, one demonstrating the authority of the covenant-making God and a new eschatological hope.

> As the "Guarantor of Restoration" . . . [the Spirit] prepares the people of God for their citizenship in the New Jerusalem and sustains them with the hope of the glorious future. . . . The outpouring of Spirit, accordingly, is "the beginning" of the progression of the Day of the Lord.[128]

This "pouring out" integrates the Spirit's qualities and effects, allowing the Jews to see the Spirit as "the true governor of Israel, and in which the transcendent God draws near to his people."[129] As Restorer of Israel, the Spirit came to have definite personal ramifications for each remnant believer. Democratization meant that believers could now begin to participate in the process of kingdom restoration through the Spirit. Haggai, for example, encouraged Temple-builders on the basis the Spirit's employment of individuals in the work of Kingdom restoration. "Take courage, all you people of the land, and work, for I am with you, says the Lord of hosts. . . . My Spirit abides among you; fear not!" (Hag 2:4). Their experience with the Spirit also led to an anticipation of a greater outpouring.

---

126. "All could participate. . . . the Spirit would supply them with supernatural help in connection with the practical tasks of preparing materials for the tabernacle that would be both useful and beautiful" (Horton, *What the Bible Says about the Holy Spirit*, 25–26).

127. "Closely associated with the temple building is the presence of God, who indwells the temple as his throne. Revelation takes place within the sanctuary, which is the symbol of blessing and God's dwelling among the people. . . . The temple expresses the political rule of God over the people" (Hildebrandt, *An Old Testament Theology of the Spirit of God*, 47–48).

128. VanGemeren, "The Spirit of Restoration," 96.

129. Eichrodt, *Theology of the Old Testament*, 61.

Indeed, their experience of the Spirit's leading became for the Jewish community virtually a pledge that they were standing on the very threshold of the age of salvation, and that all the wretchedness and poverty of their external situation were but the curtain behind which the glorious inheritance destined by God for his people was hidden.[130]

With the coming of Jesus the progress of redemption reaches a culmination point. Recognizing that the redemptive nature and power of his ministry will continue long after his ascension, Jesus proclaims in Matt 16:18, "I will build my church; and the gates of Hades shall not overpower it." Then he grants the Church the "keys of the kingdom of heaven" so that "whatever you bind on earth shall have been bound in heaven, and whatever you loose on earth shall have been loosed in heaven" (16:19). This verse seems to imply *some* notion of the Church's authority. Elsewhere in the NT a "key" (κλεῖδας) always seems to imply authority to open a door and give entrance to a place or realm (i.e. Luke 11:52; Rev 1:18). According to Grudem, "The 'keys of the kingdom of heaven' therefore represents at least the authority to preach the gospel of Christ (cf. Matt 16:16) and thus to open the door of the kingdom of heaven and allow people to enter."[131] Jesus seems to grant the Church an authority to execute the Spirit's authority in and through her ministry "practices."

The Church's "ministerial authority" is displayed and confirmed in the book of Acts. Pentecost marks the beginning of the kingdom's "presentness" within the Church. Whereas Isa 32:15–16 demonstrates that the Spirit will govern the eschatological Kingdom of God on earth with righteousness and justice, Acts 1:5–8 describes this "realm" in terms of a new "ecclesial structure." Within this structure the presence of the Spirit is equated with Christ's kingdom rule and believers are employed as "witnesses" to Christ's redemption. In the book of Acts, the Spirit is portrayed as the Church's new "Governor." The Spirit is given the authority to orchestrate events in relation to the preaching of the gospel (Acts 10), to command action for the mission of the Church (Acts 13:2), and to obstruct movement within the Church (Acts 16:6–7). Here the Spirit's activity seems to progress according to Jesus' portrayal in John 3:3–8. As the "wind" blows where it

---

130. Ibid., 61–62.
131. Grudem, *Systematic Theology*, 889.

The Lord Is the Spirit

wishes, so the Spirit is portrayed as possessing freedom with respect to redemption.[132]

Democratization and restoration progresses in the way the Spirit "dwells" in the NT Church. Paul in particular takes OT temple-building imagery and applies it directly to the Church—God's people are now "growing into a holy temple in the Lord, in whom you also are being built together into a dwelling of God in the Spirit" (Eph 2:21–22). While Christ is the "cornerstone," the Spirit is seen as the one who orchestrates the building process, assembling the "stones" (believers themselves) as a corporate "dwelling place" for God. This "dwelling" theme is also captured in Romans 8, but on an individual level: "you are not in the flesh but in the Spirit, if indeed the Spirit of God dwells in you" (8:9). Paul also speaks here of the Spirit's sanctification (8:11–13) and guidance (8:14), reminiscent of the guidance the Israelites reviewed through the cloud (Exod 40:38). The present government of the Spirit, however, is vastly superior to that of the cloud—the Spirit of the "new covenant" would transform hearts of stone into hearts of flesh (Jer 17:1; 31:31–34; 2 Cor 3:2–18).

Through such a presence the Spirit of Restoration continually invades the present, luring the Church toward her vision of the eschatological kingdom.

> At the same time, the same Spirit as giver of life and as *communio* draws into history the end time, the eschaton (Acts 2), namely, God's eternal life. Here the Church becomes the *communio* of saints in which past, present, and future, rather than being causally related, are one as the body of Christ in the communion event itself.[133]

Paul describes the authoritative "presentness" of the kingdom in the Church by using three metaphors unique to the Spirit. First, the reception of the Spirit is the "first fruits" of the kingdom to come (Rom 8:23),

---

132. According to Ladd, this means that the Spirit "cannot be pinned down to a precise time and mode" (Ladd, *A Theology of the New Testament*, 28). Calvin comments on Jesus' analogy between the effects of wind and the life of the Spirit—they are both "free, uncertain, and variable" Calvin, *Commentary on the Gospel According to John*, 116). This analogy is tighter in Greek because the same word (πνεῦμα) is used.

133. Zizioulas, "Die pneumatologishe Dimension der Kirche," 137 (author's translation from German text).

the initial evidence of the kingdom.[134] Second, believers have the "seal" of the Holy Spirit (Eph 1:13), indicating God's ownership of believers (2 Cor 1:22) as well as his authenticity of ownership (the authority of the insignia that is placed upon the one sealed).[135] Finally, Paul refers to the "down payment" of the Spirit (Eph 1:14), an eschatological term that carries an "already but not yet" presupposition, and refers to both Jews and Gentiles.[136] By pointing to the eschatological and corporate nature of redemption, these metaphors draw our attention to the Spirit as eschatological Governor of the entire Church body, while indicating that the Spirit's authoritative presence resides *within their body*. Oden captures this sense of the *presence* of the Spirit's governing authority:

> The Son placed under the governance of the Spirit not merely redeemed individuals one by one but also the redeemed community together. The Spirit works in the community to offer new life, birthing, regeneration (John 3:3; Titus 3:5), baptizing beliers into the body (1 Cor 12:13), indwelling in their hearts (1 Cor 3:16), freeing from guilt, sin, and death (Rom 7:9—8:2), strengthening the inner life amid hardships and challenges (Eph 3:16–19), bearing witness to their daughterhood and sonship with the Father (Rom 8:16), sealing believers until the day of redemption (Eph 4:30), bearing fruits of faith active in love (Gal 5:19–23; Rom 14:17; 15:13), guiding into all truth (John 16:13), directing the life of prayer

---

134. Moo argues that "the Spirit, in this sense [of firstfruits], is both the 'first installment' of salvation and the 'down payment' or 'pledge' that guarantees the remaining stages of that salvation," and that it furthers the sense of eschatological tension (Moo, *The Epistle to the Romans*, 520–21).

135. "In Paul's time, cattle and even slaves were branded with a seal by their masters to connote ownership" (O'Brien, *Ephesians*, 120). The change from first person plural in v. 12 to second person plural in v. 13 ("you also") to an inclusive first person plural in v. 14 indicates that "seal" is used in the context of Gentiles. Thus, while Joel's prophecy of the New Covenant foretold that the Spirit would not discriminate between age, sex, or social standing, this "seal" extends the Spirit's non-discrimination to ethnicity (Eph 2:11–22). Here, both Jewish and Gentile believers are "sealed" in this New Covenant of the Spirit, through whom they both have full access to God (2:18). Those who are sealed are authorized for divine service (John 14:26, 15:26–27, 20:22–23) and inspired to prophesy (Acts 4:8; 1 Cor 14:1).

136. Fee expresses this metaphor in terms of a "guarantee": "This 'fulfilled promise' is likewise the fulfillment of the promise. The Spirit, therefore, serves as God's down payment in our present lives, the certain evidence that the future has come into the present, the sure guarantee that the future will be realized in full measure" (Fee, *God's Empowering Presence*, 807).

The Lord Is the Spirit

(Rom 8:26, 27; 1 Cor 14:15; Eph 6:18; Jude 20), bringing into accurate recollection the words of Christ (John 14:26), enabling fitting proclamation of the good news of God's own coming (Acts 2:8; 1 Cor 2:1–5), revealing the deep things of God through spiritual discernment.[137]

Knowing well that the eschatological age marks the completion of the restoration process, the Church can go forth today under the government of the Spirit of Restoration so as to realize a degree of that fullness in present anticipation. God's people realize this as they submit their lives and ecclesial activities to the will of this Governor and participate in the "progress of redemption" in practical ways. The Spirit breaks through the tension created by the expectation of the eschaton, a tension that will ultimately resolved by the Spirit's judgment (John 16:8–11). In the meantime, believers are to see themselves as those under the Spirit's authority and are to be actively working with Him in the restoration process.

As we approach an investigation into systematic theology we should keep this conception of the Spirit of Restoration in the background of our thinking—as the One who governs the Church by connecting the authoritative "realm" of the Kingdom with his immanent effects, and as One who authorizes the Church to be the executor of his will.

Systematic Theology

As we have discovered thus far, the Spirit's authority within the pattern of divine authority is an *"executorial divine authority"* that is displayed in terms of not only a *veracious authority* but also a *governing authority*. This general framework will now be used to develop a biblical model of the Spirit's authority in relation to the Church. Our exegetical findings and our survey of biblical theology will now allow us to fill in the framework through the logic and analysis provided by systematic theology.

We need to be careful, however, that while filling the frame we do not move outside the framework. It is important, therefore, to begin with a brief investigation of some contemporary pneumatologies that attempt to relate Spirit and Church.

---

137. Oden, *Life in the Spirit*, 56.

The Authority of the Holy Spirit and Systematic Theology: Part 2

Moltmann's Immanent Experientialism, Hodgson's Liberationism, and Welker's Communalism

As seen in chapter two, three contemporary theologians have recently created models of the Spirit's activity in relation to the Church. In each of their theologies we are able to isolate what seems to be their most significant postmodern or contemporary concern.

Moltmann's contemporary concern is not only that of spiritual and political liberation, *but particularly of the immanent experience of the Spirit,* along with the implications of this starting point for spiritual vitality and hope. Moltmann's pneumatology contributes several positive insights into our understanding of the Spirit's eschatological Lordship. Because of the intimate connection between Spirit and Kingdom, Christians are able to think of Jesus' past and future as "eternally present." Moltmann's views the Spirit as the one "through which the future that is hoped for enters into history."[138] His eschatology advances the idea that God does indeed rule in history through the "Spirit of freedom," who looks toward the final consummation and transforms the present in accordance with this future reality. The present is liberated by the invasion of the future kingdom as well as by the eschatological events of the past (most significantly the redeeming work of Christ) through the Spirit. Moltmann surmises:

> Pneumatology is developed historically and eschatologically, in the sense that the history of the Church, the communion of saints and the forgiveness of sins are to be interpreted as the history of the future; while the eschatology of the resurrection of the body and life everlasting are to be seen as the future of history. That is why we understand this mediation of eschatology and history as the presence of the Holy Spirit.[139]

Hodgson's primary postmodern concern seems to be that of *rediscovering the Spirit's liberation in the world.* In chapter two we also examined Hodgson's *Winds of Spirit* and found the Spirit to be depicted as an immanent, panentheistic "primal energy" that appears in the form of liberating communities. The Spirit helps us to interpret the "gestalt" (i.e., forms) of Christ in the world.

138. Moltmann, *The Church in the Power of the Spirit*, 34.
139. Ibid., 198.

> The name Holy Spirit signifies the unifying and liberating power of the "infinite love that arises from infinite anguish." . . . God in the modality of Spirit *is* the redemptive, transfigurative power that indwells and constitutes a new human intersubjectivity, an intersubjectivity shaped by the paradigmatic love of Christ.[140]

Hodgson's liberation theme reminds us of the Spirit's freedom in this world "to create, shape, and enliven."[141] The focus of the Church is to exist as a "liberated communion." Hodgson proposes a model of the Spirit's "government" that highlights the Spirit's immanence but completely dismisses the Spirit's transcendence. Like Welker, the Spirit is not a Person existing in advance but an "emergent person generated out of the interrelationship of God and the world, the process by which the world is liberated and God is perfected."[142] Since the Spirit exists "as community," Hogdson prefers to speak of the Spirit's "energy" rather than the Spirit's "power" (which he thinks is too closely associated with "ruling").

> If we move back slightly from these metaphors we can say that Spirit is an immaterial vitality that enlivens and shapes material nature: It is the *energeia* that infuses all that is. For this reason Krister Stendahl proposes the metaphor of energy as best suited for the Spirit. "Energy," he says, "is a better word than power. Power is for ruling. Energy is for living." Energy is simply that mysterious power that is active and at work in things (*en + ergon*, work)—and that power (which need not be understood as ruling power) is God as Spirit.[143]

Welker's primary concern seems to be *the experience of the Spirit's powerful presence within pluralistic communities in postmodern times,* particularly in ways and places previously unexpected (i.e., places of powerlessness).[144] Welker's *God the Spirit* attempts to solve the contemporary "problem of experience" by presenting the Spirit as an expression of God's *power* in the world and particularly in the pluralistic community of believers called

---

140. Hodgson, *Winds of Spirit,* 296–97.
141. Ibid., 277.
142. Ibid., 288.
143. Ibid., 279.
144. On this theme, see also Welker, "God's Power and Powerlessness," 39–55.

the Church. Welker warns us of modern understandings of the Spirit's "government." For example, "modern, triumphalistic readings" of OT military narratives[145] "result from superficial understandings and thus obstruct important insights into the Spirit's power in the world." Such early manifestations of the Spirit demonstrate that God's Spirit "is precisely not a spirit of war, but delivers out of distress and helplessness as a 'Spirit of righteousness and mercy.'"[146] In the NT, Welker refers to the Spirit as a "force field" that liberates people from powerlessness, oppression, and bondage.[147] Since the Spirit's primary work is to invoke a unity within the Church while respecting diversity, God no longer is seen as "standing above" the world but as influencing and transforming the world through those who receive the outpouring of the Spirit and through intersubjective contexts. The Spirit's "pluralism" implies the discernment of an almost indefinable yet powerful presence of God in the world. God's Spirit characteristically acts in and through "emergent processes" which transform communities that are powerless or disparate and are either potentially or actually in conflict.[148] Thus for Welker the "Spirit" in the NT seems to work only in cooperation with the community as a "public person" rather than as an unseen Person of God who precedes and stands over the community. Indeed Welker argues that "the Holy Spirit is not something that exists in advance as a supernatural person of the Godhead."[149]

Response

As seen in chapter three, Moltmann understands the Spirit's transformation in the world to be *evolutionary*, that is, a cosmologically internal process

---

145. Cf. Judg 3:7–11, 6:33–35, 11:14, 27–29; 1 Sam 11:6–7.

146. Welker, *God the Spirit*, 55. Instead, these early manifestations of the Spirit's power demonstrate the Spirit's righteousness and mercy. "In a situation of powerlessness, . . . the bearer of the Spirit restores loyalty and a capacity for action among the people" (56).

147. Welker says, "The persons seized, moved, and renewed by God's Spirit can know themselves placed in a force field that is seized, moved, and renewed from many sides—a force field of which they are members and bearers, but which they cannot bear, shape, be responsible for, and enliven alone" (Welker, *God the Spirit*, 228–29).

148. See Welker, "God's Power and Powerlessness," 39–55; also Welker, *God the Spirit*, chapter two.

149. This is Hodgson's summary of Welker's pneumatology (Hodgson, *Winds of Spirit*, 282).

of the Spirit in creation. The Spirit's authority as a divine Person is always reduced when he is essentially thought of as an immanent involvement in the world. Eschatologically speaking, the kingdom of God is understood by Moltmann as a transforming power immanent in the open system of history, and the rule of God as the future transcending the system.[150] Moltmann's perspective on "the eschatological Spirit," however, is flawed because "God's presence" in the world through the Spirit ultimately means that the world is involved in the very being of God.[151] A panentheistic Spirit may "empower" the church but seems somewhat unable to "govern" the church.

The question that must be raised for Hodgson is whether his model aligns with the biblical evidence for the Spirit as the Church's "Governor." Hodgson's model further exposes the "panentheistic" theme found in most postmodern theology, that theme which we have seen to be a great reducer of the Spirit's divine authority. How, then, can Hodgson's model possibly align with a notion of the Spirit's governing authority? With such a model, the Spirit's Personhood is essentially equated with his work in the community; as Hodgson says, the Spirit is "God existing as community."[152]

Welker claims that the Spirit of God "recognizes, enlivens, and maintains the body of Christ in constantly new ways,"[153] but does not portray the Spirit as having any position over the Church in reforming and purifying the fellowship of Christians. As we saw in chapter two, Welker proposes a postmodern ecclesiology where the Spirit's main work is to reveal God's *power* in the structuring of *pluralistic communities*. Such a work, however, begins with the "intersubjective" witness of the community rather than with eschatological "reality." The Spirit's "power" is thereby no longer related to authority but to specific *functions* within diverse, postmodern communities.

As seen in previous sections, Moltmann, Hodgson, and Welker each demonstrate severe deficiencies with respect to the Spirit's authority. In their pursuit of a recovered *experience of the Spirit* within the church community, these essential parameters are neglected, having become for these

---

150. Moltmann, *The Church in the Power of the Spirit*, 190.

151. See ibid., 57–62; also Moltmann, *The Trinity and the Kingdom*, 61ff.

152. Hodgson, *Winds of Spirit*, 309.

153. Welker, *God the Spirit*, 278, 312. See also Bloesch, *The Holy Spirit: Works and Gifts*, 261.

The Authority of the Holy Spirit and Systematic Theology: Part 2

theologians "modern" limitations to a new paradigm for the Spirit's activity. Because the contemporary emphasis is on the Spirit's *function* within the church community (implying that the Spirit possesses authority only with respect to what he *does* or *produces*), the Spirit's "governing authority" is often displaced by that which mediates authority (i.e., doctrine or the church community itself) or by the experience of the Spirit itself. A functional perspective of the Spirit's authority is simply a result of attempting to define the Spirit's relationship to the world without incorporating the parameters provided by the pattern of divine authority. Our discussions of the Spirit's divine, executorial, and veracious authority provide a biblical framework so that the Church can properly understand the Spirit's governing authority. Any denial of these parameters will result in a reduction of the Spirit's governing authority and often an establishment of a replacement "authority" by human leaders, institutions, or doctrines.[154]

Further Discussion and Formal Description

The Spirit's governing authority can now be investigated in terms of the *activation* of the Spirit's "executorial divine authority" and veracious authority in governing the Church. As seen in chapter one, our principle of authority incorporates both *transcendence* and *immanence*. We can now infer from our exegetical conclusions that the Spirit's governing authority reflects the *transcendent/immanent* nature of the Spirit's authority *within the Church*. The *transcendence* of this governing authority is emphasized in the Spirit's eschatological *qualities* (i.e., Isa 11:2 and 32:15–16) that structure the Spirit's realm in the immediate form of the Church (i.e., Acts 1:5–8). The *immanence* of the Spirit's governing authority is emphasized in powerful *effects* wrought by the Spirit within this realm, effects that allow us to *experience and know God* (i.e., Isa 59:21; Rom 8:2; 2 Cor 3:17–18). In addition, our overview of Biblical Theology demonstrated that the Spirit of

---

154. The history of the Church is littered with communities, movements, and persons that have claimed unquestionable governing authority, but in every case the Spirit's function predominates—and often the function of passing authority onto the human leader. Many cult groups and "new age" groups rely as well on "the Holy Spirit" as their source for determining their authority. The Jehovah's Witnesses, for example, deliberately refer to the Spirit as a force or influence rather than as a person: "As for the 'Holy Spirit,' the so-called 'third Person of the Trinity,' we have already seen that it is, not a person, but God's active force" (*The Truth that Leads to Eternal Life*, 24).

Restoration correlated these qualities and effects, employing God's people in the restoration process.

In developing a formal description of the Spirit's authority as the Church's Governor, I shall first describe the Spirit's role as Governor of Christ's eschatological, redemptive kingdom—the realm of the Spirit where the Church is created and governed.[155] Within this realm the Spirit administers the Church as a present, temporal, earthly, social expression of the Kingdom, and does so according to a specific eschatological blueprint and toward eschatological restoration.

Second, I will attempt to describe the *effects* of the Spirit within this realm—specifically, *how* the Spirit creates and governs the Church—by imparting himself to *all* God's people (*democratization*), by freeing God's people from bondage (*liberation*), and by transforming the Church into the image of Christ (*transformation*).

Finally, I will examine the impact of the Spirit's governing authority upon the notion of *Church authority*. In what way do believers who are governed by the Holy Spirit—displaying the Spirit's qualities in their lives and experiencing the Spirit's effects—execute the Spirit's *authority* in and through their participation in the church? Indeed the Church as a whole acts as such an executor when she remains attentive to the pattern of divine authority in her ministry. As we shall see here initially—and in chapters five through seven more extensively—the Church's role as "executor of the Spirit's authority" can be assessed according to specific "practices" in the local church.

---

155. The Spirit's "kingdom authority" is his governing authority that reveals Jesus' eschatological authority in the present Church era. Ladd defines the kingdom as "primarily the dynamic reign or kingly rule of God, and derivatively, the sphere in which the rule is experienced." The Kingdom is never to be identified with the Church, but the kingdom, according to Ladd, creates the Church. "The dynamic rule of God, present in the mission of Jesus, challenged men to respond, bringing them into a new fellowship. . . . [The Church] is the people of the Kingdom, and yet it is not his ideal people, but it includes some who are actually not sons of the Kingdom" (Ladd, *A Theology of the New Testament*, 113). Ladd's definition of the Church, while a bit simplistic, provides a starting point: "The Kingdom is the rule of God, the Church is the fellowship of men" (111).

The Spirit's Governing Authority as an Eschatological/Immediate "Realm" of Authority in the Church

The Spirit's governing authority in the Church is first of all *messianic* (Isa 11:2) and *eschatological* (Isa 32:15–16). In other words, the Spirit governs the Church with the same authority to be displayed by the Messiah at the consummation of God's kingdom (though this is now only a partial display of that final eschatological exhibition).[156] Fee holds that in some of Paul's writings (i.e., Galatians) the fact of the present experience of the promised eschatological Spirit lies at the core of Paul's argumentation, much more than "righteousness by faith."[157] If this is correct, our understanding of the Spirit's relationship to the Church must *begin* with the discussion of Spirit's governing realm within the eschatological Kingdom and the resulting "authority" this imposes upon the Church. According to Gunton,

> The Spirit is God's eschatological transcendence, his futurity, as it is sometimes expressed. He is God present to the world as its liberating Other, bringing to it the destiny determined by the Father, made actual, realized, in the Son.[158]

This statement implies that the Spirit's realm is established according to the eschatological "blueprint" set forth by the Father. The Father's law is interpreted by the Son, who is himself the goal of all history (Eph 1:9–10). The Father who fashions history and is sovereign *over* time is thereby the

---

156. It must be admitted that the typical evangelical response to the "problem of experience" has been weak at best. Reformed theologian Sinclair Ferguson, for example, speaks of the Spirit as governor of the created order. Reflecting Calvin's emphasis on order, Ferguson refers to the Spirit as the "executive in ordering creation" and "the executive of the powerful presence of God in the governing of the created order" (Ferguson, *The Holy Spirit*, 23–24). In the end, however, he is very reluctant to say that the Spirit himself is actually to be considered "Lord" in any sense with respect to the Church (See Ferguson, *The Holy Spirit*, chapter 9). Ferguson's conclusion regarding 2 Cor 3:18—that "Lord" refers to only to Christ, who is now "Lord of the Spirit"—is posited with very little exegetical reasoning (55). As a result, Ferguson only mentions the Spirit's sovereignty with respect to regeneration (123–26), but not with respect to creation, time, hermeneutics, or even the dissemination of spiritual gifts. While rightly expounding the incompromisable truth that "to sustain us 'in Christ' . . . is the heart and soul of the Spirit's ministry," Ferguson seems afraid to grant the Spirit a full governing authority (and tends to deny the Spirit's immanence).

157. Fee, *God's Empowering Presence*, 815.

158. Gunton, *Theology through the Theologians*, 123.

Father who can grant the Spirit an authority to create the Church *in* time. The Spirit displays this governing authority *under* the Son's Messianic authority.

The Spirit's governing authority in the Church is thereby the present "rule" of the Messiah, impacting our understanding of time—of history, the present, and the future—so that we might understand the impact and relevance of future eschatological conceptions in our present time. This creates a tension in our conception of "kingdom," one that Dunn attributes to the Spirit:

> In terms of the present-future tension in the kingdom concept, we might put it this way: the presence of the Spirit is the "already" of the kingdom; the inadequacy of humanity's recognition of the Spirit's presence and submission to him explains the "not yet" of the kingdom. The importance of this formulation is that it explains the relationship between Jesus and the kingdom. For at once we see that the kingdom is present in Jesus only because he has the Spirit. It is not so much a case of Where *Jesus* is there is the kingdom, as Where the Spirit is there is the kingdom.[159]

The Spirit proclaims to us that Christ's eschatological kingdom—indeed Christ himself—is "at hand." In other words, the Spirit reveals that Christ is indeed immediately *present* in all his kingly authority, precisely because the Spirit *transcends* linear history. According to Zizioulas,

> [The] contribution of the Spirit is to liberate the Son and the economy from the bondage of history. . . . The Spirit is the beyond [of] history, and when he acts in history he does so in order to bring into history the last days, the eschaton. Hence the first fundamental particularity of pneumatology is its eschatological character.[160]

The Spirit now displays his governing authority by interpreting the reality of the eschatological kingdom for our immediate benefit (i.e., a basic *theology of presence*). "The work of the Spirit, who does not speak 'from himself,' is to bear witness to the kingdom, making its reality present to us as he elicits our faith, and making its authority bear upon us as he elicits

---

159. Dunn, *Jesus and the Spirit*, 138.
160. Zizioulas, *Being as Communion*, 130.

The Authority of the Holy Spirit and Systematic Theology: Part 2

our free obedience."[161] The Spirit's dynamic revelation of Jesus—and particularly of Jesus' redemption, forgiveness, and mercy is predominant in such a theology of presence.[162] According to Fee,

> The gift of the out-poured Spirit meant that the messianic age had already arrived. The Spirit is thus the central element in this altered perspective, the key to which is Paul's firm conviction that the Spirit was both the *certain evidence* that the future had dawned, and the *absolute guarantee* of its final consummation.[163]

In Acts 1 and 2, the Spirit's governing authority emerges as the very *presence* and *authority* of God over previous administrations of darkness (as demonstrated through the Spirit's provision of victorious power to these disciples). The Spirit appears as a dynamic presence—dynamic in that this eschatological/messianic Spirit is continually breaking into the present, displaying Christ's Lordship, effecting Christ's redemption, and creating a new eschatological/immediate realm called "the Church." In Acts 1:5–8, for example, Jesus reinterprets the *meaning* of the future Kingdom for those in his present time, a reinterpretation that hinges on the sending of the Spirit, the first non-human "ruler" that Israel could equate with the eschatological kingdom.

The Spirit's governing "realm" involves a comprehensive exercise of God's authority over all of creation. Because of its comprehensive eschatological nature, it lays claim on all history. Acts 1:7–8 deliberately demonstrates the immediate display of this realm as the Spirit "conquers" ever-increasing territory through the mission of the Church. This "realm" of authority is exposed not only in terms of *space* (i.e., Acts 1:8 and throughout the book of Acts) but also *time* (i.e., 1:7; the Spirit's authority over history). Bock interprets the idea of a "realm" today according to

---

161. O'Donovan, *Resurrection and Moral Order*, 140.

162. According to O'Donovan, "There are other ways, immanent and non-authoritative, by which past and future events enter into the present and affect it. . . . But the redemptive moment, or moments, of Christ's passion and triumph act upon our present in quite another way. They are God's final deed, the eschaton in which history is given is meaning; and as such they stand equidistant from all moments of time and determine what the reality of each moment is. 'Authority' and 'reality' are inseparable aspects of the presence of God" (O'Donovan, *Resurrection and Moral Order*, 103) (emphasis his).

163. Fee, *God's Empowering Presence*, 806.

his messianic conceptualization of kingdom. First, it refers to the invisible presence of God's authority in the community of believers.

> An operative but invisible realm is at work in the community Jesus is forming, . . . a power of God working in the midst of Jesus' absence and in anticipation of his visible return and rule . . . [and] the community that recognizes and responds to Jesus as Lord, Son of Man, Christ; . . . the place where he is Head.[164]

Second, this realm extends beyond the Church into a "claimed, potential" realm where the Kingdom makes a claim on the entirety of humanity in anticipation of its eventual scope. Here the presence of divine authority is demonstrated as a challenge to the world. Such a "realm" brings kingdom authority into the entire world through various governmental means—including political and human government, moral and judicial law, family, and individual conscience. This realm "justifies the preaching of the gospel of the authoritative Jesus to every tribe and nation . . . [and] establishes an accountability for every person before the one true God and his chosen One, so that there is only one way to God."[165]

The moral/political authority displayed by Christ within each "realm" is now displayed through the Spirit's qualities and effects. Each passage exegeted previously in some way demonstrates the "in-breaking" of these eschatological qualities into the community of God's people through the Spirit, who therein creates (or imposes) ethical structures that shape all aspects of community life. According to Bock,

> In this era, the Kingdom involves the inaugural "in-breaking" of God's power, presence and rule among a people he has claimed as his own, forming them into a community that looks forward one day to the total in-breaking of his authority expressed throughout the world. Those who are his have acknowledged their need for God and his provision by faith alone. As a result, they have entered into an enduring relationship to God. That relationship entails a

---

164. Bock, "The Kingdom of God," 29. See also Ladd, *The Presence of the Future*, 195–205.

165. Bock, "The Kingdom of God," 29–30. Bock adds, "Note how my reading does not limit the authority here to 'Christendom.' The claim is far more comprehensive in scope than this. The weeds in the world are not a reference to professing Christians, but to humanity at large in the world, including those outside of the sown word Jesus brings" (30).

call from God on the life of the disciple. Thus, in a sense all aspects of Jesus' teaching about discipleship involve teaching about the Kingdom and ethics. In sum, what Jesus presents is the idea that the in-breaking of God's rule into one's life demands a total response to that rule.[166]

The Pentecost fulfillment of the promise of Acts 1:5 in Acts 2:1–13 demonstrates that the Spirit's governing authority not only parallels the first Pentecost at Sinai (see Exod 23:16) but also *reverses the curse of Babel*. "The divisive nature of languages, Genesis' climactic symbol of man's social disintegration due to his hubris, is now overcome by the one Spirit."[167] The Spirit's "new" immediate authority breaks through the "language barrier" that previously limited Israel's witness to the world (and, in this sense, limited divine government throughout the world).

In Acts 2:33–39, Jesus' exaltation and Lordship makes him the chosen vessel for receiving and pouring out the promised Holy Spirit, and the tangible evidence is presented in "what you see and hear" (v. 33). The Davidic throne is now occupied (v. 34) and all Israel can be assured that "God has made this Jesus, whom you crucified, both Lord and Christ" (v. 36). The only appropriate response is to "repent and be baptized, every one of you, in the name of Jesus Christ for the forgiveness of your sins. And you will receive the gift the Holy Spirit" (v. 38). The Spirit is therefore a confirmation of Jesus' Lordship over the new believer, "for you and your children and for all who are far off" (v. 39).

> Jesus exercises key elements of the promised rule when He pours out the Spirit of God on His people to enable them to undertake their current tasks. . . . This is the heart of Christ's rule in the present era. He pours out the benefits of His victory, the spoils of His rule. By His Spirit He transforms people who are a part of His newly formed community, the Church. . . . His rule and their transformation begin with this distribution of the Spirit. The Spirit's presence is evidence that Jesus is Lord and Messiah, the One who rules from heaven dispensing benefits of salvation (Acts. 2:34–36).

---

166. Bock, "The Kingdom of God," 30–32.
167. Montague, *Holy Spirit: Growth of a Biblical Tradition*, 282.

> The transforming grace of Jesus Christ stands at the center of God's current dispensational activity.[168]

This passage (especially vv. 34–36) portrays Jesus as a *royal exile*—though only a temporary one. In his absence, the Holy Spirit has been sent to reveal the Messiah's kingdom rule. According to Bock,

> God's rule is expressed in terms of the exercise of his authority. Thus, Jesus' miracles evidence the in-breaking of God's authority, the presence of his power. Jesus' presence means the Kingdom's presence. We would also suggest that the mediation of the Spirit through Jesus is evidence of the presence of this rule, as the giving of the Spirit is a key, messianic work. This idea is not explicit in the gospel material, but it will show up in Acts and the epistles. Most New Testament scholars accept this "dynamic" element as central to Jesus' teaching.[169]

The Spirit's Governing Authority with Respect to the "Effects" of this Realm in Establishing and Governing the Church

A basic understanding of the Spirit's eschatological/immediate realm of authority in governing the Church naturally leads to the question of *how the Spirit acts* in creating the Church. As Christ's executor, the Spirit's executorial authority can now be expanded beyond "the execution of Christ's will" to a full "plenipotentiary authority"—a full representation of the King's will in creating the Church. This particularly involves the application of Christ's redemption to the world, an application that occurs through kingly "decrees" that appear as specific, powerful effects and that present to us a vivid, immediate picture of the glorious eschatological kingdom in the form of present church communities. These redemptive effects include the Spirit's work in *democratization, liberation,* and *transformation*. The Spirit is democratized to all believers, who are liberated and transformed so that their church "practices" can also be liberated and transformed into specific executions of the Spirit's authority. Nevertheless, while we must listen to the concerns of contemporary postmodern theologians who decry the need for a powerful restoration of each of these effects, evangelicals must be

---

168. Bock, "The Son of David and Saints' Task," 454.
169. Bock, "The Kingdom of God," 29–30.

careful to call for such a restoration only within the context of the pattern of divine authority.

Democratization

First, Welker and other cotemporary theologians decry a need for a pluralistic "pouring out" of the Spirit in present times, *so that diverse communities of the Spirit may come forth*. Welker's pneumatology cries for a "restoration of solidarity and of the community's capacity for action" (as he sees portrayed in OT deliverance through the hands of the Judges) and as a result eschews the oppressive tendencies of "modern, totalizing metanarratives" in view of the "public transformation of powerholders and of political power structures."[170] Referring to Bonhoeffer's critique of modern individualism, Welker reminds us that the Spirit,

> is not bound up with an abstract, uniform individualism that reduces everything to an unrealistic, abstract quality, reducing everything to "the ego," the subject, the decision-maker, the consumer, or the payee. The individualism of the Spirit is marked by diverse concreteness and by concrete diversity, without crumbling into the indeterminate pluralism of "pure" individuality.[171]

In our exegesis of Isa 59:21 we also saw that the Spirit's central eschatological activity involves the fulfillment of the New Covenant, a fulfillment that occurs in accordance with the Spirit of Restoration and the Word of Promise. Such activity produces the initial effect of the Spirit within the entire "remnant community"—"democratization"—which is eventually fulfilled according to Joel's vision. This specific effect of the Spirit not only allows this community to remain hopeful in a time of eschatological tension but also, in accordance with the Word of Promise, becomes an instrumental element in the Spirit's restoration activity. While this community may and should seek political/societal liberation as a tangible demonstration of the Spirit's "democratizing" effects (and as a "downpayment" of eschatological liberation), this community does not exist primarily for the purpose of societal liberation; neither is the Spirit discovered primarily as the power of God that combats differences

---

170. See Welker, *God The Spirit*, 52–83.
171. Welker, *God The Spirit*, 21–22. See also Bonhoeffer, *The Communion of Saints*, 20–25.

and creates political solidarity. Rather, the "democratizing" Spirit is for the community the guarantee of future covenantal blessings, a "governing authority" that will not only create an eschatological unity in the presence of Messiah, but is creating that unity now in the presence of the Messianic Spirit. This "covenant of the Spirit" demonstrates the initial *effect* of the Spirit of redemption—democratization—as Yahweh's covenant faithfulness to his remnant people.

The "Spirit of Restoration," as we saw in our biblical theology, brings forth such restorative effects in this community according to an eschatological "blueprint." Whereas the promise of eschatological fulfillment in Isa 59:21 (the "Covenant of the Spirit") "extends to God's people *throughout* the progression of redemptive history,"[172] the fulfillment of New Covenant is a specific action of the Spirit of Restoration does not begin until the Church age. The Spirit is both the *guarantee* of the fulfillment of God's New Covenant promises as well as the *guarantor*, the one who restores the world according to these promises. Like good parents who prepare their children to handle their inheritance well, the Spirit prepares the children of God to receive their divine inheritance.

The "pouring out of the Spirit" in Acts 2 is indeed the initial and immediate fulfillment of the New Covenant demonstrating the Spirit's "democratization." The Spirit's immediate execution of Christ's Kingdom in creating the Church is witnessed in Jesus' statement, "I will build my Church" (Matt 16:18). Paul will later use distinct metaphors (a "body" in 1 Cor 12:12–13; a "building" in Eph 2:20–22) to illustrate the Spirit's authority to construct and orchestrate the Church.

Liberation

Second, as we have seen, Hodgson desires to recover the liberating experience of the Spirit within the context of "liberated communities." In developing critique of modern oppression, Hogdson looks to Comblin, who studies individuals and communities that "had been downhearted, lacking in dynamism, resigned to the endless struggle for survival."[173] Comblin states that now these people, "discover that they are acting for themselves,

---

172. VanGemeren, "The Spirit of Restoration," 88.
173. Comblin, *The Holy Spirit and Liberation*, 20–23.

discover that they are capable of setting and seeking goals, of achieving objectives."

> Before, they gave up before they had stared: only the masters, teacher or priests knew what to do. Now they are amazed at their discovery that they themselves are acting in the compete sense of the word. . . . This experience has the effect of completely reversing their situation, of changing them from mere passivity to activity: it is like the experience of being born. It is the experience of re-birth. This is the experience that has to be attributed to the Spirit.[174]

Hodgson, however, interprets such amazing turnabouts as such:

> The Holy Spirit acts in the form of human activity and is dependent on us to actualize itself. When we find available the resources and power to go on when we have reached the end of the rope, when we are filled with hope in the midst of desperation, when we are given the courage to act in the face of fear and discouragement, then we know that the Spirit has been "poured out" upon us and that we are "standing out" into God.[175]

As we have seen, the Spirit for Hodgson is the experience of God existing *as* community, wherein which the very purpose of the Church as a liberating experience of God comes forth. The Spirit's *liberation,* however, is presented in Scripture not as an *impersonal force* that remains "dependent on us to actualize itself" (i.e., "in the form of human activity"), but is expressed by Paul in Rom 8:2 in terms of the Spirit's "binding authority" that *results* in redemptive freedom.

Whereas traditional evangelicals have often viewed eschatological "reality" or "presence" as having a static quality, contemporary theologians give them a much more dynamic (i.e., *liberating* or *public*) character. Moltmann, for example, argues that the presence of the Spirit can be found wherever men and women receive the power to enter into the struggle for the liberation of God's creation, for justice within a world of social injustice, and for freedom from oppression. While the present experience of the world is an experience of the lack of freedom, the Spirit is precisely the presence of the power of liberation, anticipations of the kingdom of God

---

174. Ibid., 21.
175. Hogdson, *Winds of Freedom*, 287.

that are experienced as resistance against the forces which bind mankind in various forms of slavery.[176]

Though such arguments re-establish the need to pay attention to the final words of Rom 8:2, "the law of sin *and death*," theologians must not forget the primacy of the personal, authoritative Spirit in the deliverance from the "law of sin" itself. Gunton points out that,

> Liberation, as some contemporary theologies seem to forget, is an essentially eschatological concept; it is only won—or rather, given—proleptically, by the Spirit. . . . The Spirit is God in his freedom to create in the here and now the conditions of the redemption of all things promised for the end.[177]

Liberation theologies blur the distinction between the Spirit's work in providence and creation (i.e., "common grace") with the Spirit's work in redemption ("salvific grace"), thus reducing the Spirit's personal *otherness*. Gunton adds, "He [the Spirit] is God present to the world as its liberating other, bringing it to the destiny determined by the Father, made actual, realized, in the Son."[178] Likewise, Barth begins his description of the "Holy Ghost as Redeemer" by presenting the necessity of the Spirit/spirit distinction:

> The Holy Spirit must be present in His total difference, if we are to be honest as theologians making a statement: the difference between the Creating Spirit and the creature's spirit, and the contrast between the Spirit who pardons and the sinful spirit, must not be left on one side: and further, this presence has to be interpreted by us in the eschatological sense: i.e. To say, as the presence of the promise.[179]

---

176. Similarly, Welker wants to re-emphasize the "concrete presence" of the Spirit, as seen in such "public" displays as Jesus' birth accounts, his baptism, and the "earthy" conditions of his life. The Spirit's liberation in public arenas, he holds, receives massive attention in the gospels in terms of Jesus' acts of deliverance from demons, an action that allows the formerly possessed to go forth and "live in a way corresponding to their creaturely possibilities and to take part in social life" (Welker, *God the Spirit*, 199).

177. Gunton, *Theology through the Theologians*, 120.

178. Ibid., 123.

179. Barth, *The Holy Ghost and the Christian Life*, 74–75.

Transformation

Third, Moltmann represents the contemporary longing for a community experience that incorporates *immanent power and transformation*. For Moltmann, the problem of the contemporary Church is the "dialectic" between transcendence and immanence (that emerged from Barth and others). Moltmann complains that Barth's conception of "The Holy Spirit and Christian Life" makes the Spirit too transcendent and does not account with an immanent rendering of human power, liberty, and transformation. After reviewing Barth's main points, Moltmann concludes, "his eschatology is not linked with the future of the new creation of all things; it is related to God's eternity, over against the temporality of human beings."[180] This is a somewhat helpful observation, particularly with respect to any over-indulgence in "transcendence" found in contemporary evangelicalism. An important distinction between Barth's thinking and Moltmann's, however, is essentially the fact that Barth, along with evangelicals, retains the distinction between the Spirit's work in justification and in sanctification. Barth's distinction carries over from Calvin, who makes clear that sanctification, not justification, involves the renewal of the Spirit. In the Catholic tradition, justification is a process in which human beings are made righteous, and retains no clear distinction from sanctification.[181] Reformation doctrine restored this distinction on the basis of the work of the Spirit through the Word, thus taking the focus off the believer—and his or her own "works"—and onto the grace of God. Human works became a matter of sanctification, and were made secondary to the work of the Spirit in the Christian life.

Whereas Moltmann's eschatology seems a bit "over-realized,"[182] Second Corinthians 3:17–18 reminds us that the Spirit brings "eschatological

---

180. Moltmann, *The Spirit of Life*, 7.

181. Calvin points out that "(the scholastics) include under the term 'justification' a renewal, by which through the Spirit of God we are remade to obedience to the law" (Calvin, *Institutes* III: xii. 11). So, if the Spirit's renewal is excluded in the doctrine of justification, what is the Spirit's role in salvation? Calvin holds that salvation involves much more than justification alone, though this doctrine itself remains central. Also at the center of Calvin's soteriology stands the doctrine of union with Christ, and this union is accomplished by the action of the Spirit of Christ.

182. Moltmann also confuses common grace (in creation) with salvific, eschatological grace. His worry that, "if redemption is places in radical discontinuity to creation, then 'the

tension" into the Church by allowing her to experience the first fruits of the New Covenant. Thorsell examines 2 Corinthians 3 in an attempt to demonstrate that within the present era of the Church there is,

> a partial and preliminary fulfillment of the New Covenant in anticipation of a complete fulfillment in the *eschaton* (and thus) within the Pauline corpus the presence and activity of the Holy Spirit among believers demonstrates that the New Covenant is currently operative, albeit in a partial and preliminary way.[183]

Transformation, therefore, is a thoroughly eschatological concept. Second Corinthians 3:17–18 presents the Spirit's initial deposit of the future eschatological transformation, vividly portrayed by the OT prophets as a total transformation that incorporates a renewal of creation. According to VanGemeren,

> Transformation demonstrates the renewal of creation, when the Lord will open up all the benefits of God's goodness to his children (Hos 2:21–23; Joel 2:19–26; Amos 9:13–15). His Spirit will also renew humans with physical and spiritual strength, consecrate them, and endow them with grace so that they may live in harmony with the kingdom of God.[184]

While Isaiah demonstrates that eschatological transformation will include the desert (32:15; 35:6–7) and vegetation (35:7), and Ezekiel predicts a total cleansing from all impurity and idolatry (36:25–28), Paul's message in 2 Cor 3:17–18 is that "the Lord is the Spirit," the one who now transforms believer into the image of Christ "from glory to glory." Such a New Covenant transformation also includes local ecclesiastical communities that are being transformed into a unified body of Christ. Paul's use of ἡμεῖς πάντες ("we all"), along with 3:6–11, indicates that the Corinthians,

---

Spirit of Christ' has no longer anything to do with Yahweh's ruach" (Moltmann, *Spirit of Life*, 8–9) is legitimate, but his over-compensation toward "panentheism" makes these two works essentially indistinguishable, as seen in the following: "To experience the fellowship of the Spirit inevitably carries Christianity beyond itself into the greater fellowship of all God's creatures. For the community of creation, in which all created things exist with one another, for one another and in one another, is also the fellowship of the Holy Spirit" (8–9).

183. Thorsell, "The Spirit in the Present Age," 397–98.

184. VanGemeren, *Interpreting the Prophetic Word*, 221.

together with Paul, are in some sense "servants of a new covenant"—that is, in the "ministry of transformation." According to Thorsell,

> Since through the gospel the Spirit works to remove "the veil" (i.e. the hardness of their minds), Paul's service of the New Covenant can be effective in transforming believers so that they, like Moses, are transformed to reflect the glory of God through the Spirit (2 Cor. 2:18).[185]

Reflecting on 2 Cor 3:3 and 3:17–18, Thorsell asserts, "When Paul proclaimed the gospel to the Corinthians, Christ had, so to speak, written on their hearts with the ink of the Spirit in fulfillment of Ezek 36:26–27."[186] Such "writing" is not only a referent to the Spirit; it also presents in vivid picture the fulfillment of the law by the act of "writing." The authority of the law, which is usurped by the Spirit of the New Covenant, actually confirms that the Spirit's action of fulfilling the New Covenant has the same authority as the written law. The Spirit's authority, however, is not veiled—it is *transformational*, reflecting the likeness of Christ with ever-increasing glory.[187]

---

185. Thorsell, "The Spirit in the Present Age," 409.

186. Ibid., 406–7.

187. Fee explains the transformational quality of the new covenant as opposed to the "deadness" of the old. The former Covenant, the Covenant of Law (or Torah), was not accompanied by the Spirit, but being written on stone tablets (which for Paul imaged its "deadness") was unable to set people free. As for the New Covenant, "the emphasis now, however, is not so much on Gentile inclusion but their inclusion apart from Torah, which served as the 'identity marker' of the former covenant. The Spirit, and the Spirit alone, Paul argues in Galatians, identifies the people of God under the new covenant. . . . [It] is written on 'tablets of human hearts' (2 Cor 3:3); its rite of 'circumcision' is that 'of the heart' (Rom 2:29. . . . The new covenant is life-giving, because its content, Christ, is administered by the Spirit, through whom also we behold—and are being transformed into—the glory of the Lord" (Fee, God's Empowering Presence, 812–13). The Law is not abolished, per se, but it does not have the transforming value associated with the Spirit's righteousness. "Thus the key to Paul's view of the Law lies with the gift of the eschatological Spirit. The fruit of the Spirit is none other than the Spirit's bearing in our lives the 'righteousness of God' (= the righteousness that characterizes God). When this is happening Torah is fulfilled in such a way that for all practical purposes it has become obsolete; however, Torah as part of the Old Testament story, of which ours is the continuation, is never obsolete. In this sense it will endure as long as this 'between-the-times' existence endures—not as a means of righteousness, nor as a means of identity, but as a means of pointing us to the 'righteousness of God,' which the Spirit brings to pass in our lives in the present expression of the eschatological future" (Fee, *God's Empowering Presence*, 816).

The Lord Is the Spirit

> The token of God's presence is the Spirit of God. He is the Spirit of transformation, assuring God's people of the victorious outcome of his intervention on their behalf. The Spirit renews humans being and internalized God's lay so that they will experience a new freedom (36:26–27).[188]

Paul's own message and ministry—which centered in gospel proclamation (1 Cor 2:1–5; 2 Cor 2:14—3:16)—was itself an operation of the New Covenant through which the Spirit transformed believers to reflect Christ's glory.[189] We can thus deduce that a critical redemptive *effect* of the Spirit of Restoration is his transformative operation in the Church with respect to this New Covenant. Rather than focusing us back on communitarian power in itself, or on a "realized eschatology" in the community, this Spirit sovereignly transforms the Church by luring her toward the eschatological vision that has been laid out. Since the Kingdom is "larger" than the Church, its transforming presence now is but a precursor to a more substantial presence in the future. The Kingdom's "invisible" and "transformative" ("claiming and potential") realm in the Church creates a "tension" sustained by the Spirit's eschatological actions. "The Lord, the giver of life, transforms the body of Jesus so that it may partake of the life of the age to come, the first-born of the new creation."[190]

The Spirit's Governing Authority and the Church's Execution of the Spirit's "Authority"

As seen above, the "in-breaking" of the Messiah's kingdom authority, first witnessed in his earthly ministry, is now exercised through the Spirit's *governing* authority within the Church today—authority that once again appears with respect to the dissemination of the gospel, the overturning of demonic "rule," and the display of moral authority as reflected in the Spirit's demonstration of righteousness and justice.[191] These ministries now become part of the Church's "mission." The Spirit's kingdom authority is

---

188. VanGemeren, *Interpreting the Prophetic Word*, 333.

189. Thorsell, "The Spirit in the Present Age," 409.

190. Gunton, *Theology Through the Theologians*, 118.

191. These activities also require cultural discernment and application, which will be taken up in chapter five.

The Authority of the Holy Spirit and Systematic Theology: Part 2

not actually *shared* with the Church; instead the Church has been delegated a "functional authority"—first by Christ and now by the Spirit.[192] Her function is essentially *administrative* or, better, *ministerial* (i.e., providing fellowship and spiritual leadership, preaching the gospel). According to Calvin, the Spirit's authority is delegated or attributed to priests, prophets, and apostles, "not in a strict sense to the persons themselves, but to the *ministry* over which were appointed."[193] Ramm proclaims, "The right of the Church to exercise a measure of administrative authority is denied by none who believe that Jesus intended a visible Church to propagate His gospel."[194]

A significant and unique feature of the Church's pneumatological dimension is the fact that the Spirit transcends the course of linear history by making the eschaton part of the *anamnesis* (i.e., the historic consciousness of past and future reality) of the Church. As a result, a church's "tradition" can, to some extent, be considered eschatological reality for those believers who "participate" in them—vis-à-vis specific church practices. These practices can become means by which believers might witness to and experience the Spirit's new life and eschatological values in the Church and to the world.[195] Evangelicals would typically believe that such traditions do not have authority in themselves (i.e., Gal 5:5–6; Col 2:8–16), but in their expression and explanation they can indeed become practical vehicles by which God's people can strengthen the Church and "witness" to the world.[196] In this light,

---

192. Ramm thinks of "functional authority" as a "substitutional authority" (Ramm, *The Pattern of Authority*, 12). It is the right to perform a specific function or task, usually in place of another, and is especially applied to the occupation of an office. It can refer to teachers who serve as an instructional guide "until the learner can know the truth for himself" (12).

193. Calvin, *Institutes*, iv.8.2.

194. Ramm, *The Pattern of Authority*, 56.

195. While examples are numerous, we might think of Eric Liddell's reasoning for choosing not to run his race in the 1924 Olympic Games that had been scheduled on the Sabbath. While the discernment of a connection between such a tradition (i.e. this particular form of Sabbath keeping) and eschatological life would involve the Spirit's authority with respect to hermeneutical interpretation and application (see next chapter), Liddell's personal commitment to this connection—thus evidencing the Spirit's righteousness as well as his liberation—is certainly done in submission to the Spirit's governing authority.

196. An example of the Spirit's governing "realm" and its expression in tradition is the early Church councils. According to Calvin, "But I maintain that he [Christ] really presides

the Church can indeed discover her functional or "executorial" authority to execute the Spirit's will as she submits to the Spirit's executorial/veracious authority and acts "under" the Spirit's governing "realm."

In an effort to clarify the various "senses of tradition" that have appeared in Church history,[197] Thiel attempts to make key connections between tradition and the authority of the Spirit. Thiel's main points are that the Spirit indeed encourages the Church to develop (and evaluate) "traditions" according to a broad sense of the word, and that the "tradition's responsibility is responsibility to the Spirit."[198] This is certainly true, if we think of this "responsibility to the Spirit" in terms of the submission of tradition to the Spirit's authority *within the pattern of divine authority*. In such an approach the Church's "tradition" would not have authority in itself but instead would perform the "function" of providing patterned activities wherein God's people might know the Father through the Son by the Spirit and in accordance with Scripture. Thiel provides helpful insight into the possible use of tradition with respect to a "functional" Church authority:

> Authority in the Church is faithfulness to God, and Jesus' life fully images that faithfulness. But as Christians share their lives with others, they meet the power of that authority and the possibilities of its concrete enactment in the presence of the Holy Spirit. God's own trinitarian being, economically disposed toward the world for salvation's sake, then, establishes a framework for considering *how*

[over the councils] only where he governs the whole assembly by his word and Spirit" (Calvin, *Institutes*, iv:9.1). Calvin also suggests that the "authority" of these councils is actually that of Christ and the Holy Spirit, and that they are to be judged by the degree to which they attain to the pattern of divine authority. "If it be inquired what is the authority of councils according to the Scriptures, there is no promise more ample or explicit than this declaration of Christ: 'Where two or three are gathered together in my name, there am I in the midst of them.' But this belongs no less to every particular congregation than to a general council . . . such councils are *directed by the Holy Spirit* . . . they are *assembled in the name of Christ*" (*Institutes*, 4.8.2; emphasis mine to show the pattern of divine authority).

197. Thiel's four "senses of tradition" explain how the traditionally old endures, how the old becomes new, how the new becomes old, or how the old occasionally ceases to be valued traditionally (Thiel, *Senses of Tradition*, preface). Thiel adds in the Preface that "the theory proposed herein is developed and illustrated with particular reference to the Roman Catholic tradition, though it could be applied, mutatis mutandis, to understand the workings of any Christian community that prized theological tradition in some way."

198. Thiel, *Senses of Tradition*, 163.

believers are responsible to God. If the presence of the Holy Spirit to creation is both the mode of encounter with God, who is Father and Son, and graceful power itself of enacted faithfulness, then authority in the Church is mediated by the Spirit who, as both divine communication and the power of believer's commitment, *is* the "how" of responsibility toward God. In other words, how authority dwells in the Church, how it is exercised, and how it is evaluated and questioned are in large measure a matter of determining how believers are responsible to the Spirit who enables their belief and action.[199]

In other words, the Church's authority is ultimately the authority of the Spirit who resides within her body and allows for the responsible discernment of tradition. Since Thiel obviously grants the Spirit "executorial authority," we must only be careful that the "how" of which Thiel speaks is also one that recognizes the Spirit's *authority* to be (1) both *immanent* and *transcendent,* and (2) a veracious authority to speak truth *through* tradition according to the final authority of God's inspired Word.

This being said, we must realize that the Spirit, who possesses plenipotentiary authority as a free, divine Person and who authoritatively resides *within* believers, can indeed grant the Church a "functional authority"—a freedom—to know God in community through the essential "practices" laid out in Scripture. Such practices include the sacraments (i.e., baptism, Lord's supper, preaching of the Word) and specific disciplines (i.e., prayer, fasting, fellowship, etc.). In addition, this Spirit can indeed grant the Church a "ministerial authority" to make Christ known in the world (by preaching the gospel).

The nature of the "practice" of the Spirit is introduced in Rom 8:2 in terms of the "law" of the Spirit and expounded in 8:3–27 in terms of the believer's "walk in" the Spirit (see especially 8:4, 6, 13; see also Gal 3:1–14 and 5:22–26). As we shall see in chapters five through seven, these practices are *means of expression* of the Spirit's new life and eschatological reality. The model proposed here incorporates the Spirit's *executorial authority* (i.e., which is "grounded" in Christ), *veracious authority* ("grounded" in Scripture), and a truly *governing authority* (i.e., "grounded" in eschatological reality). Such an appropriate "grounding" does allow for the Church to practice its traditions in joy and freedom—"earthing" its ecclesial life, so to

---

199. Ibid., 165–66.

speak, in specific traditions as means of submitting to the Spirit in practical ways.[200] The emphasis, however, must remain on discovering the *qualities* of the Spirit (righteousness, justice, peace) and experiencing his specific *effects* (democratization, liberation, transformation), rather than seeking to discover some "deeper meaning" within the traditions themselves.

Such a notion of the Church's "authority" shall be investigated further in chapters five through seven with respect to specific Church practices. In these chapters we shall see that the Spirit's authority in the Church directs us as to *how* these practices can be worked out in particular local bodies and *how* the Church can serve as a functional executor of the Spirit's authority in various ways. First, since most church "practices" (i.e., baptism, Sabbath, preaching) come wrapped in various interpretive traditions, the Spirit extends *himself* as the "interpretive authority" within those churches that rely upon his authority (within the pattern of divine authority) and thus provides "authoritative significance" (see chapter five). Second, since such practices also occur in community, the Spirit grants a "ministerial authority" to all believers and a "functional authority" to church leaders so that they might guide the church in truth and wisdom (chapter six). Third, since these practices are practical manifestations of Christian spirituality, the Spirit communicates to believers a "spiritual authority" whereby they might know God and resist evil forces (chapter seven).

Conclusion

In sum, we have discovered that postmodern theologies are often crying out for fresh, powerful experiences of God in the Church and in the world—ones that provides justice through ecclesial diversity, freedom through ecclesial and political liberation, and power through immanent encounters with God. In doing so, however, many seem to have reduced the Spirit's authority as divine Governor in the Church to a powerful force *within* the Church community (i.e., an "empowering spirit"), a liberating force or function *indistinguishable from* the community (i.e., a "community spirit") or the immanent presence of God *within* the world and *within*

---

200. Thiel adds, "The Spirit is the continuing presence of God to creation, to time and space, and even to the small durations and places of historicity.... But the Spirit's continuing presence is neither spiritual at the expense of the physical nor pneumatological in a way that prescinds from the incarnational" (Thiel, *Senses of Tradition*, 167).

life-experiences (i.e., a "world-spirit"). These postmodern understandings of "Spirit" have essentially abandoned the pattern of divine authority and with that the true authority of the Spirit as Governor of the Church.[201]

Our experience of the Spirit within the Church is restored, however, when the Spirit's personal/plenipotentiary authority begins to emerge within the Church as an activation of the Spirit's divine, executorial, veracious authority in terms of a governing authority. *This is an authority to (1) create an eschatological/immediate realm of authority under which believers honor the Spirit as their Chief Governor, (2) produce powerful effects—in terms of democratization, liberation, and transformation—that demonstrate this authority and allow believers to know and experience God, and (3) delegate a certain "authority" to the Church whereby her tradition and practices can serve as means for knowing God and making him known.*

In developing the doctrine of the Spirit's authority for systematic theology, it should be remembered that, while the Spirit's divine authority is *always* and *at the same time* executorial, veracious, and governing, it is not always recognized by us (or by history) in such an integrated manner. As in historical theology, where the doctrine of the Spirit's authority develops in stages, so has our understanding with respect to systematic and practical theology. As divine Person, Executor, Teacher, and Governor, the Spirit is obviously not known according to a purely cognitive "understanding." This being said, we can present our completed model in the form of the following chart.

---

201. Likewise, the majority of evangelicals might only recognize the Spirit's authority with respect to the Spirit's divine, executorial, and veracious authority (and even then perhaps only in terms of function rather than authority (i.e., the Father's will in the world, Christ's saving Spirit, and the Spirit who aids us in applying the Scriptures).

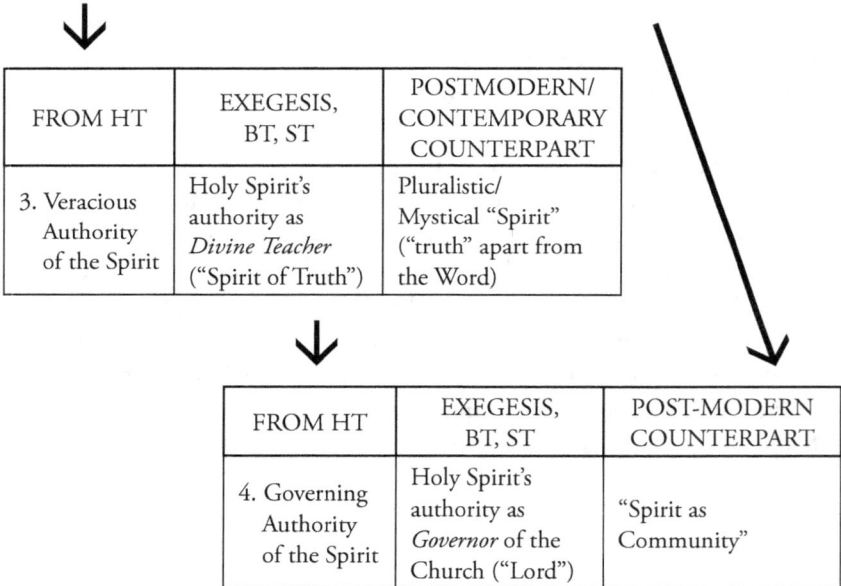

Figure 1. A Summary of Biblical and Postmodern Perspectives with Respect to the Authority of the Holy Spirit

Here we see that the Spirit's governing authority is an extension of his executorial authority and also in keeping with his veracious authority, so that—going in reverse—the Spirit as Governor always points the Church to the Word and to Christ.

As we begin to grapple with this model of the Spirit's authority *in its fullness*, we will want to apply this model to special practical issues within the Church. The authority of the Spirit is not only a theological model for systematic theology but also one that can and must find embodiment within practical theology in order to be "complete." The illustration of the butterfly that is dissected by researchers applies well to our understanding of this doctrine. The scientists perform in-depth analyses of the butterfly's composition, wing structure, molecular content, and migration patterns, and when they are finished they realize they have not studied a butterfly at all but a dead carcass! The Spirit of life, as we shall see in the next three chapters, can only be "analyzed" in places where he is found to be "alive"—that is, in the practical arenas of his influence. This *Spirit of life,* as described in Romans 8, is this sort of life that creates a dramatic paradigm shift for such practical issues as hermeneutics, Church structure and guidance, and spirituality. These issues shall become the topics of discussion in chapters five through seven, respectively.

5

The Authority of the Holy Spirit and Practical Theology: Hermeneutics

❖ WHAT DIFFERENCE DOES the authority of the Holy Spirit make in the NT Church? Lloyd-Jones proclaims that, while the authority of Christ and the authority of the Bible "do not of necessity affect our lives and our work," the authority of the Holy Spirit, "from a practical standpoint . . . is the most important [authority] of all."[1] In chapters five through seven I will use the theological model of the Spirit's authority already developed—a biblical/systematic model of the Spirit's "plenipotentiary authority" as divine Person, Executor, Teacher, and Governor—to examine three common "practices" of the Church.[2] I will use this model to demonstrate how our principle and pattern of divine authority "structure" the specific practice under investigation. I will first develop this basic structure with respect to the Spirit's *divine Personhood* and *executorial authority*. I will then do so with respect to the Spirit's *veracious* and *governing authority*, and in doing so will "listen" and respond to one or two contemporary theologians concerned with this particular "practice" of the Spirit within local church settings.

---

1. Lloyd-Jones, *Authority*, 62.

2. I previously defined "practical theology" as the application of the results of systematic theology to the development of the Church's overall "ministry," both theoretically and practically. "Practical theology" would thereby include the theory and practice of hermeneutics, church structure, and spirituality.

In this chapter I will apply our model to basic hermeneutical theory. I will first attempt to demonstrate that the Spirit as a divine Person *authorizes* Scripture, in that Scripture reveals God to us and thereby possesses "full authority" in itself as the Word of God. Second, I will try to show that the Spirit as Christ's Executor *inspires* the human authors, thus determining the content of Scripture and providing epistemological certitude to the reader with respect to the knowledge of God. Then, I will respond to two contemporary "practical" theologians introduced at the end of chapter two—Stephen Fowl (who locates the Spirit's authority within communities and Stanley Grenz and John Franke (who link the Spirit to "perlocutions")—weighing their approaches against a biblical notion of the Spirit's *veracious authority* and *governing authority*. Finally, I will attempt to build a case for the Spirit as Teacher (who provides certitude of meaning for believers today) and as divine Governor (who provides authoritative significance with respect to the application of Scripture).

Hermeneutics and the Divine Authority of the Spirit

Evangelical theologians have traditionally employed "modern" methods of interpretation that rely almost completely on rational tools for understanding the text's meaning. Such theologians often teach that we only need the Spirit of God at the point of application.[3] To understand the roots of "modern" (and "postmodern") hermeneutics we must look to the Reformation, particularly the hermeneutical models developed by Luther and Calvin. As those who generally kept the Spirit/Word relationship intact in their theologies, they gave the Spirit a proper, though somewhat limited, place in biblical hermeneutics. For Luther, the Word is the instrument of the Spirit in that the Spirit breaks the bondage of the flesh through the message of the Word as Christ lives His risen life in our midst. By this action our minds and hearts are purified and we are able to interpret the Scriptures correctly. The Spirit produces *certitudo*—a term commonly used by Luther to proclaim that we can know with certitude that we are truly saved and that the Word of God is God's truth. According to Prenter, the Spirit's role in Luther's hermeneutic is to make God present within us—

---

3. For examples of such "modern" hermeneutical methods see: Green, *How to Read Prophecy*; Kaiser, *Toward an Exegetical Theology*; Steward, *Old Testament Exegesis*.

The Authority of the Holy Spirit and Practical Theology: Hermeneutics

in such a way that his presence takes Jesus Christ out of the remoteness of history and heavenly exaltation and place [sic] him into the midst of our concrete life as a living and redeeming reality which constantly calls upon both the groaning of faith and the work of charity.[4]

For Luther, faith carries the weight of the determination of *certitudo*. Later Reformers spoke of the Bible as their primary source of *certitudo*, calling it their "singular norm" of theology (in that Scripture is self-authenticating in and of itself, bearing its own authority). In this way, Scripture was given exclusive authority over theology. The Spirit makes contemporary not only the historical Christ—who is the focal point of history—but also the entire history of Israel and the gospels. For Luther *certitudo* implies a self-authenticating authority or something that bears its own authority.[5] Only the Spirit can provide *certitudo* by transferring the certainty of the truth of the Word of God to the believer's particular context in such a way as to produce genuine faith. In this way, the Word of the living and authoritative God becomes contemporary. While the Roman Catholic theologian looks to the Holy Spirit in the development of church tradition, Luther implies that Spirit gives the Word *contemporaniety*.[6]

Calvin's approach complements Luther's in that the Spirit's role is to convince the mind of the truth of Christ and the authority of the Word of God. Calvin's doctrine of the "internal testimony of the Spirit"—a by-product of the "illumination of Scripture"—actually made the Spirit superior to reason and, as seen in chapter two, signified a shift from an essentially institution-based interpretive authority to a Spirit-based one. Protestants, as a result, believed the Holy Spirit could superintend biblical interpretation and guard the believer against error.

While Luther and Calvin were foundational in modern hermeneutics, they were not able to ward off tendencies by their followers to separate Spirit and Word. The Enlightenment would eventually lead to the subjec-

---

4. Prenter, *Spiritus Creator*; 92.

5. See Johnson, *Authority in Protestant Theology*, 14. Luther contrasted this certitudo with *securitas*, an absolute security obtained apart from the Word.

6. This is what Luther meant when he shouted, "it is written" at the Diet of Worms—the Spirit makes the Word presently effective, and God is thus able to "speak" with contemporary authority.

tion of all authority to reason,[7] and in general the hermeneutics of the eighteenth and nineteenth centuries would no longer rely upon the Holy Spirit for discovering biblical meaning. Out of Lutheranism (and Calvinism to a lesser extent) grew Protestant scholasticism, based on a version of medieval scholasticism that placed confidence in reason and resorted to scholastic logic to settle disputes. Through scholasticism,

> faith came increasingly to be thought of as *rechte Lehre* (correct doctrine). A more mechanical view of the role of the Scriptures was developed, and as a result the witness of the Spirit tended to be bypassed. Now the Word alone, without the Spirit, was regarded as the basis of authority.[8]

Another major movement during this period was Christian rationalism, which at first sought to justify the beliefs of Christianity through human reason, but eventually concluded that only those things that can be established by rational proof are credible. As the foundation for deism, rationalism came to view God as far removed from human life and neglected the need for the Spirit in hermeneutics.

As a result, twentieth-century methods of interpretation were derived mainly from the assumption that human reason was sufficient to interpret Scripture, that is, if one was careful to apply rational methods and to follow proper principles and rules. Liberal theologians developed "scientific" ways of interpreting the Bible—analyzing the Bible according to certain pre-determined criteria (i.e., "critical-historical methods") to determine what was "historically reliable" and what was not. Evangelicals, on the other hand, responded with their own "scientific" approach, the "grammatical-historical method." Yet in both cases the guiding authority for interpretation was the *mind*. In general, the Holy Spirit was not associated with the *interpretation* of the biblical text but only with its *application*. Virkler, for example, claims in his book *Hermeneutics, Principles and Process of Biblical Interpretation* that,

> The unbeliever can *know* (internally comprehend) . . . the truths of Scripture using the same means of interpretation he would use with

---

7. See Gadamer, *Truth and Method*, 278.
8. Erickson, *Christian Theology*, 870.

The Authority of the Holy Spirit and Practical Theology: Hermeneutics

non-biblical texts, but he cannot truly *know* (act on and appropriate) these truths as long as he remains in rebellion against God.[9]

Such a perspective seems to pit "head knowledge" against "heart knowledge." "Modern" hermeneuticians, likewise, tend to separate exegesis and spirituality. This "bifurcation" seems to find its roots in the philosophy of Immanuel Kant, who divided our sources for obtaining knowledge into two distinct categories—reason and revelation.[10] Much of evangelical teaching today on interpretation continues this division, proclaiming that while the Bible is the Spirit's revelation it can be interpreted through rational methodology without any actual "illumination" of the Spirit. Henry comments:

> While acknowledging that the biblical writers did not distinguish between oral and written proclamation in respect to divine inspiration, evangelicals considered the Bible, in view of its canonical authority, to be the singular important achievement of inspiration. Moreover, evangelical emphasis on the perspicuity or clarity of Scripture seemed somehow to displace the affirmation that the Spirit who inspired the Scriptures is alone their proper interpreter to us; in other words, concentration on Scripture as it stands appeared prematurely to close the hermeneutical circle in which both the Spirit's inspiration and interpretation are necessary and integral to each other.[11]

---

9. Virkler, *Hermeneutics, Principles and Process of Biblical Interpretation*, 30. If "The Chicago Statement of Faith" reflects orthodoxy, saying that "The Holy Spirit, Scripture's divine author, both authenticates it to us by his inward witness and opens our minds to understand its meaning," then Virkler's statement would seem to lie *outside* of orthodox hermeneutics (see Packer, *God Has Spoken*, 143).

10. Klooster presents a correction to the reductionism in our modern understanding of "understanding": "Understanding is not only a matter of the mind or thought or reason, as Enlightenment hermeneutics implied—although the human mind is certainly involved in interpretation. Heart-understanding does not allow for the separation between faith and knowledge, as if knowledge were reached by reason common to all people while faith is restricted to trust in what reason has achieved. This separation between knowledge and faith has been promoted by the use of Scottish realism in the Old-Princeton apologetic and appears in a new context in Pannenburg's theology. . . . Understanding rooted in the heart does include the intellect, will, and emotion; it concerns the whole person" (Klooster, "The Role of the Holy Spirit," 462–63).

11. Henry, *God, Revelation, and Authority*, vol. IV, 256.

The Bible is our "final authority," having the privileged status of judging all other disciplines and authorities, and possesses "full authority," having universal application for all times.[12] Biblical authority, however, ultimately emerges from the Spirit's divine authority (as a divine Person). As seen in chapter three, 1 Cor 2:10–13 informs us that only the Spirit has the authority to search and reveal God's mind to us. Thus biblical revelation cannot be understood simply on a cognitive level. The exegesis of this passage led to two relevant insights: (1) the Spirit has "divine access" to search the depths of God and therefore has authority to reveal God's character and will to us (vv. 10–12); and (2) by the Spirit Paul was "combining spiritual thoughts with spiritual words" (v. 13) and in doing so displayed a certain divine authority through his words. Paul makes it clear that *the Spirit* is the divine Revealer who imparts divine authority to these very words.[13]

An authentic respect for the authority of the Bible is thereby directly tied to an understanding of the Spirit's authority as the divine Revealer. When we speak of the Spirit's authority in hermeneutics we are appealing not only to the Spirit's authority *over* the human knower[14] but also to his authority to reveal the mind of God *to* the believer in and through the text of Scripture.

The implication of all this is that "divine knowledge" and "interpretation" cannot be viewed as purely cognitive terms. Hermeneutics must, according to Vanhoozer, "affirm transcendence." The transcendent/immanent Spirit must energize the entire hermeneutical process. "The Spirit's role in bringing about understanding is to witness to what is other

---

12. For fuller descriptions of "final authority," and "full authority" see Larkin, *Cultural and Biblical Hermeneutics*, 272–80.

13. See Macdonald, *The Interpreter Spirit and Human Life*, 108–25 for the role of the "Interpreter Spirit" in hermeneutics.

14. This authority, as seen in chapter three, is grounded in a view of the Spirit's divine transcendence "over" creation itself (Ps 109:29–30). Calvin, in particular, pointed out the vital connection between the physical order and the "ordering" of the mind provided by the Spirit's illumination of Scripture. MacDonald also explains that, whereas "the function or process of interpretation involves the idea of organization" and "the function of revelation was operative at creation, when the executive action of the Word of God made all things according to the Father's original plan or thought, so the function of Interpretation was operative at the creation when the Spirit of God 'moved on the face of the water' and brought order out of shoals, organizing the already created world, and so interpreting it as that which has significance and purpose" (MacDonald, *Interpreter Spirit and Human Life*, 118).

than himself (*meaning accomplished*) and to bring its significance to bear on the reader (*meaning applied*)."[15] The human interpreter, then, becomes only a secondary interpreter who must look to the Spirit for assistance in the process of interpretation. While we must acknowledge that non-believers are able to "understand" or possess a basic conceptual grasp of the meaning of Scripture at varying levels, we cannot reduce the Spirit's illumination of Scripture to the ability of the human intellect.[16] The Holy Spirit affirms the proper use of the rational mind and yet contributes an "awareness" not attainable by the rational mind alone. This is expressed by Helm:

> The internal testimony of the Spirit is not to be thought of as in some way short-circuiting the objective evidence or making up for the deficiencies in external scriptural evidence, nor as providing *additional* evidence, nor as merely acting as a mechanical stimulus, but as making the mind capable of the proper appreciation of the evidence, seeing it for what it is, and in particular heightening the mind's awareness of the marks of divinity present in the text in such a way as to produce the conviction that this text is indeed the product of the divine mind and therefore to be relied on utterly.[17]

The Spirit places our interpretation of the Bible back into the context of our relation to God, thus breaking down the division between interpretation and spirituality. In order to attain accurate interpretation we must look *beyond* the actual words of the text and engage in the authentic *spirituality* presented to us by the author. Fee expresses what this means for the exegete:

> I do not mean by this that what is often termed application or development is to be understood as part of the exegetical task itself. Rather, I mean that the biblical authors to a person were not only inspired by the Holy Spirit—or so we believe—but also brought their own spirituality to their writing of the text. My point is that

---

15. Vanhoozer, *Is There a Meaning in This Text?*, 407.

16. For an explanation of the similarities and differences between the nonbeliever's abilities with respect to the knowledge of God in comparison to the believer's, see Frame, *The Doctrine of the Knowledge of God*, 49–59.

17. Helm, "Faith, Evidence, and the Scriptures," 312–13.

true exegesis attempts to engage in the author's *spirituality*, not just in his or her words.[18]

Steiner holds that the reader encounters an "otherness" in the text that calls for a response on the part of the reader. To read for the "other" is a theological activity.[19] Vanhoozer asserts that *all* hermeneutics is theological, in that the theological virtues of faith, hope, and love allow the reader to recognize a real *presence* in the text and to respect the "otherness" of the text.[20] We could go a step further and say that all hermeneutics is *spiritual*—invoking the Holy Spirit, a secular spirit, or much worse, a *demonic* spirit.[21] Perhaps this is why we "feel" the text so vividly when reading a fiction novel or even a theological work. The text "lifts" us out of a mere physical existence, reminds us of transcendent or spiritual realities, and actually brings us into a new spiritual environment or *realm* (see section on hermeneutics and the Spirit's governing authority). In the biblical text we encounter the authoritative presence of God *made personal*. The following summary by Klooster gets to the heart of the Spirit's personhood with respect to the "personalization" of the Word of God:

> God's gracious purpose with this book is to bring about the living "encounter" with Him in an I-thou relationship for building His church and manifesting His kingdom. For the believer this I-thou relationship is not really an "encounter," with the negative implica-

---

18. Fee, *Listening to the Spirit in the Text*, 11 (emphasis his). Fee illustrates this point: "Of what earthly or eternal value is it, for example, for us to exegete Phil 1:21 ('for to me to live is Christ, to die is gain'), in purely descriptive terms, if we do not engage in Paul's further intent that the Philippians themselves share this view of present life?" (11). See also: Fee, *Gospel and Spirit*, chapter 2; Veenhof, "The Holy Spirit and Hermeneutics," regarding the need for the Spirit in "reforming the reader" in order to attain accurate interpretation.

19. See Steiner, *Real Presences*.

20. Vanhoozer states that *faith* in hermeneutics means that "there is a real *presence*, a voice, a meaning in the text"; *hope* means that "the interpretive community can, *in the power of the Spirit*, attain an adequate, not absolute, understanding"; and *love* means that "a mutual *relation* of self-giving between text and reader" (Vanhoozer, "The Spirit of Understanding," 161, emphasis mine).

21. According to Hall, the denial of *presence* in the text results in "the demonic spirit of absolute faithlessness, the exact opposite of the Christian spirit which exists in radical and absolute faithfulness" (Hall, *Word and Spirit*, 100). Postmodernism denies such a presence, and seeks instead to achieve some sort of "self-understanding."

tions of that term, but fellowship and communion with the living triune-God![22]

The Spirit's transcendence *over* the interpreter demands that he or she be in complete submission to God or to possess a desire for absolute obedience to God. "Understanding" is regularly equated in the Bible with obedience (Luke 8:15; 11:28). Because of this emphasis, Fee suggests,

> we have not entered into the full spirituality of these texts until we are ready to follow Christ so fully that we can tell those whom we have been given to teach that they should mark our lives, and the lives of those who walk as we do, and thus follow our example.[23]

The Holy Spirit convicts us of "righteousness, sin, and judgment" (John 16:8)—terms that all possess hermeneutical importance and communicate to us how little we know and how much the Spirit transcends the reach of our minds. Through the Word of God, the Holy Spirit reveals both discontinuities between God's thoughts and our thoughts (resulting in humility) as well as continuities (resulting in accountability).[24] Therefore, anything that hinders the Spirit's revelation of divine authority (i.e., pride, sin) thwarts the hermeneutical process.

An acknowledgement of the Spirit as the one who gives to Scripture its *authority* is only the beginning of the interpretive process. As we shall see in the next section, the Spirit's authority *over* the exegete is qualified by the Spirit's authority to execute Christ's will.

---

22. Klooster, "The Role of the Holy Spirit," 454.

23. Fee, *Listening to the Spirit in the Text*, 13.

24. Such discontinuities include: God's thoughts are uncreated, eternal, original, etc. (while ours are created, temporal, and unoriginal). Continuities include: both God's thoughts and ours are creative, personal, bound to standards, etc. For a fuller explanation of these discontinuities and continuities see Frame, *The Doctrine of the Knowledge of God*, 20–29. Frame also develops the idea that "knowledge" in Scripture is subject to God's authority. "Knowledge of God, in the fullest sense, is an obedient knowledge" because (1) knowledge of God produces obedience; (2) obedience to God leads to knowledge; (3) obedience *is* knowledge and visa versa; and (4) obedience is the criterion of knowledge (42–44).

The Lord Is the Spirit

Hermeneutics and the Executorial Authority of the Spirit

In our study of Isa 11:2 we saw that the Spirit anoints the Messiah with wisdom, counsel, understanding, and the fear of the Lord. These are actually supernatural hermeneutical abilities. How does the Messiah employ such attributes? In the gospels, Christ is given a hermeneutical role—to make his Father's true will "known" by re-interpreting the law according to *divine mercy*. As our "advocate," Christ re-interprets the law concerning the Sabbath (Mark 2:23—3:6) and sin (John 8:3–11). We can easily infer that when Christ sent the Holy Spirit as "another advocate" (John 14:16), and did so "in my name" (or, "with my authority," John 14:26), he was sending the Spirit as an Executor of such re-interpretations.

The implications of the Spirit's executorial authority with respect to hermeneutics, and particularly epistemology, are enormous. As Christ reveals the Father to his disciples (John 1:18) so the Spirit reveals the truth of Christ, and of Christ's interpretation of the law, to the human mind (John 15:26, 16:12–15). Whereas Jesus' ministry on earth displayed God's authority through human speech (Mark 1:22, 27) and resulted in epistemological certitude in the minds of believers, so the Spirit of truth, as Christ's authoritative agent in the world, is able to provide epistemological certitude for believers today through the Word of God. Thus, the Spirit's interpretation under Christ always correlates to God's self-revelation *in Christ*. As Christ's "advocate," the Spirit not only makes Christ's case before the world but is also "with us" in Christ's full authority.

John 16:12–15 also breathes of certitude, particularly regarding the Spirit's work in completing the act of Christ's revelation. Verses 12 and 13 inform the disciples that, since Jesus' speaking ministry will not be complete even after his earthly ministry, the Spirit "will guide you into all truth" (that is, the truth of Jesus Christ). From this passage we can infer that the certitude provided by the Spirit through the Scriptures will reflect the certitude experienced by Jesus' disciples. The idea is, "If you trust the words of Jesus (which John's readers certainly did), you can trust the Spirit's words as well."

The purpose of verse 13 is disclosed in verse 14—the Spirit's goal in speaking is to "glorify" Christ by "disclosing" (or further explaining) to the disciples what the Father has revealed in Christ. Since the redemptive work

The Authority of the Holy Spirit and Practical Theology: Hermeneutics

of Christ is the height of God's revelation in Christ, the Spirit will explain the fullness and reality of Christ's redemption and mercy to the world. Verse 15 drives the argument home: the Spirit's revelation of the Father in the Son will be completely true and adequate.[25] The epistemological certitude is vivid—there will be no diminishing of the Father's authority, or Christ's authority, in the words spoken by the Spirit and recorded by the disciples. John 15:26—16:15 must have instilled a profound certitude in the minds of the disciples that the Spirit would indeed have the authority to continue Christ's mission.

Practical application of such executorial certitude is provided in Matt 16:13–18. Foundational to one's hermeneutical activity is a genuine confession of the authority and Lordship of Christ, a confession not instigated by "flesh and blood" but by the Father through the Spirit (who is implied in the word "revealed").[26] Peter's confession demonstrates the central hermeneutical "principle" for the church—the person and redemptive message of Christ.[27] Klooster explains the trinitarian "balance" that must be retained in our understanding of Scripture.

> Scripture is really Christologically theocentric. One can state that even more accurately, for it is a pneumatically Christological theocentricity! Those complex words express what Paul stated so simply: "For through Him (Christ Jesus) we both have access to the Father by one Spirit" (Eph 2:18; cf. 2:12–13).[28]

John 15:26—16:15 and Matthew 16 thus demonstrate that the Spirit provides epistemological certitude with respect to the revelation of Christ. Such an epistemology is best described in terms of "critical realism," which holds that knowledge is not sterile belief but contains both objective and subjective elements that coincide as we are involved in the mission of

---

25. See Bruce, *The Gospel of John*, 321.

26. Matt 16:13–18 builds a strong case for the Spirit's executorial authority that is not reductionistic regarding the Spirit's personhood or speaking. Jesus trusts that the Spirit's revelation of Himself will provide Peter with a certain *authority* (v. 19) to bind and to loose.

27. This passage, however, does not mean that all biblical hermeneutics is "Christocentric" (as Barth advocates), but that Christ's own interpretive "principle"—the Father's revelation of himself through the Spirit—is the foundation for all hermeneutics (as alluded to by his statement, "upon this rock I will build my church").

28. Klooster, "The Role of the Holy Spirit," 454.

the church.²⁹ Modern exegetes claim to possess exact knowledge gained through precise interpretive methods—as with one who would create an exact replica of a city or a perfectly corresponding photograph. Postmodern exegetes hold that such correspondence to the "original" is impossible, that interpretation is subject to the mind of the exegete—as with one who would "interpret" a Rorschach test. Critical realism, however, holds that knowledge is both subjective and objective—as with the knowledge of one who would construct a topological map.³⁰ Such an approach helps us to connect our "subjective" knowledge of truth through the Spirit to the "objective" truth of Christ found in Scripture.

The development of this sort of knowledge can be illustrated in terms of the relationship between a "hyperbola" and an "asymptote." In geometry, an asymptote is an axis or line (i.e., the "x axis" of a simple graph) that is approached but never touched by a hyperbola (tangent or curve). The hyperbola is formed, for example, by plotting the numerals 1, 2, 3 . . . (to infinity) for the simple function [x, 1/y] where x=y. While Christ aligns with the objective aspect of our knowledge, the Spirit provides subjective knowledge that continually approaches a more accurate reflection of the objective knowledge of Christ. Jesus Christ is, according to Veenhof, the "permanent ground," the content and norm of faith that all interpretation refers to.

> No interpretation can be the true one which detracts from that permanent identity. This permanent identity however does not mean that the Word is bound to or even imprisoned in a past period, or restricted to a past culture. Jesus is the same, yesterday, now and in eternity (Heb 13:8). That means that he in all the phases of history is who he was during his stay on earth; the One who is surprisingly new.³¹

---

29. See Hiebert, *Missiological Implications*, 68–116. "Critical realist" hermeneutics present a somewhat helpful "compromise" between "modern" hermeneuticians (which employed a "positivistic" view of knowledge based solely on a correspondence theory of truth) and postmodern hermeneutics (which forced science and theology alike to dismiss a strict correspondence theory and adopt an "idealist" view of knowledge or an "instrumentalist" view based upon a coherence or pragmatic theory of truth).

30. Hiebert, *Missiological Implications*, 68–116.

31. Veenhof, "The Holy Spirit and Hermeneutics," 114.

Hermeneutical certitude, therefore, lies in the existence of a self-revealing God (our principle of authority) who can "personalize" his revelation in Christ through the Spirit's revelation in the Word of God (our pattern of authority). Practically speaking, the exegete must live in the mercy and justification provided by Christ and communicated by the Spirit, allowing his or her mind to be filled with the "knowledge of Christ."

Hermeneutics and the Veracious Authority of the Spirit

As seen in chapter two, Stephen Fowl believes that theological interpretation primarily involves the work of the Holy Spirit in the community. Indeed the essential nature of the community is that it is *interpretive*. For Fowl, the Spirit seems to possess an "authority" to assist local church communities to reach crucial theological decisions regarding biblical texts based on "communal consensus."[32] Fowl indeed speaks of "Spirit-inspired interpretation" rather than the Spirit's "inspiration of Scripture."[33]

Fowl therefore advocates an "underdetermined interpretation" that views Scripture as devoid of "past meaning" and thereby requiring *theological* interpretation in contemporary communities (rather than a "determinate" hermeneutic that understands "meaning" to be a specific property of the text[34]). Fowl proclaims, "our discussions, debates, and arguments about texts will be better served by eliminating claims about textual meaning in favor of more precise accounts of our interpretive aims, interests, and practices."[35] The "past" does not exist as an uninterrupted collection of sense data, but always involves "a particular sort of remembering" through the subsequent works of the Spirit.[36] For example, the Spirit allows Jesus' commands to be understood and applied in new contexts.

---

32. Fowl, *Engaging Scripture*, 203.
33. See Fowl, *Engaging Scripture*, 113.
34. Fowl defines this as an approach to the text where "meaning can be uncovered through the application of some set of interpretive procedures. On this view, the biblical text is seen as a relatively stable element in which an authority inserts, hides, or dissolves (choose your metaphor) meaning. The task of the interpreter, whether lay, clerical, or professional, is to dig out, uncover, or distill the meaning of the text" (Fowl, *Engaging Scripture*, 33–34).
35. Fowl, *Engaging Scripture*, 56.
36. Ibid., 101.

Fowl's central argument is that there remains a "complex interaction between the biblical text and the varieties of theological, moral, material, political, and ecclesial concerns that are part of the day-to-day lives of Christians struggling to live faithfully before God in the context in which they find themselves."[37] It is in this interpretive interaction that the Spirit is experienced. This is exemplified in Fowl's commentary on Acts 10–15, and particularly the Jerusalem council's decision regarding circumcision:

> While James' judgment becomes authoritative, it does so because it articulates for the community the sense of the Spirit's work. It is not authoritative simply because James, the leader of the church in Jerusalem, says so. . . . In fact, the process of coming to a decision on this matter, which ultimately is articulated by James, reflects a complex series of interactions between interpretations of the Spirit's work and Spirit-inspired interpretation and application of Scripture. Understanding these interactions will be essential for any Christian community if the Spirit is to play a significant role in the interpretation and embodiment of Scripture.[38]

The Veracious Authority of the Spirit and Recognition of the Text's "Meaning"

Fowl's hermeneutic does seem to portray the Spirit as one who grants the community a certain *interpretive authority*. The community's interpretive activity is the *means* by which the Spirit's veracious authority comes to expression. "Christians hope and expect the Spirit will guide, direct, and confirm their readings of Scripture as well as the practices generated and underwritten by such readings."[39] Such optimism is indeed refreshing, particularly in light of the myriad of "modern" straightjacketing methodologies that severely *lower* our expectations of the Spirit's ability to speak to the "common" interpreter.

Noticeably absent in this comment, however, is Jesus' proclamation that the Spirit will "guide you *into all truth*" (John 16:13). As seen in chapter three, the idea of this verse is that the Spirit will guide the interpreter

---

37. Ibid., 60.
38. Ibid., 112–13.
39. Ibid., 102.

The Authority of the Holy Spirit and Practical Theology: Hermeneutics

into the truth *already disclosed* in Jesus. When combined with our exegesis of 2 Pet 1:20–21 (namely, that inspiration is the sure basis for illumination and that Scripture has a *divine author*), we can infer that the Spirit will guide believers into the truth *fixed by Jesus—its author* (i.e., John 14:6). This understanding of inspiration requires a *determinate* interpretation, one made definite by the specific words used in a specific context. Our exegesis of John 16:13 and 2 Pet 1:20–21 (along with John 14:26 and 1 Cor 2:10–13) thereby implies hermeneutical *realism* (i.e., that meanings exist *outside* the interpreter's own mind or community).[40] Vanhoozer asks, "Is it the Spirit's role to develop or create new meaning from the text in the history and tradition of its reception? The role of the Spirit in interpretation hangs on the answer one gives to this question."[41]

Fowl seems to confuse the text's *meaning* (that which is intended by the biblical author) with its *significance* (for the community). Fowl ignores the need for interpreters to "reconstruct" the intended meaning of the text and essentially replaces this with the formation of the character or spirituality of the interpreter. Scriptural "authority" is only granted in association with "vigilant communities" where Scripture is interpreted and embodied and where believers are sanctified. Fowl claims,

> the authority of Scripture is not a property of biblical texts any more than a meaning or an ideology is a property of these texts. . . . Rather, scriptural authority must be spoken of in connection with the ecclesial community who struggle to interpret Scripture and embody their interpretations in the specific contexts in which they find themselves. . . . my account [also] demands a notion of eccle-

---

40. Quoting Hirsch, Vanhoozer suggests: "Hermeneutical realism ultimately rests on this distinction between meaning and significance, on the distinction 'between an object of knowledge and the context in which is known'" (Vanhoozer, *Is There a Meaning in this Text?* 260). Also, "The reality of meaning is ground on past action: 'Stable meaning depends, then, on pastness.' There is a determinate something 'in' the text—intended meaning—that remains fixed and unchanging through the history of its interpretation. . . . The concern for relevance—for reading with the aim of bringing a text to bear on contemporary concerns—is a concern for what Hirsch calls 'significance.' Unlike meaning, the significance of a text can change, for significance pertains to the relation between the text's determinate meaning and a larger context (i.e. another era, another culture, another subject matter)" (259).

41. Vanhoozer, *Is There Meaning in this Text?* 409.

sial authority that recognizes that the Spirit has been and still is at work in the lives of Christians and Christian communities.[42]

Fowl's "complex interaction" model essentially replaces the community's need for textual understanding with the community's own "needs," specifically, its "interpretive aims, interests, and practices." Vanhoozer also addresses such a replacement:

> It is, of course, important that Christians read the Scriptures for the sake of spiritual formation and edification. Yet this aim, while absolutely vital, must not displace the prior aim of coming to understand the text. The thrust of the present argument is, just as perlocutions can never precede but must always *proceed* from illocutions, so spiritual formation can never precede but must always proceed from the ministry of the Word—that *thought, power, deed* whose mission it is to transform those who receive it.[43]

For Fowl, the Spirit seems to have the authority to "shape" the church community by guiding her efforts to interpret and embody the Scriptures, but not the authority to illuminate the original text. In responding to Fowl and others who promote a "community-oriented" hermeneutic, we should first reflect on the fact that the Spirit's executorial authority in hermeneutics naturally implies his veracious authority. The correlation of Christ and Spirit has strong hermeneutical implications for the correlation between Word and Spirit. In other words, the Spirit of Christ and the Spirit of Truth are one and the same.[44] "Christ rules 'by His Word and Spirit.' The Spirit-inspired Scriptures reveal Jesus Christ, and the Spirit employs His Word to unite believers to Christ in true faith."[45] The "meaning" in the text points the reader to the Spirit as it "author,"[46] as the One who "speaks in"

---

42. Fowl, *Engaging Scripture*, 203.

43. Vanhoozer, "From Speech Acts to Scripture Acts," 42–43.

44. Fowl root problem may be the fact that he speaks of the Spirit "who speaks in unison with the Father and the Son" but not of the "Spirit of Truth" in developing his hermeneutical method (Fowl, *Engaging Scripture*, 99).

45. Klooster, "The Role of the Holy Spirit," 456.

46. "One way to conceive of author-text relation is to think in terms of cause and effect. The author is the historical cause of a textual effect; his or her intention is the cause of the text being the way it is. No other explanation adequately account for the intelligibility of texts. The author, an intelligent cause, is the necessary and sufficient effect of the text, an

the text (John 16:13–15). Readers are thus "invited" by Christ *to know God* by recognizing and submitting to the Spirit's authoritative and contemporary illumination of that deposited meaning, thereby "knowing the truth" (John 17:17).

With regard to hermeneutics this best translates into a "missional model of communication," based on the Spirit's continuation of Christ's mission. The Spirit "sends" messages to his "receivers."[47] The idea here is that language is a vehicle for communication, one that involves not only the speaker but also the listener. Alston, for example, re-defines communication in terms of the *use* of language, saying that "an expression's having a certain meaning consists in its being usable to play a certain role in communication."[48] If Alston is correct, the Spirit's *speaking* is a mission in itself, rather than a process of encoding. Such a "missional model" demonstrates not only the Spirit's executorial authority to "complete" Christ's revelatory mission but also the Spirit's veracious authority to deposit meaning and truth into Scripture. This authority presupposes that the Spirit demands submission to God on the part of the "hearer." The Spirit impresses the text upon our minds and hearts by the full force of the Spirit's communicative acts (i.e., "illocutions"[49]) so that the Spirit's authority can come to bear upon us in the text. No hermeneutical separation can be made between the Spirit's divine Personhood and his veracious authority as Spirit of Truth, as the one who inspires the text. Herein lies the danger of the postmodern "community-response" hermeneutic, which only attempts to retain a non-authoritative "Spirit." Such a "Spirit" seems unable to actually "confront"

---

intelligible effect. The text thus serves as a kind of surrogate presence, a reliable expression and extension, of the author" (Vanhoozer, *Is There a Meaning in This Text?* 44).

47. See Vanhoozer, "From Speech Acts to Scripture Acts," 10. The missional model dismisses the notional that human languages consist as "free-floating sign systems that enjoy an autonomous existence from their users" (9).

48. Alston, *Illocutionary Acts and Sentence Meaning*, 154. Ricoeur defines communication in terms of semantics (i.e., the science of sentences) rather than semiotics (the science of the sign). This distinction is "the key to the whole problem of language" (Ricoeur, *Interpretation Theory*, 8). Sentences, in Ricoeur's mind, are the smallest units of language that can be used to say something in a particular setting.

49. While "illocutions" have to do with textual *meaning*, "perlocutions" are *effects* or *significances* (or, roughly, "applications") that "supervene" on (or attach to) that meaning (see Alston, *Illocutionary Acts*, 31).

the community with potentially "sinful" interpretations. Such a hermeneutic ultimately amounts to the "death of the author" and, as a result, the "birth of the reader."

> Meaning is not discovered, but made, by the reader's rediscovered Nietzschian will-to-power. The text "has no rights" and "can be used in whatever ways readers or interpreters chose." With the birth of the reader, the divine has been relocated: the postmodern era is more comfortable thinking of God not as the transcendent Author but as the immanent Spirit. The Shekinah cloud has settled on the interpretive community.[50]

How, then, is a postmodern understanding of the Spirit in hermeneutics to be combated without returning to a "modern" approach? The exegesis in chapter four clearly points to the authority that the Spirit possesses with respect to the inspiration and illumination of Scripture, a veracious authority *over* the reader or exegete. John 14:17 strongly alludes to the idea that to receive (λαβεῖν) the Spirit of Truth involves an active submission to the Spirit himself, and 14:26 states that to encounter the Spirit in the text is to encounter the very words of Christ.

The Veracious Authority of the Spirit and Illumination of Scripture

As we have seen, 2 Pet 1:21 tells us that scriptural prophecy cannot be interpreted, ultimately, by anyone other than God the Spirit. In this verse it is "implicit but clear"[51] that a correct understanding of Scripture depends upon the aid of the Spirit. Since the illumination of Scripture is a function of the Spirit of Truth who inspires Scripture, a subjective certitude is available to those who "listen" to the Spirit speaking in Scripture. "Listening" to the Spirit does not simply mean understanding what the Bible said to the original audience but "hearing" the timeless truths embedded in the text, and ultimately "hearing" God speaking *to me*.

> So the Spirit places me in an *Ich-Du* relation, which God will maintain with men. This relation is brought about in the knowledge of God in Christ, which itself is owed to the illumination of the

---

50. Vanhoozer, "The Spirit of Understanding," 136–37.
51. Kelly, *A Commentary on the Epistles of Peter and Jude*, 325.

> Spirit. . . . This knowing is a tremendous thing, comparable with creation itself (cf. 2 Cor. 4:6). Just as creation has the Spirit of God as its author so the recreation has as its author the Spirit of God, who is now the Spirit of Christ. . . The Holy Spirit is ready to grasp, transform and fill also the present interpreter.[52]

This explains why the pattern of divine authority must be respected in hermeneutics—particularly the idea that divine authority is revealed through the vital connection of authoritative Spirit and authoritative Word. As Packer aptly states, "Those who would live under the authority of the Spirit must bow before the Word as the Spirit's textbook . . . those who would live under the authority of Scripture must seek the Spirit as its interpreter."[53] MacDonald comments as well about the Spirit's interpretive authority.

> To each of us the Spirit is a sword which cleaves open the stubborn and obscure passages, illumines the chambers of the mind so that dark and uncertain thoughts and conclusions become clear and effective, and supplies us with practical interpretation.[54]

Klooster introduces an "organic illumination," which requires that we keep in mind both the Spirit's sovereignty and our own need for faithful exegesis. "In organic illumination the Holy Spirit works in the believing interpreter of the inspired Scripture to enable faithful understanding of the meaning of the passage under study."[55] While "inspiration" and "illumination" must not be confused, we must remember that they both occur under the veracious authority of the Spirit. Because of this, the Spirit is able to guide us into "all truth" in a manner very similar to the way he guided the writers of Scripture into "all truth." Organic illumination occurs as the Spirit authoritatively works in and through the human aspects of exegesis. This means that the Bible's interpretation is not in the hands of an elite few or only the trained Bible scholar (cf. 1 John 2:20, 27). Illumination can be hindered by a lack of spiritual preparation or human effort as much as, and

---

52. Veenhof, "The Holy Spirit and Hermeneutics," 121.
53. Packer, *Keep in Step with the Spirit*, 240.
54. MacDonald, *Interpreter Spirit and Human Life*, 157.
55. Klooster, "The Role of the Holy Spirit," 460–61. See Klooster's definitions of "organic" on pp. 453 and 460.

perhaps more than, a lack of hermeneutical training. The two must go hand in hand. Zuck adds:

> With a heart sensitive to the Spirit, the interpreter must study the Word intensely. The point here is that the Spirit does not make study superfluous. "The more self-consciously active the interpreter is in the process, the more likely is the Spirit's illumination." The Holy Spirit works through the efforts of the individual as he reads the Bible, and studies it, meditates on it, and consults other works about it. In the inspiration of the Bible, the Holy Spirit was working but so were the human authors. In a similar way in the interpretation of the Bible, human work is involved.[56]

Organic illumination also means that interpreters cannot ignore the need for common sense and logic. "The Spirit of Truth" employs such rational means, resulting in interpretations with logical, internal consistency. The Spirit's illumination, of course, can go far beyond logic into issues of the heart, revealing the need for the love and grace of Christ to enter into the interpretive activity. Since the mind of the reader "inevitably seeks structure," the reader logically fills in the gaps of the imagined details of events not expressly presented in a narrative.[57] This does not mean that the reader *determines* or *produces* meaning or that the text is only a *potential of meaning*. The text's meaning, while unfinished, is "completed" as the reader follows textual clues and authorial instructions under the guidance of the illuminating Spirit.[58]

The advantage of *biblical* hermeneutics is that the actual author of the text is presently available to the reader to govern the illumination of the text. First Corinthians 2:12 informs us that the teacher lives within the believer, providing accurate interpretation. The Spirit can thereby point out

---

56. Zuck, "The Role of the Holy Spirit in Hermeneutics," 125–26.

57. See Archer, *Forging a New Path*, 201. Archer asserts that the plot functions on three levels: the "surface" level of story, the "arrangement of incidents and patterns" in a story, and the plot that operates within the mind of the reader. "The reader also exercises a tendency to organize and make connections between events within the narrative" (201).

58. Fowl, on the other hand, holds that "the interpretation of Scripture is guided by the testimony about the Spirit's work, rather than the other way around," and that "experiences of the Spirit's work provides the lenses through which Scripture is read rather than visa-versa" (Fowl, *Engaging Scripture*, 114). As a result, Fowl ultimately puts one's *experience* with the Spirit over the *inspiration* and *illumination* of the Spirit.

authorial instructions, ways to follow them, when to know that they are being disobeyed or ignored, inappropriate conclusions, et cetera. The Spirit convicts the reader of the need to respect the biblical text; he illumines our eyes "so that we see the Logos that is 'really present' in the letter."[59] While we often think of interpretation as a struggle with words and concepts in themselves, Vanhoozer reminds us that, "Accurate interpretation is a struggle not against flesh and blood, but against principalities and powers (Eph 6:12), as well as a struggle against ourselves."[60]

A secular, critical, or even demonic "spirit" may tempt the reader to resist any authoritative or absolute claims made by the original author. The "postmodern" reader may be a "playful producer" of meaning (where one experiences the thrill of losing oneself in the text, according to Roland Barthes), a "user" of the text (for one's own pragmatic purposes, as Richard Rorty describes), or a community member who always follows the reading strategies of the "interpretive community."[61] In each case the "death of the Author" (the Holy Spirit) is pronounced.[62] Pentecostal theologian French Arrington holds that the interpretation of Scripture requires the interpreter to submit his or her mind to God "so that the critical and analytical abilities are exercised under the guidance of the Holy Spirit." This allows the interpreter to have a conscious and "genuine openness to the witness of the Spirit."[63]

Such submission places the work of the exegete within the Christological boundaries provided by the Spirit (in his executorial authority) in expectation of the Spirit's leading (in his veracious authority). Henry proclaims that "the Spirit of God—not any private interpreter (2 Pet 1:20),

---

59. Vanhoozer, "The Spirit of Understanding," 133.

60. Vanhoozer, *Is There a Meaning in This Text?*, 413. See also McCartney and Clayton, *Let the Reader Understand*, 75–80. John connects "anointing" from the Spirit with epistemology in 1 John 2:20, 26–27, thus allowing us to win the hermeneutical struggle.

61. See Vanhoozer, *Is There a Meaning in This Text?*, chapter four.

62. In analyzing the John 4 narrative, Vanhoozer portrays the "conservative" approach to reader-response in comparison to the "radical" approach (See Vanhoozer, "The Reader in New Testament Interpretation," 318–24).

63. Arrington, "The Use of the Bible by Pentecostals," 105.

evangelical or nonevangelical—is the authoritative illuminator of the spiritually given Word."[64]

The doctrine of illumination naturally forces us into an "investigation" of divine mystery. Mystery in the NT most often refers to something that was once hidden but is now open for all who believe, to those who are willing to wrestle with the "the mystery of his will" (i.e., Eph 1:9–10). Biblical hermeneutics is the very means by which the Spirit takes possession of the soul and the mind. As the Spirit in the text "meets" the Spirit resident in our lives, God "mysteriously" takes possession of us in that Christ takes possession of us through the Spirit.

> What we become more sure of than anything else is that God has done what makes Him surer of us than we are either of ourselves or of Him. Our chief certainty is God's certainty of us in Christ. And our religious knowledge is not to know God but to know that we are known of Him.[65]

The practical advantages of this may seem elusive, but they are indeed enormous. In wrestling with such mysteries—especially with what it means to be "possessed" by Christ through his Spirit—we are delving into "the depths of God" (1 Cor 2:11). The result is a radical worldview re-orientation—not a worldview that eliminates mystery but one that, upon reading the Scriptures in order to "hear" the Spirit, encroaches upon such mystery.

The Veracious Authority of the Spirit and Certitude of Meaning

Fowl further develops "a notion of ecclesial authority that recognizes that the Spirit has been and still is at work in the lives of Christians and Christian communities."[66] He speaks of the "authority of the interpreter" which rests

---

64. Henry, *God, Revelation, and Authority*, IV: 289. See also 2 Cor 2:15.

65. Forsyth, *The Principle of Authority*, 35. Forsyth adds, "Even this certainty, resting in God's possession of us, begins in an even greater and more amazing certainty. And our certainty is, by the Holy Spirit, a most incredible thing—it is a function of the certainty which God always has of Himself. It is certainty of experience true, but it is more than experience; it is faith; it is a reflection of His own self-certainty. It is His own self-certainty immanent in us by faith. He never doubts Himself, and He lives in us. The things of God are only known by the Spirit of God, whether in Him or in us. We rise to newness of life by the very self-same power which raised Christ from the dead" (39).

66. Fowl, *Engaging Scripture*, 203.

The Authority of the Holy Spirit and Practical Theology: Hermeneutics

on the Spirit's hermeneutical priority.[67] The Spirit indeed works in the community through those given interpretive authority, as seen in Paul's letter to the Galatians. Paul provides a counter-conventional (or "allegorical") reading of Abraham in Galatians 3 and 4 based on, and judged by, the Galatians' experience of the Spirit. Fowl thereby sees the responsibility of the interpretive community to be that of "reading the Spirit" within their contemporary context, which incorporates to the community's underlying *traditions*.

> Understanding and interpreting the Spirit's movement is a matter of communal debate and discernment over time. This debate and discernment is itself often shaped by prior interpretations of Scripture and by traditions of practice and belief. . . . Experience of the Spirit shapes the reading of Scripture, but Scripture most often provides the lenses through which the Spirit's work is perceived and acted upon.[68]

Though we have pointed out Fowl's theological shortcomings (specifically, confusing *meaning* with *significance*; elevating the community's interests over the need to interpret *the text*), his attention to *context, prior interpretation* and *tradition* is indeed instructive for evangelicals. The ecclesial tradition, whether local or historical, indeed provides context for hermeneutical practice. Brown states,

> Tradition is a valid and important concept and a necessary means to be consulted and employed in doing theology, provided it is consulted and heard as *context* and not as *content*. No individual Christian or community of Christians has ever lived nor could ever live solely from the content of written Scripture or any other fixed and limited body of information and instruction.[69]

For Fowl, however, the Spirit's authority seems to be essentially *located* in tradition (in the church's "Spirit-inspired interpretation and application of Scripture"[70]) rather than in the text itself (thus replacing "content" with "context"). However, without the textual *meaning* availed to the interpreter through the inspiration of Scripture, how can the Spirit actually illuminate

---

67. Ibid., 114; see also pp. 145–51.
68. Fowl, *Engaging Scripture*, 114.
69. Brown, "On Method and Means in Theology," 163–64.
70. Fowl, *Engaging Scripture*, 113

the text so as to provide "certitude" in the mind of the believer, as described in John 16:13–15 (and reflected in protestant theology)? According to Ramm,

> [I]n the Christian religion our certainty is not derived from the rational powers of the human mind, nor from the word of the imperial Church, nor from the direct delivery of a reason within the heart. Rather, it comes only from the *testimonium spiritus sancti*.[71]

Can the Spirit's illumination produce certitude? Does illumination produce certitude of *meaning*, of *significance*, or of both? My claim is that the Spirit is able to produce certitude of meaning according to his executorial, veracious authority. In the next section I will attempt to demonstrate that the Spirit is also able to produce certitude of significance according to his governing authority.

Luther proposes a "two factor hermeneutic" (the text is distinct from the reader; the text affects the reader) which emphasizes that biblical texts are active and functional word-events, rather than passive words to be discerned. They are thereby able to illuminate, bring about clarity, and give life.[72] By this hermeneutic Luther is able to adhere to a theocentricity that produces salvific certitude.[73] Luther maintains that one may have a subjective certitude of the truth of God's Word without the objective certainty that comes through religious education.[74] Thus, it is not the strength or

---

71. Ramm, *The Witness of the Spirit*, 16.

72. See summary of Luther's hermeneutic in comparison to Riceour's in Marshall, "Luther's Two-Factor Hermeneutic," 54–55.

73. Luther explains, "But now, since God has taken my salvation out of my hands into his, making it depend on his choice and not mine, and has promised to save me, not by my own work or exertion but by his grace and mercy, I am assured and certain" (Rupp, *Luther and Erasmus*, 329). Marshall claims that Luther's concept of certitude is a bit ambiguous (because "it renders the certitude of experience insignificance in relation to the certitude of understanding or logic" [Marshall, "Luther's Two-Factor Hermeneutic," 63]); he therefore tries to make a distinction between "certitude" and "certainty" (the first referring to a state of mind, the second the objective character of propositions themselves). One may thus have certitude of experience (i.e., "I *know* that my redeemer lives . . . ") without certainty of understanding or logic.

74. According to the nineteenth century epistemologist Granfelt, "certainty" may be thought of as subjective or objective. Subjectively certain individuals are not able to present grounds that justify a belief, even though they feel that the grounds must exist. Objectively certain individuals, however, are able to clarify their beliefs. Objective certainty is attained through proper religious education. Believers have a desire for their subjective certainty to

degree of certitude of one's faith that is the basis of salvation, but rather the creation of faith in the believer by the Holy Spirit through the Word (forensically grounded in the atoning work of Jesus Christ). The Spirit's veracious authority therefore provides essential background for understanding biblical epistemology. The Spirit serves as a master Teacher who provides subjective certitude through experience, and then goes beyond experience by transforming subjective certitude into objective certainty—a certainty in the mind that blends experience and reason in the present with basic biblical concepts rooted in the past.

> The Spirit is the one who bridges the distance between the past and the present and lets us see and meet Jesus, the Son of God, sent by the Father; and in Jesus the Father himself. That is the greatness of the work of the Spirit, that in all reflection about hermeneutical questions in connection with the Bible comes to us as a surprising and overwhelming reality.[75]

Illumination produces certitude of meaning, first, through the conviction wrought by the Spirit himself that the Bible is indeed our "final authority" and that it possesses "full authority." Through his illumination, the Spirit provides a "compelling authority" that this Word is indeed authoritative—"compelling" in that, once truly "heard," one cannot help but to be convinced by and submit to its message.[76] The Spirit applies the bibli-

---

turn into objective certainty (see Luukkanen, *In Quest of Certainty*, 118–19, 124). In this light, we may evaluate Luther, who valued the subjective certainty provided by the gospel (given by the Spirit through the Word) but acknowledged that doubt plagues the Christian throughout his life, a doubt which results from the conflict between the certitude of faith and the rational experience of the law (see Kragen, "Epistemological Studies," 40–42; also Luther, *The Works of Martin Luther*, vol. 40).

75. Veenhof, "The Holy Spirit and Hermeneutics," 115. The Spirit can thereby be described in terms of relation or interaction. 1 Cor 2:10–16 "makes clear that we have to see the understanding (of the things of the Spirit) in respect of the knowing of faith." It also breaks down the "subject-object" dichotomy imposed by Des Cartes in that "the object of that knowing—the things of the Spirit—is that which determines the knowing human subject" (117). The person who knows by faith is fully dependent upon the operation of the Spirit; it is the Spirit who "knows in us" (118).

76. For a fuller description of "compelling authority" see Larkin, *Cultural and Biblical Hermeneutics*, 272–80. My understanding of the "compelling authority" of the Spirit is adapted from Larkin's definition of the "compelling authority" of the Bible (and is, in my mind, a better application).

cal message to our existential situation, compelling us to come under his "plenipotentiary authority." The Spirit compels us that the message we hear in the text corresponds with the Spirit's original, authoritative *speaking*. How does this occur? In the text we discover that the Spirit who has "spoken" to the original audience has a larger audience in mind as well—those in all times who would *hear* the Spirit's timeless message and *submit* to God in the very act of hearing.

The Spirit produces certitude of meaning, second, through *organic illumination* of the individual believer when the Spirit's sovereignty is combined with faithful exegesis of the text (as previously discussed).

Finally, the Spirit provides certitude of meaning as he confirms (or disaffirms) our interpretation through our interaction with the church community and with her "traditions." Accurate understanding of the text cannot occur in isolation. Jesus alludes to this in John 16:13, "he will guide *you* [plural] into all truth." Organic illumination must occur within the context of two important "communities." First, immediate, local church communities must embody the text through the formation of doctrines and church practices so that the text can "live again" in their own context. Critical realism demands that community investigation becomes an essential part of the hermeneutical process of searching for truth. "[Critical realism] is a powerful corrective against the subjective biases of individual scholars."[77] It also allows a basic process to develop for a workable community hermeneutic.[78]

The second hermeneutical "community" lies with believers *outside* our immediate, local context. This may consist of either the contemporary international community or, often better, the "community traditions" presented to us in historical (systematic) theology. As "Scripture interprets Scripture," other aspects of God's truth are illuminated to other bodies of believers as they attempt to embody the truth in their own practice and

---

77. Hiebert, *Missiological Implications*, 94.

78. Hiebert describes this process: First, scholars select domain of study, determine critical questions, provide categories and methods, set standards, define "proofs," and integrate theories, generate conceptual problems, and work in a worldview, explicating its larger assumptions and biases. Second, they check their research in critical interaction with one another and against the history of interpretation. Finally they deal with disagreements with humility and without fear of changing their non-essential theories (see Hiebert, *Missiological Implications*, 94).

worship. These illuminations often become a central aspect of ecclesiastical or historical tradition. According to Dorman, we need, "the Spirit-inspired attitude of openness to the results of another's exegesis of Scripture . . . [which] while not overcoming all differences of opinion, will make consensus on the meaning of the text much more likely."[79]

The global Church can become an international hermeneutical community in which Christian leaders from around the world become partners in hermeneutics. According to Hiebert, these partners must seek three things:

> to understand Scripture under the guidance of the Holy Spirit, to help one another in dealing with the problems they face in their particular contexts, and to check one another's cultural biases. Out of this process there can emerge a global theology that is increasingly freed from the influence of specific human contexts.[80]

Historical Church tradition is necessary for "balanced" theological interpretation. As seen in chapter two, Oden's "paleoorthodoxy" calls theologians to assess the texts of all traditions from the historic Church that allege to be consensual Christian teaching and to listen to their centrist interpreters. We will recognize heresy not by pure rational analysis, but "only by first knowing and sharing deeply in the language, worship, ethics and ethos of the ecumenical testimony of many cross-cultural generations of apostolic testimony."[81] Such an approach also calls for a renewed focus on the experience of the Spirit within the Church.

Thiel's proposal regarding the execution of the Spirit's authority within various "senses" of tradition (introduced in chapter four) can provide balance to those churches historically locked into only one sense. Other "traditions" can reveal other ways of experiencing the Spirit.[82] Thiel proclaims,

---

79. Dorman, "Holy Spirit, History, Hermeneutics and Theology," 429.
80. Hiebert, *Missiological Implications*, 113.
81. Oden, *Life in the Spirit*, 474.
82. "Indeed, the four senses are ways of naming tradition's pluralism within its own affirmed catholicity. But the senses of tradition offer more than a taxonomy of belief, doctrine, and practice. As *senses* of tradition, they dwell in the life of the Church as its divine experience" (Thiel, *Senses of Tradition*, 162 [emphasis his]).

> By definition, a comprehensive discernment of tradition involves an apprehension of the Spirit's presence that goes beyond tradition's literal sense as all the senses of constancy and renewal are accounted for, positively or negatively, in its discerning judgment.[83]

In light of the above considerations, "certitude of meaning" is indeed possible for biblical interpreters, particularly with respect to specific hermeneutical questions. Development of a "fuller" certitude, of course, only occurs over time, according to the "asymptote" model presented earlier.

Hermeneutics and the Governing Authority of the Spirit

Grenz and Franke attempt to develop a theology that goes "beyond foundationalism" and in doing so provide an "evangelical" slant on postmodern pneumatology and hermeneutics.[84] As seen in chapter two, Grenz and Franke maintain that the Spirit is constructing the eschatological "world" God has intended for creation as disclosed in the text.[85] Reflecting on the Westminster Confession, Grenz and Franke are particularly interested in the way the Spirit governs the church by "speaking in the Scripture."[86]

---

83. Thiel, *Senses of Tradition*, 188.

84. Though the Reformation did well to bind the Word and Spirit together—and thus eliminate any hermeneutical appeal to biblical exegesis without the Spirit or to a direct "word from the Spirit"—the *goal* or *perlocutionary effect* of the Spirit must now be addressed in postmodern times. The "modern" hermeneutic is being replaced by a "new communitarianism" that finds its roots in Hegel and in Toennies. Toennies distinguishes true community (which is marked by holistic relationships) from society (marked by contractual relationships), and many subsequent sociologists have used this distinction in order to criticize American individualism (See Grenz and Franke, *Beyond Foundationalism*, 211; also Toennies, *Community and Society*, 1887]). While standing in the Protestant framework with respect to pneumatology (i.e., they hold to *Filioque*, the Word/Spirit model of Luther, and the *testimonium* of Calvin), Grenz and Franke attempt to define what the Spirit actually *does* within the framework.

85. They cite Berger's sociological model of "world construction," which entails "the imposition of a meaningful order (a *nomos*) on our variegated experiences." These experiences include language and "knowledge"—not objective knowledge about the universe, but the "common order of interpretation society imposes on experience" (Grenz and Franke, *Beyond Foundationalism*, 76). This reflects the OT conception of the Spirit as the divine power creating and sustaining life (Gen 1:2; Ps 104:29–30), and the NT linkage of the Spirit to eschatological, new life (Rom 8:9–30).

86. *The Westminster Confession of Faith*, 1.10.

Grenz clarifies his understanding of this phrase in his article entitled "The Spirit and the Word,"[87] stating that biblical authority does not lie in the text itself but in "the authority of the Spirit whose instrumentality it is. The Bible is Scripture in that the sovereign Spirit has bound authoritative divine speaking to this text."[88]

How does Grenz connect the Spirit's "speaking" to "world construction?" "The Spirit performs the perlocutionary act of creating a world through the illocutionary act of speaking . . . by appropriating the biblical text as the instrumentality of the divine speaking."[89] "World construction," therefore, does not lie in the biblical text itself but in the Spirit's work in speaking through the text.[90] The Spirit's aim in this is to transport the contemporary reader or hearer into the text as the biblical narrative is told or re-read. The Spirit then recreates the past (as narrated by the text) within the present life of the community, both individually and corporately—a sort of re-enactment of the biblical drama in the present Church.

In this model, the Spirit seems to have an authority to govern Christ's eschatological kingdom. By "appropriating" Scripture, the Spirit uses his authority to create and govern the Church as an "extension" of the kingdom, as the present fulfillment of the eschatological New Covenant.[91]

> Through the appropriated biblical text, the Spirit forms in us a communal interpretive framework that creates a new world. . . . the Spirit creates in the present a foretaste of the future, eschatological world and constitutes us as the eschatological people who serve as a sign pointing to the eschatological community.[92]

In other words, the Spirit forms a specific interpretive framework within the Christian community, which in turn shapes our community. The Spirit authors personal identity by bringing people to reinterpret their own

---

87. Grenz, "The Spirit and the Word," 357–74.
88. Ibid., 358.
89. Ibid., 365.
90. Grenz and Franke, *Beyond Foundationalism*, 77.
91. Ibid., 225–26, 228.
92. Ibid., 81.

life-narrative in association with the Bible's "paradigmatic" narrative as re-enacted in the contemporary church.[93]

The Spirit's Governing Realm and "Authoritative Significance"

Grenz and Franke's model does seem to center on the Spirit's "governing authority." The Spirit's governing activity has been closely integrated with the Church's *dramatic application* of the text. Such a "performance" of the text is guided by the Spirit, who "appropriates" the text in somewhat the same way actors might creatively "perform" a Shakespearean script. As we shall see, "dramatic application" of the text is indeed a creative addition to any hermeneutic that has forgotten the *dynamic* quality of the Word.

For Grenz and Franke, however, the Spirit does not appropriate the "authorial discourse" of the text (that is, the illocutionary act performed by the Spirit when inspiring the text); rather, "the Spirit speaks by 'appropriating the text itself.'"[94] Textual "appropriation," however, is not the same as "application," which asks how an objective meaning comes to bear on a new situation. "Appropriation" of the text, in Ricoeur's language, has to do with how the contemporary reader experiences the text meaningfully (i.e., contextually, personally).[95] This essentially amounts to a "performance interpretation" of the text (rather than dramatic application). Vanhoozer reacts to this:

> There is no law against such performance interpretation, but neither is there any understanding. For once the attempt to infer the communicative intentions of the author is abandoned, so is the means

---

93. Grenz and Franke define the "person" as follows: "The assumption that the self is autonomous, self-determining, and unencumbered—that it exists independently of and outside any tradition or community—continues to color the manner in which many people view themselves and life itself. It is evident, for example, in the tendency to define ourselves fundamentally through reference to the choices we make, including the choice to join whatever 'communities' we prefer" (Grenz and Franke, *Beyond Foundationalism*, 207).

94. Grenz, "The Spirit and the Word," 361. Grenz critiques Wolterstorff's proposal in Wolterstorff's *Divine Discourse*. See also Wolterstorff, "The Promise of Speech Act Theory for Biblical Interpretation," 73–90.

95. Grenz and Franke quote Ricoeur, who claims that the meaning of a text always points beyond itself "toward a possible world" (Ricoeur, *Interpretation Theory*, 87). Grenz and Franke explain that the text "projects a way of being in the world, a mode of existence, a pattern of life" (Grenz and Franke, *Beyond Foundationalism*, 76).

for a meaningful interaction with the "other." This is deeply to be regretted; it is difficult to learn or grow or be transformed when one is in dialogue only with oneself.[96]

Grenz' root problem lies in his misapplication of Austin's speech act model. For Austin, the illocutionary act is not "speaking" but the certain force that is associated with an utterance (i.e., a warning). Illocutionary acts are only performed by the Spirit when *inspiring* the text and thus depositing *meaning* into the text.[97] Grenz thus falls in the subtle yet popular trap of looking to the Spirit's world-application—the text's *significance*—before recognizing the text's objective *meaning* as inspired and illumined by the Spirit. Because of this, the specific *content* of Scripture that provides the specific design necessary for the Spirit's "world construction" is not accounted for. According to Vanhoozer,

> Grenz's account fails to explain how we can infer, and to whom we should ascribe, what illocutionary acts have been performed. Consequently, he leaves unanswered the foundational question of how Scripture's actual *content* is related to the Spirit's accomplishing his further, perlocutionary, effects.[98]

Grenz' article does surface the critical problem of the Spirit's authority with respect to "significance." As we shall see in the next chapter, Grenz' essential "significance" lies in his conception of the Church's very *identity* as eschatological people of God. Grenz' introduction of the Spirit's authority to govern the Church by creating an eschatological, identity-forming interpretive framework is actually quite helpful for hermeneutical application and contextualization. In addition, Grenz conceives of the Spirit's "realm" of authority as evidenced in the culture at large:

---

96. Vanhoozer, "From Speech Acts to Scripture Acts," 40.

97. See Austin, *How to do Things with Words*, 95, 98. Vanhoozer further explains, "Because Grenz abandons the authorial model and embraces Ricoeur's premise that the text takes on a life of it own, he has difficulty specifying just what illocutionary acts the Spirit performs. Indeed, the only illocutionary act Grenz actually ascribes to the Spirit is *speaking*. . . . Speaking, however is not an illocutionary act!" (Vanhoozer, "From Speech Acts to Scripture Acts," 41 [emphasis his]).

98. Vanhoozer, "From Speech Acts to Scripture Acts," 41 (emphasis his).

the Spirit's voice can conceivably resound through many media, including the media of human culture. Because Spirit-induced human flourishing evokes cultural expression, we can anticipate in such expressions traces of the Creator Spirit's presence. Consequently, we should listen intently for the voice of the Spirit, who is present in all life and therefore who "precedes" us into the world, bubbling to the surface through the artifacts and symbols humans construct.[99]

Does the Spirit, who provides certitude of meaning, provide *certitude of significance* as well? In chapter four we analyzed the *realm* of the Spirit's governing authority as well as the Spirit's governing *effects*. When evaluating this governing authority in terms of hermeneutical *application* we discover that the Spirit's realm of authority establishes boundaries for discerning the authority of a particular application or significance of a text (i.e., hermeneutical legitimacy). Likewise, the Spirit's governing *effects* determine the authoritative force or *perlocution* of that application (i.e., hermeneutical impact). The Spirit who lives authoritatively within the believer and within the community is the same Spirit who authoritatively guides them in applying the text.

While difficult issues regarding biblical application should not be dismissed, the Spirit's governing *realm* of authority and powerful *effects* provide tremendous help and confidence to the interpreter of Scripture. The Spirit is our authoritative *guide* in applying the text, allowing us to "complete" the hermeneutical circle. The Spirit illuminates the mind regarding the meaning of the text; the Spirit then illuminates the mind regarding the very *relevance* of that meaning to the present world. The Spirit "reveals" God's mind and heart in an almost infinite number of contexts and situations, such as: "How do I preach the gospel in Portugal?" "How should our church address our Pastor's immorality?," or "What does the Word say about a difficult decision I'm currently facing?" Such "revelation" is not *new* revelation (e.g., Mark 4:15; Luke 8:11; John 10:35; λόγος generally refers to the written "Word"), but rather *new light* on biblical revelation, specifically adapted to present human contexts (e.g., Rom 10:8; Eph 6:17; ῥῆμα

---

99. Grenz and Franke, *Beyond Foundationalism*, 162–63. They also add, "Hence, while being ready to acknowledge the Spirit's voice wherever it may be found, we still uphold the primacy of the text."

generally connotes a *contemporary* "Word").¹⁰⁰ The Word (λόγος) that is "living and active and sharper than any two-edged sword" (Heb 4:12) is the Word (ῥῆμα) that can be "tasted" (Heb 6:5), can "cleanse" (Eph 5:26), and can bring forth faith through "hearing" (Rom 10:17).

Chapter four revealed the Spirit's *realm* in terms of various qualities he displays in his work of eschatological renewal. The Spirit of Yahweh anoints the Messiah-King, providing him with specific ruling qualities, such as wisdom, understanding, counsel, strength, knowledge, and fear of God (Isa 11:2). Thus the Spirit allows the King to fulfill his role as *divine interpreter* (and this will indeed be a crucial aspect of Christ's authority during his future reign). Likewise, the Spirit gives the human interpreter insight into the *significance* of the text for present times, providing him or her with these same qualities for applying Scripture. Isaiah 32:15–17 presents other qualities available to the human interpreter for applying Scripture righteously, justly, peacefully, and in accordance with the biblical idea of kingdom restoration according to a specific eschatological blueprint. The eschatological Spirit adds a "dynamic" element to biblical application that energizes and identifies the text's significance with past and future realities.

> The perfection of this inaugurated transformation in meaning and understanding is eschatological and awaits the final revelation at the end of the age, when we shall no longer "see . . . a poor reflection as in a mirror; then we shall see face to face," and "shall know fully" just as we are "fully known" (Cor 13:12).¹⁰¹

The Spirit thereby enlightens the interpreter within present contexts in anticipation of the Messiah's eschatological *reign*. The focus of Isa 32:15–17 upon physical and spiritual renewal should translate into healing and freedom from oppression, thereby providing a strong counter to human or ideological authoritarianism.¹⁰²

---

100. Though these Words are not always distinguishable in the NT, λόγος more often refers to the general "Word of God" written, particular the Word in association with Christ (e.g., 1 Pet 1:23, the "living Word"); ῥῆμά, to a specific word for a specific person (e.g., Matt 4:4, by the Word man "lives").

101. Gruenler, *Meaning and Understanding*, 171.

102. See Ramm, *The Pattern of Authority*, 19. Both hermeneutical authoritarianism and hermeneutical anarchy can be avoided through the pursuit of the sort of "hyperbolic" knowledge discussed earlier, which also has strong implications for significance. Such

The Lord Is the Spirit

The "immediacy" of the Spirit's governing authority in relation to hermeneutics is witnessed when the Word of God is made contemporaneous in the lives of present-day believers. The Spirit "exegetes" the world in *dramatic* fashion, applying the truth of the Word to all aspects of life and thought through active and creative application of the text. The Spirit acts as the reader's or exegete's "advocate" (παράκλητος) in this regard, bringing the Word to life.

> We speak of the Spirit when we make the transition from "then" to "now," when the remembered past and the unthinkable future become realities which shape our present. The work of the Holy Spirit defines an age—the age in which all times are immediately present to the time, the time of Christ.[103]

As seen in chapter four, Acts 1:4–5 demonstrates that the human interpreter must be "baptized in the Holy Spirit," which means that he or she has experienced the immediate reality of the eschatological kingdom. Experience of the Spirit becomes a qualitative foundation for NT hermeneutics as the Spirit "executes" the rule of Jesus Christ in human lives. In Acts 1:6–8 Christ responds to the disciples' desire for an "immediate" fulfillment of the Kingdom with the power of the Spirit—a power closely associated with "authority" (1:7). Much of their subsequent preaching involved the contextual development of this event's *significance*—e.g., Peter's speech in Acts 10–11; Paul's speech in Acts 17:22–23.[104] Such eschatological preaching, in fact, challenged the ideological and imperial structures of first century culture. According to O'Donovan,

> The Holy Spirit brings God's act in Christ into critical opposition to the falsely structured reality in which we live. At the same time and through the same act he calls into existence a new and true structure for existence. He gives substance to the new creation in Christ, giving it a historical embodiment in present human deci-

---

knowledge adopts a critical realist approach to hermeneutics, one that correlates *significance* derived *from* the text to the *meaning* deposited *in* the text—so that the Spirit can exegete the world without undue hindrance from the hermeneutician.

103. O'Donovan, *Resurrection and Moral Order*, 102–3.

104. In terms of legal hermeneutics, they are authoritative "witnesses" to the event and thereby able to explain the gospel in other situations. The Christ-event takes legal precedent over all other cases.

The Authority of the Holy Spirit and Practical Theology: Hermeneutics

sions and actions, so that is becomes partly visible even before its final manifestation.[105]

The Spirit provides an eschatological authority with immediate enjoyment—the past and future lived out in the present. According to Larkin, "the Spirit is an indispensable buttress for the hermeneutical bridge, serving to present the truth being transpired across it and then serving to show how the meaning may be put to work in the contemporary cultural context."[106] Forsythe also asserts:

> Apart from the Holy Ghost . . . there is no means of making the past present in the Christian sense. Only the Lord the Spirit, by the Word of the Gospel makes the person of Christ so near as to be the ever-present revelation and ever-creative redemption by God. The revelation that came to mankind in Christ, i.e. the real, intimate, and ageless act of God, comes to each man as Christ comes to him in the Holy Ghost.[107]

The Spirit's Governing Effects and Redemptive Significance

As we saw in our exegetical study and Biblical Theology, the qualities and authoritative "realm" of the Spirit are evidenced in the world according to a specific redemptive "effects." Regarding hermeneutics, these effects seem to be fashioned in the discovery of *redemptive significance*. The Spirit of Restoration forms the church as a redemptive community that experiences and participates in the progress of redemption and interprets all of life redemptively.

The Spirit creates realms of authority—realms where the kingdom of God becomes immanent—through textual application in specific contexts. Biblical application is seriously flawed if it is only a rationalistic enterprise resulting in rational application to the secular world-system. Without the governing influence of the Spirit, popular models such as "the hermeneutical spiral"[108] will likely appear more like a hermeneutical tower of Babel

---

105. O'Donovan, *Resurrection and Moral Order*, 104.
106. Larkin, *Cultural and Biblical Hermeneutics*, 303.
107. Forsyth, *The Principle of Authority*, 116.
108. See Osborne, *The Hermeneutical Spiral*, 324, 340–41. Osborne defines this spiral as a "critical realist" way of doing contextualization. The spiral is a process of developing

than a pursuit of life-producing truth. As Osborne points out, contextualization of Scripture in another culture is controlled by the Spirit when we realize that "the effects of the gospel are entirely the result of the Spirit rather than of our skill."[109]

Democratization

Isaiah 59:21 presents the Spirit/Word connection in terms of covenantal democratization and restoration. This is the "prophetic Spirit" distributed to the true remnant of Israel, empowering God's people to speak—and interpret—God's word. For them, the Spirit can now be understood as the One who indwells every believer, thereby providing *himself* as their "interpretive authority." As those living in a time of eschatological tension, the Spirit allows them to re-interpret their lives "dramatically" in light of their eschatological hope.

The governing character of God the Father, revealed in Jesus Christ, would be completely transcendent without the Spirit. Indeed there can be no effective legislation of a "constitution" without the actual *presence* of a governor who puts this legislation into effect for the benefit of all people. Such legislation was nominally present in the OT prophets, but led to dependence upon the human vessel with respect to the interpretation of God's will for personal and communal life. After Pentecost, the governing Spirit is no longer reserved for the "professional interpreter" but rather is poured out on "all flesh." Christians now take this interpretive responsibility upon themselves, acting as God's "prophets" in the world.

In our efforts to re-capture the effects of the Interpreter Spirit in today's churches, we need to re-assert a positive vision for world-engagement with Spirit-directed applications of Scripture and Scriptural principles. Stackhouse demonstrates that today's "globalization" creates a tremendous opportunity for the Church to develop a moral vision with respect to such

---

meaning and significance (fusing "the two horizons") as the interpreter interacts with the text. The text's cultural significance must be grounded in the text's context. The text also sets forth the agenda which "reshape the interpreter's preunderstanding and help to fuse the two horizons" (324).

109. Osborne, *The Hermeneutical Spiral*, 340. Osborne adds that "we can lose the Spirit's assistance through dishonesty, pride, laziness, or neglect of prayer."

"global" concerns as education, law, medicine, and the environment.[110] "The professions of education, law, and medicine, what we have called 'the authorities,' have largely defined modernity and are leading us to the new postmodernity."[111] They, however, "lack a moral rudder because, not only are they largely ignorant of their roots, they have often repudiated them, leaving these fields morally and spiritually vacuous and sometimes frightening, as the twentieth century revealed."[112]

Whereas "some strands of the theological tradition have at times been irrelevant to, overcontrolling of, or even abusive toward promising allies in the professions and regencies," Stackhouse envisions that "the authorities" might now be put into a larger moral and spiritual context shaped by a "consciousness of the Holy Spirit."[113] In other words, when these new "authorities" search for a theological/ethical framework, the Church must be ready to provide such frameworks, creatively applying them in each context. This will only happen, however, when the Church's hermeneutic reflects a renewed understanding of the Spirit's "democratization" with respect to his governing authority.

Liberation

"Liberation" must be viewed as a "redemptive effect" of the Spirit that leads to both hermeneutical liberty and moral responsibility. Romans 8:2 presents two warring administrations, the "law of the Spirit" and the "law of sin and death," that result in two opposing interpretations as well. The Spirit's administration (further explained in 8:6–11) orders the believer's life according to an eschatological kingdom blueprint, one that liberates the practice of interpretation from the "law of sin and death" (i.e., legal-

---

110. Stackhouse, "Introduction," 16. Stackhouse explains, "Globalization is proceeding, according to various opinions, on the basis of rediscovered, newly discovered, newly invented, or newly imposed universalistic values borne by a host of new social institutions and practices" (15). While these professions gained their authority on the basis of the Christian values they portrayed, modernization has secularized these "authorities."

111. Stackhouse, "Introduction," 36. Stackhouse holds that, "Professors, scholars, and teachers; lawyers, legislators, and judges; doctors, researchers, and nurses over the past two hundred years have become among the most honored authorities of the common life" (16).

112. Stackhouse, "Introduction," 29.

113. Ibid., 29, 36.

istic interpretation). "Interpretive freedom" finds its "form" in the Spirit's realm of authority, which appears in 8:3–4 as a moral sphere of influence grounded in Christ's redemption (v. 3) and "fulfilled in us" through the Spirit (v. 4).

Biblical interpretation can thus be seen as a vital part of the "drama of redemption." Balthasar speaks of Scripture in terms of a "theodrama," where God performs on the stage of world history, a history that reaches its climax in the cross.[114] God the Father is the author-producer, Jesus Christ is the main actor and "interpreter" of the Father, and the biblical text is the "script" that vividly presents the redemptive drama where we too can play our parts in its continuing "performances." The Spirit functions as "director," the one who "governs" the action and mediates between script and actors.

Vanhoozer affirms that a "creative fidelity" to the text is achieved as the director-Spirit does justice to the vision of the author and the abilities of the actors.[115] The biblical reader enters into the drama by bearing accurate witness to the text—both in its original meaning and in its present drama of personal redemption and sanctification. The Spirit directs the reader to employ "dramatic imagination" while remaining faithful to the text and in keeping with the main plot. Readers take note of particular scenes within the drama (as in "case studies"), studying and meditating upon their themes, background, tones, and subtleties in order to become familiar with the mind and heart of the author and the particular actors in each scene. As such scenes are "re-lived" in the present, they become "contemporaneous" to us. According to Balthasar, "when the Spirit proceeds from the Father and the Son and is breathed into the Church of Christ, something of God himself speaks in the mouths of the actors."[116]

Such an understanding allows for a liberty of application with respect to the biblical drama, a liberty that should result in a much closer portrayal of the actual drama of redemption in the context of life. Pinnock speaks to the need for this sort of hermeneutical liberty with biting analysis.

---

114. See Balthasar, *Theodrama*.
115. See Vanhoozer, "The Voice and the Actor," 92.
116. Balthasar, *Theodrama* I, 319.

Do we not often found ourselves resembling those Ephesians who had not heard that there was a Holy Spirit and those Samaritans on whom the Spirit was not yet poured out? (Acts 19:2; 8:16). If so, then we need, in addition to our rational training, a liberating of our spirits by the Spirit of God, so that we might be the kind of interpreters of Scripture that it deserves.[117]

TRANSFORMATION

Second Corinthians 3:7–18 is *the* key passage for developing a model of the Spirit's transforming influence through hermeneutics. The Spirit is "Lord" who "transforms" us into the image of Christ. Such a transformation occurs as we apply the text practically, "completing" the hermeneutical circle. The "completion" of hermeneutics, therefore, is not accomplished until the Holy Spirit guides the interpreter to go beyond the text, transforming their life and community.

The Spirit's "realms" of authority are places where he transforms the world as the Word is preached and applied. Such transformation begins in the mind, altering the recipient's "cognitive environment"—that set of assumed truths a person or group of people "live in." According to Sperber and Wilson, such cognitive environments create additional challenges for communicators:

> the communicator may be in a position of such authority over her audience that the success of her informative intention is mutually manifest in advance. When the communicator lacks that kind of authority but still wants to establish a mutual cognitive environment with her audience, all she has to do is adapt her informative intentions to her credibility.[118]

This second scenario seems to be a common one for the Holy Spirit, whose authority is frequently unrecognized by the interpreter. The Spirit presents his authority by "adapting" the biblical text to the interpreter's present situation. The Spirit creates an authoritative "realm" by applying the Word to the interpreter's context—bringing the *significance* of the text to bear upon their cognitive environment, transforming that environment

117. Pinnock, *The Scripture Principle*, 173–74.
118. Sperber and Wilson, *Relevance*, 63.

in accordance with the author's intentions. If the interpreter is a pastor, the entire "cognitive environment" of the church can be transformed. This amounts to a reformation in worldview or "interpretive framework." Klooster refers to this in terms of the Spirit's transformation of "preunderstanding."

> Regenerated believers are not immune from the danger of pursuing their study of Scripture with at least a partially unbiblical preunderstanding. Especially in academic work, foreign syntheses sneak in, often unwittingly. . . . The Spirit's organic illumination "by and with the Word" is indispensable in conforming one's preunderstanding to Scripture. Only from such preunderstanding can faithful biblical understanding result in real sanctification.[119]

Transformation does not need to be a forced process; rather, it is a process of communication that will "enable receivers of a language act to infer meaning that is relevant to their existence or situation."[120] Alston holds that speech acts are the "verbal exercise of authority, verbal ways of altering the 'social status' of something."[121] Laughery claims that the biblical worldview presents the interpretive task in terms of "a living hermeneutics in motion," which only finds closure "when the biblical text is acted or lived out into the world."[122] Interpreters make a mistake if they think the hermeneutical task ends with the linking of the world of the text to the world of the reader (as Ricoeur might have us think)—they must go beyond self-transformation and look to find biblical realities that "also aim at transforming the totality of the world." According to Laughery,

> [Biblical hermeneutics culminate] with the hermeneutical Spirit-illuminated "what," read and Spirit acted on [sic], which has *transforming world power* as it continues its motion through the text to the reader, and through the reader out into the animate world. . . . The world of the text and the world of the reader then must finally be in dialogue with the world God has created. . . . In this context, hermeneutical motion is to be understood as living and having the capacity to affect the world.[123]

---

119. Klooster, "The Role of the Holy Spirit," 464.
120. See Vanhoozer, "From Speech Acts to Scripture Acts," 14.
121. Alston, *Illocutionary Acts and Sentence Meaning*, 17.
122. Laughery, "Language at the Frontiers of Language," 188.
123. Ibid., 188 (emphasis his).

The Authority of the Holy Spirit and Practical Theology: Hermeneutics

Verhey sees the work of the Spirit in creating the Church as forming *communities of moral discourse* (which includes corporate reasoning and discernment) and *communities of healing* (based upon the promise of the Spirit in Rev 21:4). Such communities are formed by the Spirit *in memory of Jesus* (and particularly Jesus' ministry).[124] While the tendency in many hermeneutical circles is to subtly separate interpretation from such practical concerns, such *effects* of the Spirit are to be welcomed as foretastes of God's eschatological future. Hermeneutics performed under the Spirit's governing authority will necessarily be evidenced by transformation—of the individual, the church, and the world.

The Possibility of Certitude with Respect to "Authoritative Significance"

When such qualities and effects are released into the work of interpretation, the application of the text will itself reflect the above qualities and effects. This does not mean that each application claiming the Spirit's authority will necessarily have binding authority for other believers. Rather, the Spirit's authority in scriptural application will be recognizable by other believers when it has logical correlation to the *meaning* of the text and when it aligns with the pattern of divine authority. In other words, for the *significance* of a text to have authority for believers it must (1) glorify Christ; (2) logically correlate in their minds to the "meaning" of the text under consideration (an example of such "examining" is provided by the Thessalonians in Acts 17:11); and (3) demonstrate the Spirit's *qualities* (righteousness, justice, peace) and produce his *effects* (redemptive democratization, liberation, and transformation) in the specific application.

Thus, in order to possess the certitude of "authoritative significance," the specific application must reflect the Spirit's "plenipotentiary authority." In addition, the significance of a text will have authority only when the human interpreter trusts the Spirit to apply the Word to the world (i.e., to "exegete" the world). Pinnock gives the example of Edith Schaeffer, who once applied Isa 2:2–3 (a prophecy about the nations streaming to the mountains of God for divine teaching) to her Swiss Christian study community known as "L'Abri." Was Schaeffer wrong to do this? It could be

---

124. Verhey, "The Spirit of God and the Spirit of Medicine," 117–18.

argued, through a careful meditation on the passage, that Schaeffer was led by the Spirit to exegete her "world" according to an appropriated significance of this passage.[125] So, as Christians from all nations come to L'Abri today they reflect the day when all nations will come to Mt. Zion for divine teaching. In addition, the purpose of the extended lesson was supposedly to glorify Christ (rather than the community itself) and the community's experience of this teaching promoted the Spirit's *righteousness* (in terms of Christ's salvation) and *peace* (through the development of harmonious, international relationships). It also produced spiritual *transformation* on the part of many listeners.

We should certainly acknowledge that there are potential dangers in allotting such a "liberty" to application. Interpreters, for example, might sanctify their own biases or justify their own "sinful" applications. However, if the "significance" can be logically correlated to the text's intended *meaning*, and if it reflects the pattern of divine authority, we ought to *more readily* acknowledge the Spirit's governing authority with respect to that significance (although the correlation may sometimes require additional explanation).

Conclusion

The Spirit of Truth indeed authorizes, inspires, illuminates, and applies the written text of Scripture so that certitude of meaning and significance are possible to the faithful hermeneutician. As an essential "practice" of the church, believers can rely on the Spirit—the One who works within the pattern of divine authority—to guide them through the challenging yet incredibly rewarding work of biblical interpretation. The result is a bold confidence that the Spirit's truth can be confidently obtained and applied within each "act" of the drama of living.

---

125. See Pinnock, *The Scripture Principle*, 172.

6

The Authority of the Holy Spirit and Practical Theology: The Structure and Guidance of the Church

❖ IN THIS CHAPTER I will attempt to describe the way the Holy Spirit's plenipotentiary authority comes to bear upon the Church—and specifically the local church—with respect to her *structure* and *guidance*.[1] By "structure" I mean the organization of the church body according to her spiritual gifts and leadership. By "guidance" I refer to the Spirit's authority to guide churches into submission to the trinitarian God, into truth, and particularly into authorized ministry. These issues indeed raise very significant questions regarding the local church's *identity* and *mission*: "How *does* the Spirit structure the church?" "How does the church *know* when she is 'filled with' or 'guided by' the Holy Spirit?" "Can church leaders possess an 'authority' derived from the Spirit?" "What kind of authority does the Church have in the world?"

I will approach this subject by once again applying the theological model developed in chapters three and four. First, I will examine the essential framework provided by the Spirit's *divine Personhood* and *executorial authority*. Then I will attempt to respond to the contemporary "practical" theologians introduced in chapter two, namely, Stanley Grenz and John

---

1. I shall refer to the "Church" when speaking of the universal Church and the "church" when referring to the local church body.

Franke (who credit the Spirit with the "construction" of the church) and Reinhard Hütter (who links the Spirit with the very practices of the church). I will weigh their approaches against the Spirit's *veracious authority* (as divine Teacher) and *governing authority* (as Governor of the church), respectively, before building a case of my own in these regards.

The Structure and Guidance of the Church and the Divine Authority of the Spirit

What sort of relation does the Spirit, as a divine Person, have with local church bodies? Though the nature of this relationship has been debated throughout church history, we can delineate some secure principles for understanding the impact of the Spirit's divine Personhood and authority upon church structure and divine guidance.

Contemporary Challenges to the Spirit/Church Relationship

Augustine called the Spirit the "soul of the church," exclaiming, "What the soul is in our body, the Holy Spirit is in the body of Christ, which is the church."[2] This image certainly has some validity. As the church's "enlivening principle of empowerment,"[3] the Spirit has a life-giving role comparable to the way the soul gives life to the human body. However, this parallel has been misunderstood through the lens of Roman Catholic ecclesiology, which often creates a "fusion" of Spirit and Church based upon the "fusion" of Christ and the twelve apostles. Many Protestant theologians, such as Hendry, are rightly critical of such an over-identification of Spirit and Church.

> The Roman Catholic theory that the apostolate takes over the mission of Christ is based on the ground that since his bodily presence was withdrawn, the apostles (as representing the Church) now constitute the body through which he acts vicariously. But the Roman Catholic interpretation obliterates any real distinction between the body and Him who acts through it; the polarity which exists between Christ and the Twelve is virtually fused into an identity.[4]

2. Augustine, *Sermon*, 267.4.4.
3. Oden, *Life in the Spirit*, 292.
4. Hendry, *The Holy Spirit in Christian Theology*, 64–65.

Such a blurring of the Spirit/Church distinction drastically affects Roman Catholic pneumatology with respect to church leadership. The Spirit fulfills an essentially instrumental role—that of establishing a direct continuity between Christ and the Church—and thereby seems to lose his distinct Personhood with respect to the church and her leaders. Hendry distills the error of this view with respect to the Spirit's Lordship:

> There is no place in the Roman Catholic system for confrontation of the Church with the Holy Spirit as Lord, i.e., as witness to the Lordship of Christ over the Church. Rather, the Holy Spirit, as the soul of the Church, is the source from which the Church is inflated with its own authoritarian claim. Hence there is a loss of the sense of the "personality" of the Holy Spirit, which is rooted in the experience of confrontation with one who is Lord.[5]

Roman ecclesiology does highlight the Spirit's role as the source of gifts and graces within the church, particularly those that spring from the Spirit's personal indwelling. With a focus on the Spirit's *effects*, however, the Spirit is easily thought of as an impersonal principle or channel rather than as Lord and divine Person. The result once again is that the Spirit is granted only a "functional power" that essentially binds the Spirit to the structure and practices of the church. Catholic theologian Hans Küng, however, challenges this by re-asserting the Spirit's "freedom."

> The distinction between Spirit and Church has its basis in the divine nature. God's Spirit or, as we can also put it, in its freedom, Spirit and Church, however closely linked, are not on the same plane; the Church is subordinate to the Spirit of God. . . . The Spirit is *not* the Church. It would be dangerous to try and identify the Church and the Holy Spirit; for the Holy Spirit is the Spirit of God, not of the Church; hence the fundamental *freedom* of the Holy Spirit.[6]

The postmodern confusion of Holy Spirit and community is somewhat different from that of Roman Catholicism, but can render similar results. As we have seen, Hodgson's pneumatology stands as a prime example of

---

5. Ibid., 58.

6. Küng, *The Church*, 173–74. Küng even calls into question the *opus operatium view* of the sacraments, which is so central to Roman Catholic Church's sacramental theology, in hopes that the authorized priesthood not try to dictate or regiment the Spirit through the observation of Church canons and tenets (178).

postmodernism's reduction of the Spirit to that of a divine function or an activity of the community itself. For example, Hodgson states,

> God is "Spirit" *insofar as* God is present to, active in, embodied by that which is other than God, namely, the natural and human worlds. Thus in Scripture "Spirit" refers to that *modality of divine activity* whereby God indwells and empowers . . . the ecclesial community.[7]

Welker runs into similar trouble. Though he does provide a healthy reminder that the community of the Spirit must take into account the Spirit's "pluralism," the unity aspect of "community" is not created by the Spirit per se. Instead, church unity "becomes a reality not by imposing an illusory homogeneity, but by *cultivating creaturely differences* and by *removing unrighteous differences*."[8] Since Welker defines the Holy Spirit as "a unity of perspectives on Jesus Christ" that we actually help to constitute,[9] his intersubjective model of reality becomes imposed on the nature of the Spirit. Welker indeed concludes that God does not "stand above" the community but rather influences the community through those who receive the outpouring of the Spirit. The community does not experience the Spirit as an "authority" but as a powerful "force field" liberating people from bondage.[10]

As seen in chapter two, Moltmann views "the fellowship (κοινωνία) of the Holy Spirit" (2 Cor 13:13) as that which "draws [believers] into his fellowship, . . . into the [trinitarian] community he shares with the Father and the Son."[11] This is a quite helpful view indeed. Nevertheless, Moltmann ultimately breaks down the distinction between the fellowship amongst Persons of the Trinity and fellowship amongst believers, defining the Spirit in terms of God's presence "as community."[12] The Spirit "arrives at consciousness of itself in the human consciousness."[13]

---

7. Hodgson, *God in History*, 111 (emphasis mine).

8. Welker, "Der Heilege Geist," 140 (author's translation from German text; emphasis mine).

9. Ibid., 140 (author's translation from German text).

10. Welker, *God The Spirit*, 21–22.

11. Moltmann, *The Spirit of Life*, 217.

12. Ibid., 217. The Spirit indeed "becomes their fellowship" (218).

13. Moltmann, *The Spirit of Life*, 228–29. Such a Spirit-consciousness inevitably links

The Spirit's Divine Transcendence over the Church

As with the loss of the Spirit/spirit distinction (see chapter three), so the loss of the Spirit/church distinction in the above models seems to result in a reduction or elimination of the Spirit's distinct Personhood. Is a recognition of the Spirit's distinct, transcendent *Personhood* necessary for an experience of the Spirit in the body of Christ and for the establishment of church leadership?[14]

We have seen in our study of Ps 104:29, 30 that the Spirit, as creator and sustainer of life, has transcendence over all creation and over "recreation." The NT confirms that the Holy Spirit is also creator and "life-giver" of the church (Acts 2:17; Eph 2:18; Rev 22:1). As members of the church we "drink" the life of the Spirit and obtain spiritual sustenance (1 Cor 12:13). Gordon reflects the idea that the Holy Spirit has authority over the life of the local church in the following comments:

> The Spirit is the breath of God in the body of his church. While that divine body survives and must, multitudes of churches have so shut out the Spirit from rule and authority and supremacy in the midst of them that the ascended Lord can only say to them: "Thou hast a name to live and art dead."[15]

This biblical portrayal of the Spirit as the church's source of life thus retains a distinct sense of "authority" that "soul of the church" metaphorizing or "presence as community" theorizing cannot. John 3:3–8 reminds us that the Spirit provides "life" by remaining free to act as he wills. Küng comments on this passage in reference to the Church:

> Anyone who thinks that the Spirit can be compelled with word or sacrament, or with law and authority, power or order, is leaving out of account precisely that faith which the Spirit demands of him: faith not in his or the Church's law, authority, power or order, but in

---

human cultural systems with "the natural ecosystems of the earth" and "re-shapes the self-isolating consciousness which rules over itself and nature, into consciousness of the Spirit which creates life and community" (229).

14. Barth, *The Holy Ghost and the Christian Life*, 11ff.
15. Gordon, *The Ministry of the Spirit*, 141.

> God's free grace and faithfulness. It is true therefore of the Church too that the Spirit blows not when he must, but when he wills.[16]

First Corinthians 2:10–14 strengthens this picture by tying the Spirit's divine authority *over* the church body to *divine revelation*. While verses 10–11 demonstrate the Spirit's radical *distinction* from the spirit of man, verse 12 indicates that the Spirit, who knows the mind of God, is now revealed *corporately* in a way that reveals divine authority. The Spirit corrects any over-identification with the Church via his revelatory freedom and authority.

> This free Spirit of God is essential for our understanding of the Church, as well as for our understanding of the believer as a man made free by God's Spirit. But the free Spirit of God in no sense belongs to the Church and must in no way be confused with it.[17]

It is critical to keep the idea of the Spirit's "freedom" in mind when examining the Spirit / Church relation. Over-identification occurs when the authority of the Church (and her government, traditions, or decrees) becomes confused with the *Spirit's* authority. The Spirit becomes "domesticated" by the church and loses his freedom to confront and to reveal. Protestant theology has often sought to avoid a complete identification between the work of the Spirit and the work of the church. According to Berkhof,

> The difference with the Roman Catholic position is often sought in the emphasis on the sovereignty of the Spirit over against his means. It is a typical Reformed position to point to the freedom of the Spirit who can use all these means but who can also refuse to do so and work outside of them. His coming to us is an act of free grace. We do not dispose of it. We can pray for it.[18]

---

16. Küng, *The Church*, 177–78.

17. Ibid., 174.

18. Berkhof, *The Doctrine of the Holy Spirit*, 54–55. Küng draws appropriate analogy between the human spirit and the entire church body: "Just as the Holy Spirit, although it dwells in Christ, is not identical with the Christ's spirit, so the Spirit is not the spirit of the Church but of God" (Küng, *The Church*, 173).

Scripture does not deny a vital *connection* between the Spirit's work and the "work of ministry" (i.e., in preaching, sacraments, organization), but is clear to set forth the Spirit as the Church's "Lord" (2 Cor 3:17–18).

> In the New Testament the authority of the Holy Spirit is an authority to which the Church remains subject; it is the principle of the Church's obedience. The Council of Constantinople showed a true instinct for the essential when it defined the first of the attributes of the Spirit as "Lordship."[19]

A church that learns to always distinguish between her own body and the Holy Spirit's divine Personhood relinquishes her concern for establishing her own "authority" in the world and is "freed" to be structured and guided by the Spirit as he wills. Küng adds,

> A Church which distinguishes between itself and the Holy Spirit can face up to sin and failure in the Church soberly and humbly, but also with the liberating hope of those already justified that they will be forgiven anew. . . . the Church which humbly distinguishes itself from the free Spirit of God is for all its undeniable weakness strong, and for all its apparent unfreedom ultimately free.[20]

The Structure and Guidance of the Church and the Executorial Authority of the Spirit

Some evangelical theologians today advocate placing the Spirit "before" Christ with respect to the creation and mission of the church. John Taylor's popular book *The Go-Between God*, for example, argues that the Spirit needs to become "so central to our thoughts about God and about man that when the name 'God' is used our minds go first to the Spirit, not last."[21] Bevans, likewise, believes that "the Spirit precedes Jesus not only in our own lives but in the history of the world and in cultures that have not known him."[22] If the Church is to express its true nature, it needs to look first to the Spirit's activity.

---

19. Hendry, *The Holy Spirit In Christian Theology*, 57–58.
20. Küng, *The Church*, 175.
21. Taylor, *The Go-Between God*, 5–6.
22. Bevans, "God Inside Out," 102–3.

> Only by allying itself with the Spirit can the church live in fidelity to its Lord, who himself is allied to the Spirit in his mission. . . . It is as the body of Christ and the "face" of the Spirit that the church discovers its mission in the world.[23]

Bruner holds that Bevans' model actually reverses the apostolic sequence laid out in John 7:39: "the Spirit was not yet given, because Jesus was not yet glorified." Bruner claims that when this happens, "the church becomes pneumatocentric—the Montanist error—which has historically meant that the church was driven dizzy in a thousand 'spiritual' directions at once."[24] The church seems to lose its Christological *purpose*. Bruner, however, does try to provide a sense of the Spirit's *executorial authority* with respect to the church:

> But when the Son is given the priority, as happens in Scripture and tradition, the apostolic Spirit ultimately points the church in its worship services to her uni-center, True North, the Lord Jesus Christ, who in turn fortifies, energizes, and sends the church out, again and again into her thousand-point world service.[25]

The Spirit's Executorial Authority and the Ultimate Purpose of the Church

Technically speaking, must we say that either Christ or the Spirit comes "first" in the creation and mission of the Church? It seems more accurate to say that they "come" to the church simultaneously, yet with different roles (as delineated in chapter three). While the NT account of the creation of the Church (Acts 1 and 2) does not seem to give a *chronological* or *logical* priority to Christ or to the Spirit, we do discover a *doxological* priority that always remains with Christ (John 16:14). As the "head of the church" (Col 1:18), Christ is glorified when the Church, as an instrument of the Spirit, brings glory to him. This is indeed the essence of the Spirit's executorial authority in the Church.

Such a christologically-based authority in the church, however, has been and still is challenged by modern theology. Modernity attacks the

23. Ibid., 102–3.
24. Bruner, "The Son is Inside Out," 106.
25. Ibid., 106–8.

delicate balance between unity and diversity within church communities by seeking to "unify" all things under metaphysical abstractions. This has, in effect, discounted the Spirit's authority to create a unified Church with all her diversity.[26] Modernity's rationalism and moralism also effectually privatized the Spirit to the individual mind or will so that "the priesthood of the believer" was elevated above the church body. The individual was now free to use his or her own intellectual and spiritual capacities for discerning truth. According to Gunton, "It is when 'spirit' is reduced to or replaced by reason or will that the disastrous inhumanities and irrationalisms of the modern age take hold."[27] The beauty of the biblical conception of the church, however, is that it reflects both the unity and diversity inherent within the Trinity.

> [A]s the liberating Other, the Spirit respects the otherness and so the particularity of those whom he elects. That is why Paul's characterization of the various charismata, in 1 Cor 12, for example, is so seminal for our conception of what it is to be in community, for it implies richness and variety, not homogeneity. It is here that we find the rub of the difference between the gospel and the modern world. God the Spirit is the source of autonomy, not homogeneity, because

---

26. The "homogenizing" trends of modernism in the church was assisted by Schleiermacher, who defines the Holy Spirit as "the common Spirit of the new corporate life founded by Christ" (Schleiermacher, *The Christian Faith*, sec. 121) or, more fully, as "the union of the divine essence and human nature in the form of the common Spirit animating the life in common of believers" (sec. 123). The Holy Spirit is described as a "specific divine efficaciousness working in believers"—a common Spirit—rather than a "person" (secs. 123–25). "What Schleiermacher is attempting here is to understand how the church is founded upon a divine reality working nonsupernaturalistically in the constitution of a human fellowship characterized by redemptive love" (Hodgson and Williams, "The Church," 258–59).

27. Gunton, *The One, The Three and the Many*, 184. Another ecclesial movement worth mentioning is one that reduces the Spirit to *experience*. At times Luther is said to have more quarrels with the "enthusiasts" than the Roman Catholics. Enthusiasts tend to give prominence to the *personal* revelation of the Spirit as opposed to the revelation of *Scripture*. According to Hendry, "Enthusiasm exalts the sovereign freedom of the Spirit . . . in such a way as virtually to sever the connection between the mission of the Spirit and the historical Christ. The emphasis is laid on the immediate, subjective experience of the Spirit in the individual rather than on his appropriation of 'the redemption purchased by Christ' in the work of his incarnate life. The real attitude of enthusiasm (and this was openly avowed in its more extravagant forms such as Montanism and Joachimism) is that the dispensation of the Spirit superseded the historical revelation of Christ" (Hendry, *The Holy Spirit in Christian Theology*, 68).

by his action human beings are constituted in their uniqueness and particular networks of relation.[28]

Hegel, on the other hand, contributed to "postmodern" pneumatology with a *dynamic* conception of "Spirit" that essentially promoted *diversity* (though this diversity is related back to unity[29]) and *"interrelationship"* within community.[30] A NT conception of "interrelationship" is discovered in the concept κοινωνία, which helps the Church retain its ultimate purpose as defined by Jesus in John 17:22: "That they may be one, even as we are one." The unity of the Church demonstrates the unity of the Father and the Son—that the Father is in fact "glorified in the Son" (John 14:13)—and the "unity of the Spirit" as well.

> The Holy Spirit in the New Testament is conceived as the Spirit enabling the acknowledgment of Jesus Christ as Lord, and the One who creates the fellowship of a people acknowledging that lordship.[31]

Paul exposes God's supreme desire for a unified body in Phil 2:1b ("if there is any the κοινωνία of the Spirit").[32] This phrase, which corresponds with "unity in Christ" (2:1a), clarifies the Spirit's executorial purpose for the church's "fellowship"—to bring glory to Christ. The fellowship or community we enjoy with God and with one another is first and foremost a gift "of the Spirit." The high Christology of Philippians gives us the impression that the Spirit's purpose is to draw the Church into the "unity of Christ" and ultimately to bring her to *know* Christ (3:8–10). The implication is that the Spirit, in his "immanence," carries the transcendent authority of Christ into the κοινωνία of the church, so that all members may encounter Christ as a loving, gracious, merciful authority. Rather than referring to the

---

28. Gunton, *The One, The Three and the Many*, 183–84.
29. See Hegel, *Phenomenology of Spirit*, 236–62, 266–94.
30. Gunton, *The One, The Three and the Many*, 184.
31. Thomas, "The Holy Spirit and the Spirituality for Political Struggles," 217.
32 This phrase could mean, "If the Spirit has created a *real fellowship*" (Berkhof, *The Doctrine of the Holy Spirit*, 57–58). In light of the apparent disunity in the Philippian congregation, however, Paul's heavy emphasis on unity in Philippians 2 highlights a focus on the Spirit's unity-creating activity (in the midst of diversity). NEB has "any sharing of the Spirit."

Spirit "as community," the Spirit has been given the executorial authority to form a community that points to Christ as head.[33] Hendry states,

> [The Spirit] makes his indwelling presence known, not by inflating the Church with a sense of its own privilege and power, but by directing its attention to its living and exalted Lord and by exposing it to his grace.[34]

The Spirit's Executorial Authority and the Structure of the Church

In chapter three we observed the three-fold nature of the Spirit's "executorial" witness to Jesus as described in John 15:26. Jesus will "send" the Spirit from the Father in association with Jesus' authority; the Spirit "proceeds from" the Father to continue Jesus' mission; and the Spirit will "witness" (as the παράκλητος) "on behalf of" the Son as an authorized representative.

---

33. The "fellowship of the Spirit" implies the experience of our "oneness in Christ." This "fellowship" becomes a testimony to the risen Christ's victory over death, and provides a strong motivation to work together with common purpose and unity. Dunn expands this notion of communal experience in the Spirit: "The oneness of the body derives from the oneness of the Spirit, the unity of the body from the common experience of the same Spirit. Their experience of the Spirit was not something merely personal, the individual in his or her aloneness. It was a society-creating experience, a body-of-Christ-creating experience, an experience of being knit into a community. That is why in Eph 4:3 appeal can be made to the readers to be 'eager to maintain the unity of the Spirit in the bond of peace'—unity as something to be maintained, not created, something given, the unity of the Spirit as the base and starting point for Christian communal life. It may be significant, then, that Acts never records an occasion when the Spirit was poured out in the earliest days other than on groups—the shared experience of the Spirit providing that unifying bond and impulse without which there can be no unity" (Dunn, *The Christ And The Spirit,* 2:346).

34. Hendry, *The Holy Spirit In Christian Theology,* 65–66. Hendry continues, "This is the reason why the locus of the Holy Spirit in the Church is defined more specifically as the 'means of grace' (the Word, sacraments, and prayer)—i.e., precisely those functions of the Church in which it looks away from itself to Christ. It is not that Protestantism does not take seriously the promise of Christ's continued presence with his Church by the indwelling spirit. Only, it understands the presence of Christ as a real presence, not a fusion of identity. . . . The mission of the Holy Spirit does indeed effect the union between Christ and the Church, but in such a way that at the same time it attests the indelible distinction between them; it underscores the fact that the Christ who presents himself to the Church in the Holy Spirit is the Christ who died and rose again—'Christ clothed with his gospel,' as Calvin expressed it" (66–67).

If this verse is correlated with John 14:26 and Acts 2:1–11, we begin to see the true corporate nature of the Spirit's *executorial authority*. The Spirit will "bring to your remembrance all that I have said to *you*" (in John 14:26 the plural ὑμῖν indicates the entire believing community) and the Spirit allows all peoples to hear of "the mighty deeds of God" (Acts 2:11).

John 16:12–15 provides similar implications. Verse 12 implies that Jesus' speaking ministry will be "completed" after his resurrection and ascension. The Spirit of Truth will then "guide you into all truth." The Spirit will "open up" or apply the truth of Jesus in new contexts, that is, local church bodies. The Spirit will "glorify" (δοξάσει, "manifest") Jesus within the church by acting to "disclose" him to the disciples (v. 14), both personally and corporately.[35] The movement or pattern here is from the *one Lord* (Jesus) to the *one Spirit* to the *many disciples* within their variegated contexts and with their unique individualities. In other words, the Spirit will execute Jesus' will by making Jesus known *contextually*.[36] This general pattern is developed further in First Corinthians 12, which incorporates both unity and diversity into the Spirit's structuring of the body. The Spirit causes the resurrected Christ to become the reference point for the entire body of Christ and in so doing creates tangible demonstrations to the fullness of the person and authority of Christ.[37] This is accomplished in the church only as the Spirit's *diversity* is intimately related to Christ's *unity*, so that the unity of the Church becomes a function of its diversity.

> The members of the body have different functions, different ministries (Rom 12:4; 1 Cor 12:4–11)—otherwise the body would not be a body (1 Cor 12:17, 19). Without the diversity of charismata there

---

35. This word ἀναγγελεῖ, which can mean "announce" or "make known," in John conveys the idea of a *reporting* of that "which was from the beginning" (1 Jn 1:1), as opposed to Luke or Paul, where it generally refers to the proclamation of new revelation (see Aalen, "Proclamation," 3:47). The *context* of the Spirit's disclosure is crucial. In addition, verse 15 confirmed to us that neither the Father's authority nor Jesus' authority is reduced in the Spirit's disclosure—an important point to remember as we investigate further the nature of the Spirit's executorial authority *in the community*.

36. In our section on the Spirit's *governing authority* we will see how the Spirit seeks to *activate* the body in her diverse structure based on spiritual gifts. This governing authority, however, is rooted in the Spirit's *executorial authority* to glorify Christ as head over this body.

37. See Ferguson, who refers to the church as "the body of the resurrected Christ" (See Ferguson, *The Holy Spirit*, 248ff).

can be no unity, for without the Spirit's activity in and through each there is no unity and no body. The unity depends on the diversity functioning as such, and can be injured as much by one member taking too much to himself as by one member failing to respond to the Spirit's prompting (1 Cor 12:14–26; Rom 12:3).[38]

As the sharing in one loaf was to be an expression of the unity of the grace that knits the "many" together (1 Cor 10:17), so the Spirit acts with executorial authority to knit his gifts together into a fabric we identify as "the body of Christ." The Spirit's community-creating unity is vividly described by Paul, who shocks many of his contemporaries with the news that two bitterly-opposed groups, Jews and Gentiles, have come together to build one body. "For he is our peace, who has made us both one, and has broken down the dividing wall of hostility . . . in whom you also are built into it for a dwelling place of God in the Spirit" (Eph 2:14, 22). This "dwelling place of God in the Spirit" not only reflects the authority of the OT temple, but now transcends national and racial affinities, demonstrating to the world the Spirit's authority to unify the body under one head—Jesus Christ (Eph 1:10).

First Corinthians 12:3–30 provides an excellent framework for understanding the Spirit as the sovereign authority who structures the church "as he wills" (1 Cor 12:11). Volf comments,

> The sovereign Spirit of God allots the charismata "as the Spirit chooses" (1 Cor 12:11). The Spirit works, first, as the Spirit chooses; no church, neither an entire (local) church nor any structure in the church, can prescribe which gifts the Spirit is to bestow upon which members. Furthermore, the Spirit works *when* the Spirit chooses; the church cannot determine at which time the Spirit is to bestow its gifts. This clearly reveals that the church lives from a dynamic not drawing from itself. . . . It is not the church that "organizes" its life, but rather the Holy Spirit.[39]

The Spirit structures the community in order that diversity might display a unified purpose. Paul first lays a foundation in unity in the one confession of Jesus' lordship (prompted by the Holy Spirit; v. 3). He then spells out

---

38. Dunn, *The Christ And The Spirit*, 2:250.
39. Volf, *After Our Likeness*, 231–32.

the principle of unity and diversity in the church as an active display of the unity and diversity in the Trinity (vv. 4–6). "[T]he Triune God loves diversity. . . . God establishes his brand of harmony by a lavish grant of highly diverse gifts, each contributing to the body as a whole."[40]

Upon this principle of unity and diversity Paul develops a practical blueprint for understanding the gifts of the Spirit (vv. 7–10). The gifts listed here demonstrate the Spirit's "manifestation" for the common good (v. 7) and displays the Spirit's sovereignty in the act of distribution (v. 11). Whereas some commentators see unity as the prominent theme in this passage and others see diversity,[41] the final sense here is that "Paul continually stresses unity in diversity in order to overcome divisiveness owing to different valuations being assigned to different gifts, with tongues as the applied higher-status gift."[42] "Unity" in this passage has been located in their common *goal* (Lategan) or in the *community* itself (Martin). Collins, however, locates unity in "the same Spirit" that holds the unit together (as a parallel to Rom 12:6–8).[43]

The body is to be unified for a purpose—to represent the "oneness" of Christ (v. 12) and the one Spirit who unifies all (v. 13). The community finds its purpose in its unity in Christ as each member individually and all members corporately take responsibility for the welfare of the whole (an idea repeated in vv. 24–26). Paul's concept of the body of Christ is thereby that of a dynamic expression of Christ's unity, truth and wholeness; he exhorts all the members of different communities to teach, admonish, judge, and comfort (Rom 15:14; 2 Cor 2:7; Col 3:16; 1 Thess 5:14).

The Structure and Guidance of the Church and the Veracious Authority of the Spirit

The church that is truly *under* the Spirit's authority will thereby be *structured* and *guided* according to the Spirit's executorial authority. This leads

---

40. Carson, *Showing the Spirit*, 32.

41. Unity is the primary theme for Lategan, Harrington, and Dale Martin; diversity for Fee and G. Wright.

42. Martin, *The Corinthian Body*, 87.

43. Collins, *First Corinthians*, 449.

to the next question: "How might we discern the veracious authority of the Spirit as the one who guides the body of Christ into truth?"

Grenz and Franke's conception of "world construction" attempts to shed light on this by focusing on the Church's eschatological *identity*. As seen in the last chapter, Grenz and Franke believe that the Spirit applies the text by performing the perlocutionary act of "creating a world," which is "the eschatological world God intends for creation as disclosed in the text."[44] This construction also occurs through "paradigmatic events" that capture the community's imagination and shape the way believers conceive "the totality of reality"—particularly their history and future—in creating a meaningful present.

> The Spirit constructs our communal identity by linking us to this glorious future. The Spirit speaks to us through the text—appropriates the biblical vision of the divinely interceded new creation—so that we might view our situation in the light of God's future.[45]

Grenz and Franke assert that the Spirit "appropriates" the text of Scripture.

> Through the appropriated biblical text, the Spirit forms in us a communal interpretive framework that creates a new world. The Spirit leads us to view ourselves and all reality in light of an unabashedly Christian and specifically biblical interpretive framework so that we might thereby understand and respond to the challenges of life in the present as the contemporary embodiment of a faith community that spans the ages.[46]

In addition to Scripture, Grenz and Franke look to *historical church tradition*[47] as a secondary medium through which the Spirit's authority is

---

44. Grenz and Franke, *Beyond Foundationalism*, 77. This "world" is "nothing less than a new creation centered in Jesus Christ (2 Cor 5:17) . . . a new community comprised of renewed persons" (77).

45. Grenz and Franke, *Beyond Foundationalism*, 81.

46. Ibid., 81.

47. "[W]e can conceive of the Christian tradition as the history of the interpretation and application of canonical Scripture by the Christian community, the church, as it listens to the voice of the Spirit speaking through the text" (Grenz and Franke, *Beyond Foundationalism*, 118). The purpose of church tradition is to provide theologians with a stabilizing continuity with the past while at the same time allowing for the flexibility needed to adapt to new contexts and concerns. Tradition also provides much needed insight in the relation-

experienced and the church is established. Tradition provides "the hermeneutical context or trajectory for the Christian theological enterprise."[48] For Grenz and Franke, it is the work of the Spirit that "unifies this relationship between Scripture and the communal tradition of the church"[49] Thus, the authority of both Scripture and tradition is derived from the Spirit as an "organic unity, so that even though Scripture and tradition are distinguishable, they are fundamentally inseparable." Such a unity is critical to the Church's *identity* under the Spirit's authority.

> To misconstrue the shape of this relationship by setting Scripture over against tradition or by elevating tradition above Scripture is to fail to comprehend properly the work of the Spirit. Moreover, to do so is, in the final analysis, a distortion of the authority of the triune God in the church.[50]

Why do they say this? Their clarification is:

> A non-foundational understanding of Scripture and tradition locates ultimate authority *only in the action of the triune God.* If we must speak of a "foundation" of the Christian faith at all, then, we must speak of neither Scripture nor tradition in and of themselves, but only of the triune God who is disclosed in polyphonic fashion through Scripture, the church, and even the world, albeit always normatively through Scripture.[51]

As with Scripture, Grenz and Franke understand tradition to be the Spirit's "instrumentality" for constructing the church (i.e., "tools" in the construction). The Spirit as Constructor has a certain *veracious authority*, as her hermeneutical guide, to illuminate/appropriate both Scripture and tradition.

---

ship between worship and liturgy, provides opportunity to observe the long-term effects of a specific tradition, preserves classical theological formulations and communal practices, allows for confessional commitments, describes the church's eschatological character, and allows for the gospel to be performed in new interpretive and cultural contexts (see Williams, review of *Beyond Foundationalism*, 753).

48. Grenz and Franke, *Beyond Foundationalism*, 120.
49. Ibid., 116.
50. Ibid., 117.
51. Ibid., 117–18 (emphasis mine).

The illuminating work of the Spirit brought forth these writings [Scripture] from the context of the community in accordance with the witness of that community. This work of illumination has not ceased with the closing of the canon. Rather, it continues as the Spirit attunes the contemporary community of faith to understand Scripture and apply it afresh to its own context in accordance with the intentions of the Spirit.[52]

Spirit of Truth and the Guidance of the Church in Truth

There are at least two problems, however, with this conception of veracious authority with respect to the church. First, by "locating ultimate authority only in the action of the triune God," these authors seem to have begun with the *pattern* of divine authority (the "how") rather than with its *principle* or definition (the "who").[53] While this may only be a matter of emphasis, understanding ultimate authority in terms of its *manifestation* seems to de-emphasize the supreme *right* to act. Second, as examined in the last chapter, these authors have referred to the Spirit's "speaking" in the text as an "appropriation" rather than as "inspiration" and have thereby confused the text's *significance* with its objective *meaning*. Because of this, the specific *content* of Scripture (that which conveys *truth*) is not accounted for. Rather than defining Scripture's truth *ontologically* (reflecting God's *being*) they have reconceived it *instrumentally* (according to its *use*). By making Scripture a tool for the Spirit's construction, they have not actually told us why *this* tool is better than any other, except that it is the Spirit's chosen instrument.[54]

Nevertheless, the Holy Spirit's guidance of the church "into all truth" *can* be investigated in terms of a "hermeneutical community" that submits to the Spirit of Truth who speaks in and through the text (see chapter five,

---

52. Ibid., 116.

53. Certainly they believe that divine authority is located in divine persons, as demonstrated in chapter six—though they do opt for a "social Trinity," which for Welker implies that the Spirit may act on his own authority (See Grenz and Franke, *Beyond Foundationalism*, 188–202).

54. "As Christians, we acknowledge the Bible as Scripture in that the sovereign Spirit has bound authoritative, divine speaking to this text" (Grenz and Franke, *Beyond Foundationalism*, 65).

"The Eschatological/Immanent *Realm* of the Spirit's Governing Authority and Authoritative Significance"). As seen in chapter four, John's dualistic understanding of "Spirit" can be applied to the entire church body. Evidently the church is able to embody either the Spirit of Truth or a spirit of error (or darkness, deception, etc.), the presence of which seems to precede or determine corporate decisions regarding doctrine, hermeneutics, theology, etc. According to Breck, the divine "Mystery" spoken of by John (in reference to the eternal Logos—John 1:14, 17; 14:6) and by Paul is "communicated as revelation to the 'community of truth' and made known through correct exposition of Scripture."[55] As our παράκλητον, the Spirit of Truth serves as an advocate or "legal counselor" for the corporate body (rather than as a prosecuting attorney).[56] Though we tend to think of "counselor" individualistically, its application in John 14–16 is obviously to the entire community. The Spirit extends Jesus' own advocacy for his community of disciples to Jesus' post-Pentecost body of believers. Jesus will send his παράκλητον so that he may "teach *you* all things," "remind *you* of everything I have said to *you*" (14:26), and "lead *you* into all truth" (16:13). This repeated use of ὑμᾶς (you, pl.) indicates that the truth of Jesus will be spoken by the Spirit for the purpose of corporate guidance as well as personal interpretation.[57] Burge concludes,

> John does not say (in John 16:13–15) that the Spirit will only reiterate what Jesus has said (anamnesis): there may be future, progressive revelation. The revelation of Jesus will still continue in the community, and the Spirit Paraclete will be his authoritative channel. But these revelations must not depart from the original revelation of the historical Christ. The Spirit will recall these, interpret them, and continue their presence in the life of the community.[58]

---

55. Breck, *Spirit of Truth*, 144.

56. It is interesting to consider the Holy Spirit's role as "advocate" who defends us (and as "Spirit of Truth" who helps us to know and speak truth) in contrast to the devil's role as "prosecuting attorney" (and as "Father of lies" [John 8:44] who attacks the church with accusations and deceptions).

57. Such leading can occur because "the Spirit of Truth" refers (at least in part) to "the truth that Jesus is" and because Jesus tells us he himself will be present "where two or three are gathered in my name" (Matt 18:20).

58. Burge, *The Anointed Community*, 215.

The Authority of the Holy Spirit and Practical Theology: The Church

The veracious authority of the Spirit in the church community is thus an obvious display of his *executorial authority*, providing the church community with great confidence regarding Christ's continued guidance. Through the authority of the Spirit the church can become the sort of "hermeneutical community" wherein Jesus' words in authoritative Scripture become embodied within the life and mission of the local community.

> The historical fact of Jesus' existence is, theologically speaking, not the only significant factor. It is also significant that Christ has entered into the history of a community, which is an ongoing modeling, interpreting, expecting, and witnessing. In other words, Christ has become part of a web of belief: he is being remembered and interpreted in connection with other elements of belief as one who redirects human lives toward God and toward the coming kingdom in a unique way. Only by way of this qualitative givenness, only through the presence of the Spirit in the community, is Christ now given to history in general.[59]

In chapter five we discovered that the entire body of Christ provides an appropriate arena for corporate *guidance* and *discernment* through the Spirit of Truth. This surfaces the legitimate use of *tradition* and *church practice* as avenues for reflection on scriptural and theological truths and principles. Traditions where Scripture is spoken, meditated upon, memorized, acted upon, studied, et cetera, can all become such avenues.

As our advocate, the Spirit of Truth graciously uses such traditions in the *embodiment of* Scripture. By guiding the Church in the process of exegesis, illumination, and application such an embodiment allows the church to recover a true sense of its own "authority"—not a "magisterial authority" *possessed* by the church but a "ministerial authority" to proclaim the Word of God and particularly the gospel of Christ in the world. As the "sword of the Spirit" (Eph 6:17), this Word is best sharpened in community contexts where "iron sharpens iron" (Prov 27:17). As church communities wrestle to "work out" theological truths in the context of practical life issues, these truths become subject matters for spiritual engagement and education. In this way, the Spirit of Truth becomes "free" to shape and guide the church community according to the pattern of divine authority.

---

59. Hoedemaker, "Toward an Epistemologically Responsible Missiology," 223–24.

The Lord Is the Spirit

Spirit of Truth and Church Leadership

As concluded in chapter four, the Spirit of Truth's "reminding" extends beyond the inspiration of Scripture to the *illumination* of authoritative Scripture. Illumination can provide great confidence to church leaders in guiding the church as they "listen" to the Spirit speaking "in the church" (i.e., John 16:13; Rev 2–3). Such "listening," however, must occur within the protective parameters provided by our pattern of divine authority. This will in turn protect the local church against abuses of authority, including any "establishment" of authority by human leaders. Furthermore, leaders are responsible to guard the church and its message against the infestation of foreign idols and ideals. Paul exhorts Timothy to "Guard, through the Holy Spirit who dwells in us, the treasure which has been entrusted to you" (2 Tim 1:14). Timothy is to *guard the gospel*—for in this simple message all authority of Christ is displayed—and is to do so through the Holy Spirit's veracious, illuminating authority. According to Forsyth, if church leaders dilute the Word within the church:

> [I]t would certainly cease to be free. It would renounce the Holy Spirit, whose source and matter and liberty are historically in that Word alone. . . . It would be a renunciation of its charter Gospel, which is the repudiation of the Holy Spirit, and the suicide of a Church.[60]

Church leaders possess a "functional authority" in this regard, one that reflects the Spirit's veracious authority in the way they handle, preach, and teach the Word of God. Through this functional authority, the Spirit's veracious authority can continually confront the church with a *living Word*. According to Calvin, "The Spirit goes before the church, to enlighten her in understanding the Word, while the Word itself is like the Lydian stone, by which she tests all doctrines."[61] Paul actually laid responsibility on the community as a whole for testing the validity of words claiming to reflect divine authority (1 Cor 2:12, 15; 1 Thess 5:20–21), including Paul's own words (cf. 1 Cor 7:25, 40; 14:37). According to Dunn:

---

60. Forsyth, *The Principle of Authority*, 250–51.
61. Quoted in Johnson, *Authority in Protestant Theology*, 55.

The Authority of the Holy Spirit and Practical Theology: The Church

> [The community is] to recognize the authority of the Spirit in those ministries undertaken at his compulsion (1 Cor 16:18; 1 Thess 5:12–13), but also to evaluate and if necessary reject any word or deed, however inspired it might seem to be, which was counterfeit or did not benefit the community (1 Cor 2:15; 12:3; 1 Thess 5:21–22). In other words, the gift was not complete until it had been evaluated and received (1 Cor 12:10, 14:27–29; 1 Thess 5:19–22, NEB).[62]

The Structure and Guidance of the Church and the Governing Authority of the Spirit

We saw in chapter two how Hütter, in *Suffering Divine Things*, aligns the Spirit with the doctrines and practices of the church. They are the "mediate forms" through which the Spirit guides the Church into truth. These truths then become the "binding authority" of the church.[63] Through church practices, churches become fellowships of participation in the communion of the Father with the Son in the Spirit. Hütter describes the Spirit's actions in terms of the "*poiemata*"[64] of the *Spiritus Creator*, "works" of the Spirit through which he implements the teachings of the church. These *poiemata* are manifested in the form of "core church practices." The *Spiritus Creator* of the church fashions the church herself as his "*poiesis*." Hütter seems to grant the Spirit a profound *governing authority*:

> The end time is already present "in the Spirit" now in the economic mission of Jesus Christ and the Holy Spirit through the communion of the ecclesial body of Christ. . . . The human being is entirely the receiving party here, whereas the Spirit's own actions are genuine poiesis; for the Spirit creates a *nova creatura*, in a way hidden now, but later openly.[65]

---

62. Dunn, *The Christ And The Spirit*, 2:251.

63. Hütter, *Suffering Divine Things*, 128. Hütter adds, "As paradoxical as it may sound, the core church practices and church doctrine, precisely in their binding nature, are essential if the Holy Spirit is to lead the church to perfect truth and teach it new things by perpetually reminding it of Jesus Christ" (128).

64. "*Poiesis*" is generally defined as *performance* or *production*. "Poetic" and "poietic" have the same etymology—both emerge from *poiesis*: "to do or to make."

65. Hütter, *Suffering Divine Things*, 124–25.

Hütter's central argument highlights Luther's treatise "On the Councils and the Church" (1539), where "Luther unequivocally associates pneumatology and ecclesiology by way of the concept of 'works' of the Holy Spirit as tied to distinct church practices."[66] In this treatise, Luther outlines seven church practices that demonstrate specific *poiemata* of the Spirit in the church community, including the preached word of God, baptism, the Lord's Supper, the "office of the keys" (church discipline), "ordination and offices," public prayer/praise/instruction, and discipleship in suffering.[67] The Spirit activates these distinct practices along with the structures of learning and recollection implied in John 14:26, "the Holy Spirit, whom the Father will send in my name, will teach you everything, and remind you of all that I have said to you."

Hütter thereby aligns the "*poiesis*" of the Holy Spirit with the "pathos"[68] of the human subject. This implies that the *pathos* of core church practices "is identical to the pathos of faith itself" and that these practices of the church, as well as her doctrines, are works of the Holy Spirit rather than human constructions. These core doctrines and practices have "binding authority" precisely because they are the work of the Spirit.

> Only in a binding context of doctrine and praxis can new insights emerge, practices be reformed, and church doctrine be articulated or rethought. Without the public established by this binding authority, Christians cannot encounter God's word anew, nor make any new discoveries; without this binding authority everything becomes the object of individual evaluation and assessment. As paradoxical as it may sound, the core church practices and church doctrine, precisely in their binding nature, are essential if the Holy Spirit is to lead the church to perfect truth and teach it new things by perpetually reminding it of Jesus Christ.[69]

---

66. Ibid., 128.

67. Luther comments, "I shall let them stand as the seven principal parts of Christian sanctification or the seven holy possessions of the church" (Luther, "On the Councils and the Church," 165–66).

68. Hütter defines "pathos" in terms of the traditional use of the word "suffering"—that is, *undergoing or incurring* as opposed to *initiating*.

69. Hütter, *Suffering Divine Things*, 128.

The Authority of the Holy Spirit and Practical Theology: The Church

We might therefore think of Hütter's model as calling for a "poetic authority," the idea that the beliefs and practices initiated by the Spirit having "binding authority" precisely because they are *products* of the Holy Spirit. According to Hütter, "The church itself is nothing else than the thankful creature of God's saving word, not a proud executor but a glad recipient. Yet this receiving embodied in practices is precisely the way in and through which the Holy Spirit works the saving knowledge of God."[70] The end result is that the Church becomes the locus of divine authority. Hütter seems to be saying that participation in church practices is a way of submitting to the Spirit and to his work.

The Governing Authority of the Spirit and the Practices of the Church

Hütter is very helpful in several ways. He rightly disavows platonic misconceptions of Luther's theology, such as a distinction between a "visible" church and an "invisible" church.[71] He is particularly helpful in saying that the Spirit works out his authority by making the church and its theology a *public practice*, particularly in the sense that it is continually in dialogue with all elements of politics and culture.[72] Certainly Hütter's insistence that the mission of the Spirit (and its soteriological *poiesis* of sanctification and renewal) is performed through specific church practices can be helpful today in the re-integration of pneumatology back into specific ecclesiological practices.

However, we must investigate the *way* Hütter attaches the Spirit's "binding authority" to core church practices. The Spirit is said to take on the "mediate form" of church practices in such a way that these practices have a "binding authority" of their own. Is this in keeping with Paul's "law

---

70. Hütter, "The Church," 23.

71. Hütter surmises, "Precisely the *externality* of that which constitutes the church as church is to be understood *pneumatologically*. This concrete externality of the Spirit's 'holy possession,' however, in no way involves the otherwise justified distinction between the 'visible' and 'invisible' church" (Hütter, *Suffering Divine Things*, 131).

72. See Hütter, *Suffering Divine Things*, part four. This indeed needs to be explored further.

of the Spirit" derived from our exegesis of Rom 8:2 (which we concluded meant "binding authority"[73])?

Hütter's understanding of *poiemata* is in fact somewhat different than Paul's. In Eph 2:10 Paul calls *believers*, rather than "practices," God's ποίημα (this word is often translated "workmanship"), emphasizing that "church" is always *people*.[74] Church practices and doctrines are indeed *means* or *tools* or *forms* through which the Spirit's authority is executed. In their execution, divine authority is displayed *in* the Church and world. These practices indeed serve as *horizontal channels* for disseminating divine authority. However, they have no binding authority with respect to believers as if to establish a *vertical* authority *over* them.

Indeed the believer's reception of the *knowledge of God*, as discerned in the Spirit's "works" within the church, always occurs within a specific context and nearly always involves the use of specific forms, traditions, and practices that make this knowledge "concrete." While these practices are *means* for knowing God, the very knowledge of God itself is the *end*, and is a gift of the Spirit (1 Cor 2:10–12).

As seen in chapter four, the Spirit's governing authority in the church is intimately associated with his *veracious authority* in the church. The Spirit is not simply a "poetic authority" or functional guide into the knowledge of God through "lived knowledge." He is also a divine *Teacher* who inspires and illuminates the text. Hütter's model seems to forget the Spirit's *veracious authority* with respect to the Word of God (or what Barth refers to as "the freedom of the Word" with respect to the Church) in light of the Spirit who becomes the "power" (and "practice") of Christian tradition.

Hütter rightly refers to church practices as "mediate forms,"[75] without which "Christians cannot encounter God's word anew, nor make any new discoveries"). It seems, however, that church tradition now *stands between* or *mediates between* the Spirit's authority with respect to the Word and the

---

73. Specifically, "binding" as in "subjecting" or a "mastery" one must obey (see chapter four).

74. See Luther, *The Works of Martin Luther*, 41:xi, xiv.

75. "Although church doctrine and the core practices definitely do not 'possess' the Holy Spirit in any way such that they simply coincide with its activity, they nonetheless do constitute the indispensable 'mediate forms' of its activity through which the Holy Spirit guides the church to truth" (Hütter, *Suffering Divine Things*, 127–28).

believer within the church. It also seems that this could easily translate into a *loss* of the Spirit's authority. Hütter opts for this approach because, in his mind, the only alternative is a "Platonic republic" ecclesiology.[76]

The Spirit's governing authority in the context of the church, however, must be incorporated and activated in connection with the entire pattern of divine authority. The Spirit who "guides" the church in practical matters does so as the church submits to God, glorifies Christ, and honors the authority of Scripture.

In chapter four, we developed a biblical model for understanding the Spirit's authority to establish and govern the Church. Do the "practices" of the church account for this governing authority? To answer this, the Spirit's governing authority will be examined according to: (1) his administration *in the church*, particularly in guiding her "life" and mission (in the next three sub-sections), and (2) his administration *through the authority of church leaders* (in the final section).

The Spirit's Eschatological/Immediate Authority and the Administrative Guidance of the Church

As Hütter points out, the church receives administrative guidance from the Spirit in the context of her corporate *life*, *mission*, and *practices*. In chapter four I discussed the Spirit's governing authority in the church in terms of an eschatological, immediate *realm* of authority. The Spirit's realm displays God's "righteousness," "justice," and "peace" in the world (Isa 32:15–18), even through such imperfect vessels as the local church and individual believers. In the NT, these qualities are discovered in the person of Christ and the cross of Christ, and are then displayed in the Church as foretastes of Christ's future kingdom community. They are also displayed in her witness of Christ in the world. Believers participate in the Spirit's governing authority as their minds and hearts are captured by an eschatological vision of history and the future,[77] a vision that naturally leads to the adventure

---

76. See Hütter, *Suffering Divine Things*, 125 (see also his note on 244).

77. The church's vision of her *history*—captured in the linear development of her *origin* (in Christ and his promises) along with a vision of her eschatological *destiny* (of all things being "summed up in Christ" [Eph 1:10] and of "reigning with Christ" [Rev 20:6])—provide her with an indelible sense of *identity* and *security* by which she lives in contemporaneity with these visions.

of the church's corporate *life* and *mission*. According to Hoedemaker, "Eschatology draws out those dimensions of pneumatology that highlight the adventure character of the Christian community in a pluralist world."[78] The body of Christ is governed by the Spirit *as a whole,* and as a union of individual members, activating her calling to be witnesses to Christ by granting her a *ministerial authority* in the world. Thomas proclaims that the Holy Spirit creates a fellowship acknowledging Christ's lordship and that this fellowship becomes a powerful sign of the kingdom to the ends of the earth until the end of time.

> The Holy Spirit provides the people of Christ the power for spiritual resistance against the powers of self-righteousness, which destroys the *koinonia* of mutual forgiveness created by divine forgiveness (Col. 3:13), and against the spirit of idolatry working universally and turning every human creativity into destructivity and every human ethos into a law unto itself.[79]

In chapter four we also studied the Spirit's "immediate" authority as portrayed in Acts. The Spirit is to be revealed as the Church's *administrator* from the day of Pentecost onward. Cumming is well known for his conviction in this regard:

> The Holy Ghost, from the Day of Pentecost, has occupied an entirely new position. The whole administration of the affairs of the Church of Christ has since that day devolved upon Him. He is the medium of communication through whom the Mediatorial work is carried on. This is "the Dispensation of the Fullness," which has been committed unto Him.[80]

---

78. Hoedemaker, "Toward an Epistemologically Responsible Missiology," 223–24.

79. Thomas, "The Holy Spirit and the Spirituality for Political Struggles," 217.

80. Cumming, *Through The Eternal Spirit*, 98. Cumming also points out the five occurrences of *oikinomia*: "once (Eph i.10) quite generally; once (Eph iii.2) as 'the dispensation of grace'; once (1 Cor ix.17) as a 'stewardship' given to Paul; once (Col i.25, see R.V. margin) as a 'stewardship' of God given to Paul; and once (1 Timothy i.4, see R.V margin) as a 'stewardship of God which is in faith.' The word employed for 'the ministration (the ministry and the administration) of the Spirit' is quite different (*diakonia*, 2 Corinthians ill. 8)" (98).

The Effects of the Spirit and the Administrative Guidance of the Church

Though the Church never attains a status of "magisterial authority," within the Spirit's realm she is given a "ministerial authority" to demonstrate that the eternal, almighty God is "present" today in his powerful "effects"—*democratization*, *liberation*, and *transformation*. These effects demonstrate the reality of God's authority in the world and in the Church, especially in and through specific church *practice* (i.e., lived knowledge). Isaiah's vision of the Spirit's eschatological restoration (Isa 32:15–16) begins with *democratization* (Isa 59:21). Whereas in the OT the Spirit primarily provided judges, kings, and prophets with a special anointing "authorizing" them to fulfill their mission, the Spirit is now "democratized" to the entire church so that all believers possess a ministerial authority to fulfill their Christ-authorized mission.

In the NT Church, democratization is realized in terms of corporate *liberation* and *transformation*. First, the "binding authority" of the *liberating* Spirit, in Rom 8:2, is expanded to the corporate level in 8:4 (by use of the first person plural pronoun, ἡμῖν). In contrast to the law's mastery, which leads to ecclesial bondage and condemnation, the Spirit provides a liberation in conjunction with Christ's redemption (Rom 8:3–30) that infects the entire body and its witness to the world. Paul portrays the Spirit not only as the giver of human freedom but also as the one who actually leads God's people *through* this freedom (e.g., Rom 8:14).

> According to this conception, the freedom of Christians derives from their institution into a new particular network of relationships: first with God through faith in Christ, and then with others in the community of the church. Just as the Spirit frees Jesus to be himself, so it is with those who are "in Christ," that is, in the community of his people. The church is a community, not a collective: that is, a particular community into which particular people are initiated by the leading of the Spirit.[81]

Second, we see in 2 Cor 3:17–18 why the "administration" of the Spirit is more glorious than the "administration" of the law (2 Cor 3:8). The Spirit in his "covenant headship" produces *corporate transformation*

---

81. Gunton, *The One, the Three, And the Many*, 183–84.

(3:17–18). The entire body experiences the Spirit as "Lord," the One through whom all believers are "beholding as in a mirror" the glory of the Lord, and are being "transformed into his likeness with ever-increasing glory" (3:18).

> In some very profound teaching in 2 Cor. 3 we seem to have a hint as to how we hear the voice of the Lord in guiding the affairs of the church. There the administration . . . of the Spirit is distinctly spoken of in contrast with the administration of the law.[82]

A Model for the Spirit's Administrative Guidance

As the Spirit leads the democratized church into his *liberation* and *transformation*, these become the basic ingredients for developing a model of the Spirit's administrative authority within the practices of the church. Church leaders certainly need a legitimate, workable model for granting the Spirit an appropriate *freedom* to lead and govern the church in accordance with the pattern of divine authority. Such a model, however, seems to be so underdeveloped in traditional protestant "systematic theology" that we need to look elsewhere to develop it. This model needs to: (1) urge churches and leaders to trust the Spirit to lead the church through his work of *liberation*—freeing, activating, and orchestrating all believers to employ their spiritual gifts within the entire body; and (2) take seriously the Spirit's *transformation* of both individual believers and corporate communities through the church's ministry, doctrine, preaching, decisions, discernment, etc. To develop this two-fold model I will employ modified forms of charismatic/Pentecostal theology and evangelical missiology. Space will only allow a brief investigation.

First, charismatic theology is generally characterized by an emphasis on the Spirit's "freedom" in the body. At its best, charismatic theology is grounded in an OT understanding of the Spirit's endowment of "charismatic leadership." Many of the gifts and abilities found in such leadership (i.e., prophecy) are democratized in the NT to every believer and to be employed in an ordered liberty (cf. 1 Cor 12–14).[83] Dunn believes that the

---

82. Gordon, *The Ministry of the Spirit*, 138. This contrast of διακονία is found in 3:7–8.

83. Sartori points out, however, that "'charism' cannot be equated with 'liberty' and thus be set again authority; nor can it be thought of as 'spontaneity' and as an alternative to the

charismatic movement has challenged the paradigms of Church government that set up an incision between clergy and laity. It takes seriously Paul's teaching that the health of the church depends on each member functioning properly, with the church supporting each individual in their ministry and in their diversity. This exercise of God's grace through individual "charisms" is "the opposite of hierarchical status and authority."[84]

> And yet that, it seems to me, is precisely the challenge and question of the Charismatic renewal—to rethink our traditional conceptions of ministry and the ministry from the bottom up, to rework our whole theology of ministry, not on the basis that the ordained ministry is a given, an established fixed point, but from first principles where any concept of "special ministry" truly grows again from a thoroughly thought out understanding of the ministry of the whole people of God as the basis. The attempt to graft a concept of the ministry of the people on the established root of the ordained ministry has not really worked. Now it is time to reaffirm that the root of all ministry is the charismatic Spirit given variously to members of Christ's body, to recognize that our starting point is the new covenant of the Pentecostal Spirit and not an old covenant institution of priesthood.[85]

Herein is the basic idea Paul wishes to make plain in 1 Cor 12:11. The Spirit sovereignly and freely orchestrates the gifts: "All these are the work of one and the same Spirit, and he gives them to each one, just as he determines." Bloesch sees one of the greatest contributions of Pentecostalism to be the way it gives "poignant expression to the priesthood of all believers."

> The Reformation had rediscovered this biblical concept but was unable to avoid a hierarchical church in which all major responsibilities are assumed by the pastor. Pentecostals remind us that all Christians share in the ministry of Christ, including laity and women.[86]

---

rule of law and order; nor can it cover the whole area of pluralism and be placed in opposition to the 'judiciary' as synonymous with unity and uniformity; still less can one refer to the 'divine' or the 'spirit' as if the structure either of the law or any other institution were 'human' or the 'flesh'" (Sortori, "The Structure of Juridical and Charismatic Power," 57).

84. Dunn, *The Christ and the Spirit*, 2:308.
85. Ibid., 298.
86. Bloesch, *The Holy Spirit*, 205.

The Lord Is the Spirit

Second, evangelical missiology is very helpful in that it is often produced by those missiologists who have continually confronted situations where the Spirit's authority becomes the most "practical resource" with respect to the transformation of cultures. Whether the issue is church growth or developing a healthy sense of "order" in a newly-established church, these missiologists know that such growth and order must emerge from the Spirit's authoritative work in the midst of "contextualized chaos." Missionaries that respect the Spirit's governing authority, according to Bevans, "can avoid the danger of preaching the Gospel as if one controlled its message, or as if that message could be exhaustively expressed in objective, rational categories."[87]

Burrows critiques Western missiology, which tends to confine the Spirit in missions "to the status of mysterious energy making for the efficacy of ecclesiastical activities."[88] Instead, we need to learn all we can from evangelical missiologists, such as William Smalley and Roland Allen, who have asked us to trust the Holy Spirit with the growth, structure and guidance of churches planted in foreign cultures. Smalley, for example, aims to replace western "paternalism" with the Spirit's authority.

> It is not until we are willing to let churches grow also that we have learned to trust the Holy Spirit with society. We are treating him as a small child with a new toy too complicated and dangerous for him to handle. Our paternalism is not only a paternalism toward other peoples; it is also a paternalism towards God.[89]

Allen argues that Paul's method contrasts the modern Western approach in many ways. His central conviction regarding missions is founded in Paul's unwavering trust in the missionary Spirit who governs the Church:

> St. Paul constructed elaborate systems of religious ceremony, and grasped fundamental principles with an unhesitating faith in the power of the Holy Ghost to apply them to his hearers and to work out their appropriate external expressions in them. It was inevitable that the methods which were the natural outcome of the mind of

---

87. Bevans, "God Inside Out," 104.
88. Burrows. "A Seventh Paradigm?," 128.
89. Smalley, "Cultural Implications of an Indigenous Church," 501–2.

The Authority of the Holy Spirit and Practical Theology: The Church

St Paul should appear as dangerous to us as they appeared to the Jewish Christians of his own day.[90]

Allen's application of Paul's "method" to missions can and should be applied to the universal church as well. The following principles are particularly helpful.

> (1) The test of all teaching is practice. Nothing should be taught which cannot be so grasped and used. . . . ; (2) A sense of mutual responsibility of all the Christians one for another should be carefully inculcated and practiced. . . . ; (3) Authority to exercise spiritual gifts should be given freely and at once. Nothing should be withheld which may strengthen the life of the church. . . . The liberty to enjoy such gifts is not a privilege which may be withheld but a right which must be acknowledged. The test of preparedness to receive the authority is the capacity to receive the grace.[91]

The Spirit leads established churches as well according to his *liberation* and *transformation* (rather than by an authoritative control). It is particularly within cultures and tribes that demonstrate bondage to oppressive and abusive rituals or ideologies that such effects have greatest impact. Such a leading of God's people enables churches to develop group expressions of the Spirit's diverse gifts because these gifts "require group participation and the pooling of resources in a unified, harmonious expression."[92] While the OT focuses on the Spirit's enabling of specific individuals for specific situations and particular needs, the NT paints a portrait of leadership, gifts, abilities, and individuals functioning together for the benefit of all members and their effectiveness in the church. "Just as temple artisans required tools to accomplish the construction of God's dwelling, so NT leaders require spiritual gifts to accomplish the construction of God's people (1 Cor 12)."[93]

---

90. Paton and Long, *The Compulsion of the Spirit*, 6–7.
91. Ibid., 10–11.
92. Hildebrandt, *An Old Testament Theology of the Spirit of God*, 201–2.
93. Ibid., 201–2. See also Dunn, *Jesus and the Spirit*, 199–258.

THE LORD IS THE SPIRIT

The Administration of the Spirit and the "Functional Authority" of Church Leaders and Church Offices

Church leaders are not to "establish authority" but are to fulfill their offices (as pastors, elders, teachers, etc.) in submission to the Spirit. This means they are to honor the Spirit's *executorial authority* by encouraging a diverse body to develop within the unity of Christ, his *veracious authority* by properly understanding and interpreting Scripture, and his *governing authority* by living within the *realm* of the Spirit and enjoying its *effects*. Church leaders possess a special ministerial authority to participate in the Church's execution of the Spirit's authority through specific Spirit-led practices. They must remember that Christ, as head of the Church, possesses all Kingdom authority and that the Spirit possesses all authority to govern churches. Because of their fallen nature, leaders can easily forget this governmental pattern, especially when attempting to "organize" the church, and can even begin to abuse their authority.[94] This is why the pattern of divine authority

---

94. While abuse of the pattern of authority appears in every form of church government, Pentecostal theologian Hodges admits that he sees it emerging more often in "independent" churches, which tend to misuse the Spirit's "liberation": "By using the term 'independent' something different from the independence of the congregational churches is meant. Rather, we are referring to those 'charismatic' leaders who declare themselves independent from all kinds of church government on the basis that God has called them to do a certain work and they must not be bound by human legislation or organization. . . . Often times such a leader himself will be the owner of the church property and, while he may name a committee with whom he occasionally consults, this committee usually has no authority, but is limited to an advisory role. Such a leader will often appeal to the 'liberty' in the Holy Spirit and claim he is free from the bondage of men and organizations. He may claim he is only obligated to obey Christ and that the Scriptures are his only authority" (Hodges, *A Theology of the Church and its Mission*, 63–64). "Postmodern" abuse of ecclesiastical power, on the other hand, seems to be more ideological. Contemporary leadership "may bind on the church the 'political correctness' of secular society, or it may enforce total control over subjugated disciples" (Clowney, *The Church*, 203). Such an attitude may stem from an agenda rooted in "liberation theology." Thomas astutely points out the "spiritual enemy of the liberation movement," which is found "within its very claim not only to be a sign of the kingdom but to establish the kingdom." Thomas adds, "[Liberation Theology] turns its programme into a scheme of ultimate salvation, and political struggles become instruments of justification by works and holy crusades. Here the politics of the liberation of people from oppression not only has a positive element, but acquires also a negative relation to the movement of redemption in Jesus Christ; it takes on a messianic character in opposition to the messianism of the Crucified and Risen Lord. Here appear idolatrous spirits that need to be resisted spiritually." Thomas sees a way of liberation for the liberation movement in "a spirituality

must be continually emphasized, preached and reiterated in the church so that its truth might grip the hearts of both leaders and laity.

The ministerial authority possessed by church leaders is a "functional authority" to fulfill their ministerial office.[95] It is *functional*, as opposed to intrinsic, personal, or hierarchical, in that church leaders are "servant-managers who use their authority only to advance the interests of those they represent and serve."[96] According to Clowney,

> While chosen and recognized by the people, church elders receive their authority through the Holy Spirit who called them, endued them, and appointed them for service (Acts 20:28). Service, not power or prestige, is the purpose of church officers, as of all believers.[97]

Calvin affirms that the authority of Church leaders is delegated by the Spirit to the *ministry* that is appointed:

> Whatever authority and divinity is attributed by the Holy Spirit, in the Scripture, either to the priests and prophets under the law, or to the apostles and their successors, it is all given, not in a strict sense to the persons themselves, but to the ministry over which they were appointed, or to speak more correctly, to the word, the ministration of which was committed to them.[98]

The "functional authority" of church leaders is rooted in the nature of "apostolic authority." Even so, while the apostles possessed a special authority to function as foundational "stewards" in the establishment of

---

rooted in the sense of human solidarity in sin and grace and also in the church as the community of divine and mutual forgiveness, with faith in the eschatological givenness of the kingdom" (Thomas, "The Holy Spirit and the Spirituality for Political Struggles," 224).

95. Once again, "functional authority" is the right to perform a specific function or task, usually in place of another, and is especially applied to the occupation of an office. Ramm notes that some refer to "functional authority" as "substitutional authority" (Ramm, *The Pattern of Authority*, 12), and that it can refer to teachers who serve as an instructional guide "until the learner can know the truth for himself" (12).

96. Clowney, *The Church*, 202. Clowney adds, "Better by far are imperfect structures in the hands of devoted servants of Christ than the most biblical form of church government practiced in pride or in a loveless and vindictive spirit" (202).

97. Clowney, *The Church*, 205–6.

98. Calvin, *Institutes*, iv.8.2.

the church and in the mediation of the NT (Rom 12:7), they were never actually *established* as "authorities."[99] According to Hendry,

> The role of the apostles is correlated with the world of the Spirit. It is their commission to bear witness to the Lordship of Christ. But it is not in their power to establish [that Lordship] among men, because it consists not just in an authority to teach and to give commands, but in a work of salvation which he completed by his exaltation. They can confess it and testify to it; but without the testimony of the Spirit who comes from the exalted Lord, it cannot be established among men. It is the recognition of the Lordship of the Spirit and the abiding polarity in the relation between the Spirit and the Church that distinguished the Protestant doctrine.[100]

This functional role of the apostles is confirmed by the fact that Jesus chose twelve apostles but evidently no apparent *leader* among them to succeed him. Though some have claimed this for Peter, he was not chairman of the Jerusalem council (Acts 15:3–22). Instead, Paul and Barnabus appointed a plurality of elders in their church plants (Acts 14:23). The book of Acts provides rather detailed snapshots of leaders who display the Spirit's qualities in specific decisions they make: in moral and practical issues and decisions (Acts 4:8; cf. 2:14–36, 8:29, 9:17), in praying for the Spirit's assistance in healing (4:22), in the choosing of Pastors and teachers (20:28), and in the selections of Deacons (upon the criterion that they be filled with the Spirit of wisdom as needed for their administrative roles) (6:1–10).

Rather than seeking to attain "power," leaders are to find their point of contact with the Spirit's governing realm as they become servants within this realm. Leaders do not stand *outside* the Spirit's realm in order to aid in its establishment; rather, they stand *inside* as participants with the entire body of Christ in its specific practices and traditions and in the enjoyment of the Spirit's effects. The leader's functional authority is not a political authority.[101] Clowney clarifies the spiritual nature of this "authority."

---

99. Ramm defines "apostolic authority" as "the authority it possessed as a witness to Jesus Christ. . . . [T]he authority was a delegated authority, for the authority pertained to the revelation mediated and to that alone" (Ramm, *The Pattern of Authority*, 51).

100. Hendry, *The Holy Spirit in Christian Theology*, 65–67.

101. Church government is never to employ political sanctions, physical force, or pragmatic means (John 18:36–37; Matt 22:16–21; 2 Cor 10:36).

> Equipped with the keys of the kingdom, church government represents the authority of Christ the Lord, who will judge the living and the dead. Though church government is fallible in applying Christ's Word, Christians must submit to it (Heb 13:17; 1 Cor 4:21; 2 Cor 13:2, 10).[102]

Human church government is an authority to be exercised by those with recognized and appropriate gifts (Acts 20:28–29; 1 Tim 5:17; 1 Cor 12:28). Church leaders are to be respected and submitted to by church member in so far that their words and actions correspond to the pattern of divine authority (Heb 13:17; 1 Cor 4:21; 2 Cor 13:2, 10; 1 Thess 5:12–13).

As for specific "offices" in the church, we must first acknowledge that all Christians can be rightly said to hold an "office," since all are in the body of Christ and gifted for his service. The governing authority of the Spirit anoints every believer with a "ministerial authority" to build up the body and to witness to Jesus' redemption.[103] "Special" offices, therefore, are to be seen as ministries of the *whole* church for the purpose of "equipping the saints for the work of ministry." According to Dunn,

> In Ephesians Paul's concept of the local church as a charismatic community is universalized . . . and the ministries of apostles, prophets, evangelists, pastors, and teachers are presented as ministries of the whole church (Eph 4:11–16). The authority of these various ministries lay primarily in the act of the ministry itself. . . . Paul did not vest authority in one individual or group. The authority of prophets and teachers was evidently limited to the sphere of their ministries (2 Cor 10:13–16).[104]

As servants labored together for the benefit of the church, the early Church enjoyed the fruits of such Spirit-led leadership: "Then the church throughout Judea, Galilee and Samaria enjoyed a time of peace. It was strengthened; and encouraged by the Holy Spirit, it grew in numbers, liv-

---

102. Clowney, *The Church*, 203–4.

103. Clowney explains this "gospel authority" as a calling to build up, not cast down (i.e., 1 Cor 10:8). It is based on the idea that "publicly recognized gifts differ only in degree, not in kind, from gifts possessed by every believer" (Clowney, *The Church*, 204). See Matt 23:7–12.

104. Dunn, *The Christ And The Spirit*, 2:251–52.

ing in the fear of the Lord" (Acts 9:31).[105] Leadership offices are presented in Acts as activities of ministry—Apostles (4:8, 31, 9:17), prophets (21:4–11), evangelists (8:29, 39), pastors and teachers (20:23, 28), and deacons (6:3–10; 7:55). Such giftings were recognized as they emerged from within the context of the whole body's ministry. The gifts associated with special leadership offices need public recognition in order to be used effectively (the gift of "Pastor-teacher" for example). This recognition by the community allows gifts and offices to become conjoined in the Spirit's act of calling.[106] The Spirit, who "has in His own gift the permanent qualifications of the rulers of the Church,"[107] calls specific persons with such qualifications and with specific giftings into these offices.

> Ideally there should be a harmonious synergism of gift and office, a dialectic of charism and institution, for the Spirit is given not only to officeholders but to the whole congregation. Laity should respect leaders, but everyone should also listen to prophets and honor gifts of faith. The work of officeholders is to foster the charisms of the community and harmonize them for the common good.[108]

The only difference leaders have from laity is their unique "stewardship": to "oversee" the administration of the church and to further its mission, so that the Spirit might be recognized as the Church's true governor. Cumming asserts:

> The actual Rule of the Holy Ghost within the Church, which is under His control . . . at once opens up regarding what we might call the Business of the Church. There is, for one thing, the question of its government. . . . "He gave some to be apostles; and some, prophets; and some, evangelists; and some, pastors and teachers" (Eph. 4:8–12). All these are "governments" set over the Church by the authority and decision of the Holy Ghost.[109]

---

105. See Hildebrandt, *An Old Testament Theology of the Spirit of God*, 203.

106. Clowney posits, "Without the support of the whole body, the work of those with greater gifts for leadership would not be effective, or even possible. We submit to the authority of others while exercising our own" (Clowney, *The Church*, 205). See also p. 210.

107. Cumming, *Through The Eternal Spirit*, 101.

108. Pinnock, *Flame of Love*, 140.

109. Cumming, *Through the Eternal Spirit*, 100.

Acts 13:2 demonstrates the Spirit's "administration" through his choosing of specific leaders: "While they were ministering to the Lord and fasting, the Holy Spirit said, 'Set apart for Me Barnabas and Saul for the work to which I have called them.'" The precious truth here is that we must commit the selection of leadership to the Holy Spirit, because through these leaders we are, in a sense, putting ourselves under his direction (cf. Heb 13:17). As "functional authorities," their offices and duties are to be placed under the care and charge of the great Administrator. This precedence is first presented at the "Council of Jerusalem," which was called to consider the question of Jewish rites and ordinances.

> [This] first great Synod . . . closes with a decree which none can read without thankful wonder. "It seemed good" (say the Apostles, Acts 25:28)—"it seemed good to the Holy Ghost, and to us." There was one council of the Church that knew where to get guidance, and whom to choose as President and Head! The Holy Ghost took charge, and the decree which settled the hard question came from Him.[110]

Church leaders and laity should find common ground in their need to submit to the Spirit's governing authority in all their affairs. Such a submission can often be a bit unsettling, particularly for church bodies that have operated according to rigid procedures and methods. Such a commitment may also result in a certain level of unexpected disorder, occasional excesses, abuse of gifts, and exposure of immaturity—the same problems encountered by Paul in Corinth. First Corinthians 12–14 provides no better example of the challenges wrought by an abandonment to the Spirit's governing authority. This passage makes plain that the Spirit's authority does not fit neatly with our preconceived notions of "Church." Packer says,

> For whatever evils these chapters may confront us with, they do in fact show us a church in which the Holy Spirit was working in power. Reading them makes one painfully aware of the degree of impoverishment and inertia that prevails in churches today. If our reaction as readers is merely to preen ourselves and feel glad because our churches are free from Corinthian disorders, we are fools indeed. The Corinthian disorders were due to an uncontrolled overflow of Holy Spirit life. Many churches today are orderly sim-

---

110. Ibid., 102.

ply because they are asleep, and with some one fears that it is the sleep of death. It is no great thing to have order in a cemetery! The real and deplorable carnality and immaturity of the Corinthian Christians, which Paul censures so strongly elsewhere in the letter, must not blind us to the fact that they were enjoying the ministry of the Holy Spirit in a way in which we today are not.[111]

Conclusion

The Holy Spirit, understood within the pattern of divine authority, provides local churches with an impressive display of authority with respect to their structure and guidance. Churches that look to the Spirit's authority can expect to experience a true freedom to be the sort of body that Christ intended. They will operate with the assurance that Christ is indeed "head" of the body in a full and dynamic way, produce powerful signs and "foretastes" of Christ's future kingdom within their present community, and serve as his chosen vessel for advancing Christ's future kingdom in this present world.

---

111. Packer, *Keep in Step with the Spirit*, 249.

7

The Authority of the Holy Spirit and Practical Theology: Christian Spirituality

❦ "Spirituality" is difficult to define precisely. Not only has the term been associated with a myriad of perspectives in the history of the Church, but contemporary theology (as we shall see) seems to promote the idea that one's "truth" can now take the form of the particular spirituality to which one ascribes. Williams asserts:

> Spirituality has seized cultural attention in our time to an extent that few other religious phenomena could claim. This popularly is evident not only in bookstore shelves closely packed with titles on angels, mediation and spiritual growth, or in the constant outpouring of magazine articles on such subjects, but also in the frequency with which one hears declarations that spirituality is important to people's lives, often people who have no connection to any organized religion and are indeed often contemptuous of such organizations. The books, the articles, the testimonials all exhibit a common characteristic: they use "spirituality" to designate any number of forms of religiosity undifferentiated with respect to other doctrinal foundations. One may adopt Native American prayer forms, the teachings of a master and Julian of Norwich, making use of all simultaneously.[1]

As a result, Christians may begin to wonder how a "true spirituality" could possibly be secured. In this chapter we shall discover that our model

---

1. Williams, "Mystical Theology Redux," 53.

of the Holy Spirit's authority is indeed sufficient to provide a framework for the practice of Christian spirituality. The purpose of this chapter is to develop a conception of Christian spirituality *in* and *under* the "plenipotentiary authority" of the Spirit. I will apply my theological model (from chapters three and four) to Christian spirituality, first, by examining the framework provided by the Spirit's *divine Personhood* and *executorial divine authority*. Then I will respond to the two contemporary "practical" approaches to spirituality introduced in chapter two—Buckley and Yeago's *Knowing the Triune God* (which seeks to develop spirituality with respect to church "practices") and Jones and Buckley's *Spirituality and Social Embodiment* (which seeks a socially-embodied spirituality). I will weigh these two approaches against the Spirit's *veracious authority* and *governing authority*, respectively, before building a case of my own.

Our study of the church community (chapter six) should not overshadow the importance of the Spirit's authority with respect to the individual believer within that community. Paul's epistle to the Galatians makes this plain. His primary imperative for these believers is "walk in the Spirit" (Gal 5:16). God's people are "led by the Spirit" (5:18), are to display the "fruit of the Spirit" (5:22–23), and must *behave* in keeping with the Spirit (5:25). Believers now "sow and reap by the Spirit" (6:8). Paul seems to be saying that the whole of the ongoing Christian life is to be lived out in terms of the Spirit. Because of this, Fee rightly proclaims that "any careful reading of Paul's letters makes it abundantly clear that the Spirit is the key element, the *sine qua non*, of all Christian life and experience."[2]

According to Wood, "Spirituality," when understood in biblical terms, "may be defined as the response of the human spirit when activated by the Spirit of God."[3] Wood elaborates as follows:

> Spirituality is not to be regarded simply as an effort of man to reach out to God. It is rather the outcome of God's initiative in reaching out to man in grace and enablement. Spirituality, then, has to do with the inner life of the Christian. That inner life will affect, and indeed control, active service and witness in the world, but its operations remain largely hidden from view.[4]

2. Fee, "Some Reflections on Pauline Spirituality," 99–100.
3. Wood, "Spirit and Spirituality in Luther," 311.
4. Ibid., 311.

The Authority of the Holy Spirit and Practical Theology: Christian Spirituality

This definition is very helpful because it not only places the Spirit in primary relation to the human "spirit" but also contains a recognition of the Spirit's authority.[5] It will therefore serve as our working definition for this chapter. Simply put, the basis for Christian spirituality is the Spirit. Spirituality is then a continuous awareness of God's spiritual and eternal realities, particularly the Holy Spirit's authoritative place in those realities, and an entire mindset and "lifestyle" lived in response to those realities. According to Henry,

> The spiritual person is personally and individually aware that his final destiny relates to his eternal decision, and is alert to the invisible immaterial realities—first and foremost deeply aware of God who is Spirit.[6]

---

5. The Spirit's authority is easily forgotten in the theology or practice of spirituality, as seen in several "modern" works that contain little or no reference to the Spirit. McGrath's "Distinguishing Features of Reformed Spirituality," for example, contains no references to the Spirit (McGrath, *Spirituality in an Age of Change*, 42–57). Hendry is on target in claiming that "the problem of the relation between the Holy Spirit and the human spirit is one that has been curiously neglected in the main stream of Christian theology" (Hendry, *The Holy Spirit in Christian Theology*, 96).

6. Henry, "Spiritual? Say it Isn't' So!" 10. This being said, we must remember that the Spirit's sovereignty is logically prior to any tendency toward spiritual receptivity. Armerding surveys the notion of the "spiritual personality" in the Old Testament: "Popular theories of spirituality generally hold to the belief that spiritual encounters come to individuals who already have some bent toward God. In contrast, the period of charismatic spirituality, represented by the judges, was a time marked by little or no such human initiative. The theological framework of Judges (2:10–19) depicts a nation with a penchant for forgetting the ways of the Lord, and what break there is in this pattern reflects communal desperation in the face of cruel enemies. Moving from the theological framework of Judges to the individual 'hero accounts,' we find equally slender evidence for the seeking, spiritual personality. Throughout the book, and on into the common period in early monarchy days, the narrative seems dominated by characters (Gideon, Jephthah, Samson, Saul) who did not take initiatives toward God. In other words, they were creatures of their time, and shared the common habit of forgetting Yahweh's covenant. Even where more seemingly sensitive personalities arise (e.g., Samuel and David),the initiative seems still to be in divine hands. Charismatic spirituality, then, is marked by divine initiative, in response to nothing more than God's sovereign commitment to maintain his covenant faithfulness toward a nation which, when conditions were sufficiently bad, had the sense to cry out in distress" (Armerding, "When the Spirit Came Mightily," 43).

THE LORD IS THE SPIRIT

Christian Spirituality and the Divine Authority of the Spirit

As we have seen, postmodern perspectives on "Spirit" are more often "panentheistic" than "theistic" and thus usually result in a breakdown of the "Spirit/spirit distinction" (see chapter three). What is the effect of this breakdown upon spirituality?

Spirituality is closely associated with perspectives regarding *creation* and *history*. The postmodern denial of "metanarratives" coincides with a dismissal of a purposeful creation account or understanding of world history. Whereas the biblical account presents an obvious divine design (i.e., Gen 1:1–28) and a clear *telos* or goal by which divine sovereignty is displayed in history and all things find their meaning (Eph 1:9, 10), postmodernism draws the "logical" conclusions from modernity that the physical universe is devoid of any "design" and that "history" is chaotic. As a result, neither *nature* not *history* can "speak" to us meaningfully.[7] Any "revealed" notion of human origin, destiny, or identity is also dismissed. Soon the "self" is considered a meaningless term as well. Foucault, for example, asserts that the independent "self" is a modern metaphysical conception that is now unraveling.

> It was the effect of a change in the fundamental arrangements of knowledge. As the archeology of our thought easily shows, man is an invention of recent date. And one perhaps nearing its end.[8]

Whereas the pressures of "modern homogenizing," according to Gunton, "take away our individuality and particularity and make us all alike,"[9] Van Kaam observes that many people in postmodern culture feel they have lost their individual "self" and are now rejecting such homogenization.[10] With the transcendental origin of "self" or "being" dismissed,

---

7. Some postmodernists have a vague sense of nature "speaking" to us. Borgman, for example, decries that "rivers are muted when they are damned; prairies are silenced when they are stripped for coal; mountains become torpid when they are logged" (Borgmann, *Crossing the Postmodern Divide*, 118–19). This "speaking," however, is not usually associated with a divine "voice."

8. Foucault, *The Order of Things*, 386–87.

9. Gunton, *The One, the Three, and the Many*, 180.

10. Van Kaam, *Formative Spirituality*, 5.

however, postmodernists readily discover that the "self" has been severely fragmented and that its recovery is indeed a daunting task.

> The self is "decentered": Under postmodern conditions, persons exist in a state of continuous construction and reconstruction; it is a world where anything goes that can be negotiated. Each reality of self gives way to reflexive questioning, irony, and ultimately the playful probing of yet another reality. The center fails to hold.[11]

According to Houston, "It is precisely the spiritual sterility engendered by modernity's tendency to identify the ego in functional rather than relational terms that has forced modern man to look for 'spirituality.'"[12] Dissatisfied with "mere identification in a functional society," some postmodernists are now proposing various forms of spirituality "in search of their deepest self in God."[13] Postmodern spirituality, however, can offer no substantial solution to the "fragmented self" except spiritualities grounded in personal construction (i.e., determined by the *self*)[14] or social construc-

---

11. Gergen, *The Saturated Self*, 7.
12. Houston, *The Holy Spirit in Contemporary Spirituality*, 16.
13. Van Kaam, *Formative Spirituality*, 5.
14. I.e., ones founded in "constructing" one's own "spiritual self" or "spirituality" according to personal preference alone. Such "spirituality" is typical of such popular television figures as Oprah Winfrey who regularly hosts (and promotes) the spiritualities of postmodern and new age "spiritualists" such as Iyanla Vanzant and Marianne Williamson (see Taylor, "The Church of O"). "New age spirituality" (i.e., eastern mysticism that has been "westernized") typically presents a postmodern or even "Christianized" version of the Hindu concept of "spirit," and is often so subtle that the average Christian may never discern its influence. Vanzant, for example, describes in striking language a "Holy Spirit" who seems to possess a certain authority with respect to spirituality: "There are times when what you think is good for you and what the Holy Spirit knows is good for you are two different things. What you think is usually based on what you know and what you can see. What the Holy Spirit knows is always based on God's plan and purpose for your life. The question is, *are you willing and available to follow the light of the Holy Spirit*? . . . At just the right time, in just the right way, the Holy Spirit will shine its light into your life to show you where to go and what to do. You may see it and not believe it. You may feel it and find the feeling uncomfortable. When this happens, you become resistant. You talk yourself out of the very thing the Holy Spirit is pushing you into. Your knowledge is never a match for the Holy Spirit's knowledge!" (Vanzant, *Until Today!*, November 17 entry). Though Vanzant's portrayal of the Spirit initially seems positive, it is indeed outside the pattern of divine authority. Vanzant seems to adopt the "Socratic" and "eastern" notion that everything we really are has always been true of us—we only did not know this truth "until today." She continues: "Everything you have

tion (i.e., determined by one's predominant community).[15] Some forms of postmodern spirituality can be traced to Heidegger, whose rejection of transcendence led him to investigate the human "being" (*Dasein*) through a purely phenomenological approach. Human "being" became so secularized that it could now be redefined according to the present moorings of secular thought or personal preference.[16]

---

ever desired for yourself already exists in the realm of the Holy Spirit. . . . The provisions for the manifestation of your dreams and illusions exist right now. . . . If you have done all you can do to prepare yourself in the physical realm, the light of the Holy Spirit will do the rest" (November 17 entry). Another example is Williamson's "Course in Miracles," where the Spirit is granted a sort of "authority" as well: "Our comfort zones are the limited areas in which we find it easy to live. It's the Holy Spirit's job not to respect those comfort zones, but to bust them." Her "new age" tendencies, however, soon become apparent: "In order to insure our progress toward the goal of enlightenment, 'the Holy Spirit has a highly individualized curriculum for everyone.' . . . He translates between our perfect cosmic self and our worldly insanity. . . . Everyone is on a spiritual path; most people just don't know it. The Holy Spirit is a force in our minds that knows us in our perfectly loving, natural state—which we've forgotten—but enters into the world of fear and illusion with us, and uses our experiences here to remind us who we are. . . . The Holy Spirit uses everything to lead us into inner peace" (Williamson, *A Return To Love*, 40–41).

15. According to Hutcheon, "Just as reality is a social construct . . . so also is Homo autonomous. . . . Just as 'we only know the world through a network of socially established meaning systems' or 'the discourses of our culture,' so also such meaning systems and discourses 'structure how we see ourselves and how we construct our notions of self in the past and in the present'" (Hutcheon, *The Politics of Postmodernism* , 7). Middleton and Walsh, however, define "homo autonomous" more along the lines of the independent subject: "[We are] self-reliant, self-centered and self-integrating rational subjects. This is a fundamentally heroic understanding of human subjectivity. We are who we are by overcoming all that binds or inhibits us and by determining for ourselves who we will be" (Middleton and Walsh, *Truth is Stranger Than it Used to Be*, 47).

16. Heidegger challenges Christianity's "metaphysical" approach to philosophical anthropology: "What stands in the way of the basic question of Dasein's Being (or leads it off the track) is an orientation thoroughly coloured by the anthropology of Christianity and the ancient world" (Heidegger, *Being and Time*, 74). Ingraffia responds, "Ironically, Heidegger claims that theology must use his phenomenological analysis of Dasein in order to make its claims about the nature of man conceptually understood. Thus Heidegger calls upon theology to repeat the mistake he has just charged it with, i.e. turning to philosophy to gain conceptual understanding of faith. . . . This definition of transcendence as belonging to man, as defining his essence, is central to Heidegger's description of Dasein. And it is my contention that Heidegger in fact takes much more from Christian theology than this one clue. But like all the 'clues' Heidegger takes from Christianity, Heidegger excludes God and therefore secularizes the, borrowed concept. In this case, "transcendence," which in Being

The pneumatology of Hegel seemed to extend Heidegger's thinking into the notion of a "world spirit." Hegel's "idealism" (the subsumption of the world into God) offers a way of comprehending "Spirit" as a "final reality" that can be spoken of in phenomenological terms.[17] Many postmodern theologians now begin their spirituality with Hegel (i.e., Welker, Hodgson). Nevertheless, the Hegelian "Spirit" ultimately leads to a loss of "particularity"—the very thing Hegel is trying to avoid. Gunton comments on Hegel's dilemma:

> To make everything spirit is to bring about a loss of particularity, or so it would appear, because it is the material shape of the objects of our experience that is the means of their individuation and the mark of their particularity, so that I recognize someone by the shape of his head, the distinctive character of their walk. In Hegelian terms, however, matter, time and space are finally abolished as a result of Spirit's relentless movement.[18]

Spirituality and the Spirit's Divine Transcendence over the Human Spirit

The Spirit as a divine Person implies that the Spirit retains divine transcendence *over* the human spirit along with the immanent revelation of divine authority to one's entire *being* (1 Cor 2:10–14). The Spirit reveals that the transcendent origination of the true "self," as both *spiritual* and *individual*, is indeed from the Spirit, who as "relational other" maintains and even strengthens individuality along with relationality.

> It is not a spirit of merging or assimilation—of homogeneity—but of relation in otherness, relation which does not subvert but establishes the other in its true reality. This is especially evident in biblical characterizations of the work of the divine Spirit, the perfecting cause of the creation.[19]

---

and Time Heidegger equates with the 'spiritual' (BT 4I), is explained as a basic constitutive feature of 'Dasein' rather than as a gift from God" (Ingraffia, *Postmodern Theory and Biblical Theology*, 128).

17. See Hegel, *Phenomenology of Spirit*, 263–409.
18. Gunton, *The One, the Three, and the Many*, 186.
19. Ibid., 182.

The Spirit's "relational otherness" (expressing both divine transcendence and immanence) provides an appropriate foundation for the recovery of the true "self" in proper relation to God. According to Gunton:

> In his holiness, he manifests the Otherness of God, as Creator over creature. Yet as Spirit, he is the life-giving breath, breathed into the nostrils of Adam, and from whom all that is life-giving to creation depends. Moreover, as Spirit, he is able to discern the thoughts and intents of our hearts, as the Samaritan woman could confess. "He told me everything that I did" (John 4:39). Thus the transcendence and immanence of the Holy Spirit are conjoined, in the person of the Holy Spirit, to reveal the God-of-gods. . . . It is the Holy Spirit who can change our individualism to make us truly persons-in-relationship with God. He is truly the source of all personal nature to our persons.[20]

"True spirituality," or spirituality developed within the framework of the pattern of divine authority, is only recovered in association with this "relational otherness." According to Houston, "The fatal flaw of much contemporary spirituality is that it is man-centered, even narcissistic, rather than originating from God. It does not come *from* the Father, *through* the Son, *by* the Holy Spirit."[21] Our principle of authority retains the Spirit's authority as a divine Person in relation to our selves as spiritual persons. This should result in a deep respect for God's authority. According to Morris,

> We must not drift into the habit of thinking of Him as no more than a vague force or power or stream or effluence making for good. Nor must we allow ourselves to separate Him from the Father and the Son, outwardly subscribing to all the orthodox formulas, but practically reducing Him to a lower status. The Trinitarian view of the Spirit is absolutely essential. When the Spirit comes into our lives, and gives us a strength not our own, then that is as fully an action of God as it is possible for an action to be. In the Spirit we have access to the infinite divine resources of God himself. It is imperative that we do not lose sight of the dignity of Him with whom we have to do.[22]

---

20. Houston, *The Holy Spirit in Contemporary Spirituality*, 18.
21. Ibid., 14.
22. Morris, *Spirit of the Living God*, 101. Trinitarian spirituality is witnessed at the "initiation" of our spiritual journey in our baptism "in the name of the Father, and of the Son,

The Authority of the Holy Spirit and Practical Theology: Christian Spirituality

As we respond to the Spirit as Director of our lives, we must therefore keep in mind a genuine sense of the "Spirit/spirit distinction"—never as a *separation* but always involving the Spirit's gracious *appropriation* of divine authority to the human spirit.[23] Since the believer cannot "conjure up" his or her own spirituality, it must be constructed by the Spirit. The Spirit accommodates one's entire humanity by appropriating divine authority to the human spirit.[24] Though this appropriation occurs in accordance with the pattern of authority, a "Spirit/spirit distinction," along with an accompanying moral accountability, is always retained in the appropriation. As we have seen, Ps 104:29–30 depicts human "spirits" as creations of God in a place of divine accountability, in that they are utterly dependent on Yahweh's continued creative activity. Though this accountability is appropriated by the Spirit to the entire being of the human person (in the *imago dei*), initial contact occurs by means of the human spirit. In other words, the human spirit is the means by which the Spirit accesses the believer's entire *being*.

> In the affirmation that the Spirit speaks to our spirit is to be found part of that mystery—the revealed mystery—of what it is to be a human being in relation to our maker. . . . God's Spirit enables the human being to be open to him.[25]

An "appropriated" model of the divine authority is best developed in the context of a modified "trichotomy" understanding of human personhood, one where some kind of actual distinction exists between the human

---

and of the Holy Spirit" (Mt. 28.19), in our experience of God as "the grace of our Lord Jesus Christ, and the love of God, and the fellowship of the Holy Spirit" (2 Cor 13:14), and in the diverse "spiritual gifts" that reflect the Trinity's threefold unity (1 Cor 12:4–6). Indeed our spirituality is marked by coming "under" the divine authority associated with of the Holy Spirit's otherness, and, in doing so, experiencing the intimacy found in identification with the "relational" aspect of the Trinity.

23. "Appropriation" might be thought of as the conceptualization or personalization of the transcendent Spirit with respect to the human being in the *imago dei*.

24. Augustine's view of the Spirit as "relation" is somewhat helpful here. Though (as deduced in chapter three) Augustine's pneumatology does reduce the Spirit's divine authority, his view of the Spirit as the relation of God (within the Trinity) that resides in the Old Testament temple, the church, and the individual believer allows for an *appropriation* of the Spirit to the human spirit.

25. Gunton, *The One, The Three and the Many*, 185.

soul and human spirit (and human body).[26] According to McDonald, "this distinction and contrast is always with reference to two specific functions of man's psychical nature, not to two separate substances."[27] McDonald's trichotomy distinguishes these two functions in the following way:

> From different points of view, soul and spirit appear as two aspects of man's inner nature. Spirit denotes life as having its origin in God; and soul denotes life as connoted in man. Spirit is the innermost of the inner life of man, the higher aspect of his personality; while soul expresses man's special individuality. Soul is spirit modified by its union with body. The *pneuma* is man's non-material nature look-

---

26. The human "spirit" might be best thought of as the aspect of the human that sets him into a *distinctive relationship to God* (one not shared by other "ensouled" creatures). Much of theology today, however, seems to prefer "dichotomy" over trichotomy, mainly because of the seeming interchangeability of the terms "soul" and "spirit" in the NT (i.e., Luke 1:46–47). This can be compared, however, by those passages that clearly distinguish and contrast the *function* of these two terms (i.e., Heb 4:12). Hendry holds that "trichotomy" is evidenced in our moral responsibility before God: "The point is that a distinction must be observed between man's existential dependence on God, which he shares with all living creatures and which applies to him as an 'ensouled body,' and man's personal *relation* to God, which can be realized only at the level of spirit. The difference is that man's creaturely dependence on God is inherent in the structure of his being; his relation to God at the level of spirit involves his free and conscious act. At the same time, however, the freedom of the spirit in man must not be separated from the structure of the soul; for it is only in the light of the relation between them that we can understand the nature of creaturely freedom, which is always structured freedom. That is to say, the spirit of man, as the spirit of the creature whom God created for himself, has the true goal of its aspiration in God; yet, as spirit is free, its direction to God appears in a phenomenological view, as only one possibility" (Hendry, *The Holy Spirit in Christian Theology*, 107). For Hendry, the spirit can also be distinguished from the soul as that entity possessed by those who no longer wish to be "under" the Spirit's divine authority. "Is it not precisely in fallen man, the man whose communion with God is broken, that the human spirit comes to consciousness of itself in its distinctness from the Spirit of God? It would seem to be more plausible to represent the Fall as a fall into trichotomy, not in the sense that spirit becomes distinct from soul at the Fall, but that they no longer point in the same direction. The structure of man's being, i.e., the dependence of his creaturely existence (his soul) upon God, remains unchanged; but his relation to God is changed, inasmuch as the created spirit no longer responds in freedom to the Spirit of God. Yet spirit remains spirit, and the essential quality and dimension of spiritual activity continue to manifest themselves in sinful man" (116). Hoekema reminds us that neither dichotomy nor trichotomy can completely describe the complexity of human personhood: "The Bible's primary concern is not the psychological or anthropological constitution of man but his inescapable relatedness to God" (Hoekema, *Created in God's Image*, 209–10).

27. McDonald, *The Christian View of Man*, 79.

ing Godward; and *psyche* is the same nature looking earthward and touching the things of sense.[28]

A "modified trichotomy" seems to provide a clearer understanding of the Spirit's authority *over* the entire human person. First, the human spirit is a primary aspect of the "image of God" that reflects the divine *being* (i.e., "God is Spirit"; John 4:24) and allows the human person to "connect" with God. Second, the Spirit's transcendence *over* the human person can only be appropriated via the human spirit, which is able to relationally "go beyond" itself. "It is precisely the spirit that furnishes the key to the Biblical understanding of man's self-transcendence; it is spirit that keeps the relation between God and man essentially free and personal."[29] Finally, the human spirit is correlative to the Spirit's overriding communication of human purpose, the orientation of all of life toward God. The Spirit/spirit relationship thereby confirms the personality, dignity, and moral responsibility of the human person.[30]

The Spirit's authority is appropriated to the human spirit of both believers and non-believers in many ways, but perhaps most notably through *creation* and through *the law*. Psalm 104:29–30 presents the transcendence of Yahweh's Spirit over the "breath of life" in parallel to his transcendence over creation. The Holy Spirit's authority over the human spirit is therefore a reflection of his dominion over all creation. According to Houston, spirituality begins with creation as the domain of the Spirit (Gen 1:2).

> It was at the beginning that the Spirit "brooded over creation," when it was still unformed in darkness, boundless and unproductive, as chaos represents. The same Spirit that ruled over the primordial chaos likewise can be allowed sovereignty over the chaos of our lives, to enlighten us and reveal his grace towards us (2 Cor

---

28. Ibid., 79.
29. Hendry, *The Holy Spirit in Christian Theology*, 105.
30. Macaulay and Barrs conclude, "We are not totally passive in relationship to God. At this point the analogy of the parents begetting the child breaks down, for the child has no say as to whether he or she is to be born. It is not the same for us. But, sadly, some have taught that because we are dead in sin and need the life-giving work of the Spirit, we therefore cannot seek for God and put our trust in him. They have said it is useless to encourage others to consider the evidence for Christianity in order to persuade them of the truth of the gospel" (Macaulay and Barrs, *Being Human*, 106).

4.6). Spirituality has concern and relevance then, not only for our redemption, but also for the care and well-being of all creation, through our redeemed lives.[31]

The practice of spirituality, then, is initially an embrace of Yahweh's providential care of the human spirit, where his dominion is seen in terms of "renewal" in the Spirit (Ps 104:30b). This Hebrew vision of divine providence means that the Spirit, who provides cosmic order, also "recreates" and nurtures spiritual life through his contact with our "spirit." According to Winslow:

> As he is the Author, so he is the Supporter. He breathed the spiritual life, and He keeps, and nourishes, and watches over it. Let it not be supposed that there is anything in this life that could keep itself. There is no principle in Divine grace that can keep this life from decline and decay. If it be not watched over, nourished, sustained, and revived perpetually by the same omnipotent power that implanted it there, it is liable to constant decline.[32]

Such "re-creation" demands a continual re-evaluation of the Spirit's relationship to our spirit. In doing so we will discover that the Spirit's holiness, transcendence, and omnipresence stands in stark contrast to the human spirit's sinfulness, immanence, and limitations. The Old Testament law is employed by the Spirit to expose this contrast. The law's original intention, to be a blessing to the Jews, was based on one condition: "Be Holy as I am holy" (Lev 11:44–45). The Holy Spirit's conviction points out one's failure to keep the law (most pointedly through the human conscience).[33] For the believer, however, the law is not to be seen as the enemy or the master, but as a reminder of the "law of the Spirit."

> Paul continually puts the law and the Spirit together in this passage (Rom. 8). He first contrasts the Spirit and the sinful nature (8:6), and then shows how the law and sinful nature are opposed (8:7). Paul thus links the Spirit and the law. As Christians, then, we are

---

31. Houston, *The Holy Spirit in Contemporary Spirituality*, 17.

32. Winslow, *The Work of the Holy Spirit*, 71–72.

33. As seen in chapter three, the human conscience invokes an "accountability of the Spirit" in and through the concept *theios*, which becomes a "law" unto the gentiles. Through the Spirit, divine attributes such as *omnipotence* are "understood through what has been made" (Rom 1:20, 2:1).

to submit to God's law because the law tells us what is pleasing to God, tells us what the things of the Spirit are and tells us what it means practically to walk in the Spirit.³⁴

The law, in other words, is a point of accountability between Holy Spirit and human spirit that allows us to perceive ourselves rightly before God, specifically as sinners in need of grace. The "profound disparagement" between Spirit and spirit should lead to a continual acknowledgement of sin, followed by a deep sense of confession, contrition, and repentance.

"Quench not the Spirit"

The Spirit/spirit distinction brings the nonbeliever under *divine judgment* without a corresponding revelation of divine *mercy*. The Spirit has been removed, resulting in "terror" (Ps 104:29). Though the nonbeliever may encounter the Spirit's *revelation* they are not able to understand it (1 Cor 2:10–14).

> The man who is incapable of receiving and discerning the things of the Spirit of God, and whom Paul describes as the "natural" man (*psychikos*), is not to be thought of as one who is constitutionally devoid of this capacity but rather as one who by his misuses of the freedom of the spirit has forfeited it; for the alternative to receiving the Spirit of God is not complete unspirituality, but to receive the spirit of the world. For Paul it is with our spirit that the Spirit of God bears witness.³⁵

Since the Spirit is the only means of attaining true spiritual knowledge (1 Cor 2:11–12), no person in their own "spirituality" can take credit as such a means. The profound disparagement set up by Paul—between πνεῦμα in reference to the "spirit" of man (2:11a) and πνεῦμα in reference to the Holy Spirit (2:11b)—can only be resolved by the Spirit's "searching" and "revealing" activities (2:10). The believer must trust the Spirit of revelation in order to know the mind of God afresh and attain spiritual knowledge (2:15–16).³⁶ The primary indication of the spirituality

---

34. Macaulay and Barrs, *Being Human*, 89–90.
35. Hendry, *The Holy Spirit in Christian Theology*, 108.
36. Wood also defines "spirituality" in such simple terms as "the contact between the Spirit of God and the spirit of man" (Wood, "Spirit and Spirituality in Luther," 327). Houston

of the "spiritual man" (3:1) is therefore one's reception of divine revelation through the Spirit (2:12) within one's own particular context.

Such a dependence on the Spirit's revelation leads Paul to instruct the Thessalonians, "Do not quench the Spirit; do not despise prophetic utterances" (1 Thess 5:19–20). This reference to the Spirit's "fire" brings an admonishment against certain conduct (i.e., idleness, impurity) that "quenches" the Spirit. The Spirit retains the right to "burn" within the believer, who is a "temple of the Holy Spirit." According to Morris:

> The bright burning of the fire of the Spirit and a willingness to engage in sin are absolutely inconsistent with each other. It is a very solemn thought that God allows men in some degree to thwart His Spirit in this way. It impresses upon us that we must not take the good gift of God for granted. It is well that we reflect on the condition that Scripture lays down for the effectual working of the Spirit and that we ensure, as far as in us lies, that these conditions are completely fulfilled. God does not view our reaction to the good gift of the Spirit with equanimity.[37]

Since the immediate context of this passage warns us not to "despise prophetic utterances" (1 Thess 5:20), we can understand 5:19 in terms of the quenching that occurs when believers are unyielding to the *revealed will of God*.[38] The Spirit's authority with respect to revelation thus stands in direct

---

thinks a proper relation of Spirit to spirit creates the need for two sets of "knowledge" by which we can perceive our own selves for who we truly are. "Within this openness of spirit to the Holy Spirit, we are created with a double need of knowledge: the knowledge of self and the knowledge of God. As Augustine prays in his Soliloquies: 'Let me know you, O God, let me know myself, that is all!' Bernard of Clairvaux repeats the need for the double knowledge which modern psycho-analysis has overlooked. He observes that without the one we have despair, and without the other we have pride. Indeed, all the great thinkers of the Church have recognized this double knowledge as needful for the spiritual life. So John Calvin introduces his Institutes with this theme" (Houston, *The Holy Spirit in Contemporary Spirituality*, 17).

37. Morris, *Spirit of the Living God*, 98–99. The "fire" is the Lord in association with his Spirit of power and authority is seen in Deut 4:24 ("For the LORD your God is a consuming fire, a jealous God") and Isa 30:27, 30, 33 ("His tongue is like a consuming fire. . . . And the Lord will cause His voice of authority to be heard. . . . The breath of the Lord, like a torrent of brimstone, sets it afire").

38. Though the exact nature of "prophetic utterances" cannot be developed here, we may conclude that this passage highly exalts the *freedom of the Spirit*, and yet without dismissing the Word's *testing* (1 Thess 5:21 adds, "But *examine* everything carefully; hold fast to that which is good").

opposition to an attitude of self-sufficiency. Houston addresses the heart of Paul's warning:

> This reflects upon the vital significance of conscience before God. As one of the desert fathers, Dorotheos, commented, "in creating man God implanted in him something divine—a certain faculty—to illumine the mind and show what is good and what is bad. This is called conscience." . . . Like a thought coming to him from within, that the desert fathers called a *logismos*, the Holy Spirit gives moral direction through the conscience. So the seriousness of "quenching" the Spirit is to forfeit moral direction, and lead instead to a state of lostness in autonomy, and a self-directed life. This is ultimately self-enclosure, pride, and the denial of God's relatedness to us, as made in the image and likeness of God.[39]

Spirituality that begins with the Spirit's authority challenges non-relational notions of the self and calls us to go "outside" or "beyond" ourselves (vis-à-vis our "spirit") to receive the Spirit and his nourishing/convicting/transforming fire of revelation.[40] The Spirit holds non-believers, and believers alike, responsible for their need to *seek God.*

> The New Testament writers clearly did not shrink from placing human responsibility side by side with the sovereignty of the Spirit in bringing us to new life. . . . The individual is to be active in looking and believing. . . . Paul is aware that the way he behaves will affect people's response to the truth (1 Cor. 9:19), he spends months trying to persuade people of the truth of Christianity (Acts 19:8; 18:4; 17:2), and he commands his listeners to repent. This is the pattern throughout the New Testament and the conclusion is clear: humans have the responsibility to repent and believe because they're significant.[41]

---

39. Houston, *The Holy Spirit in Contemporary Spirituality*, 17–18.

40. In contrast to the spirituality implanted by the Holy Spirit, Houston holds that "the 'New Age' often uses spirituality merely to reinforce the egotism of the self. It excludes the Other, the source of true personhood. It is contrasted then to the Christian ethic which is always for the other" (Houston, *The Holy Spirit in Contemporary Spirituality*, 18).

41. Macaulay and Barrs, *Being Human*, 107.

THE LORD IS THE SPIRIT

Christian Spirituality and the Executorial Authority of the Spirit

The Spirit's executorial authority implies that "true spirituality" always has a definite Christological focus. Christian spirituality therefore invokes, first and foremost, the knowledge of Christ. Packer asserts that the Spirit asks us questions like, "Do you know Jesus Christ?" and "Do you know him well?"

> His ministry is a floodlight ministry in relation to Jesus, a matter of spotlighting Jesus' glory before our spiritual eyes and of matchmaking between us and him. He does not call attention to himself or present himself to us for direct fellowship as the Father and the Son do; his role and his joy is to further our fellowship with them both by glorifying the Son as the object for our faith and then witnessing to our adoption through the Son into the Father's family.[42]

While Packer gives the Spirit the highest place with respect to sanctification, he also warns of two evils that immediately result when shifting from knowing Jesus to "knowing the Spirit."

> On the one hand, like the Colossian angel worshipers, we should impoverish ourselves by "not holding fast to the Head from whom the whole body, nourished and knit together through its joints and ligaments, grows with a growth that is from God" (Colossians 2:19). On the other hand, we should enmesh ourselves in a world of spurious "spiritual" feelings and fancies that are not Christ related and do not correspond to anything that actually exists except Satan's web of deceptions and his endless perversions of truth and goodness. We should not take one step down this road.[43]

John makes the initial "test" for the Holy Spirit one's acknowledgment of the person of Jesus. "This is how you can recognize the Spirit of God: Every spirit that acknowledges that Jesus Christ has come in the flesh is from God" (1 John 4:2, NIV). Macaulay and Barrs relay the *simplicity* of such a test:

---

42. Packer, *Keep in Step with the Spirit*, 92.
43. Ibid., 92.

The Authority of the Holy Spirit and Practical Theology: Christian Spirituality

> John does not leave us wondering how to tell whether or not the Spirit is in us. This could begin a process of inward questioning: Do I feel the Spirit living in me? Am I feeling so weak and sinful and empty because the Spirit is not really in me?" Being a good pastor, John gives us a clear test. . . . Notice that his test for recognition of the Spirit's presence a doctrinal one—does the person (whether myself or someone else) acknowledge that Jesus Christ has come in the flesh? If the answer is "yes," then the teaching or the person is from God and has his Spirit. Conversely, anyone who denies Jesus does not have the Spirit of God.[44]

The Spirit's Executorial Authority and Identity in Christ

Western Christianity now seems to be seeking to rebuild a sense of *spiritual traditions* based on *identity* and *internal character* as central themes for spirituality. The Spirit's executorial authority indeed provides an *identity in Christ* that results in a new internal character. Such an identity begins with Spirit-baptism, where believers are "united with Christ" in his death and resurrection (Rom 6:3–4). Del Colle understands "Spirit-baptism" in terms of the existential experience of our identify in Christ, in that Jesus "is the mediator of life, mission and our deepest human identity, what we can describe in the language of election as our calling to exist in graced filial relation to God, the source of all reality."[45] Because the NT emphasizes the entire experience of our identity in Christ through the Spirit, Fee believes (contrary to historic Protestantism) that "justification by faith" is actually *not* the central theme of Pauline theology.

> That is but one metaphor among many, and therefore much too narrow a view to capture the many-splendored richness of God's eschatological salvation that has been effected in Christ. For Paul the theme "salvation in Christ" dominates everything, from beginning to end. . . . God the Son, through his death on the cross, has effected it, and thereby accomplished for his people adoption, justification, redemption, sanctification, reconciliation, and propitiation, to name the primary metaphors. But it is God the Spirit who has effectively appropriated God's salvation in Christ in the life

---

44. Macaulay and Barrs, *Being Human*, 114–15.
45. Del Colle, "Spirit-Christology," 93.

of the believer and of the believing community. Without the latter, the former simply does not happen.[46]

Luther understood salvation in such terms, seeing the Spirit particularly as a "legacy" of Christ to be identified with and experienced. "Although spiritual gifts are given by the Spirit, he himself is a gift from God as a legacy from Christ's death. The Holy Spirit was only bestowed after the victory of the cross, when in His body Christ had overcome all."[47] As Christ's "legacy," the Spirit possesses a specific executorial authority to change one's status before God (Rom 6:18). This change in status is rooted in the Spirit's application of God's *righteousness* in Christ. In chapter three we saw that Isa 32:15–18 speaks of the Spirit's *righteousness* and Isa 11:2 of the Messiah's *beneficiary sovereignty and rule* through the Spirit. The Messiah's rule makes his subjects *benefactors* of his righteousness.[48] The Messiah has "corrected" the law (re-interpreting it through *equity* and *mercy*), and the Spirit now applies this corrected law so that it can fulfill its original purpose—to assist in making us *righteous*.

This is the ultimate "appropriation" of the Spirit to our spirit. John 15:26 implies that the Spirit possesses the authority to apply Christ's redemption. The Spirit "becomes" our salvation, our point of identification, so that God's presence is "with us" in Christ.[49] Everything bound up in the

---

46. Fee, "Some Reflections on Pauline Spirituality," 98–99.

47. Luther, *The Works of Martin Luther*, 23:375.

48. Isa. 11:1–16 depicts the Messiah as a king in whose hands the concerns of the weakest will be safe.

49. This challenges the popular "new Pentecostal" mandate to invoke or "call down" the Spirit (for gifting, empowerment, etc.) so that the "self" might enter a "higher level" of spirituality. Rooted in "transcendental spirituality" (i.e., James, *The Varieties of Religious Experience*) and particularly "New Thought Metaphysics" (i.e., Ralph Waldo Trine, *In Tune with the Infinite*), these false teachers view the "Spirit" as a power to be invoked rather than a *Person* who indwells, and thereby exchanges the authority of the Spirit with the authority of *self*. Trine, for example, sounds strangely similar to the message given at healing services hosted by "new Pentecostals": "*Don't shut out the divine inflow.* Do anything else rather than this. Open yourselves to it. Invite it. In the degree that you open yourself to it, its inflowing tide will course through your bodies a force so vital that the old obstructions that are dominating them today will be driven out before it" (55). James recognizes and seems to respect theology's claim that, through the "spirit" ("of God") "an absolutely new nature is breathed into us, and we become partakers of the very substance of the Deity" (222), but in the end opts as well for a depersonalized "spirit": "Summing up in the broadest possible

life, work, and continuing ministry of Jesus is now given *to* us and worked *in* us by the Spirit. In John 14:23, Jesus speaks of those who love him, "we will come to him and make our abode with him." Commenting on this verse, Luther explains that the Spirit dwells in believers "not merely according to His gifts but according to His own substance."[50] Because of this internal presence, Paul calls us "temples of God, in that the Holy Spirit dwells in you" (1 Cor 3:16). The believer's body, soul, and spirit are to be included in this NT allusion to the OT temple. Winslow describes the identity of this "temple" for NT believers.

> Through the incarnation, obedience, death, and resurrection of Christ, a way was opened by which God could again dwell with man, could resume His abode in the very temple that sin had destroyed, and show forth the riches and glory of His grace far more illustriously than when this temple stood in its original perfection and grandeur. Here was the *foundation* of every successive temple that grace was about to raise.[51]

Paul takes this "temple" metaphor a step further in referring to the "sealing" of the Holy Spirit in Eph 1:13. As we have seen, this connotes an authority to execute a contract or will made by another, in this case, Christ. Ephesians 1:3–12, which lays out our foundational identity in Christ (i.e., election, adoption, redemption, knowledge of God's will), gives context to this "sealing." In this light, Paul later warns the Ephesians, "Do not grieve the Holy Spirit of God, by whom you were sealed for the day of redemption" (Eph 4:30). To deny or dismiss the Spirit's "sealing" (in one's thoughts or actions) is to live according to another identity and thereby to "grieve the Holy Spirit" who has been given the executorial authority to unite us to Christ.

---

way the characteristics of the religious life, as we have found them, it includes the following beliefs: . . . That prayer or inner communion with the spirit thereof—be that spirit "God" or "law"—is a process wherein work is really done, and spiritual energy flows in and produces effects, psychological or material, within the phenomenal world" (475). See also Macaulay and Barrs, *Being Human*, 67–69.

50. Luther, *The Works of Martin Luther*, 12:377. Luther claims that the experience of the Spirit's indwelling is independent of any emotional awareness (Luther, *The Works of Martin Luther*, 29:85). Though the Spirit's gifts are felt, "one does not feel it when the Holy Spirit Himself is poured out richly."

51. Winslow, *The Work of the Holy Spirit*, 95–96.

> So whatever is destructive of the will and purposes of God for human personhood, will "grieve" his Spirit, in his holiness. For sin destroys his Spirit's influence in our lives. Thus we are called to open confession and repentance. . . . To grieve his Spirit is then disloyalty, idolatry, to be unconsecrated to him. . . . Chastity, that is to say the exclusive love we have for God alone, is then the first mark of true spirituality.[52]

Spirituality and Participation in Christ's Life and Mission

The Spirit's application of Christ's redemption confirms the "dual nature" of the Spirit/spirit relation, which is to be seen as a relation of unity. The Spirit in his freedom applies Christ's redemption, a "downreach," and thereby frees our spirits to be re-oriented *toward* the Spirit, thus enabling "upreach" as well.[53] This answers the question, "how is the believer's identification *experienced*?" The Spirit's "appropriation" of Jesus' salvation becomes crucial not only in terms of an intimate identification with Jesus' life, death, and resurrection, but also a "participation" in Christ's continuing life and mission *by faith*. Whereas modern metaphysics posited that "personal" knowledge of divinity is beyond our experience (i.e., Kant), the trinitarian Spirit opens the possibility of a full "participation" in the life and purposes of God once again.

In chapter three, I introduced the notion of "Spirit-Christology" as a complementary model to logos Christology. The living reality of Spirit-Christology, however, is not seen until we investigate its implications for "participatory spirituality." Several authors have explicated this connection extensively. E. P. Sanders, for example, sees Spirit-Christology as the hallmark of the believer's "participation" in salvation.

---

52. Houston, *The Holy Spirit in Contemporary Spirituality*, 18.

53. According to Hendry, "Barth interprets the *filioque* as precluding not only the notion of a Spirit which proceeds from the Father alone, and which would furnish the basis of a relation between God and man apart from Christ, but also the conception of a created spirit in man. The relation of man to God is established solely and exclusively by the downreach of the Spirit who proceeds from the Father and the Son, i.e., the Spirit who 'makes us partakers of the redemption purchased by Christ.' There is no other relation between God and man apart from this, and in this relation there is no place for the upward reach of a spirit of man. The question we have to ask is whether *sofu gratia* necessarily entails these two negative consequences" (Hendry, *The Holy Spirit in Christian Theology*, 108–9).

The Authority of the Holy Spirit and Practical Theology: Christian Spirituality

> The prime significance which the death of Christ has for Paul is not that it provides atonement for past transgressions (although he holds the common Christian view that it does so) but that, by sharing in Christ's death, one dies to the power of sin, to the old aeon, with the result that one belongs to God. The transfer takes place by participation in Christ's death. . . .[54]

The nature of "spiritual participation" can be seen in the book of Hebrews, where Jesus is portrayed as a forerunner who entered God's holy sanctuary and now serves as the pioneer and perfecter of our faith (6:19–20, 12:2). In the Spirit we now enter as well, "participating" in Christ's previous entrance. John 16:12–15 demonstrates that such participation can only occur through the aid of the Spirit, who becomes intimately identified with Jesus by *executing Jesus' will*. Through the Spirit's executorial authority the believer identifies with Jesus and actively participates in Jesus' death and present life and mission by faith. Here we discover the beginnings of true spirituality as our spirit is "awakened" to God.

This "participation" is captured in Paul's command to "walk in the Spirit" (Gal 5:25), a verse not specifically commanding obedience per se but *participation* in the life of God by faith. According to Houston,

> The inestimable privilege of the Christian life is the gift of eternal life, which is no less than the participation of the believer in the life and communion of the Father, Son and Holy Spirit. So to walk in the Spirit is to benefit from the triune resources of eternal love and friendship. It is, in fact, to make a mysterious exchange of our natural state of alienation for his divine fellowship. This is what is meant by "regeneration," the re-making of human nature to be inter-penetrated by the divine Spirit of God.[55]

To "walk in the Spirit" requires an active engagement in the promises of Scripture regarding one's identity in Christ. This answers the question regarding what the believer must actually *do* to participate in Jesus' mission. First, the believer needs to "listen" to the Spirit as the one who exposes our need to identify with Christ in specific ways (John 16:12). In this way the Spirit "completes" Jesus' revelation in us, appropriating it to every aspect

---

54. Sanders, *Paul and Palestinian Judaism*, 549.
55. Houston, *The Holy Spirit in Contemporary Spirituality*, 18–19.

of our lives. Such an engagement and continual re-consideration of our identity in Jesus can be captured through biblical meditation.[56] Paul, for example, attempts to "commend" and "persuade" the Corinthians to think rightly regarding their identity, proclaiming a promise he hopes will be "made manifest also in your conscience" (2 Cor 5:11), namely, that "when one died, all died" (2 Cor 5:14).

> It is clear that the test of Christ-likeness as applied by Paul to the experience of the Spirit in his Christian congregations is profound. This is likeness to Christ on the cross, not yet to the exalted, heavenly Christ; in the realm of the Spirit of Christ there are no short cuts to heaven; the way of the cross is the way for all. And the test is not only one to be applied to individual charismatic acts or utterances in the congregation, but to the character of the Christian life as a whole.[57]

Second, because Jesus is our representative, believers can share in Christ's death and resurrection by the Spirit, participating in the Son's obedience to God, as well as his adoption, justification, and sanctification, through our obedience to him.[58] "Participation" in such promises, and the hope provided therein, occurs in accordance with the Spirit's executorial authority in that the Spirit allows believers to experientially *know Christ* through their obedience to him.

Christian Spirituality and the Veracious Authority of the Spirit

As introduced in chapter two, Buckley and Yeago (in *Knowing the Triune God*) seek to construct a spirituality they call "evangelical catholicity," one

---

56. The Hebrew word for meditation, וְהָגִיתָ, is given by the Lord to Joshua (1:8) as a commandment that Joshua should "*mutter*" the book of the law, seemingly unto himself, in order that his "way should be made prosperous" as he enters the land of Jordan. In the sort of "participation" engendered by such meditation, Joshua, who is a *type* of Christ who could enter the land, might be contrasted with Moses the lawgiver, who could not enter the land and receive its blessings.

57. Dunn, *The Christ And The Spirit*, 2:351. Dunn adds, "The forces of death are grappling with the Spirit for every believer. So our life in this time between the ages must be marked as much by death as by life, by the dying, whether quickly or slowly, of what is at odds with the Spirit of life, for it is only through death that we share in Christ's life" (Dunn, *The Christ And The Spirit*, 2:354).

58. Ferguson, *The Holy Spirit*, 104–7.

The Authority of the Holy Spirit and Practical Theology: Christian Spirituality

that goes beyond the modern "inner vs. outer" dichotomy. Their goal is to unify God's action and Church practices, making them *one beginning point* for spirituality within the Spirit's unity. In such a unified spirituality we are able to *know God*.

> Saying that we hope to *know* the triune God by the gift of the Spirit in the practices of the Church is a dangerous claim . . . because modernity as well as postmodernity include a luxurious garden, or desert wilderness, of theories and practices of "knowing" that all too often eclipse the singular habits of mind and heart required to know *this* God. In such a context, knowing and believing become competitors.[59]

Yeago, in his chapter "The Bible," looks to the spirituality of St. Hilary of Poitiers in order to "revisit" the doctrine of the inspiration of Scripture, examining the way it functions within Christian community. "To describe the biblical texts as 'inspired Scriptures' is thus to affirm that the Holy Spirit has made the discourse of these texts his own."[60] The function of inspiration is,

> to specify the Christian community's distinctive knowledge of the biblical texts and their role in the economy of salvation . . . [rather than] to ground the doctrine of perspicuous propositional revelation, according to which God speaks by propounding universally accessible true propositions for our belief.[61]

The latter view ("the older Protestant doctrine of inspiration") was developed "with surprisingly little reference to the larger economy of the Spirit." Yeago thereby proposes a renewed account of Scriptural inspiration, which "must locate the Scriptures within the redemptive economy of the Spirit, and thereby recover the church's distinctive knowledge of these texts."[62] In this way, Scripture takes on a specifically *spiritual* function, which Yeago describes in several ways:

---

59. Buckley and Yeago, "Introduction," 6.
60. Yeago, "The Bible," 63.
61. Ibid., 61–62.
62. Ibid., 62.

The Lord Is the Spirit

> The textual character of the Scriptures is thereby taken up and put to work *sacramentally*. . . . Scripture brings to bear the Spirit's transcendence of the church's life and understanding. . . . The texts serve as a sacramental locus of the Spirit's presence as perpetual *giver of life* in the church.[63]

"Spirituality" for Yeago consists of the Spirit's work *within the church*, particularly within the practice of interpretation. Yeago thus argues for a sacramental or "distinctly ecclesial practice of interpretation" of the Bible as a central means for knowing God. "Scripture functions as a quasi-sacramental instrument of the Holy Spirit, through which the Spirit makes known the mystery of Christ in order to form the church as a sign of his messianic dominion."[64]

> The church's knowledge of Scripture as inspired has therefore interpretive consistency; it calls for a specific or perhaps a concatenation of arts, of faithful reading, exposition, and application by which Christ is glorified and the church built up in its distinct life and mission.[65]

The Spirit's Inspiration and Illumination of the Word as Central for "True Spirituality"

Buckley and Yeago should be applauded in attempting to construct a trinitarian theology that highly affirms the traditional practices of the church and describes these practices in such a way that they can be *lived*. Yeago's chapter in particular advocates a spirituality where *Scripture* can be lived in the context of a unified ecclesiology.

However, in developing his ecclesial spirituality, does Yeago's understanding of the Bible and interpretation give respect the Spirit's veracious authority as *Teacher* of the church? Yeago's argument hinges on Luther's critical distinction between Scripture's twofold clarity: the "inward clarity" ("located in the heart's understanding" and ultimately the work of the Holy

---

63. Ibid., 64–65.
64. Ibid., 51.
65. Ibid.

The Authority of the Holy Spirit and Practical Theology: Christian Spirituality

Spirit) and the "outward clarity" ("located in the ministry of the word").[66] Yeago observes:

> But in reality Luther does not present the outward clarity [of Scripture] as a single property of the text; he describes it rather as "located in the ministry of the word" (*in verbi ministerio posita*), that is, in the network of ecclesial communicative practice within which both the text and interpreter are situated.[67]

While this seems to be true, Yeago appears to go *beyond* Luther by then making interpretation primarily dependent on ecclesial situatedness rather then the Spirit's inspiration and illumination. Yeago concludes,

> The knowledge of God provided by the Spirit is thus inscribed in the concrete institutions and practices of the ecclesial life that the Spirit displays before the nations; knowing "the only true God and Jesus the Messiah whom he has sent" (John 17:3), and so experiencing a foretaste of eternal life, is not separable from participation in the "sanctification" (v. 17) of the disciples.[68]

Rather than the knowledge of God being "inscribed" within the hearts of believers (Jer 31:33), it is inscribed within institutions and practices themselves. Yeago's "ecclesial" view of inspiration is exposed in his misrepresentation of 2 Tim 3:16, "the Scriptures are 'God-breathed' or 'inspired' *in that* they are 'useful for teaching, for reproof, for correction, and for training in righteousness.'"[69] He adds,

> the Spirit has appropriated [the Scriptures] and invested them with the specific *auctoritas* proper to his saving mission. The texts written by Isaiah or Matthew or Paul have been appropriated by the Spirit, so that we now rightly read them as the Spirit's own discourse, backed by the Spirit's authority, and directed towards the Spirit ends.[70]

---

66. Ibid., 57.
67. Ibid.
68. Ibid., 63.
69. Ibid., 64 (emphasis mine). Nearly every version has "and" rather than "in that."
70. Yeago, "The Bible," 70.

As with Grenz and Franke, the language of "appropriation" has been employed here to demonstrate the Spirit's "authority" in the text. What sort of authority does Yeago's model suggest? Certainly not a *veracious* authority, for the Spirit is not held responsible to fix its *meaning*. Rather, the Spirit seems to have an *authorizing* or *delegating* authority (to invest authority in another's writings) and perhaps an *executorial* authority (to use the Scriptures to accomplish God's will and to "inscribe" the knowledge of God in concrete institutions and practices). Finally, the Spirit seems to possess a *governing* authority (to form the church as a sign of Christ's messianic dominion).

But why not grant the Spirit *veracious authority* as the "Spirit of Truth" within the community? We have seen that Welker's understanding of "inspiration" develops on the basis of the diverse testimonies of the intersubjective community that "point to the reality of God." Though Yeago does not reduce the Spirit's role in inspiration to that of a "force field," he does reflect Welker's "intersubjectivity" theory by linking inspiration to the unity of God's people around the church's *practices*. In other words, since our ecclesial/traditional practices are the Spirit's "inscription" of the knowledge of God, these practices actually "participate" in the original inspiration of Scripture.[71]

How are we to assess such a notion of "participation"? As seen earlier, "participatory spirituality" explains how we now "participate" in Christ's death and present life and mission, namely, through the Spirit's present application of Christ's salvation and sanctification. This occurs as we "listen" to the Spirit regarding the reality of and our need for such identification. As mentioned earlier, "participation" in Christ's continuing life and mission ultimately occurs not by "practice" in itself but *by faith realized in practice*, not in *our* faithfulness to Christ but in *Christ's* faithfulness to us.

The Holy Spirit was a focal point of Luther's theology as it was a main focus of his spirituality. "I, too, have been in the Spirit and have seen the Spirit, perhaps even more of it . . . than those fellows which all their boasting will see in a year," he declares.[72]

---

71. See Yeago, "The Bible," 62–63.

72. Luther, *The Works of Martin Luther*, 45:365–66. He said this as a warning to the Councilmen of Germany in 1524 against the "enthusiasts" who boasted of their experience in the Spirit but considered the Scripture of little worth (even imagining that they were

The Authority of the Holy Spirit and Practical Theology: Christian Spirituality

However, as seen in chapter two, Luther always sought to hold the Spirit and the Word in tension. This means, that the aims of the one should never supersede those of the other,[73] but also that the Spirit must always be tethered to the "sensus literalis" of Scripture.[74] Such a tension counters a strictly "allegorical" hermeneutic or a strictly "moral" one. "Word and Spirit" thereby became a continual theological rallying point for post-reformation movements. The Puritans, for example, strove to retain this balance by basing their spirituality on their "first principle"—that the Scriptures are the inspired Word of God—as well as on the Spirit's sovereign work in establishing this principle in the heart.[75] The Spirit, in other words, must be present in the believer for the Word to have real spiritual impact. Puritans keenly observed this as a "double light." For there to be any spiritual understanding, the Spirit that is in the Scripture must also have residence in the believer. Sibbes states:

> The breath of the Spirit in us is suitable to the Spirit's breathing in the Scriptures; the same Spirit doth not breathe contrary motions. As the spirits in the arteries quicken the blood in the veins, so the Spirit of God goes along with the word, and makes it work.[76]

As seen in chapter one, Word and Spirit together form a *pattern of divine authority* centered in Christ. One of John's "tests" for determining whether or not one's spirituality indeed proceeds from the Holy Spirit is in fact based on one's response to the New Testament's teachings (1 John 4:4–6). While the presupposition of John's argument is the Spirit's divinity (v. 4), he concludes that "listening" to apostolic teaching is the simple distinguishing point between "the Spirit of Truth and the Spirit of error"

---

superior to Scripture and could indeed improve upon it).

73. For example, in his comment on John 16:13 Luther declares, "Although the gospel came and still comes through the Holy Spirit alone, we cannot deny that it came through the medium of languages" (Luther, *The Works of Martin Luther*, 45:358), and thereby exhorts ministers to study the languages voraciously.

74. See Luther, *The Works of Martin Luther*, 10:7, 54, 56, 95, 155.

75. Puritan Richard Sibbes indeed exclaims that "there must be an infused establishing by the Spirit to settle the heart in this first principle" and that the Word is central to spirituality only in that it is "the Spirit's bedrock" (Nuttall, *The Holy Spirit in Puritan Faith and Experience*, 23).

76. Nuttall, *The Holy Spirit in Puritan Faith and Experience*, 23.

(v. 6). "The test of whether God's Spirit is living and working in us is whether we listen to the apostles' teaching or disregard it. If we listen, then we know we have the Spirit of truth."[77]

As deduced in chapter four, the Spirit's veracious authority is displayed through these two interrelated "truth-telling" activities: inspiration of Scripture and illumination of Scripture. The "Spirit of Truth" is vividly characterized by John as the one who creates a practical spirituality diametrically opposed to the "Spirit of Perversity." We saw in John 14:16 that the Spirit will not only bear witness to Jesus by inspiring and illuminating the Scriptures, but in doing so will activate a practical spirituality *in* the believer to be worked out in accordance with the Word of God. The Spirit does this by guiding the disciples "into all truth" (16:13), and in doing so brings the weight of Jesus' authority to bear on our humanity (through the Scriptures).[78] True spirituality thereby recognizes that the Spirit's primary form of speaking and guidance is the authoritative illumination of the Scriptures. Morris affirms such guidance for spirituality.

> The Spirit is regarded as the Author of the Bible. Therefore we will chiefly look to Scripture to guide us on our way. There are references to the Spirit as "speaking" (e.g. Acts 21:11; 1 Tim 4:1) so that we may well feel that His Spirit within the believer moves him, and applies the basic revelation to the needs of the day. But we will not look to some extraordinary disturbance within ourselves as the usual mode of guidance. Rather we will expect that the Bible will provide us with the great principles that we need. "Men spake from God, being moved by the Holy Ghost" (2 Pet 1:21). And the Spirit-inspired Book will be the chief means of affording us guidance.[79]

The Spirit, therefore, has veracious authority with respect to the believer's spirituality—to govern, order, and process the ministry of the Word of God to the human heart so that it will impact *behavior*. The Spirit's ministry is authoritative for a reason often missed in contemporary evangelical circles: it is the ministry of the Spirit through the Word *bringing forth the very identity and internal character of the believer* (as presented in

---

77. Macaulay and Barrs, *Being Human*, 115.

78. As seen in chapter four, this "guidance" extends to all believers through the Spirit's illumination of the Word of God.

79. Morris, *Spirit of the Living God*, 80.

The Authority of the Holy Spirit and Practical Theology: Christian Spirituality

the previous section). The Spirit of Truth guides and affirms this process by activating, confirming, and "externalizing" one's new internal identity in Christ, and does so in conjunction with the believer's meditation *on* the Word and (as we shall see below) discipleship *in* the Word. The "spiritual man" *lives* through the Spirit's activation of the Word of God. The result is the development of a spiritual mindset (i.e., the mind of Christ), a view of humanity that relates spirituality to every area of life and thought.

We also saw that John 14:17 contains three faith-related terms—*receive, behold,* and *know*—and that these verbs have strong implications for actively receiving and submitting to divine revelation and truth. Such submission allows the development of one's spiritual life "under" the Spirit of Truth to result in *wisdom*.[80] John 14:26 makes a "spiritual correlation" between the Spirit of Truth and wisdom, pointing to the Paraclete's authoritative mission as one that involves "teaching" and "reminding." The Spirit's mission thereby provides spiritual nurturance, sustenance, and guidance through the Word for pursuing a life of wisdom.

The Spirit accomplishes this mission by activating the Word's "speech acts" (Isa 55:11). The reception of the Word of God (John 14:17) allows the believer to go *beyond himself or herself* to the Spirit as the genuine *other* in the text, so that the perlocutionary effects of Scripture might drive the believer toward a spirituality marked by active obedience. Recognizing speech acts for what they are (i.e., Paul's directive to "be filled with the Spirit"; Eph 5:18) allows the Spirit to guide our behavior (i.e., "in psalms and hymns and spiritual songs"; Eph 5:19). According to Vanhoozer, "The text can become more than a dialogue partner: it can become a pedagogue that illumines one's existence and opens up new ways of living in the world."[81]

As we have seen, the "multi-faceted" authority of Scripture (seen in the forms of assertives, directives, etc.) demonstrates the complexity of the Spirit's veracious authority to speak "truth" in and through the many canonical vehicles of Scripture (i.e., narratives, propositions, poetry, prophecy, etc.). It also has practical implications for the development of

---

80. Breck's view of the Spirit as speaker of Wisdom—which is grounded in Job's depiction of the Spirit as director of the development of "understanding" (32:8)—helps us see the Spirit as the one who both illuminates the Word and enlightens the mind in the pursuit of wisdom.

81. Vanhoozer, *Is There a Meaning in This Text?*, 375.

a "multi-faceted spirituality" (i.e., prayer, solitude, worship, fasting, listening, remembering, acting) in that the Spirit guides the believer to specific principles of Scripture in the development and practice of such disciplines. The "understanding" spoken of in Job 32:8, provided by the Spirit of Truth, ensures that the Spirit's illumination will result in a *practical theology* that invigorates spirituality.

The many "traditions" of spirituality are often developed as responses to the Spirit's "acts of speaking" through the Word, dynamically applying and affirming its theological truths in particular space/time contexts and situations. While these traditions are not "authoritative" in themselves, they naturally become the means for spiritual identification and formation. Surely a rich interrelationship between spirituality and theological "tradition" can develop under the authority of the Spirit. Here Del Colle is instructive:

> Spirituality may not just enliven theology but enable theology to breathe in a new way. . . . Theology is enabled to speculate anew in the light that a living spirituality affords. Likewise, spirituality nourished by theology penetrates and enhances life in the Spirit when it clearly understands the full contours and implications of the logos from God. Without sounding simplistic, there is a reciprocal relationship between theology and spirituality.[82]

Discipleship "Under" the Spirit's Veracious Authority

Perhaps the best "medium" in the Church through which the Word's truth becomes illuminated and practiced by the Spirit is *discipleship relationships*. The Spirit's veracious authority provides a biblical framework for discipleship "under" the Spirit of God (i.e., a discipleship with intentional structures and within a believing community). Discipleship relationships provide the context within which the reception of the Word of God, through the Spirit's illumination, might result in a "living theology." John 15:26–27 and 16:13–14 are to be *practiced* within the context of discipleship relationships in order to ground the believer's entire spirituality in the shared Word of God. The Spirit of God "speaks" through these relationships (even though the spirituality or theological understanding of the discipler may be flawed)

---

82. Del Colle, "Spirit-Christology," 94–95.

The Authority of the Holy Spirit and Practical Theology: Christian Spirituality

if they exist within communities that esteem the final authority of the Word of God and the veracious authority of the Spirit. When this Spirit/Word "balance" is neglected, the community will likely amass a myriad of inconsistencies, as we see in the Corinthian church. According to Fee, "They [the Corinthians] speak in tongues, to be sure, which Paul will not question as a legitimate activity of the Spirit. But at the same time they tolerate, or endorse, illicit sexuality, greed, and idolatry."[83]

Communities that retain such "balance," however, are able to "test" the "spirits" of the world through the Spirit's illumination of the Word of God. Houston sees the Spirit as the one who "stands guard" in the revelation of his will against the opposition of the spirits of the world.

> When we discern therefore the spirits of the world around us, it is primarily to see "if they be of God" or not. The test is really, do they point to the Holy Trinity or not? For if God is God, then he is incomparable with all else, for it is never fitting to be content with what is merely analogous to God, as myth has done in the history of other religions. For the biblical God is self-revealing, God as revealed by God. Thus the Holy Spirit stands guard over the sovereignty of the Lordship of God, in the revelation of himself.[84]

The Spirit's veracious authority requires that believers "hear" his discernment regarding such world spirits as legalism or licentiousness, spirits that often gain attention through fleshly approaches to scriptural interpretation (i.e., "rationalism" or "enthusiasm"). In pursuit of a "deeper" spirituality there is a constant danger we might interpret our own feelings and opinions as the Spirit's guidance. According to Morris,

> Our best defense against this temptation is a real humility joined with a genuine readiness to hear and obey the Spirit. If we are sincerely seeking to know God's will, and are ready to follow it, wherever it may lead, then His guidance will certainly be afforded us.[85]

---

83. Fee, *God's Empowering Presence*, 198–200. See 1 Cor 5:9–10; illustrated in 5:1–5; 6:1–11, 12–20; and 8:1—10:22.

84. Houston, *The Holy Spirit in Contemporary Spirituality*, 17–18.

85. Morris, *Spirit of the Living God*, 80. When confronting the childish thinking of the Corinthians, for example, Paul demonstrates a bit of irony regarding "speaking in tongues" (1 Cor 13:1–2 and 14:20). Though tongues "serves as evidence of their new transcendent spirituality and thus marks off the spiritual quality of their gatherings, they actually evidence

Christian discipleship forms a "bridge" between the Spirit's illumination of Scripture and practical spirituality by providing the relational framework necessary for spiritual discernment in today's world. It does not substitute for the Spirit's veracious authority but instead provides a human context through which the Spirit dynamically fills the framework with contemporary discernment.

In the last chapter we investigated the Spirit's guidance of the church "into all truth" in terms of a "hermeneutical community," determining that the Spirit of Truth is indeed able to lead the community toward corporate decisions regarding doctrine, hermeneutics, theology, et cetera. "True spirituality" needs such a "hermeneutical community" because, as Houston affirms, it is in our "personal relationships" that true spirituality is distinguished.

> If we try to communicate the faith impersonally, we are most betraying its truth. For it is "the fellowship of the Holy Spirit" that distinguishes true from false spirituality. For the fellowship of the Holy Spirit is what reveals the love of God and the grace of our Lord Jesus Christ.[86]

The blessing of the Spirit's veracious authority is the illumination of the entire Word of God in the formation of a rich, communal spirituality that matures within the context of the church community. The full activation of this spirituality, however, is not accomplished without an awareness of the Spirit's governing authority as well.

Christian Spirituality and the Governing Authority of the Spirit

As introduced in chapter two, Jones and Buckley's goal (in *Spirituality and Social Embodiment*) is to confront "modern spirituality" with a "socially-embodied spirituality." The Spirit allows us to go "beyond ourselves" and live within concrete reality. Yeago builds on this in his chapter, "A Christian, Holy People: Martin Luther on Salvation and the Church." Here Yeago's ecclesial *spirituality* emerges, which is once again derived from his interactions with Luther. Yeago praises Luther for having "liberated spiritu-

---

all kinds of ethical/behavioral aberrations" (Fee, *God's Empowering Presence*, 238).

86. Houston, *The Holy Spirit in Contemporary Spirituality*, 21–22.

ality and faith from dependence on community in the form of the Roman Church and the pretensions of its priesthood."[87] Looking to Luther's *Large Catechism*, Yeago states: "Luther maintains that we are not saved by the work of Christ except by way of the completed work of the Holy Spirit." Yeago clarifies:

> Our salvation is just as dependent on what we may call the "economy of the Spirit" as it is on the "economy of the Son." Without the economy of the Spirit, who brings us to Christ, the treasure which Christ has for us would lie buried and dead, doing us no good. Christ has won our salvation through his incarnation, death, and resurrection, but the Spirit must distribute this salvation through the Christian church and through the forgiveness of sins imparted in the church.[88]

With this in mind, Yeago seems to comprehend the Spirit's "inward" work of incorporating us into the church to be a function of the Spirit's work within "outward" church practices.

> By faith the Spirit brings us into a *corporate* union and communion with Christ, and so with one another. Moreover, the inward is not given except through the outward: sharing in the hidden mystery of the church's union with Christ takes place in, with, and through participation in the church's communion life and its holy practices.[89]

What emerges is a "Lutheran" spirituality that understands all doctrine in light of a *corporate* "priesthood of all believers" (rather than an individualistic priesthood).

> Justification by faith is not, for Luther, the establishment of a private, individual relationship to God which may subsequently find expression in adherence to the church. Justification is incorporation into the communal priesthood of the church, into the unity of the Body of Christ with its Head.[90]

---

87. Yeago, "A Christian, Holy People," 108.
88. Ibid., 115.
89. Ibid., 116.
90. Ibid.

This perspective in turn leads to interdependence and mutual accountability within an ordered community (1 Cor 14:29). To make this point Yeago quotes Luther:

> Of this assembly I too am a part and member, a sharer and partner in all the good which it has, brought in and pointed through the same Holy Sprit, through the fact that I have heard God's word and still hear it, which is the beginning of entering into it.[91]

Eschatological/Immediate Spirituality and the Authority of the Believer

As with our analysis of Yeago's "ecclesial" understanding of inspiration, Yeago does seems to go a bit beyond Luther's exact words in ways that do not seem to resonate with the vast body of Luther's writings. This is evident in the statement that, "Christ has won our salvation through his incarnation, death and resurrection, but the Spirit must *distribute* this salvation *through the Christian church* and through the forgiveness of sins imparted *in* the church."[92] Yeago goes on to quote Luther in this regard,[93] but noticeably absent in Luther's theology are the words "distributes" or "imparted"—words that add a certain "magisterial" tone to the discussion (the idea that salvation and forgiveness are the *church's* holy possessions rather than the Spirit's). Also, Yeago is a bit misleading regarding Luther's view of justification as "incorporation" into the assembly, portraying that this statement expresses Luther's entire thinking on the subject. However, when examining Luther's works, he does in fact refer to a "personal" notion of justification.[94] In other words, while the *inward* work of the Spirit is given lip-service, the Spirit's *outward* work dominates the conversation.

91. Luther, *Die Bekenntnisschriften der Evangelisch-Lutherischen Kirche*, 657.

92. Yeago, "A Christian, Holy People," 115 (emphasis his).

93. "In the first place, he [the Spirit] has a singular assembly (*gemeine*) in the world, which is the mother which begets and bears every Christian through the word, which he reveals and urges, so that hearts are illumined and kindled, so that they grasp it, accept it, hang on it, and abide with it" (Luther, *Die Bekenntnisschriften der Evangelisch-Lutherischen Kirche*, 115).

94. In his commentary on Gal 3:23, for example, Luther makes a connection between the effective work of sanctification and the church. He is essentially saying that sanctification works in the church and that the two are not entirely distinct. Luther makes this point by

The Authority of the Holy Spirit and Practical Theology: Christian Spirituality

Though Yeago seems to respect the executorial character of the Spirit's work, we must ask Yeago (as we would theologians who seem to advocate the church's "magisterial authority"): Is the Spirit's authority within the Church *mediated* by its traditions and practices, or do these practices simply become forms of expression for executing the Spirit's authority (so that it can be experienced *directly*)?

While we could answer this by simply quoting Paul: "there is only one mediator between God and man, the man Jesus Christ" (1 Tim 2:5), we must ask ourselves where the Spirit falls into this discussion. The answer can be found by looking to the "eschatological Spirit" as our appropriate foundation for the practice of spirituality. Hebrews 12:22 provides an eschatological vision that can be read as an immediate, spiritual reality: we "*have* come to Mount Zion and to the city of the living God, the heavenly Jerusalem" (emphasis mine). In drafting an *actual identity* between those believers in heaven and those remaining in this life (through the use of the perfect verb προσεληλύθατε) this passage seems to allude to the "down-payment" or "earnest" of the Holy Spirit. Schaeffer asserts that the Spirit provides believers with an experience that can be considered "equal reality" with the experience of those already in heaven.

> They are there, they see Christ face to face, they are dead, and we have the earnest of the Holy Spirit. . . . They are equal reality. They are two streams of present reality, both equally promised. The Christian dead are already with Christ now, and Christ really lives in the Christian. Christ lives in me. . . . Here is true Christian mysticism.[95]

---

saying that by the creed's phrase "I believe in the holy church" we understand that Christ's work of justification (and consequently sanctification) happens in the church. But Luther does make a distinction between the ecclesiological body and the work of justification in the believer. "Therefore faith justifies because it takes hold of and possesses this treasure, the present Christ" [Luther, *The Works of Martin Luther*, 26:130]. For Luther, there is a difference between the Word and the Church, but the Spirit publically binds the two together (or better, the Spirit is publically bound to the Word); hence the efficacious activity/presence of the Spirit wherever the Word is preached *just is* the Church. (Luther, *The Works of Martin Luther*, 26:140, 285). In the Finnish school of interpretation, for Luther, to be "justified" means to participate in God's being in a mystical fashion, to have a "personal relationship." For a general introduction to and summary of the Finnish school of interpretation, see Mannermaa, "Justification and *Theosis*," 25–41.

95. Schaeffer, *True Spirituality*, 53–55.

Believers, likewise, can now know Christ without any official mediation. The believer's eschatological vision, therefore, is not to be thought of as completely future-oriented but as also one obliging immediate realization.[96] The Spirit's "contemporaniety" not only applies to biblical hermeneutics but also to the hermeneutics of *self*, imposing a new eschatological vision with respect to the self's *identity*. The Spirit in his governing authority activates the believer's spirituality by bringing the authority of God into all aspects of life and faith. The Spirit not only affirms the believer's *purpose*[97] through the Spirit's *governing authority*, but also activates within the believer a certain authority in accordance with his or her established eschatological destiny. Because the Spirit's governing realm is both *eschatological* and *immediate* it has implications for bringing the very rule of Christ into the believer's entire spiritual life. Christ's authority, which is now "far above all rule and authority and power and dominion" (Eph 1:21–22), in a sense becomes the believer's authority as well, in that believers have been "raised up with Him, and seated with Him in the heavenly places, in Christ Jesus" (Eph 2:6). This "spiritual authority" goes beyond the original "dominion" over the earth that God granted to Adam (Gen 1:28), though that might be considered the foundation of the believer's authority.[98] The "authority of the believer" in the NT not only demonstrates a *restoration* of this original dominion over the physical earth but also a certain *spiritual identity*,

---

96. Without such a view toward *immediacy* we would end up with what Moltmann refers to as a Gnostic "religion of redemption." "To the extent to which Christianity cut itself off from its Jewish roots and adapted itself to the ancient world, it became a religion of redemption. . . . God's Spirit was no longer viewed as 'the source of life'; it was now the Spirit who redeems the soul from the prison of the mortal body. In the same measure as redemption was spiritualized, the realm of 'the flesh' was reduced to the body and its earthly drives and baser needs. The Platonic dualism of body and soul and the Gnostic contempt for the body forced Christianity into the mould of a corresponding religion of redemption" (Moltmann, *The Source of Life*, 74–75).

97. Spiritual *purpose* seems to include: knowing one's *origin* under the Spirit's divine authority, grasping one's *identity* in Christ through the Spirit's executorial authority, and deriving spiritual *wisdom* and *guidance* through the Spirit's veracious authority.

98. Notice, however, that immediately preceding this mandate is God's act of "breathing" his Spirit of life into Adam. Though we should not make too much of this association, some correlation between God's נְשָׁמָה ("breath") in creation and man's dominion must be observed in light of the *responsibility* Adam is given as a steward over God's creation (see Schaeffer, *Genesis in Space and Time*, 33).

The Authority of the Holy Spirit and Practical Theology: Christian Spirituality

through the Spirit, with Christ's present dominion over all spiritual powers. Since believers are now "glorified" in Christ (Rom 8:29–30), their authority is derived from their identity with Christ's authority and activated by the Spirit who governs the "immediate" kingdom of God.

The believer's authority is activated in two specific ways. First, as the *eschatological* Spirit identifies Christ's authoritative rule with the immediate reality of the believer, the Spirit confers to the believer *some degree of "authority" over spiritual forces*. As seen in chapter four, the Spirit of Yahweh provides ruling qualities to the Messiah (including judgment, rulership, justice, wisdom, strength, knowledge, and fear of God; Isa 11:2). As the agent of restoration, the Spirit creates an eschatological realm of authority for all creation and humankind (establishing the kingdom in terms of the Messiah's "righteousness" and "justice"; Isa 32:15–16). We have also seen how Acts 1:3–8 portrays the *immediacy* of this eschatological kingdom through the Spirit.

As a result, we can now say that the experience of the Spirit's power with respect to spirituality is an *immediate demonstration and display* of Jesus' eschatological kingdom and glorious reign. The *practice* of spirituality is to be understood as the reality of the eschatological Spirit *lived today*. Grudem proclaims,

> We also share in part now in the kingly reign of Christ, since we have been raised to sit with him in the heavenly places (Eph 2:6), thus sharing to some degree in his authority over evil spiritual forces that may be arrayed against us (Eph 6:10–18; James 4:7; 1 Peter 5:9; 1 John 4:4). God has even now committed to us authority over various areas in this world or in the church, giving to some authority over much and to some authority over little. But when the Lord returns those who have been faithful over little we'll be given authority over much (Matt 25:14–30).[99]

---

99. Grudem, *Systematic Theology*, 630. MacMillan, in his popular little book *The Authority of the Believer*, also points to Eph 1:19–22 and 2:4–6 in this regard. "They (believers) are made to sit with Christ in the heavenlies. Christ's session is at the right hand of God. His people, therefore, occupy 'with Him' the same august position. This honor is not to a chosen few, but is the portion of all those who share the resurrection of the Son of God" (MacMillan, *The Authority of the Believer*, 17).

The Lord Is the Spirit

The believer's "spiritual authority" is therefore an outflow of his or her identity in Christ, which is given through the Spirit by "power of appointment."[100] There are, however, major qualifications necessary for this Kingdom authority to be activated.[101] As we have seen, believers in this present age are marked by the Spirit's eschatological qualities (*justice, righteousness,* and *peace*). Jesus details his interpretation of these kingdom qualities in Matt 5:3–9.[102] "Poverty of spirit" is listed first, likely because of its foundational contribution, and Jesus distinctly associates this quality with the Messiah's eschatological Kingdom (v. 3). The Spirit, who administers the Kingdom's eschatological structures in the world, confirms the believer's authority through this "poverty of spirit" by providing moral and spiritual vision and vitality in association with the Messiah's glorious reign. The believer's spirituality is thereby structured according to the eschatological "vision" of the Messiah's reign, now brought into "governing authority" by the Spirit.[103] Jesus also mentions another quality with strong ties to the

---

100. Legally speaking, the believer's "spiritual authority" is conferred by the Spirit by "power of appointment" from Christ. "Power of appointment" is "a power or authority conferred by one person or deed or will upon another to appoint, that is, to select or nominate the person or persons who are to receive and enjoy an estate or an income therefrom or from a fund, after the testator's death . . . " (*Black's Law Dictionary,* "Power of Appointment," 1054).

101. The believer is an "ordinary agent" whose authority is limited by the Word of God. An ordinary agent's authority is always designated (or "authorized") by the terms and conditions within a document or word provided by the "Principal" or "source of authority" (see *Black's Law Dictionary,* "Principal," 1073–74). The Spirit is not a Principal but an Agent with "plenipotentiary authority" (i.e., complete identity with the Principal), and is thus granted authority to lay forth these conditions in the Word of God.

102. The Sermon on the Mount is thereby the penultimate eschatological spirituality. See Carson, *The Sermon on the Mount,* 16–21.

103. According to Carson, "poverty of spirit" is the primary spiritual attitude combining *lowliness* and *humility* (i.e., Prov 16:19; Isa 57:15, 66:2). See Carson, *The Sermon on the Mount,* 17. "Poverty of spirit is the personal acknowledgment of spiritual bankruptcy. It is the conscious confession of unworthiness before God. As such, it is the deepest form of repentance. . . . It is not surprising, then, that the kingdom of heaven belongs to the poor in spirit. As the very outset of the Sermon on the Mount we learn that we do not have the spiritual resources to put any of the Sermon's precepts into practice" (Carson, *The Sermon on the Mount,* 17–18). "Poverty of spirit" also stands in opposition to spiritual "Platonism," which "teaches that as we become absorbed in the spiritual realm we become careless of the world below. . . . Spirituality (however) involves the whole of human life; nothing is unspiritual. But wherever Platonism has affected Christian teaching there has been a separation of the

The Authority of the Holy Spirit and Practical Theology: Christian Spirituality

eschatological kingdom: "Blessed are the peacemakers, for they shall be called sons of God" (Matt 5:9). In Romans 8 we see that the Spirit confirms the privileges and authority associated with *sonship* (i.e., as participants in God's *family*). Del Colle holds this to be the ultimate eschatological manifestation with respect to our "immediate" Christian spirituality (see Rom 8:18–25; Eph 4:11–16).[104]

The Effects of the Spirit and "The Authority of the Believer"

The second way the believer's authority is activated through the Spirit's governing authority is demonstrated with respect to the specific *effects* of the eschatological Spirit of God in the world. *The Spirit confers a "ministerial authority" to the believer* as a reflection of the Spirit governing authority and as part of the universal Church. Since believers live within the Spirit's eschatological *realm*, they can demonstrate the Spirit's immediate *effects* as specific manifestations of their ministerial authority. The Spirit produces such powerful effects in and through God's people, including democratization, liberation, and transformation. It is therefore appropriate to examine the nature of these effects in relation to the believer's authority.[105]

Democratization

The Spirit's *democratization*, as seen in chapter four, means that the Spirit is now available to all of God's "remnant" people. Isaiah 59:21, along with Joel 2:28–32, confirms the progressive "democratization" of God's Spirit to his true followers, so that they might interpret their life in light of this

---

sacred and secular . . . . This mentality subtly affects Christ thinking in numerous ways. For example, someone might say, 'If only I could be involved in something really spiritual like witnessing rather then peeling these potatoes.'" (Macaulay and Barrs, *Being Human*, 54).

104. Del Colle explains, "If Spirit-Christology mutually relates the Sonship of Jesus with his anointing with the Spirit, then the font and fullness of life in the Spirit is to manifest in word, life and deed our graced adoption by the Father, to share in the communion of his Son's paschal mystery amidst a world that groans for the *parousia* and the redemption that the promised kingdom will usher in" (Del Colle, "Spirit-Christology," 112).

105. In doing so, we must keep in mind that we are attending to the individual as a member of the local church community and in cooperation with it (see chapter 6). The believer's authority (somewhat like the authority of the church leader) is *functional* and *spiritual*, rather than *established*.

eschatological hope. "The Spirit that is upon you, and this Word that I have put in your mouth" means that God's "remnant" people and their "seed" were granted a certain "ministerial authority" by the Spirit in the spoken Word of Promise. This *authoritative Word* is captured in the democratized sense by Paul, who repeatedly uses "word" (either λόγος or ῥῆμα) in connection with the powerful proclamation of the gospel of Christ (i.e., "word of faith" in Rom 10:8; "word of truth" in Eph 1:13; "word of life" in Phil 1:14, 2:16) and His kingdom. This Word of Promise continually points forward to the eschatological Kingdom and, in correlation with the Spirit of Restoration, results in a word that is alive, "living and active and sharper than any two-edged sword" (Heb 4:12).

The Spirit and the Spirit's governing authority have thereby been democratized to all believers, who possess ministerial authority in association with the spoken Word of God. Democratization allows believers to participate with the Spirit in his work of restoration through the spoken Word. Acts 1:3–8 and 2:3–21 presents the ministerial authority of believers in terms of Jesus' continuing mission. Jesus imparts *leadership* in association with the Spirit of Restoration, as seen in Jesus' choice of the twelve Apostles (1:2–4), to speak the gospel as Christ's "witnesses" (1:8a). The Spirit's empowerment will also lead to specific geographical *vision*: Jerusalem, Judea, Samaria, the remotest part of the earth (1:8b and throughout the book of Acts). The disciples' mission thereby demonstrates a "localization" of the Spirit's governing authority.

Spiritual gifts present one of the strongest evidences of the Spirit's democratization. First century believers knew that only Israel's "Charismatic" leaders had possessed the Spirit and special endowments of the Spirit. To discover that the Spirit and his gifts were now indwelling *them*, providing them with gifts for servant-leadership within the body of Christ, would create a humble sense of linkage to their Old Testament leaders. According to Hill and Walton,

> The empowerment function (given to certain leaders) did carry over to the New Testament as we understand the Holy Spirit to empower people to holy living and to bestow spiritual gifts. And in

both the Old and New Testaments, the Spirit gave people the ability or authority to do what they normally could not have done.[106]

Spiritual gifts, however, should not be placed into the sort of "platonic" categories described earlier. The Spirit's democratization, as seen in chapter six, does not create a sharp division between "supernatural" gifts and "natural" ones.

> It is wrong to label particular gifts extraordinary and say these are the *really* spiritual ones. That a gift like tongues or healing or working miracles is more obviously given directly by the Spirit, does not put it on a higher place. Nor does it demonstrate that the person who exercises such a gift is more open to the Spirit or knows a fullness of the Spirit not enjoyed by others who have more ordinary gifts.[107]

The democratization of the Spirit thereby informs us that spiritual gifts are both expressions of the Spirit's governing authority as well as demonstrations that each believer has a particular "dominion" within their own church body—a giftedness to be used for building up Christ's body.

LIBERATION

The believer's ministerial authority, secondly, is one that witnesses to the "freedom of the Spirit" in the practice of spirituality. Far from destroying the freedom of our spirit, the Holy Spirit restores this freedom by changing its false freedom from God into true freedom for God. This is in keeping with "the glorious liberty of the children of God" (Rom 8:21).[108] The believer who receives the Spirit's application of Christ's redemption experiences a restoration of the *imago dei*, in that the human spirit's freedom "reflects" the Holy Spirit's freedom. According to Houston,

> In the order of creation man is a being destined for fellowship with God, and, since this is a relation to be realized in freedom, man, as God's creature, is endowed with freedom in the form of created spirit. The image of God in man becomes intelligible when it is understood in this sense, not as indicating some kind of amnity with

---

106. Hill and Walton, *A Survey of the Old Testament*, 179.
107. Macaulay and Barrs, *Being Human*, 55–56.
108. See Hendry, *The Holy Spirit in Christian Theology*, 117.

God inherent in man's creaturely structure, but as a relation freely willed by God and to be received by man in freedom. Now, when this relation is realized in the free correspondence of created with uncreated Spirit, the communion between them is of such a nature that, while the human spirit is not displaced by the divine, it is so open and receptive to the divine that it gladly yields place to it.[109]

Such restoration of freedom, as a gift of the Spirit, coincides with a liberation *from* the bondage of this world and *for* spiritual life. We have seen that Rom 8:2 presents such a liberty under the "law" or mastery of the Spirit, the One who "sets you free from the law of sin and death." With the law of God written on the heart, the believer's liberty now defines their *spirituality* in terms of an authority to claim one's freedom from external impositions. According to Morris,

> Other religions may press men down with a multitude of burdensome requirements. Other religions may interpose an indispensable hierarchy between the seeking soul and God. But Christianity introduces us to a sphere where all is of grace not law (did not Augustine say, "Love God and do what you like?"), a sphere where even the humblest believer has the right of immediate access to the Very Presence of God Himself (Heb. 10:19). The Spirit of God is within him. The Spirit of God informs and guides him. And where the Spirit is, there is freedom from pressing restraints. . . . The Christian feels himself subject indeed to the law of God. But this is a matter of inner conviction as well as of the Word of God. The Spirit of God within him works the necessary changes. As far as outward things are concerned he is completely free.[110]

Paul goes on to develop Romans 8 around this "law of the Spirit" theme, expanding on and describing the glorious freedom of God's children who live under the Spirit's authority. Such a liberty *from* the world translates into a ministerial authority *in* the world. Taylor explains how such a translation takes place through the assistance of the Spirit:

---

109. Hendry, *the Holy Spirit in Christian Theology*, 115–16. Hendry adds, "It is in the freedom of his spirit that man changes his freedom for God to a freedom from God. But man cannot in the freedom of his spirit reverse this change. That is the essential limitation upon the freedom of his spirit as created. Created spirit cannot choose the Creator as a possibility" (Hendry, *The Holy Spirit in Christian Theology*, 117).

110. Morris, *Spirit of the Living God*, 75.

The Authority of the Holy Spirit and Practical Theology: Christian Spirituality

> The person who is not free is the one who is always having to refer to some other source of authority and always having to look for someone else's approval. This means that he or she is always looking away from the business in hand to an external point of reference, like a child in a school play who cannot keep her eyes off the mistress-producer. . . . When the play takes over or the inner reality of persons . . . takes over, these [children] have their own authority to dictate how one is to respond to them. Then the response will be independent of external authority and may even be in defiance of it. Intrinsic truth will have set them free. This, moreover, is the only kind of authority which can demand obedience without diminishing the autonomy of the one who obeys. This is because the truth of another being addresses itself to the truth of oneself, and draws it out, compelling one to discover one's own truth more deeply and live it out more freely. . . . To be made alert towards that self-validating truth of "the other" is an annunciation of the Holy Spirit. That is how he shows "where wrong and right and judgment lie" (John 16:8).[111]

The Spirit's governing authority creates a *realm* of authority where the believer's liberty emerges in association with his or her vision of the eschatological kingdom. Paul indeed wants to make sure believers ground their thinking about the Spirit in the present eschatological order of things. Romans 8:22–23 connects the future liberation "of our bodies" with the present "firstfruit" of the Spirit. Fee points out that this metaphor elicits an eschatological vision based on the imagery of "harvest," one that "verifies that for Paul the Spirit was an essentially eschatological reality."[112] While this passage appears to portray *bondage* ("we ourselves groan within ourselves"), it begins Paul's integrative argument that moves toward his monumental conclusion that "nothing shall be able to separate us from the love of God, which is in Christ Jesus our Lord" (Rom 8:39).[113]

The believer's liberty *from* the world allows for a counter-cultural influence *in* the world marked by the Spirit's order, beauty, and creativity. Counter-cultural leadership is, of course, highlighted by genuine *risk* under

---

111. Taylor, *The Go-Between God*, 174–75.
112. Fee, *God's Empowering Presence*, 573.
113. This argument "pulls together, with the present reality of the Spirit as the key element, several feature of this eschatological tension" (Fee, *God's Empowering Presence*, 574).

the governing Spirit. The secure basis for this risk is the fact that the Spirit, as the believer's true "Governor," shapes his or her eschatological vision and brings forth this vision into present reality.

> The Spirit of God, however, enables us to risk dreams of an alternative world that can capture our imaginations and thereby liberate us from the constrictions of the dominant culture. It is only when we can imagine the world to be different from the way it is that we can be empowered to embody this alternative reality which is God's kingdom and resist this present nightmare of brokenness, disorientation, and confusion.[114]

Transformation

The "restoration" of the image of God in the believer necessitates a *spiritual transformation*. The "Spirit of Restoration" accomplishes this through sanctification. With a vision of the eschatological Kingdom intact, the Spirit works to sanctify believers by drawing them into and toward that vision. This occurs when one's *active submission* to the Spirit is hinged to the pattern of divine authority. As we have seen, the Spirit's sovereignty over our "spirit," "identification with Christ" through the Spirit, and the Spirit's illumination of Scripture are the foundational pieces of true spirituality. Nevertheless, if the believer's *praxis* of spirituality under the governing authority of the eschatological Spirit is not woven into this spiritual tapestry—particularly with respect to sanctification—there remains a static mysticism that does *not* result in transformation.

The believer's "ministerial authority" thereby appears to the world as evidence of the Spirit's governing authority through the believer's *praxis* of spirituality. Romans 8 indeed presents such a *praxis* as one that is activated by yielding to the sovereign Spirit who conducts our sanctification (8:2–11) and by actively "putting to death the deeds of the body" (8:12–13). Ironically,

---

114. Middleton and Walsh, *Truth is Stranger Than it Used to Be*, 192. Middleton and Walsh add, "Pentecost serves to remind us anew that no historical dead ends are final in God's scheme of things. The story of redemption can be opened up again—even after modernity—and a new dream of God's redemptive purposes can be imagined. But imagination and dreams are dangerous things. We have had enough experience of dreams being dashed on the cold rocks of reality or of their frightful transposition into nightmares" (192).

Paul appeals to the Spirit's sovereignty (i.e., Titus 3:5–6; Phil 2:12) not to discourage human participation in sanctification but instead to insist on it.

> The sovereignty of the Spirit and the principle of humanness are affirmed side by side in the New Testament. Indeed, far from nullifying it, the sure knowledge that the Spirit will work in me to change me and strengthen me establishes the necessity of my working out my own salvation. Rather than discouraging me, making me feel that I can only wait helplessly for the Spirit to work, the knowledge that the Spirit is the sovereign Lord over my life is a source of comfort and encouragement.[115]

Second Corinthians 3:17–18 speaks of those who are "being transformed" by the Spirit, as well as the manner in which this transformation becomes increasingly visible, "from glory to glory." Transformation is visible to all because in human weakness "the *glory* of the Lord" is exposed (3:18a). Believers exhibit a *non-fading reality* vis-à-vis "the Lord who is the Spirit" (3:18b), whereas "the letter" of the Old Covenant is fading away (3:6–7). While the Old Covenant was glorious but temporary, the glory of the New Covenant will remain forever. Since the *internal* sanctification of the Spirit trumps a purely *external* sanctification of the "letter," transformation demonstrates to the world that the Spirit has authority *over* human or religious effort and striving.[116]

Conclusion

The Holy Spirit is indeed "Lord" of the believer in every aspect of the word. His "plenipotentiary authority" creates an authoritative framework wherein the believer is able to develop to spiritual maturity. Whereas the Spirit provides a foundation for spirituality "under" his plenipotentiary authority, this spirituality is developed according to a specific pattern of divine authority. This includes a specific *identity* in accordance with his executorial authority, *guidance* in the context of discipleship relationships through his veracious authority, and an *activation* of the believer's "spiritual authority"

---

115. Macaulay and Barrs, *Being Human*, 103.

116. Sanctification demonstrates the contributions of the Spirit's divine authority, executorial authority, and veracious authority in the activation of his governing authority (as seen in Lev 22:32; 1 Cor 6:11; and 2 Thess 2:13, respectively).

in the world through his governing authority. Certainly the *experience* of spirituality in and under the Spirit's authority finds a spiritual depth and richness unknown without a sufficient understanding of this doctrine.

8

Conclusions and Implications of the Doctrine of the Authority of the Holy Spirit

❖ THE PURPOSE OF this book, as stated in chapter one, has been to discern how evangelicals might recover a biblical conception of the Holy Spirit's authority in and over the Church, one that could serve to provide a response to contemporary misconceptions of "Spirit." My aim was to recover this conception in systematic theology—both theoretically (by discerning the nature of the Spirit's authority within the overall pattern of authority) and practically (by showing how the Spirit's authority is brought to bear in hermeneutics, the structure of the church, and Christian spirituality).

In chapter one, this purpose was first addressed by defining the principle and pattern of divine authority and identifying the Spirit's place within this pattern. For those who may have viewed "authority" as essentially *transcendent*, chapter one asserted that divine authority is located in and yet immanently revealed by the three Persons of the Triune God (our *principle* of authority), and that this immanent revelation incorporates Christ, Scriptures, and the Holy Spirit (our *pattern* of authority).

In chapter two, several historical debates regarding the nature and work of the Holy Spirit were discussed, and provisional definitions of the Spirit's authority that seemed to emerge from these debates were identified. Those who wonder if church history has wrestled with questions relevant to the discussion of the Spirit's authority will find this chapter enlightening. This chapter also demonstrates that twenty-first century believers now stand in a privileged position—the Spirit's place within our "pattern of authority" indeed seems to have "played out" in theological history and can now be understood essentially *in its completion.*

In chapters three and four, an exegetically-based defense of the Spirit's authority was made. Our exegetical analysis led to formal descriptions for systematic theology—descriptions that (1) could serve to clarify a specific model of the Spirit's "plenipotentiary authority" as a "divine Person," "Executor," "Teacher," and "Governor," and (2) could effectively and correctively respond to various perspectives on the Spirit as proposed by postmodern and contemporary theologians. Many evangelical theologians will find that this model provides a needed defense of the Spirit's authority, one that can be substantiated biblically and within evangelical orthodoxy. In addition, many evangelical ministers will find these clarifications to be very helpful in discerning and exposing the basic presuppositions of postmodern and contemporary pneumatologies that appear today within a myriad of popular trends and ideologies.

Chapters five, six, and seven demonstrate that the model developed in chapters three and four is indeed applicable to "practical theology"—the theory and practice of hermeneutics, church structure and guidance, and Christian spirituality. For those who wrestle with these issues in the "praxis" of faith and ministry, these chapters will provide building blocks for developing a positive practice of theology that respects the Spirit's "plenipotentiary authority" within their particular context.

Further implications of this doctrine can now be examined in three crucial areas of concern: the "place" of this doctrine within evangelical theology, the "concerns" of postmodern and contemporary theology, and broader implications of this doctrine for other critical aspects of life and faith.

Implications for Evangelical Theology

Implications of the doctrine of the authority of the Holy Spirit for evangelical theology include the need for attention to the long-standing neglect of this doctrine as well as the need to find a more appropriate place for this doctrine within evangelical systematic theology.

Conclusions and Implications of the Doctrine of the Authority of the Holy Spirit

The Neglect of the Doctrine of the Spirit's Authority in Evangelical Theology

The neglect of the Holy Spirit can be seen as far back as Paul's encounter with the Ephesians, of whom he asked, "Did you receive the Holy Spirit when you believed?" They responded, "No, we have not even heard that there is a Holy Spirit" (Acts 19:2). Karkkainen indeed calls the Holy Spirit the "Cinderella of Theology."[1] When the two "sisters" went to the ball, she was left at home. According to Farley,

> Unlike the doctrine of the Trinity or the Church, the discussion of the Spirit has not stood on its own feet, so to speak. Most often pneumatological topics have been incorporated into the doctrine of salvation (soteriology).[2]

The Spirit has been called *theos agraptos* ("the God about whom nobody writes"), "the forgotten God" (by nineteenth century Catholics), and "the Unknown Third." According to Hiberath, our Western "forgetfulness" goes back to Augustine, who "de-personalized" the Spirit[3] (see chapter 2).

Indeed the "subtlety" of the doctrine of the Spirit's authority has often been missed by evangelical theologians as well, and this has resulted in a body of theology that often remains shortsighted in a number of ways. The neglect of this doctrine not only left the Church unprepared for the onslaught of postmodern pneumatologies, but also, and even more fundamentally, led to deficiencies within evangelical theology itself. Today there is not so much a complete forgetfulness of the Spirit as there is an unrelatedness of the Spirit to many of the other doctrines of theology, such as Christology, bibliology, etc.

The emphasis on the "work" or "function" or "economy" of the Spirit by contemporary theologians and popular preachers seems to have diminished our concern for the Spirit's *nature*. The Spirit seems to have become the easiest prey within some local churches for creating a *God in our own image*—an image of our experiential desires. Local churches thus need to re-emphasize the *personal and authoritative presence* of the Spirit, re-asserting

---

1. Karkkainen, *Pneumatology*, 16.
2. Ibid., 19.
3. Hilberath, "Identity through Self-Transcendence," 2–4.

the notion that *who he is* must be our biblical starting point for understanding *what he does*.

Due to the "subtle" nature of this doctrine, the authority of the Holy Spirit is not always recognized by the "untrained eye" (even though most Christians recognize that the Holy Spirit must possess some sort of authority). The Spirit shows up in places—and in doctrines—we might not always expect. In what specific ways has the Spirit's authority been subtly neglected in evangelical theology?

First, the Spirit's *divine authority* is neglected when we fail to recognize that the Holy Spirit who is *within* believers or *within* the fellowship of believers is also transcendent *over* believers, and in fact remains transcendent as he does his work in the world. Thus, the Spirit's work must always be recognized within the larger context of his divine personhood (rather than defining his nature by his work). The Spirit's authority as a *divine Person* can be identified in his roles as life-giver and as transcendent revealer of God's nature to the world. As we have seen, any view of the Spirit that diminishes his full divine personhood will lead to a reduction of our understanding of the Spirit's authority in its entirety. This is experienced in evangelical circles when our language of the Spirit's "filling" or "baptism" or "presence" takes precedent over any discussion of his *divinity* or *personhood*. This subtle shift in focus can be seen in dozens of popular evangelical books that wrestle to explain the doctrine and work of the Spirit in contemporary settings.[4]

Second, the Spirit's *executorial authority* is neglected when we speak of Christ's authority in relation to believers without referring to the Spirit who is sent "in my name" (John 14:26)—that is, with Christ's authority, to fulfill Christ's will in the world, and to bring glory to Christ. Since the Spirit is clearly presented in Scripture as *Christ's Executor*, we must not think of the Spirit simply as a *functional* agent in our salvation but rather as Christ's *authoritative* agent.[5]

---

4. Prater's book neglects the *nature* of the Spirit with respect to his eternality, transcendence, and role in creation (which he relegates to the Father alone). The only substantial role the Spirit fulfills is that of being "poured out on all flesh" (Prater, *The Presence*). Coleman's book similarly errs, asserting that "God is the Father in administration; God is the Son in revelation; but God is the Spirit in operation" (Coleman, *The Spirit and the Word*, 16).

5. See Ferguson, *The Holy Spirit*, 55.

Conclusions and Implications of the Doctrine of the Authority of the Holy Spirit

Third, the Spirit's *veracious authority* is neglected when the Bible is granted an "authority" not derived from the Spirit but one that is essentially self-authenticated or established on shallow descriptions. An example of this second error and its subtlety is provided by popular preacher John Piper, who asserts, "Today the New Testament stands where the apostles stood."[6] While this assertion is somewhat true, it neglects the Spirit of Truth who stands behind, inspires, and indeed *connects* these two authorities. Any "biblical authority" that is disconnected from the veracious authority of the Spirit will become a dry rationality. Speaking of the Boyle Lectures of the early eighteenth century, Lloyd-Jones states: "They were endeavouring to restore the authority of the Bible and the gospel, and to establish the Christian faith rationally. 'We must do something to get back the old authority,' they said."[7] Yet it was the Spirit speaking through the preaching of Whitefield, Wesley, and Edwards that brought forth revival. As we have seen, the Spirit is presented in Scripture as *Divine Teacher* or *Spirit of Truth*. Neglect occurs when the doctrine of the Spirit is placed "under" the doctrine of the Word rather than *over* the Word as the one who "reveals" God's mind *in the text* (i.e., as its inspirer) and *through the text* (as its illuminator).

Finally, the Spirit's *governing authority* is neglected when the Spirit is given a limited authority with respect to the church—that is, when "Lordship" refers to Christ and not the Spirit,[8] when "eschatological" refers to our future destiny but has little or no bearing on present church vision, or when the "authority" of God in the church is associated with the Father and the Son, but not the Spirit (i.e., the Spirit is viewed only *functionally* as the power to maintain fellowship or evangelize non-believers). In such cases the Church suffers from a subtle yet pervasive *deism*—a disconnection from the authority of the Triune God in the Church. The God who possesses sovereignty *over* the Church and displays authority *toward* the Church is not thought of as actually communicating this authority *within* the Church (i.e., as an immanent *Governor* guiding her affairs; as a blessing to be *experienced*). In the twentieth-century, efforts to restore the church's "authority" often included planned revivals and attempts to elevate the

---

6. Piper, "The Authority and Nature of the Gift of Prophecy," par. 6.
7. Lloyd-Jones, *Authority*, 67.
8. See Ferguson, *The Holy Spirit*, 55

authority of the preacher. In many cases, the result was a grave neglect of the Spirit's "realm" of authority within the Church and of the powerful "effects" only he can produce (i.e., democratization, liberation, transformation). Redemption is generalized as a work of God, forgetting that it incorporates such effects and that these redemptive effects display the magnitude of the Spirit's authoritative realm. As we have seen, the Spirit is presented in Scripture as "Governor" who rules in Christ's kingdom. In an effort to establish the church's "authority," the Spirit's governing authority has often been squelched.

> Now this is what grieves me. I very rarely hear any Christians today, even Evangelicals, praying for revival. What do they pray for? They pray for their own organized efforts, either at home or in various other lands. . . . I suggest seriously that we are neglecting the authority of the Holy Spirit. We are so interested in ourselves and in our own activities that that we have forgotten the one thing that can make us effective.[9]

How should all these aspects of the Spirit's authority be understood *together*? As we have seen, the Spirit's "plenipotentiary authority" incorporates all aspects, resulting in a single "authority" that cannot be divided except for the purpose of discussion. We must hold these aspects together in order to recognize whether or not the Spirit's fully integrated authority has been "unleashed" in the church. Whereas many ministers fear "chaos" may result if and when such an unleashing occurs, the Spirit's plenipotentiary authority actually ensures the precise order and balance presented to us in our pattern of divine authority. The Spirit *opens up* this divine pattern so that it can now find practical bearing *in relation to us*. The Spirit has the authority to demonstrate God's *Person, Mercy, Truth, and Power* in real church contexts. His authority allows us to understand God as the one who penetrates all aspects of life, to know God the Father intimately, and to bring forth glory to Christ in the fullest degree possible.

---

9. Lloyd-Jones, *Authority*, 92–93.

Conclusions and Implications of the Doctrine of the Authority of the Holy Spirit

The Place of the Doctrine of the Spirit's Authority in Evangelical Systematic Theology

Since our pattern of authority determines and prescribes the starting point for theology and hermeneutics, as Ramm has aptly pointed out,[10] this pattern needs to be given a place within systematic theology with respect to *theological prolegomena*. The doctrine of the Spirit's authority should therefore be incorporated as well into our prolegomena for evangelical systematic theology. The parameters of the Spirit's authority as divine Person, Executor, Teacher, and Governor indeed provide a *practical test* for assessing evangelical "orthodoxy" with respect to the doctrine of the Spirit. These parameters are particularly useful as local churches analyze and discern the veracity of a particular understanding of the Holy Spirit—particularly when hermeneutics, ecclesiology, and spirituality come into play. They also provide a test for other doctrines of the Christian faith that substantially confer the need to incorporate the Spirit's work (i.e., the doctrine of salvation or of sanctification).

The doctrine of the authority of the Holy Spirit provides theologians and ministers with a theological tool for discerning the myriad of perspectives encountered in church settings, particularly those congregations that have a profound hunger for spiritual *experience* but also seem confused with respect to the precise biblical boundaries for these experiences. A beauty of this doctrine is that the Spirit who provides boundaries for spiritual experience is the same Spirit who provides the experience itself. In fact, the Spirit is most fully released within the local church to move "where it wishes" (John 3:8) when such theological boundaries are secured.

The usefulness of such a doctrinal tool can be applied to an incredibly wide variety of discussions, and indeed the doctrine of the Spirit's authority often contributes to the shaping of the entire discussion. Here I will briefly illustrate its application to (1) spiritual gifts within the local church body, and (2) religious pluralism. First, spiritual gifts are not to be thought of as emerging from the believer's *own power or natural abilities*. Because of the Spirit's divine authority, there is always a distinction to be kept between spiritual gifts and one's own "natural gifts" and talents.[11] Second,

---

10. See Ramm, *The Pattern of Authority*, 20–26, 40–62.

11. There may certainly be a strong *correlation* between one's spiritual gifts and natural

spiritual gifts are always to be seen as a means of *glorifying Christ,* since the Spirit who disseminates spiritual gifts to us does so in accordance with his executorial authority. Third, the use of spiritual gifts can only occur under the Spirit's veracious authority, as the Spirit teaches us through the Word of God what it means to use our gifts *in truth* and for the purpose of "building up the body." Finally, spiritual gifts are to be *governed* by the Spirit, meaning that they will be disseminated under the Spirit's "realm" of authority ("as he wills," 1 Cor 12:11) and will provide "foretastes" of the eschatological kingdom through the display of specific "effects." These effects are, in fact, signs of the Spirit's democratization (they are given to all believers), liberation (believers are generally free to employ them in ways they see best), and transformation (they assist in the transformation of the body of Christ into the likeness of Christ).

As for religious pluralism, the evangelical trend today seems to be moving toward some sort of modified "inclusivism," where the Holy Spirit can indeed be found *in* other religions. Does such an understanding honor the Spirit's plenipotentiary authority, or is this simply a universalized version of the postmodern "Spirit?"

One of the most recent contributions to this discussion is Amos Yong's *Beyond the Impasse.* Yong's aim is to develop a "pneumatological approach to the theology of religions,"[12] and his essential message is that the Spirit is indeed at work outside the Church. At the same time, Yong proclaims that he is "not an exclusivist if one means by this not only that salvation is dependent in an ontological sense on the person and work of Christ but also that one has to cognitively recognize that dependence."[13] While there is not space to discuss Yong's overall work in depth, how might we use our model of the Spirit's authority as a "test" for this approach to the theology of religions? First, Yong emphasizes the Spirit's "omnipresence" and "universality" but neglects the Spirit's *transcendence, omniscience,* and *sovereignty.*[14] Second, Yong essentially rejects any subordination of the Spirit's mission within the present economy of salvation to Christ's mission

---

abilities, but the Spirit's empowerment will provide a qualitative difference in their use and purpose.

12. Yong, *Beyond the Impasse,* 20.
13. Ibid., 27.
14. See Yong, "Beyond the Impasse," 37–42.

(referring to Irenaeus' "two hands" of the Father as Word and Spirit, and essentially agreeing with the "inclusivist" model of Clark Pinnock with only mild reservations).[15] Third, Yong's approach to "the hermeneutics of discernment" seems to be "phenonemologically"—rather than textually—driven.[16] Finally, the Spirit in Yong's assessment does not appear to be "Governor" or "Lord" of the Church, but rather the one who facilitates "the mystery of communication."

Implications for Contemporary Theology

Stereotypical conceptions of Plato and Aristotle are that their bodies of philosophy can be summed up in terms of *transcendence* and *immanence*, respectively. Indeed some philosophers hold that all of philosophical history can be reduced to the ongoing struggle between these two opposing poles. Perhaps these stereotypes were most evidenced in the Middle Ages, with *realists* (who held to real universals—eternal archetypes of the things we see and touch) following Plato and *nominalists* (who rejected universals) following Aristotle.[17] Contemporary theologians, in general, feel that both of these models should be dismissed.

The "Problem of Authority"

Kant summarized the above debate by pitting "noumenal" (supernatural) knowledge against "phenomenal" (natural, rational) knowledge. In doing so, Kant stated what philosophy had refused to admit—that there could no longer be an integration of these dichotomous epistemologies within philosophy itself. He did not envision a resolution within theology either, and because of this his philosophy led to Deism and skepticism (and ultimately, despair). "[Kant] has built his own trap: having located satisfaction in phenomenal (temporal) reality, how can he still acknowledge hope for happiness in the noumenal life?"[18]

Kant's epistemological impasse seems to be confirmed in scripture, which openly admits the inability of "non-believers" to receive and un-

15. Ibid., 43–44, 106–27.
16. Ibid., 149–61.
17. See Brown, *Philosophy and the Christian Faith*, 19.
18. Rutler, *Christ and Reason*, 13.

derstand revelation (1 Cor 2:10–14). Schaeffer points to the modern (and postmodern) despair painted by Kant:

> Modern man is left either downstairs as a machine with words that do not lead either to value or facts but only to works, or he is left upstairs in a world without categories in relation to human values, moral values, or the difference between reality and fantasy. Weep for our generation![19]

While Hegel's "philosophy of the Holy Spirit" did make a slight dent in "Kant's box" (reminding us that the nature of "Spirit" is ultimately *dynamic*) it could not go beyond the actual *words* of philosophy (and its reliance upon rationality) to "get at" the divine *Being* in self-revelation. Though Hegel's rendering of "Spirit" does attempt to discover the "revelation" of the nature of things noumenal within the realm of things phenomenal, Hegel could not comprehend a "Spirit" that reveals the mind or nature of God, nor could he attain a notion of the essential Personhood inherent in the biblical conception of the Holy Spirit. As a result, Hegel was *not* able to speak of the Spirit's "authority," but only of "Spirit" in terms of "absolute real being," "immediate truth," or "actuality of [ethical] substance."[20] These concepts, however, are phenomenologically, rather than revelationally, discovered. As a result, many contemporary philosophers now proclaim that the "problem of philosophy" today is a problem of *authority* (and specifically *hermeneutical authority*).[21]

Listening to Postmodern Pneumatology

How have postmodern and contemporary perspectives on "Spirit" attempted to address this problem of authority? As we have seen, postmodern pneumatology looks to develop a modified version of the Hegelian project,

19. Schaeffer, *He is There and He is Not Silent*, 58.
20. See Hegel, *Phenomenology of Spirit*, 263–66.
21. Sociologically speaking, this problem is evidenced in the *loss of institutional power* associated with medieval hegemony and the loss of *unity* associated with modernity. Such "medieval" and "modern" approaches to authority included: (1) the Roman Church (an authority of *tradition*), (2) the Protestant Church (the authority of *scripture alone*), and (3) science (authority of *reason* and *empiricism*). As a result of this abandonment of these authorities, postmodern "authorities" are essentially political (authority resides with the one who has the power).

adopting his idea of a dynamic "Spirit" for theology (one that is understood phenomenologically) while criticizing Hegel's extreme reliance on *rationality*. Most contemporary pneumatologists (i.e., Moltmann, Welker, Hodgson), as well as most "postmodern" believers in general, are crying for an *experience* of the Spirit in the world. This seems to be particularly true of those in previously "sterile" religious circles, where "revelation" was only thought of in terms of the biblical text, and the Spirit only as its Inspirer.[22] Postmodern pneumatology seeks to recover the experience of God by moving beyond the transcendence of the Father and the Son and by looking now to the Spirit as the one who proffers *immanence*.[23] In effect, such pneumatology seeks a fullness of the Spirit's *governing authority*—one that can be experienced as a spiritual "realm" with powerful "effects"—without adequate biblical discussion regarding the Spirit's divine, executorial, veracious authority.[24] We need to listen closely to such postmodern voices in that they hold out to us the *genuine needs and deficiencies* experienced within many churches—particularly the need for the experience of the Spirit as God's *immanent power* (i.e., Moltmann), as *liberator* (i.e., Hodgson), and as "community" (i.e., Welker).

22. As we have seen, Moltmann represents the postmodern desire for a theology that overcomes a form of "revelation" that cannot be experienced and wants to avoid "the false alternative between divine revelation and human experience of the Holy Spirit" (Moltmann, *The Spirit of Life*, 5).

23. Moltmann says, "But the real phenomenon is to be found neither in the Spirit's immanence nor in its transcendence, neither in the continuity nor in the discontinuity. It is to be found in God's *immanence* in human experience, and in the *transcendence* of human beings in God. Because God's Spirit is present in human beings, the human spirit is self-transcendently aligned towards God. Anyone who stylized revelation and experience into alternatives ends up with revelations that cannot be experienced, and experiences without revelation." (Moltmann, *The Spirit of Life*, 7).

24. In particular, by forgetting the Spirit's divine transcendence, this approach runs the danger of encountering the Triune God in his full divine authority but without the redemption of Christ. When the *Spiritus Creator* reveals himself as divine authority to sinful humanity, the results are "conviction" (John 16:8) and frustration (1 Cor 2:10–14). The presence of the *Holy* Spirit without the mercy of Christ certainly *will* result in a vivid experience—the *judgment of God*. This sort of contemporary approach to the resolution of the problem of authority deserves our attention (and compassion), for in their present search for experience (i.e. "peace with God" or "spiritual power") contemporary theologians may well end up with the exact *opposite* of what they seek.

The Solution

As we have seen postmodern pneumatology often opts for panentheistic redefinitions of God—as one who *becomes* Spirit in and through relationship with the world.[25] In this study we have learned that the Spirit's governing authority—and the postmodern desire for the *experience of God* within the church—can only be realized within the context of the Spirit's "plenipotentiary authority" as it emerges from the principle and pattern of divine authority.

Our pattern of divine authority, however, resolves the "problem of authority" in a way that accounts for these postmodern concerns. Our pattern first informs us that Jesus Christ, as the "Word made flesh," embodies this solution by revealing God incarnationally, reinterpreting the law through *mercy*. Our pattern then tells us the fullness of the person and truth of Christ is *still available* through the Spirit, who reveals Christ to the church in all his glory and authority. This pattern of authority is thereby a sufficient revelation of the character of God in the world. Christ's redemptive power, when applied by the Spirit in conjunction with the Scriptures, brings forth the experience of God's power, liberation, and community. In particular, the doctrine of the Spirit's authority resolves the contemporary problem of authority in philosophy (i.e., transcendence vs. immanence) by searching out and revealing the mind of God to us (1 Cor 2:10–11), thus eliminating the problem by allowing us to "know the things freely given to us by God" (2:12b). The postmodern search for "Spirit" ends in a recovery of the Holy Spirit "who is from God" (2:12a), who is both transcendent *and* immanent. To speak only of his transcendence leads to a deistic or idealistic understanding of the Spirit. To speak only of his immanence leads to a process or open theism, a "god of the world," or a world-spirit. The authority of the Spirit, however, provides what philosophy cannot—a transcendent/immanent reality accessible by humanity. The answer to the "problem of authority" is the authoritative Spirit *revealing* the character, knowledge, and will of God in our immediate context and *governing* our lives, churches, and ministries so that we might fulfill the purposes of the Father and glorify the Son.

As a result, re-introducing the Holy Spirit as one having authority may come as a welcomed surprise to many postmodern sympathizers.

---

25. Hodgson, *Winds of the Spirit*, 140.

Conclusions and Implications of the Doctrine of the Authority of the Holy Spirit

"Postmodern" ministries, with their concern for the holistic needs, passions, and contexts of people should find in this doctrine a "non-oppressive" authority that provides for both firm boundaries and rich experience in local ecclesial settings.

Further "Practical" Implications

A prevailing sense of "ambiguity" regarding the authority of the Spirit—particularly in some evangelical, charismatic, and Pentecostal movements—often leads to either an attempt to "control" the Spirit or to a general dismissal of definitions regarding "Spirit." What results is a lack of understanding of the Spirit's work in the church. How might this be resolved?

Theocentric Living and the Praxis of Theology "Under" the Spirit's Plenipotentiary Authority

A "practice of theology" within the pattern of authority results in a true integration of the practices of biblical hermeneutics, church structure and guidance, and Christian spirituality under the Spirit's authoritative realm. While our model indeed becomes a vital tool for discerning "practical theology," the actual working out of this model *in* practical theology is just as integral to the reality of the model itself. The illustration of a hunter who studies, cleans, loads, and cocks his rifle comes to mind. Unless he pulls the trigger, there is *no* purposeful impact. In fact, all the preparation was essentially *wasted*. So we must now choose to *live* in and under the authority of the Spirit, both individually and corporately.

Theocentric living involves an abandon of all of life to the glory and honor of God. This is accomplished only by living "under" God's authority so that each step of our spiritual journey can be informed by his Word and directed by his Spirit. Being "under authority," however, is impossible without the *presence* of the one in authority. A ruler, teacher, or ethic that remains irrelevant to life or disconnected from "real issues" will only invite rebellion. The "authority of the Spirit" resolves this dilemma by *re-presenting* the authority of the Father and the Son *to us*. In this respect, the Spirit is the true *Lord* of our lives as well (in that we understand "Lordship" to include control, authority and *presence*). With this perspective of the Spirit's authority, we can embrace the Spirit as the *divine authoritative presence* that also incorporates God's heart, passions, and emotions—including his joy, grief, wrath, love, compassion, tenderness, care—and even his suffering.

Understanding the Spirit's authority with respect to one's personal "life span" opens the door for developing life-purpose. Whereas an "existential" (or "nihilistic") view of history and reality only leads to a personal sense of meaninglessness and a "pantheistic" (or cyclical) view to a sense of hopelessness, a theistic perspective restores a sense of "linear" purpose (according to God's eschatological purposes) "under" the Spirit. "Purpose" in this light might be defined as the integration of all activities toward a single focal point, one that gives meaning to each activity. It answers the "why" questions of life. The spiritual connection between one's purpose and activities (mission) can only be established in the Spirit, who integrates each aspect of the "heart," including *mind*, *soul*, and *actions* (generally speaking, this integration occurs through the Spirit's authority with respect to hermeneutics, the local church, and Christian spirituality, respectively). This brings forth integrity of life, thought, and convictions as a full witness to the Spirit's authority.

Other "Practical" Areas Requiring Further Study

Still to be investigated are the implications for developing the doctrine of the Spirit's authority with respect to several other crucial issues. First, how does the Spirit provide moral and administrative influence and structure with respect to the various aspects of *natural* and *human government*? Specifically, how does the Spirit govern the cosmos (i.e., physical and electromagnetic laws; see Gen 1:1–2; Ps 104:29–30), the nations (i.e., their structure, law, and, policies, dominion, economics, environment, defense; see Num 11:17; 1 Sam 16:3), families (i.e., marriage, child-raising, elderly care, death and dying; see Jer 31:1; Isa 59:11; 63:11), and the "self" (i.e., conscience, mind, psychology; see Rom 8:2–6, 9, 13)? Second, how might we recognize the Spirit's authority with respect to the development of the cultures of the world (Acts 17:24–28) and in the artist's skills (Exod 31:3)? Finally, how will the Spirit display his authority in the eschatological kingdom? In what way will his authority be of vital importance to those enduring a "Great Tribulation" (1 Thess 1:6; Rev 14:13)?

Bibliography

Aagaard, A. M. "The Holy Spirit in the World." *ST* 28 (1974) 154.
Aalen, S. "Glory." In *NIDNTT*, 2:44–46.
Alexander, Donald L., editor. *Christian Spirituality: Five Views of Sanctification.* Downers Grove, IL: InterVarsity, 1988.
Alexander, Joseph Addison. *The Psalms: Translated and Explained.* Grand Rapids: Zondervan, 1964.
Alston, William P. "The Indwelling of the Holy Spirit." In *Philosophy and the Christian Faith*, 121–31. Notre Dame: Univ. of Notre Dame Press, 1988.
———. *Illocutionary Acts and Sentence Meaning.* Ithaca, NY: Cornell University Press, 2000.
Anderson, A. A. *Psalms 100–150.* New Century Bible Commentary. Grand Rapids: Eerdmans, 1981.
Archer, Kenneth J. "Forging a New Path: A Contemporary Pentecostal Hermeneutical Strategy for the Twenty-First Century." PhD diss., St. Andrews University, 2001.
Armerding, Carl Edwin. "When the Spirit Came Mightily: The Spirituality of Israel's Charismatic Leaders." In *Alive to God: Studies in Spirituality Presented to James Houston.* Downers Grove, IL: InterVarsity, 1992.
Arrington, French L. "The Use of the Bible by Pentecostals." *Pneuma* 16 (Spr 1994) 101–7.
Athanasius. "First Letter to Serapion." Translated by C. R. B. Shapland. *The Letters of Saint Athanasius Concerning the Holy Spirit.* London: Epworth, 1951.
———. "Third Letter to Serapion." Translated by C. R. B. Shapland. *The Letters of Saint Athanasius Concerning the Holy Spirit.* London: Epworth, 1951.
Augustine. "De Trinitate." In *The Fathers of the Church* 45. Translated by Stephan McKenna. Washington DC: Catholic University of America Press, 1963.
Authority, Conscience, and Dissent. Christchurch, New Zealand: National Council of Churches, 1971.
Averbeck, R. E. "Holy." In *NIDOTTE*, 3:687–89.
Badcock, Gary D. *Light of Truth and Fire of Love: A Theology of the Holy Spirit.* Grand Rapids: Eerdmans, 1997.
Balthasar, Hans Urs von. *Theodrama* I. Translated by Graham Harrison. San Francisco: Ignatius, 1988.
Barrett, C. K. *The First Epistle to the Corinthians.* Black's New Testament Commentaries. Peabody, MA: Hendrickson, 1968.
———. *The Gospel according to St. John.* London: SPCK, 1955.
———. *The Holy Spirit and the Gospel Tradition.* London: SPCK, 1970.

Bibliography

———. *The Second Epistle to the Corinthians.* Harper's New Testament Commentaries. New York: Harper & Row, 1973.
Barrs, Jerram, and Ronald Macaulay. *Being Human.* Downers Grove, IL: InterVarsity, 1978.
Barth, Karl. *Church Dogmatics*, I, III. Translated by Geoffrey W. Bromiley. Edinburgh: T. & T. Clark, 1960.
———. *The Holy Ghost and the Christian Life.* Translated by R. Birch Hoyle. London: Muller, 1938.
Bartholomew, Craig, et al, editors. *After Pentecost: Language and Biblical Interpretation.* Grand Rapids: Zondervan, 2001.
Bauckham, Richard J. *Jude, 2 Peter.* WBC 50. Waco, TX: Word, 1983.
Bauer, Walter. *A Greek-English Lexicon of the New Testament and Other Early Christian Literature*, 2d ed. Edited by William F. Arndt, F. Wilbur Gingrich and Frederick W. Danker. Chicago: University of Chicago, 1958.
Baxter, Richard *The Practical Works of Richard Baxter* V. Ligonier, PA: Soli Deo Gloria, 1990.
Beasley-Murray, George R. *John.* WBC 36. Waco, TX: Word, 1987.
———. "John 3:3, 5: Baptism, Spirit and the Kingdom." *ExpT* 97 (1986) 167–70.
Becker, U., and D. Muller. "Proclamation." In *NIDNTT*, 2:44–46.
Berkhof, Hendrikus. *The Doctrine of the Holy Spirit.* Richmond: John Knox, 1964.
Berman, Harold J. *Law and Revolution: The Formation of the Western Legal Tradition.* Cambridge: Harvard University Press, 1983.
Betz, O. "Might." In *NIDNTT*, 2:606–8.
Bevans, Stephen B. "God Inside Out: Toward a Missionary Theology of the Holy Spirit." *IBMR* 22 (1998) 102–5.
Bloesch, Donald. *The Holy Spirit.* Downers Grove, IL: InterVarsity, 2000.
Bock, Darrell L. "Current Messianic Activities and OT Davidic Promise: Dispensationalism, Hermeneutics, and NT Fulfillment." *TJ* (1994) 57–87.
———. "The Kingdom of God in New Testament Theology: The Battle, The Christ, The Spirit-Bearer, and Returning Son of Man." Unpublished paper presented at 51st Annual Meeting of the Evangelical Theological Society, Danvers, MA (Nov. 19, 1999).
———. "The Son of David and the Saints' Task: The Hermeneutics of Initial Fulfillment." *BibSac* 150 (1993) 452.
Bolich, Gregory G. *Authority and the Church.* Washington DC: University Press of America, 1982.
Bonhoeffer, Dietrich. *The Communion of Saints: A Dogmatic Inquiry into the Society of the Church.* Translated by R. G. Smith et al. New York: Harper & Row, 1963.
Borgmann, Albert. *Crossing the Postmodern Divide.* Chicago: University of Chicago Press, 1992.
Braaten, Carl E., and Robert W. Jenson, editors. *Union with Christ: The New Finnish Interpretation of Luther.* Grand Rapids: Eerdmans, 1998.
Bray, Gerald. "The Double Procession of the Holy Spirit in Evangelical Theology Today: Do We Still Need It?" *JETS* 41 (1998) 415–26.
Breck, John *The Spirit of Truth: The Origins of Johannine Pneumatology.* Crestwood, NY: St. Vladimir's Seminary Press, 1991.

Brito, Emilio. "Hermeneutique et Pneumatologie selon Schleiermacher." *EphTL* 69 (1993) 88–117.
Brown, Colin, editor. *New International Dictionary of New Testament Theology*. Grand Rapids: Zondervan, 1986.
———. "Revelation." In *NIDNTT*, 3:315.
———. *Philosophy and the Christian Faith*. Downers Grove, IL: InterVarsity, 1968.
Brown, Francis, S. R. Driver, and Charles A. Briggs, *The New Brown-Driver-Briggs-Gesenius Hebrew and English Lexicon with an Appendix Containing the Biblical Aramaic*. Peabody, MA: Hendrickson, 1979.
Brown, Harold O. J. "On Method and Means in Theology." In *Doing Theology in Today's World*, 147–70. Grand Rapids: Zondervan, 1991.
Bruce, F. F. *The Acts of the Apostles: The Greek Text with Introduction and Commentary*. 2d ed. London: Tyndale, 1952.
———. *The Gospel of John*. Grand Rapids: Eerdmans, 1983.
Bruner, Dale. "The Son is Inside Out: A Response to Stephen B. Bevans, S.V.D." *IBMR* 22 (Jl 1998) 106.
Buchanan, James. *The Office and Work of the Holy Spirit*. New York: Carter, 1849.
Buckley, James J., and David S. Yeago. "Introduction." In *Knowing the Triune God*, 1–22. Grand Rapids: Eerdmans, 2001.
———, editors. *Knowing the Triune God*. Grand Rapids: Eerdmans, 2001.
Bullinger, E. W. *Word Studies on the Holy Spirit*. Grand Rapids: Kregel, 1979.
Bultmann, Rudolf. *Theology of the New Testament*. Translated by Kendrick Grobel. New York: Scribners, 1951.
Burge, Gary M. *The Anointed Community*. Grand Rapids: Eerdmans, 1987.
Burrell, David B. "The Spirit and the Christian Life." In *Christian Theology*, 302–27. Philadelphia: Fortress, 1986.
Burrows, William R. "A Seventh Paradigm? Catholics and Radical Inculturation." In *Mission in Bold Humility: David Bosch's Works Considered*, 121–38. Maryknoll, NY: Orbis, 1996.
Calvin, John. *Commentary on the Gospel according to John*. Translated by William Pringle. Grand Rapids: Eerdmans, 1949.
———. *Institutes of the Christian Religion*. Translated by Ford Lewis Battles. Philadelphia: Westminster, 1960.
Campenhausen, Hans von. *Ecclesiastical Authority and Spiritual Power*. London: Adam and Charles Black, 1969.
Carlson, Arnold E. "Luther and the Doctrine of the Holy Spirit." *LQ* 11 (1959) 135–46.
Carson, D. A. *The Gospel according to John*. Pillar New Testament Commentary. Grand Rapids: Eerdmans, 1999.
———. *The Sermon on the Mount*. Grand Rapids: Zondervan, 1978.
———. *Showing the Spirit: A Theological Exposition of 1 Corinthians 12–14*. Grand Rapids: Baker, 1987.
Carson, D. A., and John D. Woodbridge, editors. *Hermeneutics, Authority, and Canon*. Grand Rapids: Baker, 1995.
———, editors. *Scripture and Truth*. Grand Rapids: Baker, 1992.

Bibliography

Champion, Leonard G. "The Baptist Doctrine of the Church in Relation to Scripture, Tradition, and the Holy Spirit." *Foundations* 2 (1959) 27–39.

Chatman, Seymour. *Story and Discourse: Narrative Structure in Fiction and Film*. Ithaca, NY: Cornell University Press, 1978.

Chen, Chantel. "Tabernacle of Moses: What is it?" GoodSeed International. No pages. Online: http://www.the-tabernacle-place.com/tabernacle_articles/what_is_the_tabernacle.aspx

Chilton, Bruce. "God in Strength: Jesus' Announcement of the Kingdom." In *SNTU* 1. Freistadt: Plöchl, 1979.

Clarke, A. *Christian Theology*. Salem, OH: Schmul, 1990.

Clowney, Edmund P. *The Church*. Downers Grove, IL: InterVarsity, 1995.

Clyde Johnson, Robert. *Authority in Protestant Theology*. Philadelphia: Westminster, 1959.

Coleman, Robert. *The Spirit and the Word: Bible Lessons for Spirit-filled Christians*. Old Tappan, NJ: Spire, 1975.

Collins, Raymond F. *First Corinthians*. Sacra Pagina 7. Collegeville, MN: Liturgical, 1999

Comblin, José. *The Holy Spirit and Liberation*. Translated by Paul Burns. Theology and Liberation Series. Maryknoll, NY: Orbis, 1989.

Congar, Yves M. J. *I Believe in the Holy Spirit*. 3 vols. Translated by David Smith. New York: Seabury, 1983.

———. *The Word and the Spirit*. Translated by David Smith. San Francisco: Harper & Row, 1986.

Cottrell, Jack. *What the Bible Says about God the Creator*. Joplin, MO: College Press, 1983.

Cragg, Gerald R. *Freedom and Authority: A Study of English Thought in the Early Seventeenth Century*. Philadelphia: Westminster, 1975.

Crenshaw, James L., and Samuel Sandmel, editors. *The Divine Helmsman: Studies on God's Control of Human Events Presented to Lou H. Silberman*. New York: Ktav, 1980.

Cross, Terry L. Review of *Flame of Love*, by Clark Pinnock. *JPT* 13 (1998) 18–20.

Cumming, James Elder. *Through The Eternal Spirit*. Minneapolis: Bethany Fellowship, 1985.

Curran, John T. "The Teaching of II Peter 1:20: On the Interpretation of Prophecy." *TS* 4 (1943) 351–52.

Dahood, Mitchell. *Psalm III: 101–150*. AB 17A. Garden City, NY: Doubleday, 1970.

Dallavalle, Nancy A. Review of *God the Spirit*, by Michael Welker. *TS* 56 (1995) 796.

Dana, H. E., and Julius R. Mantey, *A Manual Grammar of the Greek New Testament*. New York: Macmillan, 1927.

Danker, Fredrick William, editor. *A Greek-English Lexicon of the New Testament and other Early Christian Literature*. 3d ed. Chicago: University of Chicago, 2000.

Davies, Rupert. *Religious Authority in an Age of Doubt*. London: Epworth, 1968.

Davison, A. B. "The Person and Work of the Holy Spirit." *London Quarterly Review* (April 1905) 211.

DeGeorge, Richard T. *The Nature and Limits of Authority*. Lawrence: University Press of Kansas, 1985.

Deissler, Alfons. "The Theology of Psalm 104." In *Standing Before God: Studies on Prayer in Scriptures and in Tradition with Essays in Honor of John M. Oesterreicher*, edited by Asher Kinkel and Lawrence Frizzell, 31–40. New York: Ktav, 1981.

Bibliography

Del Colle, Ralph. "Spirit-Christology: Dogmatic Foundations for Pentecostal-Charismatic Spirituality." *JPT* 3 (1993) 93–112.
Dorman, Ted M. "Holy Spirit, History, Hermeneutics and Theology." *JETS* (1998) 427–38.
Dowey, Edward A., Jr. *The Knowledge of God in Calvin's Theology.* Grand Rapids: Eerdmans, 1994.
Dumbrell, William J. "Spirit and Kingdom of God in the Old Testament." *RTR* 33 (Jan-April 1974) 1–10.
Dunn, James D. G. "1 Corinthians 15:45: Last Adam, Life-giving Spirit." In *Christ and Spirit in the New Testament*, 127–41. Cambridge: Cambridge University Press, 1973.
———. *The Christ and the Spirit, Vol. 1: Christology.* Grand Rapids: Eerdmans, 1998.
———. *The Christ and the Spirit, Vol. 2: Pneumatology.* Grand Rapids: Eerdmans, 1998.
———. *Jesus and the Spirit.* Grand Rapids: Eerdmans, 1975.
———. "Spirit and Kingdom." *ExpT* 82 (1970) 36–40.
Dupre, Louis. "Hegel's Absolute Spirit: A Religious Justification of Secular Culture." *Revue de l'Universite' d'Ottawa/University of Ottawa Quarterly* 52 (1982) 555.
———. "The Absolute Spirit and the Religious Legitimation of Modernity." In *Christian Spirituality and the Culture of Modernity*. Stuttgart: Klett-Cotta, 1984.
Easley, Kendall H. "The Pauline Usage of πνευματι as a Reference to the Spirit of God." *JETS* 27 (1984) 299–313.
Eichrodt, Walter. *Theology of the Old Testament.* Vol. 1. Translated by J. A. Baker. Old Testament Library. Philadelphia: Westminster, 1961.
———. *Theology of the Old Testament.* Vol. 2. Translated by J. A. Baker. Old Testament Library. Philadelphia: Westminster, 1967.
Eno, Robert B. "Pope and Council: The Patristic Origins." *ScEs* 28 (1976) 183–211.
Erickson, Millard J. *Christian Theology.* 2d ed. Grand Rapids: Baker, 2000.
———. *Concise Dictionary of Christian Theology.* Grand Rapids: Baker, 1994.
Elwell, Walter A., editor. *Evangelical Dictionary of Theology.* Grand Rapids: Baker, 1984.
Esser, H. H. "Grace." In *NIDNTT*, 2:123.
Evdokimov, Paul. *La Nouveaute' de l'Espirit.* Translated by D. Bloesch. Begroes en Mauges: Abbaye Bellefontaine, 1977.
Farley, Edward. *Ecclesial Reflection: An Anatomy of Theological Method.* Philadelphia: Fortress, 1982.
Farrer, Austin Marsden. *Saving Belief: A Discussion of Essentials.* New York: Morehouse-Barlow, 1964.
Fee, Gordon D. *God's Empowering Presence: The Holy Spirit in the Letters of Paul.* Peabody, MA: Hendrickson, 1994.
———. *The First Epistle to the Corinthians.* NICNT. Grand Rapids: Eerdmans, 1987.
———. *Gospel and Spirit: Issues in New Testament Hermeneutics.* Peabody, MA: Hendrickson, 1991.
———. *Listening to the Spirit in the Text.* Grand Rapids: Eerdmans, 2000.
———. "Some Reflections on Pauline Spirituality." In *Alive to God: Studies in Spirituality Presented to James Houston.* Downers Grove, IL: InterVarsity, 1992.
Feenstra, Ronald J., and Cornelius Plantinga, Jr., editors. *Trinity, Incarnation, and Atonement.* Notre Dame: University of Notre Dame Press, 1989.
Feinberg, J. S. "Theism." In *EDOT*, 1082.

Bibliography

Ferguson, Sinclair B. *The Holy Spirit*. Downers Grove, IL: InterVarsity, 1996.
Fiddes, Paul S. *Participating in God: A Pastoral Doctrine of the Trinity*. London: Darton, Longman and Todd, 2000.
Fisher, John. *La Documentation Catholique* 942 (8 July 1945) col. 481.
Forde, Gerhard O. "A Lutheran Response." In *Christian Spirituality: Five Views of Sanctification*. Downers Grove, IL: InterVarsity, 1988.
Forsyth, P. T. "The Divine Self-Emptying." In *God the Holy Father*. London: Independent Press, 1957.
———. *The Principle of Authority in Relation to Certainty, Sanctity, and Society*. London: Independent Press, 1952.
Fortman, Edmund. *The Triune God*. Grand Rapids: Baker, 1972.
Foucault, Michel. *The Order of Things: An Archaeology of the Human Sciences*. New York: Random House-Pantheon, 1970.
Fowl, Stephen E. *Engaging Scripture: A Model for Theological Interpretation*. Malden, MA: Blackwell, 1998.
Frame, John M. *The Doctrine of the Knowledge of God: A Theology of Lordship*. Phillipsburg, NJ: Presbyterian and Reformed Publishing, 1987.
Franklin, S. T. "Panentheism." In *EDOT*: 819–20.
Gadamer, Hans Georg. *Truth and Method*. 2d rev. edition. Translated by Joel Weinsheimer and Donald G. Marshall. New York: Crossroad, 1989.
Garland, David E. *2 Corinthians*. NAC 29. Nashville: Broadman & Holman, 1999.
Garner, Bryan A., editor. *Black's Law Dictionary*, 7th ed. St. Paul, MN: West, 1999.
Garrett, Duane A., and Richard R. Melick, Jr., editors. *Authority and Interpretation: A Baptist Perspective*. Grand Rapids: Baker, 1987.
Gaybba, Brian. *The Spirit of Love*. London: Chapman, 1987.
Gergen, Kenneth J. *The Saturated Self: Dilemmas of Identity in Contemporary Life*. New York: Basic Books, 1991.
Gordon, A. J. *The Ministry of the Spirit*. Minneapolis: Bethany Fellowship, 1964.
Green, Joel B. *Hearing the New Testament*. Grand Rapids: Eerdmans, 1995.
———. *How to Read Prophecy*. Downers Grove, IL: InterVarsity, 1984.
Green, Michael. *2 Peter and Jude*. TNTC. Grand Rapids: Eerdmans, 1991.
———. *The Second General Epistle of Peter and the General Epistle of Jude*. Grand Rapids: Eerdmans, 1991.
Greenwood, D. "The Lord Is the Spirit—Some Considerations of 2 Cor. 3:17." *CBQ* 34 (1972) 467–72.
Gregg, Robert C., and Dennis E. Groh. *Early Arianism*. London: SCM, 1981.
Gregory of Nazianzus. *On the Holy Spirit*. Nicene and Post-Nicene Fathers (Second Series) 7. Edited by Alexander Roberts, et al. Peabody, MA: Hendrickson, 1994.
———. *Select Orations of St. Gregory Nazianzen: Five Theological Orations*. Translated by Charles Brown and James Swallow. Edinburgh: T. & T. Clark.
Gregory of Nyssa. *On the Baptism of Christ*. Nicene and Post-Nicene Fathers, 2d Series 5.
Grenz, Stanley, and John R. Franke, *Beyond Foundationalism: Shaping Theology in a Postmodern Context*. Louisville: Westminster John Knox, 1991.
Grenz, Stanley J. *A Primer on Postmodernism*. Grand Rapids: Eerdmans, 1996.
———. *Divine Discourse*. Cambridge: Cambridge University Press, 1995.

———. *Revisioning Evangelical Theology: A Fresh Agenda for the Twenty-first Century.* Downers Grove, IL: InterVarsity, 1993.
———. "The Holy Spirit: Divine Love Guiding Us Home." *Ex Auditu* 12 (1996) 1–10.
———. "The Spirit and the Word: The World Creating Function of the Text." *TTo* 57 (2000) 35–74.
Griffith Thomas, W. H. *The Holy Spirit of God.* Grand Rapids: Eerdmans, 1955.
Grudem, Wayne. *Gift of Prophecy in 1 Corinthians.* Washington DC: University Press of America, 1982.
———. "Scripture's Self-Attestation and the Problem of Formulating a Doctrine of Scripture." In *Scripture and Truth*, 19–64. Grand Rapids: Baker, 1992.
———. *Systematic Theology.* Grand Rapids: Zondervan, 2000.
Gruenler, Royce Gordon. *Meaning and Understanding.* Grand Rapids: Zondervan, 1991.
Gunton, Colin E. Review of *The Spirit of Life*, by Jürgen Moltmann. *JTS* 45 (1994) 789.
———. *The One, The Three and the Many.* New York: Cambridge, 1993.
———. *Theology through the Theologians.* Edinburgh: T. & T. Clark, 1996.
Guthrie, Donald. *The Pastoral Epistles.* TNTC. Grand Rapids: Eerdmans, 1991.
———. *The Pastoral Epistles: An Introduction and Commentary.* Grand Rapids: Eerdmans, 1990.
Guthrie, Shirley C. Review of *Winds of the Spirit*, by Peter C. Hodgson. *TTo* 53 (1996) 379–80.
Hafemann, S. J. *Paul, Moses, and the History of Israel: The Letter/Spirit Contrast and the Argument from Scripture in 2 Corinthians 3.* Peabody, MA: Hendrickson, 1996.
Hall, Francis. *Authority: Ecclesiastical and Biblical.* Pelham Manor, NY: The American Church Union, 1968.
Hall, Ronald J. *Word and Spirit: A Kierkegaardian Critique of the Modern Age.* Bloomington: Indiana University Press, 1993.
Hansen, Guillermo. Review of *The Spirit of Life*, by Jürgen Moltmann. *CurTM* 21 (1994) 220–21.
Hanson, R. P. C. "Basil's Doctrine of Tradition in Relation to the Holy Spirit." *VC* 22 (1968) 241–55.
Hart, Larry. "Hermeneutics, Theology, and the Holy Spirit." *PRS* 14 (Winter 1987) 53–64.
Hartshorne, Charles, and W. L. Reese, editors. *Philosophers Speak of God.* Chicago: University of Chicago, 1953.
Hawthorne, Gerald F. *The Presence and the Power.* Dallas: Word, 1991.
Haykin, Michael "The Spirit of God: The Exegesis of 1 Cor 2:10–12 by Origen and Athanasius." *SJT* 35 (1982) 513–28.
Hegel, Georg Wilhelm Friedrich. *Phenomenology of Spirit.* Translated by A. V. Miller. Oxford: Clarendon, 1977.
Heidegger, Martin. *Being and Time.* Translated by John Macquarrie and Edward Robinson. New York: Harper & Row, 1962.
Helm, Paul. "Faith, Evidence, and the Scriptures." In *Scripture and Truth*, 303–20. Grand Rapids: Baker, 1992.
Hendry, George Stuart. *The Holy Spirit in Christian Theology.* Philadelphia: Westminster, 1956.

Bibliography

Henrich, Dieter, and Rolf-Peter Horstmann, editors. *Christian Spirituality and the Culture of Modernity*. Stuttgart: Klett-Cotta, 1984.

Henry, Carl F. H. *God, Revelation and Authority*. Vol. 4. Wheaton, IL: Crossway, 1979.

———. "Spiritual? Say it Isn't So!" In *Alive to God: Studies in Spirituality Presented to James Houston*. Downers Grove, IL: InterVarsity, 1992.

Heron, Alasdair. *The Holy Spirit*. Philadelphia: Westminster, 1983.

Hesselink, I. John. "Governed and Guided by the Spirit: A Key Issue in Calvin's Doctrine of the Holy Spirit." In *Das Reformeirte Erbe: Festschrift für Gottfried W. Locher,* 2:161–71. Zurich: TVZ, 1993.

Hiebert, Paul G. *Missiological Implications of Epistemological Shifts*. Harrisburg, PA: Trinity, 1999.

Hilary. "On the Trinity." Edited by H. Wace and P. Schaff. *A Select Library of the Nicene and Post-Nicene Fathers of the Christian Church*, vols. 2, 14. New York: Christian, 1887–1900.

Hilberath, Bernd Jochen. "Identity through Self-Transcendence: The Holy Spirit and the Communio of Free Persons." In *Advents of the Spirit*, edited by Bradford E. Hinze and D. Lyle Dabney, 265–92. Marquette Studies in Theology 30. Marquette, WI: Marquette University Press, 2001.

Hildebrandt, Wilf. *An Old Testament Theology of the Spirit of God*. Peabody, MA: Hendrickson, 1995.

Hill, Andrew E., and John H. Walton, *A Survey of the Old Testament*. Grand Rapids: Zondervan, 1991.

Hodge, Charles. *An Exposition of the First Epistle to the Corinthians*. Grand Rapids: Eerdmans, 1950.

Hodges, Melvin L. *A Theology of the Church and its Mission*. Springfield, MO: Gospel, 1977.

Hodgson, Peter C. *God in History: Shapes of Freedom*. Nashville: Abingdon, 1989.

———. *Revisioning the Church: Ecclesial Freedom in the New Paradigm*. Philadelphia: Fortress, 1988.

———. *Winds of the Spirit: A Constructive Christian Theology*. Louisville: Westminster John Knox, 1994.

Hodgson, Peter C., and Robert H. King, editors. *Christian Theology: An Introduction to Its Traditions*. Philadelphia: Fortress, 1985.

Hoedemaker, Bert. "Toward an Epistemologically Responsible Missiology." In *To Stake a Claim: Mission and the Western Crisis of Knowledge*, edited by J. Andrew Kirk and Kevin J. Vanhoozer, 217–32. Maryknoll, NY: Orbis, 1999.

Horton, Stanley. *What the Bible Says about the Holy Spirit*. Springfield, MO: Gospel, 1976.

Houston, James M. *The Holy Spirit in Contemporary Spirituality*. Grove Spirituality Series 47. Bramcote, Eng.: Grove, 1993.

Hryniewicz, Waclaw. "Der Pneumatologishe Aspekt der Kirche aus Orthodoxer Sicht." *Catholica* 31.2 (1977) 137–38.

Hütter, Reinhard. "The Church." In *Knowing the Triune God*, edited by James J. Buckley and David S. Yeago, 23–48. Grand Rapids: Eerdmans, 2001.

———. *Suffering Divine Things: Theology as Church Practice*. Translated by Doug Stott. Grand Rapids: Eerdmans, 2000.

Inch, Morris A. *Saga of the Spirit: A Biblical, Systematic, and Historical Theology of the Holy Spirit.* Grand Rapids: Baker, 1985.

Ingraffia, Brian D. *Postmodern Theory and Biblical Theology: Vanquishing God's Shadow.* Cambridge: Cambridge University Press, 1995.

James, William. *The Varieties of Religious Experience.* New York: Modern Library, 1929.

Janes, Burton K. "Taking a Step Toward Pentecost: The Holy Spirit in the Thought of Karl Bath." *Paraclete* (Winter 1991) 24–28.

Jensen, Robert W. *The Holy Spirit.* Edited by Carl E. Braaten and Robert W. Jenson. Christian Dogmatics 2. Philadelphia: Fortress, 1984.

———. *Systematic Theology, Vol. 1: The Triune God.* New York: Oxford University Press, 1997.

Jewett, Robert. *Paul's Anthropological Terms: A Study of the Use in Conflict Settings.* Leiden: Brill, 1971.

Johnson, Robert Clyde. *Authority in Protestant Theology.* Philadelphia: Westminster, 1959.

Jones, L. Gregory. "A Thirst for God or Consumer Spirituality." In *Spirituality and Social Embodiment*, 3–28. Malden, MA: Blackwell, 1997.

Jones, L. Gregory, and James J. Buckley, editors. *Spirituality and Social Embodiment.* Malden, MA: Blackwell, 1997.

Kaiser, Walter C. "A Neglected Text in Bibliology Discussions: 1 Corinthians 2:6–16." *WTJ* 43 (1981): 315.

———. *Toward an Exegetical Theology.* Grand Rapids: Baker, 1981.

Kanzer, Kenneth S., editor. *Applying the Scriptures: Papers from ICBI Summit III.* Grand Rapids: Academie, 1997.

Karkkainen, Veli-Matti. *Pneumatology: The Holy Spirit in Ecumenical, International, and Contextual Perspective.* Grand Rapids: Baker, 2002.

Kasper, Walter. *The God of Jesus Christ.* Translated by Matthew O'Connell. London: SCM, 1984.

Keck, Leander E. "The Law and 'The Law of Sin and Death' (Rom 8:1–4) Reflections on the Spirit and Ethics in Paul." In *The Divine Helmsman: Studies on God's Control of Human Events Presented to Lou H. Silberman*, 41–78. New York: Ktav, 1980.

Kelly, J. N. D. *A Commentary on the Pastoral Epistles.* New York: Harper & Row, 1964.

———. *A Commentary on the Epistles of Peter and Jude.* Grand Rapids: Baker, 1981.

———. *Early Christian Creeds.* 3d ed. London: Longman, 1972.

Kidner, Derek. *Psalm 100–150.* Downers Grove, IL: InterVarsity, 1975.

Kierkegaard, Søren. *On Authority and Revelation.* Translated by Walter Lowrie. Princeton: Princeton University Press, 1955.

Kinkel, Asher, and Lawrence Frizzell, editors. *Standing Before God: Studies on Prayer in Scriptures and in Tradition with Essays in Honor of John M. Oesterreicher.* New York: Ktav, 1981.

Kirk, J. Andrew, and Kevin J. Vanhoozer, editors. *To Stake a Claim: Mission and the Western Crisis of Knowledge.* Maryknoll, NY: Orbis, 1999.

Klooster, Fred H. "The Role of the Holy Spirit in the Hermeneutics Process: The Relationship of the Spirit's Illumination to Biblical Interpretation." In *Hermeneutics, Inerrancy, and the Bible: Papers from ICBI Summit II*, 451–72. Grand Rapids: Academie, 1984.

Bibliography

Kragen, K. David. "Epistemological Studies in the Thought of Martin Luther Concentrating on Faith, Reason, and Certainty." M.A. thesis, Conservative Baptist Theological Seminary, Portland, OR, 1982.

Kümmel, Werner Georg. *Man in the New Testament.* Translated by John Vincent. Philadelphia: Westminster, 1963.

Küng, Hans. *The Church.* Translated by Ray Ockenden and Rosaleen Ockenden. New York: Sheed & Ward, 1967.

Kuyper, Abraham. *The Work of the Holy Spirit.* Translated by Henri De Vries. Grand Rapids: Eerdmans, 1946.

LaCugna, Catherine Mowry. *God with Us: The Trinity and Christian Life.* San Francisco: HarperSanFrancisco, 1991.

Ladd, George Eldon. *A Theology of the New Testament.* Grand Rapids: Eerdmans, 1974.

———. *Crucial Questions About the Kingdom of God.* Grand Rapids: Eerdmans, 1952.

———. *The Presence of the Future: The Eschatology of Biblical Realism.* Grand Rapids: Eerdmans, 1971.

Larkin, William J., Jr. *Culture and Biblical Hermeneutics: Interpreting and Applying the Authoritative Word in a Relativistic Age.* Grand Rapids: Baker, 1988.

Larson, Duane H. Review of *God the Spirit*, by Michael Welker. *Dialogue* 36 (Winter 1996) 70.

Laughery, Gregory J. "Language at the Frontiers of Language." In *After Pentecost: Language and Biblical Interpretation*, edited by Craig Bartholomew et al., 171–94. Grand Rapids: Zondervan, 2001.

Leupold, H. C. *Exposition of Isaiah.* Grand Rapids: Baker, 1968.

Lewis, G. R. "Attributes of God." In *EDOT*, 453–58.

Levinson, Jon D. *Creation and the Persistence of Evil.* San Francisco: Harper & Row, 1988.

Limburg, James. "Down to Earth Theology: Psalm 104 and the Environment." *CurTM* 21 (1994) 344–45.

Livingston, James C. *Modern Christian Thought.* New York: Macmillan, 1971.

Lloyd-Jones, D. Martin. *Authority.* Downers Grove, IL: InterVarsity, 1960.

Loder, James E. *The Logic of the Spirit: Human Development in Theological Perspective.* San Francisco: Jossey-Bass, 1998.

Long, Charles H., and David Paton, editors. *The Compulsion of the Spirit: A Roland Allen Reader.* Grand Rapids: Eerdmans, 1983.

Lundin, Roger, editor. *Disciplining Hermeneutics: Interpretation in Christian Perspective.* Grand Rapids: Eerdmans, 1997.

Luther, Martin. *Luther's Works.* 55 vols. Edited by Jaroslav Pelikan and Helmut T. Lehmann. Philadelphia: Muhlenburg, 1955–86.

———. "On the Councils and the Church." In *Luther's Works.* Vol. 41. Translated by Eric W. Gritsch. Philadelphia: Fortress, 1966.

———. *A Commentary on St. Paul's Epistle to the Galatians.* 4th ed. Translated by Theodore Graebner. Grand Rapids: Zondervan.

———. *Commentary on the Epistle to the Romans.* Translated by J. Theodore Mueller. Grand Rapids: Zondervan, 1954.

Luukkanen, Tarja-Liisa. "In Quest of Certainty: Axel Fredrik Granfelt's Theological Epistemology." PhD diss., Helsinki, 1993.

Bibliography

Lyotard, Jean-Francois. *The Postmodern Condition: A Report on Knowledge*. Translated by Geoff Bennington and Brian Massumi. Minneapolis: University of Minnesota Press, 1984.

Ma, Wansuk. *Until the Spirit Comes: The Spirit of God in the Book of Isaiah*. JSOT Supplement Series 271. Sheffield: Sheffield Academic, 1972.

Macdonald, A. J. *The Interpreter Spirit and Human Life: A Study of the Doctrine of the Holy Spirit in the Old Testament, the Wisdom Books and the New Testament*. London: SPCK, 1944.

MacMillan, John A. *The Authority of the Believer*. Camphille, PA: Christian Publications, 1980.

Mannermaa, Tuomo. "Justification and *Theosis* in Lutheran-Orthodox Perspective." In *Union with Christ: The New Finnish Interpretation of Luther*, 25–41. Grand Rapids: Eerdmans, 1998.

Marshall, I. Howard. *The Acts of the Apostles*. TNTC. Grand Rapids: Eerdmans, 1991.

———. "The Hope of a New Age: The Kingdom of God in the New Testament." *Themelios* (1995) 5–15.

Marshall, Ronald F. "Luther's Two-Factor Hermeneutic." *LQ* (Fall 1976) 54–69.

Martin, Dale. *The Corinthian Body*. New Haven: Yale University Press, 1995.

Martin, Ralph P. *2 Corinthians*. WBC 40. Word: Waco, TX, 1986.

McCartney, Dan, and Charles Clayton. *Let the Reader Understand: A Guide to Interpreting and Applying the Bible*. Wheaton, IL: Victor, 1994.

McConville, Gordon J. "ברית." In *NIDOTTE*, 1:752

McDonald H. D. *The Christian View of Man*. Westchester, IL: Crossway, 1981.

McGrath, Alister E. *Christian Spirituality*. Malden, MA: Blackwell, 1999.

———. *Spirituality in an Age of Change*. Grand Rapids: Zondervan, 1994.

McKim, Donald K. "Authority." In *A New Handbook of Christian Theology*, edited by Donald W. Musser and Joseph L. Price, 47. Nashville: Abingdon, 1992.

Menzies, Robert P. *Empowered for Witness: The Spirit in Luke-Acts*. JSNT Supplement Series 54. Sheffield: Sheffield Academic, 1991.

Merrill, Eugene H. "Old Testament History: A Theological Perspective." In *A Guide to Old Testament Theology and Exegesis*, 65–82. Grand Rapids: Zondervan, 1997.

Middleton, J. Richard, and Brian J. Walsh. *Truth is Stranger Than it Used to Be: Biblical Faith in a Postmodern Age*. Downers Grove, IL: InterVarsity, 1995.

Molnar, Paul D. "The Function of the Immanent Trinity in the Theology of Karl Barth: Implications for Today." *SJT* 42 (1989) 367–99.

Moltmann, Jürgen. "Christianity in the Third Millennium." *TTo* 51 (1994) 75–89.

———. *God in Creation: A New Theology of Creation and the Spirit of God*. Translated by Margaret Kohl. 1985. Reprinted, Minneapolis: Fortress, 1993.

———. *The Church in the Power of the Spirit: A Contribution to Messianic Ecclesiology*. 1977. Reprinted, Minneapolis: Fortress, 1993.

———. "The Fellowship of the Holy Spirit—Trinitarian Pneumatology." *SJT* 37 (1984) 287–300.

———. *The Source of Life*. Translated by Margaret Kohl. Minneapolis: Fortress, 1997.

———. *The Spirit of Life*. Translated by Margaret Kohl. 1992. Reprinted, Minneapolis: Fortress, 2001.

Bibliography

———. *The Trinity and the Kingdom*. 1991. Reprinted, Minneapolis: Fortress, 1993.
———. *Theology of Hope*. Translated by James W. Leitch. 1967. Reprinted, Minneapolis: Fortress Press, 1993.
———. "Theology of Mystical Experience." *SJT* 32 (1979) 501–20.
Monroe Starkey, Lycurgus. *The Work of the Holy Spirit*. New York: Abingdon, 1962.
Montague, George T. *Holy Spirit: Growth of a Biblical Tradition*. Peabody, MA: Hendrickson, 1994.
Moo, Douglas J. *The Epistle to the Romans*. Grand Rapids: Eerdmans, 1996.
Morris, Leon. *Spirit of the Living God*. London: Intervarsity, 1973.
———. *The First Epistle of Paul to the Corinthians*. TNTC. Grand Rapids: Eerdmans, 1958.
———. *The Gospel according to John*. NICNT. Grand Rapids: Eerdmans, 1995.
Morrison, Karl F. *Tradition and Authority in the Western Church 300–1140*. Princeton: Princeton University Press, 1969.
Mullins, Edgar Young. *Freedom and Authority in Religion*. Philadelphia: Griffith and Rowland, 1913.
Musser, Donald W. and Joseph L. Price, editors. *A New Handbook of Christian Theology*. Nashville.: Abingdon, 1992.
Nestle-Aland Greek New Testament, 27th ed.
New American Standard Bible, 1995 ed.
Nielsen, Charles Merritt. "Clement of Rome and Moralism." *CH* 31 (1962) 131–50.
Nuttall, Geoffrey F. *The Holy Spirit in Puritan Faith and Experience*. Chicago: University of Chicago Press, 1992.
Oberman, Heiko A., et al, editors. *Das Reformeirte Erbe: Festschrift für Gottfried W. Locher*. Zurich: TVZ, 1993.
O'Brien, Peter T. *The Letter to the Ephesians*. Pillar New Testament Commentary. Grand Rapids: Eerdmans, 1999.
Oden, Thomas C. *Life in the Spirit*. Systematic Theology: Vol. 3. San Francisco: HarperSanFrancisco, 1992.
O'Donnell, John J. *Trinity and Temporality: The Christian Doctrine of God in Light of Process Theology and the Theology of Hope*. New York: Oxford University, 1983.
O'Donovan, Oliver. *Resurrection and Moral Order: An Outline for Evangelical Ethics*. Grand Rapids: Eerdmans, 1994.
Orchard, Father Bernard. *A Catholic Commentary on the Holy Scriptures*. New York: Nelson, 1953.
Osborne, Grant. *The Hermeneutical Spiral*. Downers Grove, IL: InterVarsity, 1991.
Osterhaven, M. Eugene. "John Calvin: Order and the Holy Spirit." *RR* 32 (Fall 1978) 23–44.
Oswalt, John. *The Book of Isaiah, Chapters 1–39*. Grand Rapids: Eerdmans, 1982.
Oswalt, John. "נוח." In *NIDOTTE*, 3:56–59.
Packer, J. I. "The Holy Spirit and His Work." In *Applying the Scriptures: Papers from ICBI Summit III*, 51–76. Grand Rapids: Academie, 1997.
———. *God Has Spoken*. Toronto: Hodder & Stoughton, 1979.
———. *Keep in Step with the Spirit*. Grand Rapids: Baker, 1984.

Bibliography

Packer, J. I. and Loren Wilkinson, editors. *Alive to God: Studies in Spirituality Presented to James Houston.* Downers Grove, IL: InterVarsity, 1992.

Palmer, Ian S. "The Authority and Doctrine of Scripture in the Thought of John Calvin." *EvQ* 49 (1997) 30–39.

Pazmino, Robert. *By What Authority Do We Teach?* Grand Rapids: Baker, 1994.

Pearson, Birger. *The Pneumatikos-Psychikos Terminology in 1 Corinthians: A Study in the Theology of the Corinthian Opponents of Paul and its Relation to Gnosticism.* Society of Biblical Literature Dissertation Series. Missoula, MT: Scholars, 1973.

Piggin, F. S. "Cause." In *EDOT*, 200.

Pinnock, Clark H. "An Inclusivist View." In *Four Views on Salvation in a Pluralistic World*, 93–123. Grand Rapids: Zondervan, 1996.

———. *Flame of Love: A Theology of the Holy Spirit.* Downers Grove, IL: InterVarsity, 1999.

———. *The Scripture Principle.* San Francisco: Harper & Row, 1984.

Piper, John. "The Authority and Nature of the Gift of Prophecy, Part One." Sermon on Acts 2:14–21. *www.desiringgod.org/library/sermons/90/032590.html.*

Prater, Arnold. *The Presence: The Ministry of the Holy Spirit.* Nashville: Nelson, 1993.

Prenter, Regin. *Spiritus Creator.* Translated by John M. Jenson. Philadelphia: Muhlenberg, 1953.

Pritchard, James B. editor. *Ancient Near Eastern Texts Relation to the Old Testament.* Princeton, NJ: Princeton University, 1955.

Pyne, Robert A. "The Role of the Holy Spirit in Conversion." *BibSac* 150 (1993) 203–18.

Radmacher, Earl D., and Robert D. Preus, editors. *Hermeneutics, Inerrancy, and the Bible: Papers from ICBI Summit II.* Grand Rapids: Academie, 1984.

Ramm, Bernard. *The Evangelical Heritage.* Waco, TX: Word, 1973.

———. *The Pattern of Authority.* Grand Rapids: Eerdmans, 1957.

———. *The Witness of the Spirit.* Grand Rapids: Eerdmans, 1959.

Ramsey, Ian T. *Models for Divine Activity.* London: SCM, 1973.

Raus, Clyde Norman. *The Authentic Witness.* Grand Rapids: Eerdmans.

Richard, Lucien. "The Enigma of Theologians in the Roman Catholic Church." *Encounter* 42 (1981) 329–51.

Ricoeur, Paul. *Interpretation Theory: Discourse and the Surplus of Meaning.* Fort Worth: Texas Christian University Press, 1976.

Ridderbos, Herman. *Paul: An Outline of His Theology.* Translated by John Richard de Witt. Grand Rapids: Eerdmans, 1975.

Rigby, Cynthia L., editor. *Power, Powerlessness, and the Divine: New Inquiries in Bible and Theology.* Atlanta: Scholars, 1997.

Robertson, A. T. *Word Pictures in the New Testament, III: Acts.* Grand Rapids: Baker, 1930.

Rogers, Jack. *Biblical Authority.* Waco, TX: Word, 1977.

Roman Catholic-World Methodist Council Joint Commission, "The Holy Spirit, Christian Experience, and Authority: Further Catholic/Methodist Reflections." *One in Christ* 16, vol. 3. (1980).

Rosato, Philip J. *The Spirit as Lord: The Holy Spirit in the Theology of Karl Barth.* Edinburgh: T. & T. Clark, 1981.

Bibliography

Rupp, E. Gordon, editor. *Luther And Erasmus: Free Will And Salvation*. Translated by Gordon E. Rupp. Library of Christian Classics 17. Philadelphia: Westminster, 1969.
Rutler, George W. *Christ and Reason: An Introduction to Ideas from Kant to Tyrell*. Front Royal, VA: Christendom, 1990.
Ryle, Gilbert. *The Concept of Mind*. London: Hutchinson, 1949.
Sabatier, Auguste. *The Religions of Authority and the Religion of the Spirit*. London: Williams and Norgate, 1904.
Sanders, E. P. *Paul and Palestinian Judaism: A Comparison of Patterns of Religion*. Philadelphia: Fortress, 1977.
Sarna, Nahum M. *Genesis*. The JPS Torah Commentary. Philadelphia: Jewish Publication Society, 1989.
Schaeffer, Francis A. *Escape from Reason*. Wheaton, IL: InterVarsity, 1968.
———. *He is There and He is Not Silent*. Wheaton, IL: Tyndale, 1972.
———. *True Spirituality*. Wheaton, IL: Tyndale, 1971.
Schleiermacher, Friedrich. *The Christian Faith*. Edited by H. R. Mackintosh and J. S. Stewart. Philadelphia: Fortress, 1976.
Schner, George P. "Louis Dupre's Philosophy of Religion: An Indispensable Discourse on Fragments of Meaning." In *Christian Spirituality and the Culture of Modernity: The Thought of Louis Dupre*, 225–75. Grand Rapids: Eerdmans, 1998.
Schwöbel, Christoph. *Trinitarian Theology Today: Essays on Divine Being and Act*. Edinburgh: T. & T. Clark, 1995.
Seitz, M. "Seek." In *NIDNTT*, 3:533.
Shelley, Bruce. *By What Authority: The Standards of Truth in the Early Church*. Grand Rapids: Eerdmans, 1965.
Seevers, Boyd V. "ירה." In *NIDOTTE*, 3:527–31.
Smail, Thomas. *Reflected Glory: The Spirit in Christ and Christian*. Grand Rapids: Eerdmans, 1975.
Smalley, William A. "Cultural Implications of an Indigenous Church." In *Perspectives on the World Christian Movement: A Reader*. Pasadena, CA: William Carey Library, 1983.
Sortori, Luigi. "The Structure of Juridical and Charismatic Power in the Christian Community." In *Charisms in the Church*. New York: Seabury, 1978.
Sperber, Dan, and Deirdre Wilson. *Relevance*. Malden, MA: Blackwell, 1999.
Stackhouse, Max L., editor. *God and Globalization: The Spirit in the Modern Authorities*. Harrisburg, PA: Trinity, 2001.
———. "Introduction." In *God and Globalization: The Spirit in the Modern Authorities*, 1–2. Harrisburg, PA: Trinity, 2001.
Steiner, George. *Real Presences*. Chicago: University of Chicago Press, 1989.
Stell, Stephen L. "Hermeneutics in Theology and the Theology of Hermeneutics: Beyond Lindbeck and Tracy." *JAAR* 62 (1993) 679–703.
Steward, D. *Old Testament Exegesis: A Primer for Students and Pastors*. Philadelphia: Westminster, 1984.
Sundermeier, Theo. "Pluralismus, Fundamentalismus, Koinonia." *EvT* 54 (1994) 293–310.
Swete, H. B. *On the Early History of the Doctrine of the Holy Spirit*. London: Bell, 1873.
———. *The Holy Spirit in the Ancient Church: A Study of Christian Teaching in the Age of the Fathers*. London: MacMillan, 1912.

Bibliography

Taylor, John V. *The Go-Between God: The Holy Spirit and the Christian Mission.* New York: Oxford University Press, 1979.
Taylor, LaTonya. "The Church of O." *Christianity Today* 46 (April 1, 2002).
The Truth that Leads to Eternal Life. Brooklyn, NY: Watchtower Bible and Tract Society, 1968.
Thiel, John. *Senses of Tradition: Continuity and Development in the Catholic Faith.* New York: Oxford University Press, 2000.
Thiselton, Anthony C. *The First Epistle to the Corinthians.* NIGTC. Grand Rapids: Eerdmans, 2000.
———. *Interpreting God and the Postmodern Self.* Grand Rapids: Eerdmans, 1995.
———. *The Two Horizons: New Testament Hermeneutics and Philosophical Description with Special Reference to Heidegger, Bultmann, Gadamer, and Wittgenstein.* Grand Rapids: Eerdmans, 1980.
Thomas, Madathilparampil. "The Holy Spirit and the Spirituality for Political Struggles." *Ecumenical Review* 42 (1990) 217.
Thomas, Owen C., editor. *God's Activity in the World: The Contemporary Problem.* Chico, CA: Scholars, 1983.
Thompson, John. *Modern Trinitarian Perspectives.* New York: Oxford University Press, 1994.
———. *The Holy Spirit in the Theology of Karl Barth.* Allison Park, PA: Pickwick, 1991.
Thorsell, Paul R. "The Spirit in the Present Age: Preliminarily Fulfillment of the Predicted New Covenant according to Paul." *JETS* (1998) 397–413.
Toennies, Ferdinand. *Community and Society.* Translated by Charles P. Loomis. East Lansing: Michigan State University Press, 1887.
Torrance, Thomas F. *The Christian Doctrine of God: One Being Three Persons.* Edinburgh: T. & T. Clark, 1988.
———. *The Trinitarian Faith.* Edinburgh: T. & T. Clark, 1988.
Trench, R. C. *Synonyms of the New Testament.* Grand Rapids: Eerdmans, 1958.
Trine, Ralph Waldo. *In Tune with the Infinite.* New York: Dodge, 1910.
Van Engen, J. "Tradition." In *EDOT*, 1106.
Van Kaam, Adrian. *Formative Spirituality.* Crossroads: New York, 1983–87.
VanGemeren, Willem A., editor. *A Guide to Old Testament Theology and Exegesis.* Grand Rapids: Zondervan, 1997.
———. *Interpreting the Prophetic Word.* Grand Rapids: Zondervan, 1990.
———, editor. *New International Dictionary of Old Testament Theology and Exegesis.* Grand Rapids: Zondervan, 1997.
———. *The Progress of Redemption.* Grand Rapids: Baker, 1988.
———. "The Spirit of Restoration." *WTJ* 50 (1988) 81–102.
Vanhoozer, Kevin J. *Is There a Meaning in This Text?: The Bible, the Reader, and the Morality of Literary Knowledge.* Grand Rapids: Zondervan, 1998.
———. "From Speech Acts to Scripture Acts." In *After Pentecost: Language and Biblical Interpretation*, edited by Craig Bartholomew et al., 1–49. Grand Rapids: Zondervan, 2001.
———. "The Reader in New Testament Interpretation." In *Hearing the New Testament*, 301–28. Grand Rapids: Eerdmans, 1995.

Bibliography

———. "The Semantics of Biblical Literature: Truth and Scripture's Diverse Literary Forms." In *Hermeneutics, Authority, and Canon*, 53–104. Grand Rapids: Zondervan, 1986.

———. "The Spirit of Understanding: Special Revelation and General Hermeneutics." In *Disciplining Hermeneutics: Interpretation in Christian Perspective*, 131–66. Grand Rapids: Eerdmans, 1997.

———. "The Voice and the Actor: A Dramatic Proposal about the Ministry and Minstrelsy of Theology." In *Evangelical Futures: A Conversation of Theological Method*, 61–106. Grand Rapids: Baker, 2000.

Van Pelt, M. V., et al. "רוח." In *NIDOTTE*, 3:1073–78.

Van Pelt, M. V. and W. C. Kaiser, Jr. "ירא." In *NIDOTTE*, 2:527–533.

van Rooy, H. F. "פנים." In *NIDOTTE* 3:638–39.

Vanzant, Iyanla. *Until Today! Daily Devotions for Spiritual Growth and Peace of Mind*. New York: Fireside, 2000.

Veenhof, Jay. "The Holy Spirit and Hermeneutics." *SBET* 5 (Spr 1987) 114.

Veith, Gene Edward. "Out-Clintoning Clinton." *World* (Dec. 2, 2000) 21.

Verhey, Allen. "The Spirit of God and the Spirit of Medicine." In *God and Globalization: The Spirit and the Modern Authorities*, 107–38. Harrisburg, PA: Trinity, 2001.

Virkler, Henry. *Hermeneutics: Principles and Process of Biblical Interpretation*. Grand Rapids: Baker, 1981.

Waltke, Bruce K. *Creation and Chaos*. Portland, OR: Western Conservative Baptist Seminary, 1974.

Watt, E. D. *Authority*. New York: St. Martin's, 1982.

Webster, Noah, and Jean L. McKechnie, editors. *Webster's New Universal Unabridged Dictionary*. 2d ed. United States of American: William Collins, 1983.

Welker, Michael. "Der Heilege Geist." *EvT* 49 (1989) 139–40.

———. *God the Spirit*. Translated by John F. Hoffmeyer. Minneapolis: Fortress, 1994.

———. "God's Power and Powerlessness: Biblical Theology and the Search for a World Ethos in a Time of Short-Lived Moral Markets." In *Power, Powerlessness, and the Divine*, 39–55. Atlanta: Scholars, 1997.

———. *Gottes Geist: Theologie des Heiligen Geistes*. Neukirchen-Vluyn: Neukirchener, 1992.

Westermann, Claus. *Genesis 1–11: A Commentary*. Translated by John J. Scullion. Continental Commentaries. Minneapolis: Augsburg, 1984.

The Westminster Confession of Faith. Glasgow: Free Presbyterian, 1976.

Whybray, R. N. *Isaiah 40–66*. Grand Rapids: Eerdmans, 1981.

Widmert, G. P. *Gloire au Pere, au Fils et au Saint-Esprit*. Neuchatel, 1963.

Wildberger, Hans. *Isaiah 1–12: A Commentary*. Translated by Thomas H. Trapp. Continental Commentaries. Minneapolis: Fortress, 1991.

Williams, A. N. "Mystical Theology Redux: The Pattern of Aquinas' *Summa Theologiae*." In *Spirituality and Social Embodiment*, 53–74. Malden, MA: Blackwell, 1997.

Williams, David Alan. Review of *Beyond Foundationalism*, by Stanley Grenz and John Franke. *JETS* 44 (2001) 753.

Williams, Stephen N. "Pneumatologies Have Consequences: Review of *Flame of Love*." *Books and Culture* 5 (Mar/Apr 1999) 36.

Bibliography

Williamson, Marianne. *A Return To Love: Reflections on the Principles of a Course in Miracles.* New York: HarperCollins, 1993.

Winslow, Octavius. *The Work of the Holy Spirit.* Carlisle, PA: Banner of Truth, 1961.

Winter, Ralph D. and Steven C. Hawthorne, editors. *Perspectives on the World Christian Movement: A Reader.* Pasadena, CA: William Carey Library, 1983.

Wolff, Christian. *Der erste Brief des Paulus an die Korinther.* Theologischer Handkommentar zum Neuen Testament 7. Leipzig: Evangelische Verlagsanstalt, 1996.

Wolterstorff, Nicholas. "The Promise of Speech Act Theory for Biblical Interpretation." In *After Pentecost: Language and Biblical Interpretation*, edited by Craig Bartholemew et al., 73–90. Grand Rapids: Zondervan, 2001.

Wood, A. Skevington "Spirit and Spirituality in Luther." *EvQ* 61 (1989) 311–27.

Woodhouse, H. F. "The Authority of the Holy Spirit." *SJT* 20 (1967) 183–197.

Wright, John H. "Authority in the Church: A Theological Reflection." *Communio* 7 (1980) 364–82.

Yeago, David. "A Christian, Holy People." In *Spirituality and Social Embodiment*, edited by L. Gregory Jones and James J. Buckley, 101–20. Malden, MA: Blackwell, 1997.

———. "The Bible." In *Knowing the Triune God*, 49–94. Grand Rapids: Eerdmans, 2001.

Yong, Amos. *Beyond the Impasse: Toward a Pneumatological Theology of Religions.* Grand Rapids: Baker, 2003.

Young, Edward J. *The Book of Isaiah.* Vol. 2. *NICOT.* Grand Rapids: Eerdmans, 1969.

Zizioulas, John D. "Die pneumatologishe Dimension der Kirche." *IKZ Communio* 2 (1973) 137.

———. "The Doctrine of the Holy Trinity: The Significance of the Cappadocian Contribution." In *Trinitarian Theology Today: Essays on Divine Being and Act*, 50–55. Edinburgh: T. & T. Clark, 1995.

———. *Being as Communion—Studies in Personhood and the Church.* London: Darton, Longman and Todd, 1985.

Zuck, Roy B. "The Role of the Holy Spirit in Hermeneutics." *BibSac* 141 (1984) 120–30.

www.ingramcontent.com/pod-product-compliance
Lightning Source LLC
Chambersburg PA
CBHW071230290426
44108CB00013B/1361